What Is Happening to State Trial Court Civil Filings?

Alan Carlson and John Greacen

AMERICAN BAR ASSOCIATION
Judicial Division

Cover design by Jill Tedhams/ABA Design

Printed in the United States of America.

28 27 26 25 24   5 4 3 2 1

A catalog record for this book is available from the Library of Congress.

ISBN 978-1-63905-404-6

Contents

Acknowledgments

The authors would also like to acknowledge the assistance of the following individuals and organizations in obtaining and understanding case filing data, assisting in the analysis of filing data, or reviewing drafts of the manuscript.

California

Judicial Council of California—Martin Hoshino, Millicent Tidwell, Robert Oyung, and, in particular, Leah Rose-Goodwin

Orange County Superior Court—Darren Dang and Nicole Li

The State Bar of California—Leah Wilson and Yun Xiang

Michael Maguire, Attorney at Law

Illinois

Administrative Office of the Illinois Courts—Marcia Meis, Skip Robertson, Nathan Jensen, Jacque Huddleston, Katie Blakeman, and Amy Patterson

22d Circuit Court—Dan Wallis

Clerk of the Circuit Court, McHenry County—Katherine M. Keefe

Illinois State Bar Association—Robert E. Craghead and Donna M. Leonard

Illinois Attorney Registration and Disciplinary Commission—Brittany Bowater

Illinois Bar Foundation—Stacey Jonas Weiler

Chicago Bar Foundation—Bob Glaves

Maryland

Administrative Office of the Courts—Pamela Harris, Jamie Walter, and Kathleen Maher

Minnesota

State Court Administration Office—Grant Hoheisel

Minnesota State Bar Association—Louise M. Copeland

Judge Kevin Burke, Marcy Rasmussen Podkopacz

Ohio

The Supreme Court of Ohio, Administrative Division—Stephanie E. Hess and Brian C. Farrington

Judge Richard Frye

Tennessee

Justice Cornelia A. Clark

Administrative Office of the Courts—Ann Lynn Walker

Texas

Texas Office of Court Administration—David Slayton, Jeffrey Tsunekawa, and Angela Garcia

State Bar of Texas—Cory Squires and Trey Apffel

Virginia

Supreme Court of Virginia—Karl Hade and Chris Wade

National Center for State Courts

Diane Robinson

Institute for the Advancement of the American Legal System (IAALS)

Becky Love Kourlis (in particular for her willingness to sponsor the study and obtain preliminary funding), Brittany K. T. Kauffman, Logan Cornett, James Swearingen, Brooke Meyer, Natalie Knowlton, and Janet Drobinske

The Pew Charitable Trusts and the Pew Civil Legal Systems Modernization team for their early support of this study

Individuals

Judge Ira Kaufman (ret.), Barry Mahoney, Ticien Sassoubre, Marcus Reinkensmeyer, Thomas M. Clarke (ret.), Prof. Stacy Butler, Prof. Christopher Griffin, and Prof. Fernando A. Wilson

American Bar Association for willingness to publish the book and their work to produce it

Jeffrey Salyards

Morgan Ewald and her staff for the editing and preparation of the manuscript.

In Memoria

Alan would especially like to acknowledge and thank Larry L. Sipes, past president of the National Center for State Courts, who recently passed away. Larry hired me as a recent law graduate with an engineering degree to work on a groundbreaking study of delay in urban trial courts. The study collected and analyzed case processing time data in civil and criminal cases in 21 state trial courts. The data provided a strong quantitative basis for the findings reported in JUSTICE DELAYED: THE PACE OF LITIGATION IN URBAN TRIAL COURTS. This book is a continuation of the belief that quantitative data about courts can lead to better-managed courts and a higher quality of justice. Thank you, Larry, for your trust, foresight, and support.

1

Introduction

"What gets us into trouble is not what we don't know.
It's what we know for sure that just ain't so."

—Mark Twain

Both of us have spent the bulk of our careers in the field of court administration. Alan served as court executive officer of the Superior Courts of Monterey, San Francisco, and Orange Counties in California; served as president of the Justice Management Institute (performing court consulting and research for state courts throughout the United States); and worked for the Western Regional Office of the National Center for State Courts (NCSC), participating in its groundbreaking research on trial court delay and the benefits of strong case management.[1] John also worked for the National Center (as deputy director for programs in Williamsburg), and served as clerk of the U.S. Court of Appeals for the Fourth Circuit and of the U.S. Bankruptcy Court for New Mexico, before becoming director of the Administrative Office of the Courts for New Mexico, and then working as a court consultant in 36 states and four foreign counties over the past 22 years.

A fundamental tenet of court administration since its creation as a profession by Ed Gallas and Ed McConnell, and one that has informed our work for half a century, has been the inevitability of growth. The workload of the courts has always grown and will always continue to grow. There will always be more cases of every type that will require ever larger courthouses, more judges, more staff, and better technology. And that will require more money—ever increasing court budgets.

In 2017, on the occasion of his acceptance of the Ernest C. Friesen Award of Excellence[2] at a meeting of the National Association of Presiding Judges and Court Executive Officers in Phoenix, John first publicly voiced his suspicion that the number of civil filings in state trial courts were falling rather than rising. In 2019, the two of us undertook

1. Thomas Church, Jr., Alan Carlson, Jo-Lynne Lee & Teresa Tan, *Justice Delayed: The Pace of Litigation in Urban Trial Courts*, NAT'L CTR. FOR STATE COURTS, 1978.

2. Alan received the same award two years later.

a detailed examination of that issue. Our journey was longer and more surprising than we imagined and complicated by the worldwide COVID-19 pandemic.

Our most fundamental conclusion is that the world of court administration is not the one we thought we were in during our careers. Filings do not keep going up. For four of the five states we studied, filings actually declined during the period we studied. In all five jurisdictions, filings moved up and down in ways that appear to us to be unpredictable. Nationwide data maintained by the NCSC shows the same trends nationally that we found in four of our five states.

We are stunned at the disparity in per capita filings from state to state, both with respect to total filings and with respect to civil filings.

We have not settled on a single factor, nor group of factors, that explain to our satisfaction why state court civil filings are in decline. We do not even attempt to articulate a set of "testable hypotheses" to explain what we have documented in what follows. Given the extraordinarily varied filings experiences in the various states, we doubt that a single factor or consistent constellation of factors determines the yearly filings or multi-year filings trends for the nation as a whole.

However, we believe that the state judiciaries, state legislators, and the legal profession should pay very close attention to two phenomena—vast disparity and overall declining state court civil, and other, filing levels. In any sector of our economy, a decline in the public's interest in its service or product is a matter for concern. The filings decline we document clearly marks a declining importance of civil lawsuits in the economic life of our country. If it denotes that our citizens have found better, cheaper ways to resolve civil disputes, we should celebrate. If it denotes declining public trust and confidence in our system of justice, the conclusions are much darker and foreboding.

Our data is all pre-pandemic. We believe that the changes the pandemic wrought in how our state courts function create a discontinuity between our data, data for the pandemic years, and filings data for the post-pandemic years. We urge our professional colleagues to monitor post-pandemic filings and continue to explore the issues that we raise.

We have made a number of recommendations for improvements in the ways in which we collect and report data on civil cases. In order to derive more definitive findings from court data, we need better data. More detailed data will allow much more thorough analyses of the impact and efficacy of substantive and procedural laws and court rules, case management programs, and court business practices. Obtaining it has, in the past, been constrained by the existence of multiple case management systems used by courts within a state and the use of inconsistent categorization processes for case types. Data consistency has been possible only at the highest levels of data aggregation. But those constraints—use of disparate case management systems and of inconsistent naming conventions—are not inevitable and perpetual. Court managers and leaders currently have the tools to generate consistent, fine-grained case filing data capable of producing better answers about the efficacy of our court processes.

Because of our past assumption that filings have always gone up and will continue to go up, we as a profession have not really thought that we needed better data. Our most important finding is, as Mark Twain quipped, one of those things that "just ain't so." And we do need that data to know why.

1.1 Our Journey: Investigating the Recent Experience of State Court Civil Filings

Court filings have always been viewed as *the* measure of court workload. Court workload, in turn, is often the basis for court funding. In some states, the court's need for judgeships has been based on "weighted caseload" formulas based on the number of filings, with different weights assigned to each case type based on empirical measurement of the average amount of judicial time spent on each type of case. Similar studies have been used to determine the number of administrative staff needed to support a court's operations and trial court funding. Caseload projections are also a significant factor in planning for the size and layout of a new courthouse.

Court budgets depend, in part, on court filing fees—in particular, the payment that must accompany the filing of a new case. A new case will not be accepted unless the requisite fee is paid, or waived, based on applicable rules of court or statutes.

Courts have not been alone in seeking to cash in on this revenue stream. Fee increases have been enacted for multiple non-court purposes, such as law enforcement training and free legal services for the poor. Consequently, falling filings mean falling revenues—for courts and for these other agencies that receive filing fee revenues. So long as filings kept rising, this formulation of fund accumulation and resource allocation worked well for all entities affected by it.

1.1.1 Early Indications That Our World Was Changing

The first sign that a change in the fundamental "fact" of ever rising filings came when John did a study for Los Angeles County of the funding needs of LA area legal services organizations to provide self-help centers in many of the larger courthouses outside of the downtown area. He was shocked to find that Limited Civil filings (cases seeking $25,000 or less) had decreased from roughly 210,000 to 100,000 from fiscal year 2007–08 to 2015–16 (Figure 1.1).

FIGURE 1.1 LOS ANGELES COUNTY LIMITED AND FAMILY LAW FILINGS, FY 2007–08 TO 2015–16

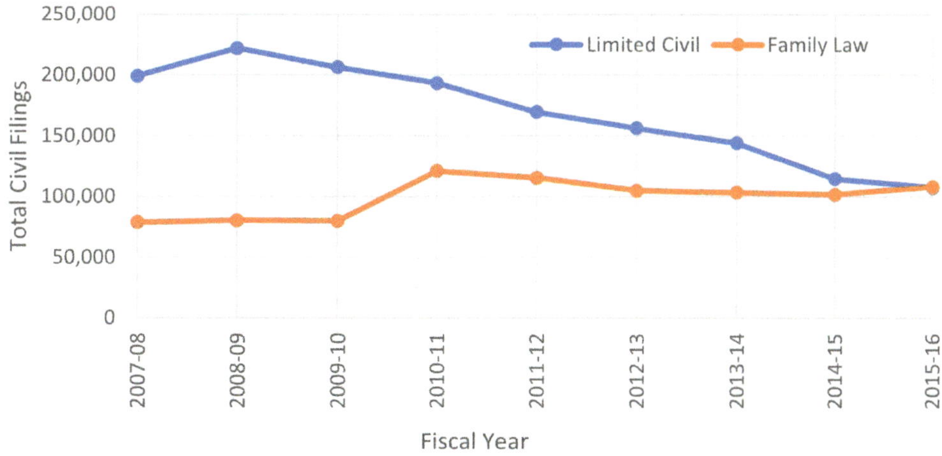

John advised the county that no increase in funding for court-based self-help centers was warranted when the number of cases most typically handled by these centers was declining.

While helping Ohio, in 2017, to develop a strategic plan for a new statewide legal information website (which has expanded into a full service portal over the past half dozen years), John learned that civil filing fee-based revenue for Ohio civil legal services had fallen by 40 percent since 2008.

At the same time, the decline in filings in California was becoming apparent to Alan during the annual budget process. The formulas for judgeships and trial court funding showed an unprecedented reduction of need in some California courts.

Discussions of these observations at professional conferences with persons such as Ray Billotte, the court administrator for the superior court in Maricopa County, Arizona, confirmed that civil filings declines were not unique to California and Ohio. While Maricopa County civil filings had not declined in absolute numbers, the per capita filings had fallen significantly in recent years. Ray referred to this issue as the "elephant in the room that no one wants to talk about."

In 2018, the NCSC put out a bulletin noting that state court filings in *every major case category* had declined from 2008 to 2016 in the 39 states reporting filing data.[3] The reported results are displayed in Figure 1.2.

FIGURE 1.2 NATIONWIDE STATE COURT FILING TRENDS, 2008–16

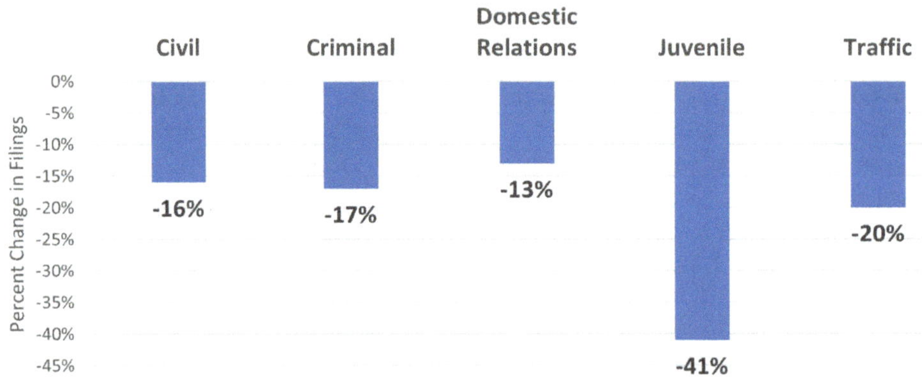

Source: Data from National Center for State Courts

1.1.2 Initiating a Study

What eventually resulted in this book began as an exploratory study at the Institute for the Advancement of the American Legal System at the University of Denver (IAALS), where John at the time was doing consulting and Alan was serving on an advisory board. With the support of the director, Rebecca Kourlis, they began a study working with several members of the IAALS staff. What is happening? Why?

The IAALS team, led by John and Alan, chose to focus on civil filings, and obtained the cooperation of four states—California, Minnesota, Ohio, and Texas—who agreed to

3. Nat'l Ctr. for State Courts, Court Statistics Project, Caseload Highlights, 2020 Incoming Cases in State Courts, Jan. 2020.

provide extensive data sets from their statistical archives. The pandemic interrupted the study. IAALS pursued its own interests, producing a report released in May 2023.[4] They authorized John and Alan to use the data collected to pursue their own interests in the data. That pursuit, with the help of numerous colleagues noted in the acknowledgments section, produced this book.

1.1.3 Choosing a Case Type

The first decision was the case type(s) on which to focus. Addressing all case types was beyond the resources of IAALS and beyond the scope of an exploratory research design. Civil cases, not including family, probate, or mental health, made the most sense—most trial courts handle some or all types of civil matters. The processing of criminal, juvenile delinquency, juvenile delinquency, and traffic cases varies widely from state to state and from community to community within a state. Domestic relations cases showed the lowest percentage change of the case types reported by NCSC. Traffic case filings are highly influenced by local law enforcement policies.

We initially felt that the filing of civil cases was more discretionary in its nature than for other case types. You have no choice about using a court to obtain a verdict in a criminal or delinquency matter. Only a court can grant a divorce, or resolve a probate. One does not have to get a court judgment to resolve a civil matter.

On closer analysis, the discretionary aspect of filing a civil case is time limited. The statute of limitations makes the court process just as obligatory in civil cases as in the other case types. The only way to stay the running of the statute of limitations is by initiating a lawsuit within the statutory time limit. Failure to file within that time period renders a contract or debt unenforceable or an injury non-compensable.

1.1.4 Choosing Our States

The IAALS research staff, using the five most recent NCSC annual statistical reports (2012 through 2016) and population data from the U.S. census, prepared a report showing the total state court civil filings and per capita civil filings for each state.

That report produced the first major finding from the study—the stunning disparity in per capita filings from state to state. That topic is covered in detail later in this chapter.

The IAALS team sought initially to pick states with complete and consistent filings data that varied widely in the numbers of per capita filings. After detailed study of data from seven states, we settled on California, Minnesota, Ohio, and Texas, all of whom agreed to participate. The extent of the data set each provided was delimited by the time period within which the states' statistical gathering system had been consistent regarding civil case reporting categories.

California provided us with 41 years of data, broken down by broad civil filings categories: Limited Civil, Unlimited Civil, and Small Claims. There was also greater case category detail for Unlimited Civil cases. A separate file analyzable by county was also provided. Minnesota provided 26 years of data, Ohio 21, and Texas 16.

---

4. Inst. for the Advancement of the Am. Legal Sys., The Past and Future of State Court Civil Filings, 2023.

After we began our independent investigation, we were able to obtain 25 years of civil filings data for the state of Illinois.

These states are not necessarily representative of the United States as a whole. With the exception of Ohio, they fall at the low end of the per capita civil filings range. None is a small state, in size or in population. They do not represent all geographic and cultural parts of the country.

1.1.5 Other Data

Alan researched the court reports and literature for all five states for the entire period of the data we analyzed. We also obtained extensive information from the NCSC's website. Additionally, we collected supplemental data on court fees and the composition of the active bar of each state.

1.1.6 The Journey within the Data

Alan took the lead in analyzing the data, starting with the state with which he was most familiar—California. The first step was to look at the statewide civil filings trends over the entire period for which data was made available. The 41-year data series for California shows a roller coaster with recurring civil filings increases and decreases. However, the overall trend over 41 years is downward. The actual number of civil filings in California in fiscal year 2018–19 was lower than 41 years prior. And, of course, the per capita filings have fallen much more steeply.

California's assumption of ever-growing filings was documented in an earlier study of filings by a futures commission[5] conducted during a period in which total filings were in fact increasing—see gray "Overlap Years" in Figure 1.3.

FIGURE 1.3 CALIFORNIA FILINGS—ALL CIVIL CASE TYPES

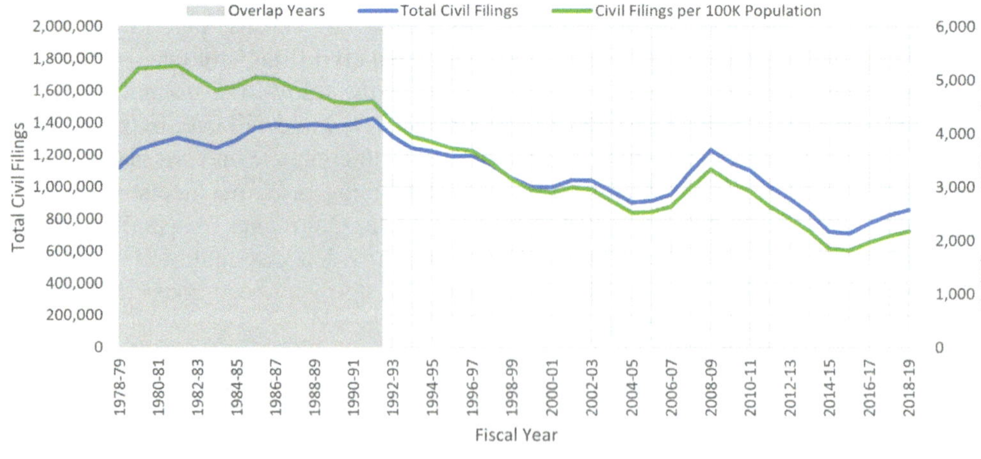

5. Comm'n on the Future of the Cal. Courts, Justice in the Balance 2020, 1993.

In contrast, the period from fiscal years 1991–92 to 2015–16 showed a consistent downward slope, consistent with the NCSC's report for the post-2008 period, with one significant exception—the period from 2005–06 to 2009–10. The official start of the Great Recession was 2008. We hypothesized that the "hump" centered on fiscal year 2008–09 had something to do with the business cycle. But it seemed completely counterintuitive; civil filings increased during boom times—when credit was easily accessible and employment was high—and then decreased during times of economic hardship. One would think that debt collection and eviction and other consequences of hard times, for example, defaults on contracts, would rise, not fall, during a recession.

This "hump" also appeared in the data for the other states we studied—to one extent or another. The phenomenon was a major focus of our attention during the study. This is addressed in Chapter 9.

Detailed study of the California data disclosed a number of other interesting facts about this 41-year time period:

- County by county variations are just as unpredictable as state-by-state variations. We could find no consistent patterns.
- Data for the largest jurisdictions was not a predictor of statewide trends.
- Changes in court organization, in amount in controversy limits on the jurisdiction of limited courts, statutes of limitations, and in court case processing initiatives had no lasting impact on civil filings.
- The most dramatic filings decline appeared in small claims cases.

These same phenomena also appeared in the data for the other states.

All of these topics are addressed in their own chapters.

1.2 Per Capita Filings in the State Courts: Do We Live in the Same "Legal Country"?

Our first major revelation came early in our efforts—as we researched state court systems to decide which states to invite to participate in the study. For this purpose, we looked at total civil case filings. And we thought it might be interesting to look at per capita filings, defined as filings per 100,000 population, as well as total filings. We were frankly astonished at the disparity in per capita filings from state to state that the data showed. Our subsequent further investigation of this data not only confirmed the disparity but also documented that the filings decline we see in the five states we studied in detail is also present in the national filings data.

The NCSC maintains a national database of state court caseload statistics going back to the 1970s. The data we originally reviewed for the purpose of choosing states for inclusion in our study was from 2016. For this book, we chose to present the data for the most recent year available (2021) and for four and eight years prior (2017 and

2013), presenting the most current data for those years.[6] The NCSC data includes per capita measures as well as overall totals for all new filings, then new filings broken down into five basic reporting categories—civil, family, juvenile, criminal, and traffic, and finally into subcategories following the State Court Guide to Statistical Reporting.[7]

1.2.1 Filing Levels of All Case Types

Figures 1.4, 1.5, and 1.6 show the total annual new case filings (including all five case types) per 100,000 population for roughly two-thirds of the states for 2013, 2017, and 2021. The NCSC's statistics do not include states that do not report filings data for all of the case types—ensuring that the data is roughly comparable from state to state (though there are unavoidable differences arising from reporting on a calendar or fiscal year basis or variations in the categories of cases from state to state).

1.2.1.1 2013: Filings per 100,000 Population across States

For 2013, Figure 1.4 shows that the total filings per 100,000 population of all case types ranges from a high of 83,966 in New Jersey (or roughly 0.8 filings per person in the population) to 11,713 in New Hampshire (or 0.1 filings per person). The ratio is roughly 7 to 1. The average per capita filing level for the 37 states[8] whose data is displayed by the NCSC is 29,219, or almost 0.3 filings per person. New Jersey is obviously a statistical outlier. If New Jersey and New Hampshire are removed from the calculation, the ratio comes down to roughly 4 to 1.

---

6. Trial Court Caseload Overview, Caseload Detail—Total Civil, https://www.courtstatistics.org/court-statistics/interactive-caseload-data-displays/csp-stat-nav-cards-first-row/csp-stat-civil (last visited Mar. 4 and 5, 2023).

7. Nat'l Ctr. for State Courts, State Court Guide to Statistical Reporting, version 2.2.2, https://www.courtstatistics.org/__data/assets/pdf_file/0031/88735/State-Court-Guide-to-Statistical-Reporting.pdf (last updated Jan. 2023).

8. The states for which this data is not reported for 2013 are Arkansas, Mississippi, Montana, North Carolina, North Dakota, Oklahoma, Oregon, South Carolina, South Dakota, Tennessee, Virginia, West Virginia, Wisconsin, and Wyoming.

FIGURE 1.4 2013 TOTAL FILINGS OF ALL CASE TYPES PER 100,000 POPULATION IN 37 STATES

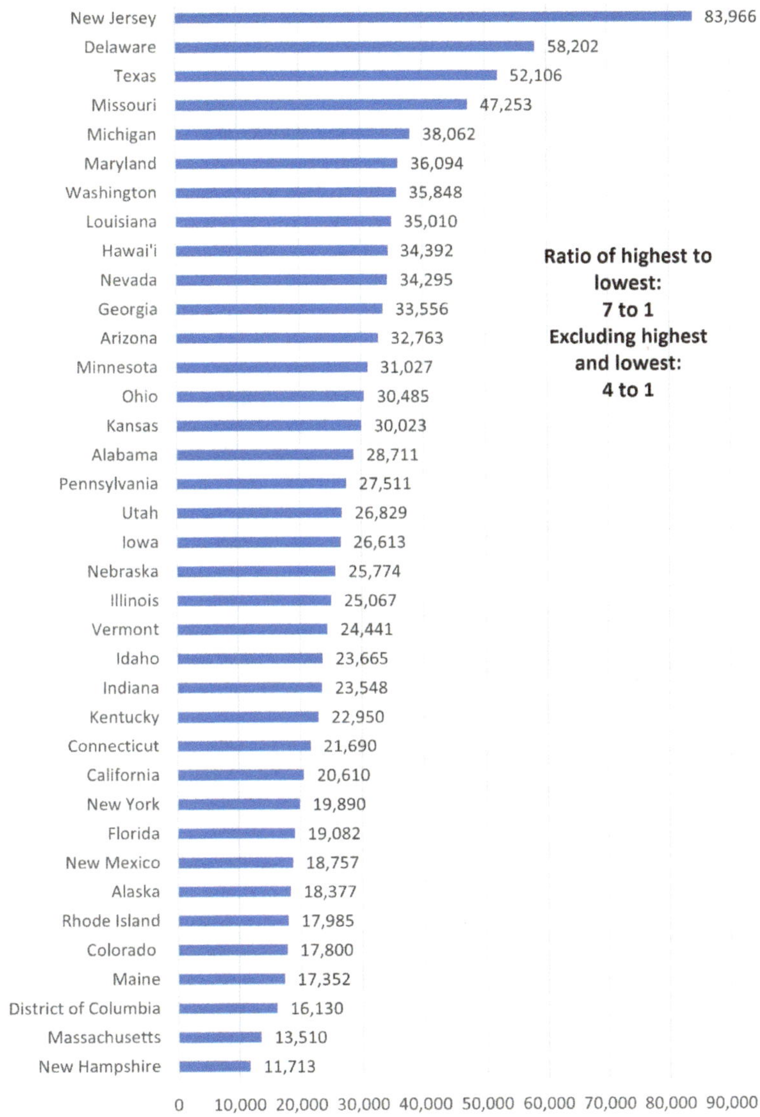

1.2.1.2 2017: Filings per 100,000 Population across States

The filings disparities for 2017, displayed in Figure 1.5, are only slightly less striking. New Jersey is again the state with the highest total filings per 100,000 population with 80,631 filings per 100,000 population, or roughly 0.8 filings per person. In 2017, Massachusetts had the lowest per capita rate: 9,831 per 100,000, or 0.09 per person. The ratio of highest compared to lowest state is 8 to 1. If New Jersey and Massachusetts are removed from the calculation, the ratio is the same as in 2013: 4 to 1. The average of the 38 states[9] was 25,595 per 100,000 population—a decrease of 12 percent from 2013.

FIGURE 1.5 2017 TOTAL FILINGS OF ALL CASE TYPES PER 100,000 POPULATION IN 38 STATES

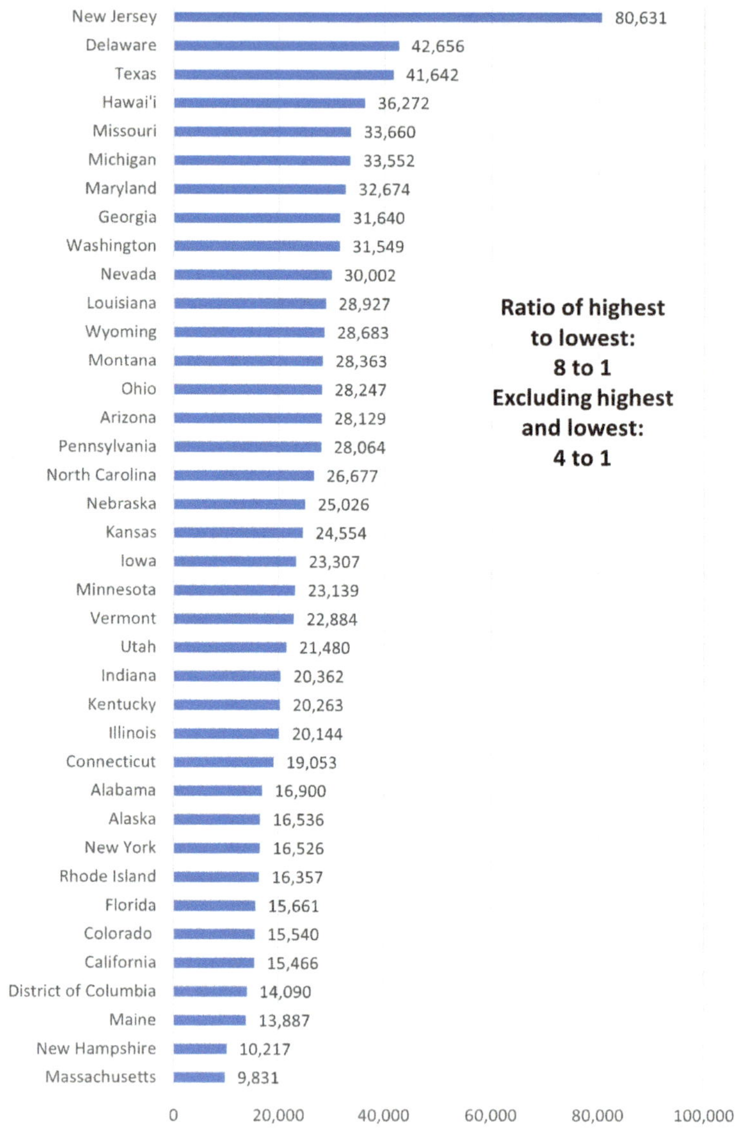

9. The states not included in 2017 were Arkansas, Idaho, Mississippi, New Mexico, North Dakota, Oklahoma, Oregon, South Carolina, South Dakota, Tennessee, Virginia, West Virginia, and Wisconsin.

1.2.1.3 2021: Filings per 100,000 Population across States

For 2021, Figure 1.6 shows a disparity of 12 to 1 between the state with the highest total filings per 100,000 population (again New Jersey) and the lowest (District of Columbia). New Jersey had 62,454 filings per 100,000 population—or more than 0.6 filings per person. The District of Columbia had 5,389 filings per 100,000 population, or roughly 0.05 filings per person.

FIGURE 1.6 2021 TOTAL FILINGS OF ALL CASE TYPES PER 100,000 POPULATION IN 38 STATES

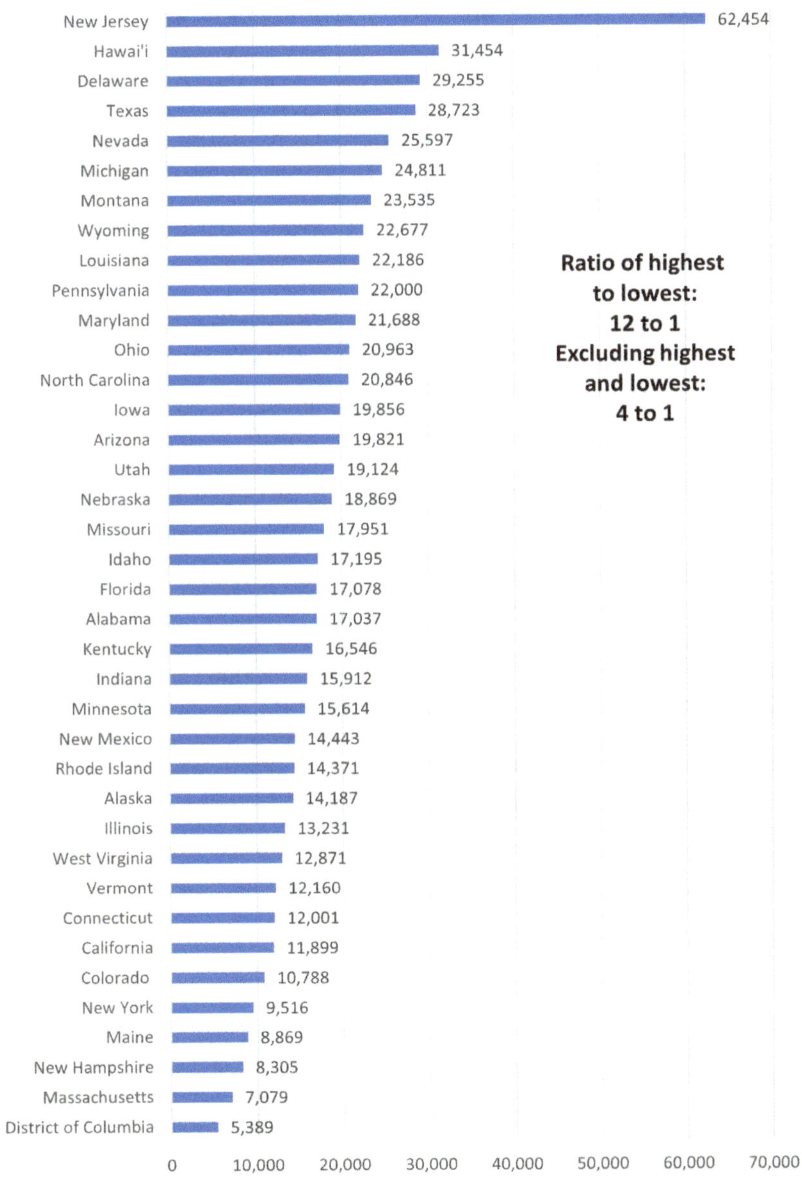

If we remove both New Jersey and the District from the calculation of disparity in filings, the ratio falls to 4 to 1, with Hawaii having roughly 0.3 filings per person and Massachusetts having 0.07 filings per person. The average per capita filings for the 38 states[10] was 18,587, a drop of 27 percent from 2017, and of 36 percent from 2013.

The per capita filings differences are not easily explained. Texas, the second most populous state, appears near the top in all three years. California, Florida, and New York, the other most populous, appear in the bottom ten. Connecticut, Maine, Massachusetts, New Hampshire, Rhode Island, and Vermont appear frequently in the bottom ten. No New England state appears in the top ten in any of the three years. New Jersey, Delaware, and Hawaii, along with Texas, appear at or near the top in each of the three years. But there are northeastern, midwestern, southern, and western states in the top ten each year.

In sum, per capita court filings levels for all case types differ dramatically from state to state for no obvious reason. Across the United States, per capita filings have been declining over the past eight years. The decline from 2017 to 2021 was undoubtedly influenced by the pandemic. But the decline from 2013 to 2017 was clearly independent of any pandemic effect.

1.2.1.4 Total Civil Filing Levels

Focusing on just civil cases, the data for total civil filings reported by the NCSC contains three categories of cases that we did not include within "civil filings" for purposes of our study—probate, conservatorship, and mental health. The filing numbers also include reopened, transferred, and remanded cases, not just new cases. Therefore, the civil filing data shown here will not be consistent with total civil filing data reported elsewhere for the five states we studied in detail.

1.2.1.5 2013: Civil Filings per 100,000 Population across States

The comparable filings per 100,000 population data for only civil cases for 2013 is shown in Figure 1.7. The disparity between Maryland and Hawaii is roughly 7 to 1, with Maryland having 17,654 civil filings per 100,000 population, or 0.2 per person. Hawaii had 2,500 such filings per 100,000 persons, or 0.03 per person. Maryland is the obvious statistical outlier for this data set.[11] If Maryland and Hawaii are removed from the calculation, the ratio falls to 3.8 to 1. The national average civil filings per 100,000 population was 5,274 for the 42 states[12] for which the NCSC reported civil data in 2013.

10. The states not included in 2021 were Arkansas, Georgia, Kansas, Mississippi, North Dakota, Oklahoma, Oregon, South Carolina, South Dakota, Tennessee, Virginia, Washington, and Wisconsin.

11. Alan Carlson studied Maryland civil case data extensively for consideration as one of the states in our study. He found no category of Maryland civil case filings that were not counted as civil filings in the other states.

12. The states not included were Massachusetts, Mississippi, Montana, North Carolina, Oklahoma, Oregon, South Dakota, Tennessee, and Virginia.

FIGURE 1.7 2013 TOTAL CIVIL FILINGS PER 100,000 POPULATION IN 42 STATES

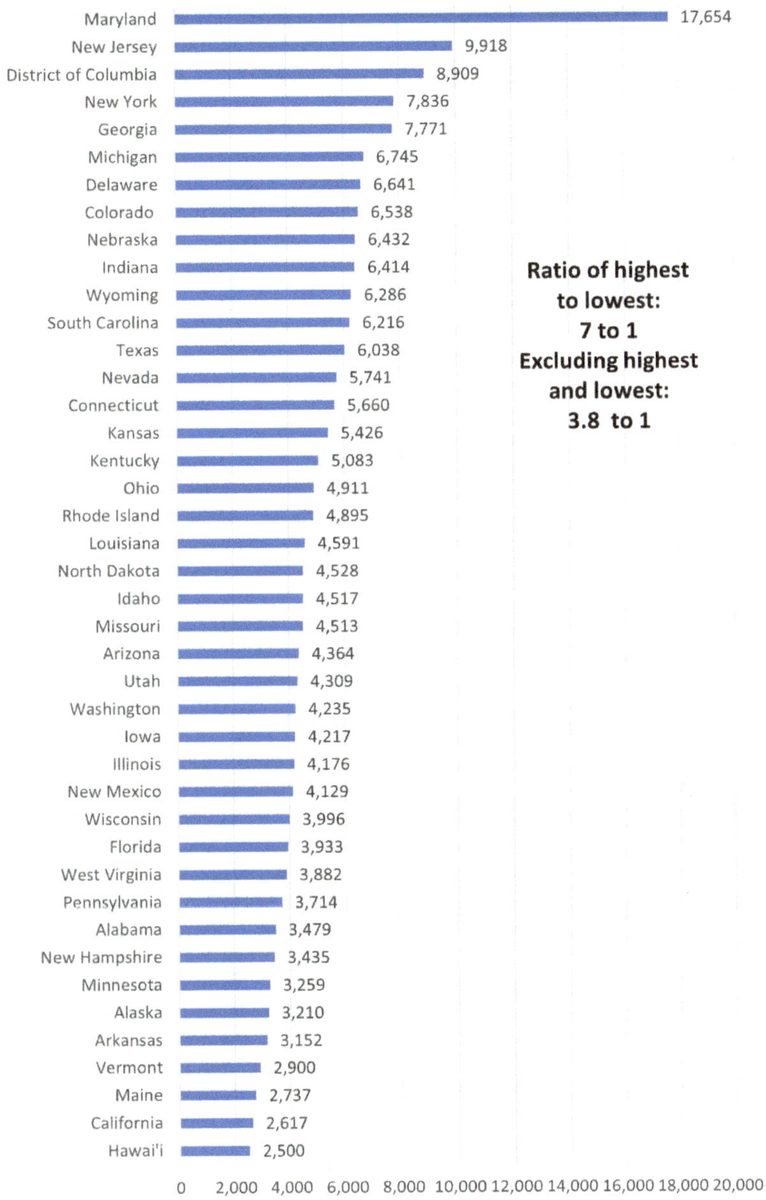

1.2.1.6 2017: Civil Filings per 100,000 Population across States

In 2017, Maryland once again had by far the highest per capita filing level: 16,951, or almost 0.2 filings per person (Figure 1.8). This year Maine was the lowest, with 2,174 per 100,000 population, or 0.02 civil filings per person. The ratio between the two states was 8 to 1. If Maryland and Maine are removed from the calculation, the ratio between New Jersey and California is 3.9 to 1. The average per capita filings for the 43 states reported was 5,075—a 3 percent reduction from 2013.

FIGURE 1.8 2017 TOTAL CIVIL FILINGS PER 100,000 POPULATION IN 43 STATES

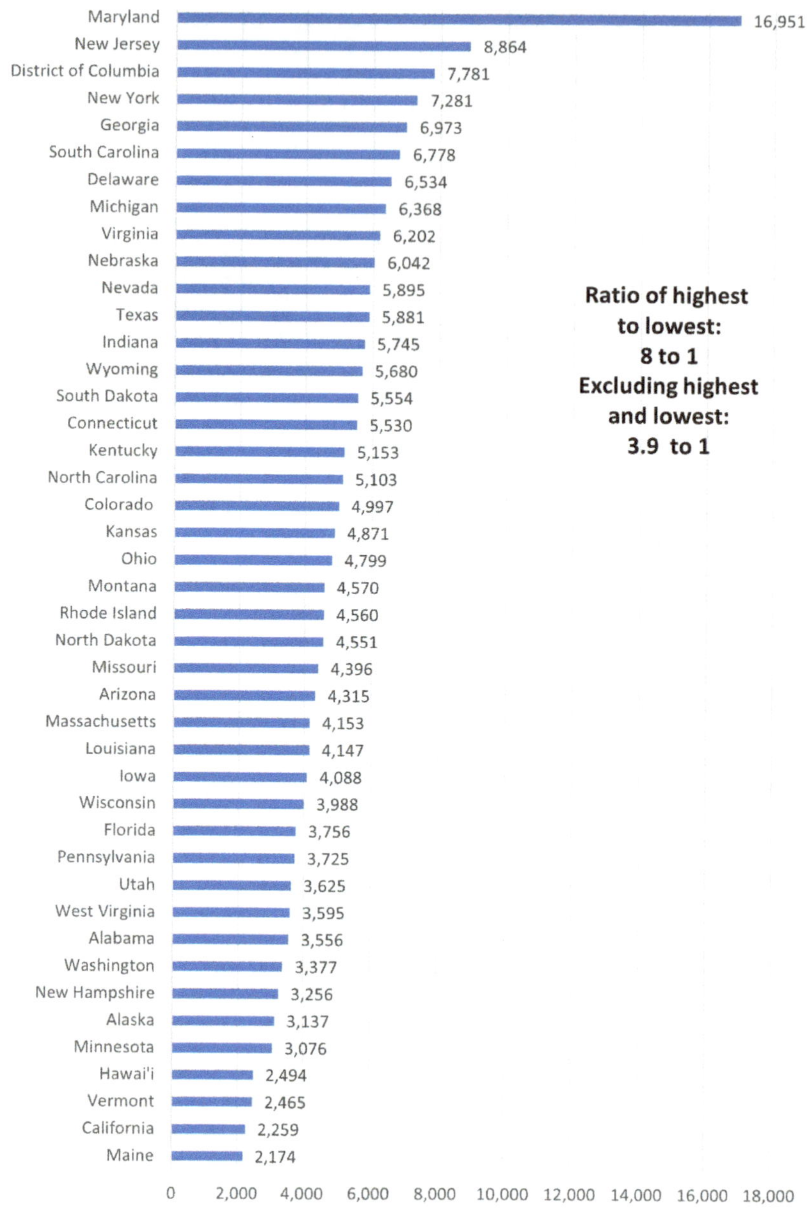

1.2.1.7 2021: Civil Filings per 100,000 Population across States

In 2021, Maryland again led the nation in per capita civil filings, but had far fewer than in 2013 and 2017 (Figure 1.9). It had 10,480 filings per 100,000 population, or 0.1 filings per person. Maine again had the lowest: 1,674 per 100,000 persons, or 0.02 per person. The ratio between these two states was 6 to 1. Excluding the highest and lowest produced a ratio of 3.3 to 1. The average for the 43 states[13] for which data was included was 3,879 per 100.000 population, 24 percent lower than in 2017 and 26 percent lower than in 2013.

FIGURE 1.9 2021 TOTAL CIVIL FILINGS PER 100,000 POPULATION IN 43 STATES

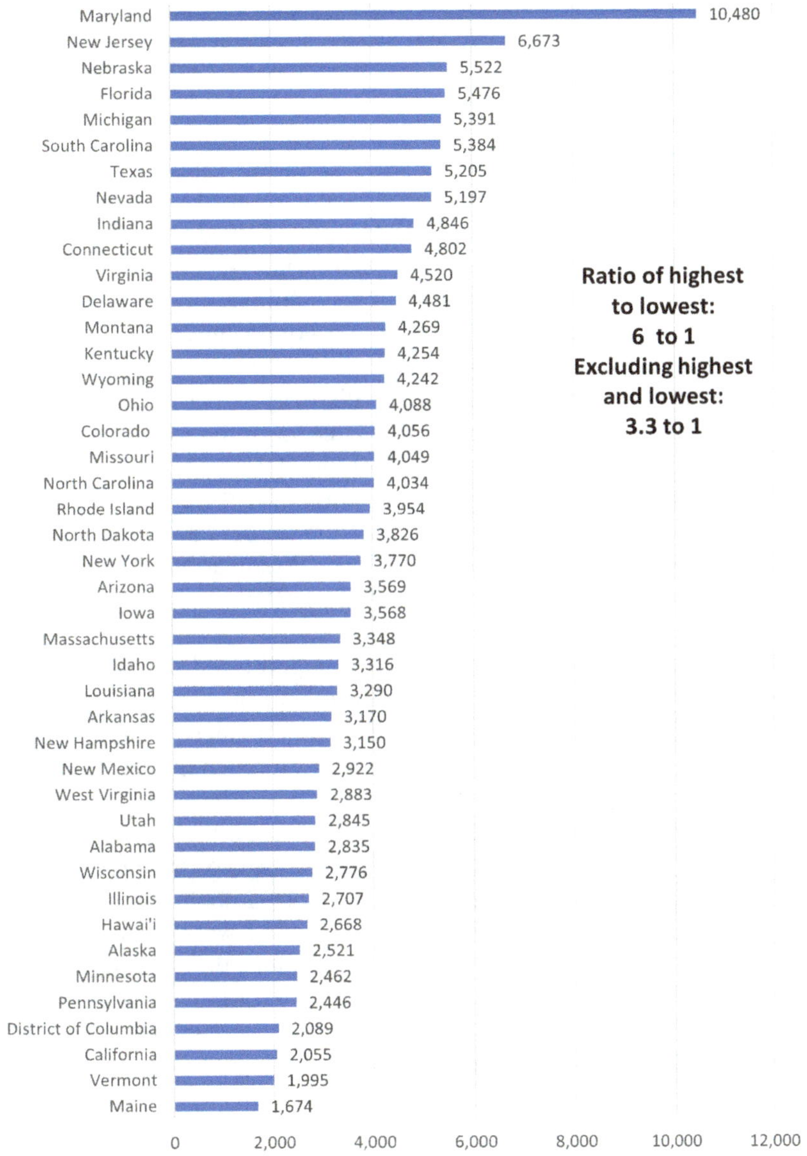

13. The states not included were Georgia, Kansas, Mississippi, Oklahoma, Oregon, South Dakota, Tennessee, and Washington.

1.2.2 Summary of Total and Per Capita Civil Filing Levels Nationwide

Maryland and New Jersey ranked first and second in per capita civil filings for each of the three years. Delaware and New York ranked in the top ten in 2013 and 2017, but not in 2021. California, Hawaii, Maine, Minnesota, and Vermont ranked in the bottom ten of the per capita civil filings all three years.

There is little consistency between the two data sets for total filings and for total civil filings. Hawaii, which ranked consistently near the top for total filings ranked in the bottom ten for civil filings all three years. Nebraska ranked in the top ten all three years (third in 2021) in civil per capita filings, but in the middle of the pack on total filings. New Jersey was the only state that consistently ranked very high on both scales. Maryland was in the top ten in both categories in two of the three years, but not in total filings in 2021. Michigan was in the top ten in both categories in two of the three years. The District of Columbia ranked very low in total filings, but in the top ten in civil filings in the first two years (but fourth from the bottom in 2021). Maine was in the bottom ten in both categories in all three years.

What can we say from this data? First, the disparity in per capita filings from state to state is shocking. Can we be living in the same legal system if Maryland has six, seven, or eight times as many filings per person as Maine? In a nation with generally consistent laws and court systems, how is it possible that there are four times as many court cases per person filed in one state compared to its next door neighbor? Why does Michigan have more than twice as many filings per person as Minnesota? Why is California near the bottom? Its economy, as measured by GDP, was the fourth largest in the world in 2021.

This information is not secret. The NCSC has published it regularly. It is accessible at no cost to anyone on the NCSC's website. But it is never discussed in court administration circles. Nor is it studied by researchers. Is there a more important topic for us to try to understand than this extraordinary difference in our legal system from state to state?

In the end, the five states we chose did not represent a high level of per capita filings diversity. Four of the five ranked in the bottom third of the preceding per capita charts. But there was nonetheless considerable diversity. Looking at just civil cases, the range of per capita filings across the five states studied was 2.2 to 1 at the peak of the recession in 2008. Among the 19 counties with more than one million population in the five states, the range of comparable per capita civil filings was 5.2 to 1 in 2019.

We found significant variance in per capita civil filings within the five states and even between adjacent counties within each state.

While this report focuses on the reality that civil case filings are not consistently rising in state courts, we have to begin with this profoundly surprising observation that state court per capita case filings exhibit such startling differences from state to state that there does not appear to be a commonality of experience from one state to the next that would make it likely that we, or anyone else, would be able to attribute observed changes in civil filings to a common set of causes.

On the other hand, this review of per capita filings over the past eight years enables us to establish that the general downward trend that we observed in civil filings in five states is more generally true across all states and across all case categories.

1.3 Case Filings as a Measure of Court Workload

What do new court filings measure? They measure the work yet to be done by a trial court. New filings are not a measure of activity, performance, efficiency, or quality of justice. Rather, performance and efficiency are often measured relative to filings, for example, clearance rates, the ratio of dispositions to filings.[14] However, filings may be a performance measure to the extent that a change in filing levels reflects a gain, or loss, of public trust and confidence in the judiciary's ability to fairly and timely resolve legal disputes.

The total number of cases filed in all trial courts in a year is a common measure reported in state judiciary annual reports. The number of filings is a single, simple, seemingly easy to understand measure. In annual reports, the total filing numbers may be compared to total filings in the prior year, over the last five years, or over the last ten years. The total filing numbers may be included in the press release for the annual report, and they may be used during budget season when courts appear before the legislature or local funding body. The number might be highlighted in media stories about the judiciary, for example, in a story about a "litigation explosion." To the extent the definition of a new filing is comparable, it also allows a crude comparison of courts across states.

But what does the total number of new filings really measure or represent? The total filings in a trial court include many types of cases, each involving different types of litigants, a different type of dispute, and requiring a different amount of time and resources to resolve, at different paces.

Consider two trial courts with the same number of total new civil filings in a year—100,000 cases. In a hypothetical River County Court, a limited jurisdiction court, the 100,000 new civil filings might include:

58,605 debt collection filings,

25,735 evictions and landlord/tenant disputes,

4,727 other types of civil filings, and

10,933 small claims filings.[15]

In a hypothetical Prairie District Court, a general jurisdiction court, the 100,000 new civil filings might include:

14,957 personal injury or property damage cases other than malpractice,

1,104 professional malpractice filings,

30,210 foreclosure cases, and

53,729 other types of civil cases.[16]

---

14. Nat'l Ctr. for State Courts, Trial Court Performance Measures, https://www.courttools.org/trial-court-performance-measures (last visited Oct. 30, 2023). *See also* Thomas M. Clarke & Paula Hannaford-Agor, Measuring the Impact of Access to Justice Programs: An Assessment Tool for Funders and Policymakers (NCSC, 2020).

15. Case type proportions based on 2019 filings in all Ohio municipal and county courts.

16. Case type proportions based on 2019 filings in all Ohio courts of common pleas.

These are very different incoming workloads. Debt and eviction cases are often decided by default without a hearing because the defendant fails to file a response to the lawsuit or fails to appear at a hearing. Small claims hearings are short, many can be heard in a typical court day. In contrast, a percentage of the general jurisdiction court cases will involve a jury trial that could last several days. Typically, cases filed in a general jurisdiction court take more court resources and last longer than cases filed in a limited jurisdiction court. The total number of new filings may be the same, but they are not equivalent or comparable as a measure of work now needing to be done.

Courts report the number of filings. What do private companies report? A comparison to measures found in a typical annual report of a private company is instructive. A company might manufacture a variety of products, analogous to the variety of cases filed in a court. However, a company's annual report would generally not report:

> Last year the company sold 10,000 products, consisting of 750 stoves, 700 refrigerators, 550 dishwashers, 3,000 coffee makers, and 5,000 water purifiers.

Rather, the annual report would say that total annual sales last year were $1,750,000. The number of products sold would be converted into a number, total sales dollars, which is a more meaningful measure of the company's overall work and economic performance, and for comparison to prior periods and to other companies. Note that the measure of total dollar sales is a measure of the company's completed activities—one element of an "outcome" measure, not an "input" measure. Nor is total dollar sales a performance measure by itself. Total sales does not measure the quality of outcomes, such as the satisfaction of customers or the benefits of the products to the public. Even the description of the number of products sold does not measure the amount of work requested of the company. A measure more comparable to new court filings would be the number of orders for each product or service.

There is no single measure for the trial courts that is comparable to a total sales figure or a net profit figure. It is not even clear what the goal of a single measure would be. Total filings, at best, is a measure of litigant "orders," not the judiciary's completed activities, outcomes, or performance. Moreover, since different cases require different amounts of judicial time, a comparable measure would require "weighting" filings by the work required to resolve them. This is discussed further Chapter 2, Section 2.5 and in the recommendations in Chapter 10.

When analyzing new filings in search of possible explanations of changes in filing levels, it is important to understand the nature of the decision to sue and the timing of lawsuits. The decision to sue is an individual decision by a litigant. Total new case filings are therefore an aggregate of decisions by literally thousands of individuals across a state depending on their specific circumstance, the nature of their claim, and the remedies sought. They do not reflect a consensus decision of a group of people. Class actions are an exception, but they are rare and declining as a result of recent laws and decisions. Finally, not all incidents that have legal aspects and are justiciable end up as lawsuits.[17] As such, evaluating a possible explanation of changes in filing levels needs to consider

17. Rebecca L. Sandefur & James Teufel, *Assessing America's Access to Civil Justice Crisis*, 11(3) U.C. Irvine L. Rev. 753, 763 (Feb. 2021), https://scholarship.law.uci.edu/ucilr/vol11/iss3/7.

the impact of societal or economic changes from the perspective of an individual contemplating whether to respond to a perceived injury or injustice by filing a lawsuit.

The timing of a suit is also relevant to examining possible explanations. A new case filing necessarily lags the event triggering the filing. Most states have statutes of limitations requiring a case to be filed within a certain period of time from the triggering incident. For example, two years is a typical limitation for filing cases involving personal injury or property damage, and four to six years for contract cases. Lawsuits are seldom filed immediately after the incident giving rise to the case. Often it takes time to determine potential defendants, assess damages, and engage in settlement discussion. Consequently, the incident triggering a new court filing may have occurred years before the filing. In analyzing the possible impact of events occurring outside the courts or a change in law on filing levels, one must remember there may be a delay before the effect of the change becomes fully apparent in filing levels.

Our perspective is that filings are a measure of the public's demand for court services, not a measure of a court's activities or outcomes. If that overall demand is falling, it is cause for concern. Consider an analogy. If an automobile dealer experiences a decline in the number of customers buying a car, that is a matter that must be addressed to stay in business. What were the causes of the reduced demand? Was the model of car the dealer sells going out of fashion, or was it a failing reputation of the car model's quality. Was it losing market share because of the introduction of cheaper products by a competitor? Perhaps it was a failing reputation for the dealership's post-sales service. Was it the manufacturer's or the dealer's lack of advertising, or effective advertising, or of advertising using the best medium for reaching potential customers?

Courts should adopt a similar approach in response to observed changes in filing levels. Rising or falling new case filings may indicate a change in the economy, in the nature of social and familial interactions, in public attitudes toward dispute resolution, or in the community's social contract. For instance, increases in civil protection order requests over recent decades is undoubtedly a reflection of increased societal attention to inappropriate behavior rather than an actual increase in its frequency or severity. Changes in filing levels could also be the result of public and bar perceptions of the effectiveness of court processes to deliver timely and effective remedies, or, perhaps, a change in the cost/benefit calculus relating to going to court.

Within this framework, this study examines the changes in new civil filings in the trial courts in five states over extended periods of time. Filing levels are expressed both as raw total numbers and as per capita filings—filings per 100,000 population. The per capita measure allows comparisons across states and across courts and regions within a state with different populations and demographics. Filing levels are also examined relative to changes in substantive and procedural law, in jurisdictional limits, in case management practices, in court structure, and in the national economy.

The results of the analysis presented here are often surprising. They are inconsistent with the generally accepted notion of ever-rising trial court filings. The unexpected results cry out for explanation. We have done our best to identify and explore plausible hypotheses for what we observed. But we have not been able to reach any definitive conclusions about "why" the civil filings pattern is what we observe it to be.

Far more case filing data from more states would be needed to begin to support findings of causation. At most, we have identified changes in filing levels, or the lack of changes in filing levels, that are associated with several factors. Moreover, the analysis looks at the factors one at a time, not in combination. Obviously, there can be multiple factors, simultaneously interacting, causing fluctuations in filing levels.[18] Hopefully, the analysis here provides a simple map for others to use in exploring the impact of these factors. On the other hand, the large disparity in per capita filings from state to state causes us to express caution to researchers seeking a generalizable explanation of declining civil filings. The wide variation in the use of the court system from state to state suggests basic differences in the attitudes and behaviors of the population as well as of the local legal profession.

Readers should be careful to distinguish the validity of the filing numbers from our speculations concerning possible explanations for their variance from expectations. We have accepted the numbers as reported by the courts every month or quarter. The judges and courts had no knowledge of how the numbers would be analyzed. We have taken great care to report them accurately, to explain any exclusions, and to inform our readers of their limitations. The analysis here is offered as much to stimulate a discussion of what is counted as to provide possible explanations for shifts in filing levels.

Perhaps this analysis will cause case filings to be treated in the future as an indicator, if not as a measure, of public trust and confidence in state trial courts as well as changes in the role of the state trial courts in the life of its community. The extent to which this could occur depends on the refinement in the recording and reporting of filings, discussed in the recommendations.

1.4 Organization of the Book and Chapters

The chapters in the book begin with a high level view—how did total civil filings change over the long term in five states? The analysis then explores several factors that, over the course of our careers, have been said to explain fluctuations in filing levels or that were adopted in whole or in part to influence filing behavior both across and within these five states. First, the impact on filing levels of external factors—the environment of trial courts, such as population, geography, and, to a limited extent, demographics within a state—are examined. The analysis then shifts to the judiciary itself. How does the composition of the civil caseload vary across and within states over time? What is the impact of variations in case flow management programs and practices on filing levels? What happens to filing levels when statutes of limitations and monetary jurisdiction boundaries are altered? What is the impact of differences in how the trial courts are organized, what initial filing fees are charged, and the number of lawyers in a state? Finally, there is a preliminary look at what happened to filing levels during economic recessions. Based on these analyses, we propose a number of recommendations concerning the case categories courts should count and how the information could be used to better manage the judicial branch and assess its impact on the communities it serves.

Each chapter begins with an introduction of the topic. It notes typical assumptions and expectations in the field of court administration regarding new civil case filings in

18. Henry N. Schreiber, *Innovation, Resistance, and Change: A History of Judicial Reform and the California Courts, 1960–1990*, 66 S. Cal. L. Rev. 2049, 2066 (1992), citing Richard Lempert, *Docket Data and Local Knowledge: Studying the Court and Society Link Over Time*, 24 Law & Soc'y Rev. 321, 327 (1990).

the context of the chapter's topic. The overview is followed by a summary of the major findings from those states among the five for which data about the topic was available. The chapter concludes with a more detailed discussion of the findings in each these states. Recommendations arising from the findings are provided in the final recommendations in Chapter 10.

If you are only interested in a particular topic that has its own chapter, we would recommend you read Chapter 2 first to provide a context for the discussion about a particular topic. It will provide a long-term overview of new filings that is relevant to the impact of the particular topic on filing levels that is of interest to you.

2

Trends in Civil Filing Levels across Five States over the Long Term

2.1 Total Filings in the Five States

During the final decades of the 20th century, there were often pronouncements of a "litigation explosion" in civil cases. For example, in 1993 the Commission on the Future of California Courts published a report that looked at civil filings over the previous 30 years. The Commission report stated, "It is generally known that California's courts have seen a massive increase in civil litigation in the last 30 years. . . ."[1] The case filing data analyzed in the five states here suggests the "explosion," if there ever was one,[2] had not only dissipated but had also reversed in at least some states.

Civil filing data from five states suggests that filings have fluctuated significantly over time, but there is no pattern of a long-term continuous rise in filings. Figure 2.1 displays the total annual civil filings for five states over the last 16 to 41 years. Table 2.1 provides percentage changes for specific periods. The total civil filing levels in California, Illinois, and Minnesota exhibited a similar filing pattern of a long-term decline. Texas and Ohio exhibited different filing patterns. Ohio experienced a significant increase in total filings during a portion of the study period, but ended with only a modest growth over the long term. Texas experienced appreciable growth during the most recent five years and was the only one of the five states to have filing levels in 2018 higher than the peak filing levels around 2008.

1. Comm'n on the Future of the Cal. Courts, Justice in the Balance 2020 at 133 (1993).

2. Marc Galanter, *Reading the Landscape of Disputes: What We Know and Don't Know (and Think We Know) about Our Allegedly Contentious and Litigious Society*, 31 U.C.L.A. L. Rev. 4 (1983).

FIGURE 2.1 TOTAL CIVIL FILINGS—COMPARABLE CASE CATEGORIES

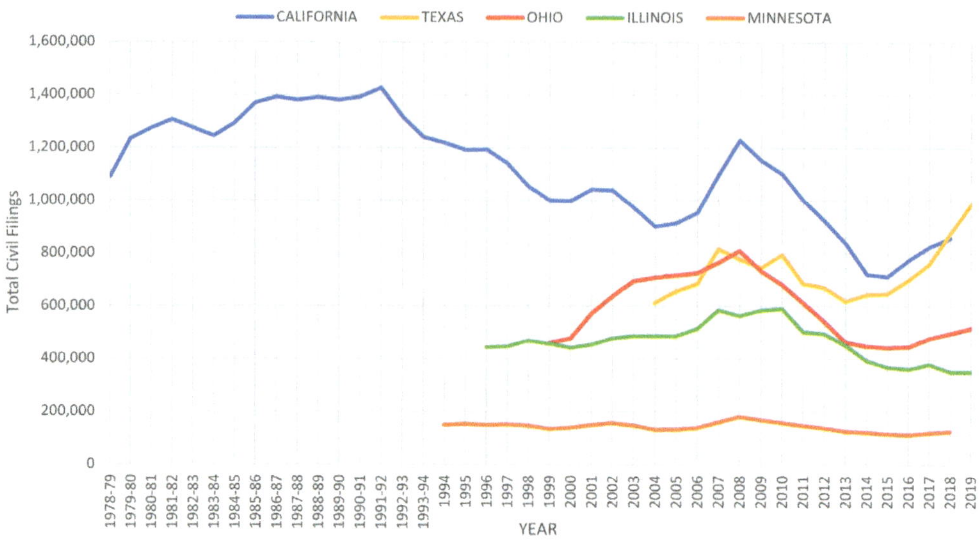

All five states experienced a surge during the first decade of this century leading up to the Great Recession. Thereafter, filing levels dropped to historic lows in four states. Texas was the exception. Ohio's surge started earlier and lasted longer. The Texas surge had two peaks, one in 2007 and a second in 2010. Minnesota's surge was less pronounced. While California's filings had steadily increased in the distant past, the highest total filing level was in Fiscal Year 1991–92. From that time forward, filings in California dropped. Although there was a surge from 2004 to 2014, filings subsequently dropped to levels lower than before the surge. Across four states the drop in total filings from the peak in the first decade of this century to the end of the period was substantial—it ranged from 25 percent to 38 percent; see the last row of Table 2.1. In contrast, Texas filings in 2019 were 21 percent higher than in the peak year of 2007.

Recently, all five states, especially Texas, showed renewed growth, starting as early as 2013. However, it remains to be seen what impact the pandemic that began in 2020 had on total civil filings. California's annual statistical report for Fiscal Year 2019–20 reported more than a 12 percent drop in total civil filings.[3] Minnesota's annual report for 2020 reported a 34 percent drop in total civil filings.[4] A 26 percent drop in new civil case filings in several states was reported by the National Center for State Courts (NCSC) Court Statistics Project.[5]

The data analyzed here suggest caution when looking at changes in filing levels over different time frames. For example, total civil filings in FY 2018–19 in California were up 2 percent over the last five years, down 30 percent over the last ten years, down 19 percent over the last 20 years, and down 21 percent over the last 40 years. The last

3. Jud. Council of Cal., 2021 Court Statistics Report, Statewide Caseload Trends, 2010–11 through 2019–20, tbl. 4a, at 96.

4. Minn. Jud. Branch, Annual Report 2020, at 17.

5. Nat'l Ctr. for State Courts, Court Statistics Project, Caseload Highlights, 2020 Incoming Cases in State Courts, Jan. 2020.

row of Table 2.1 shows the change over the last 20 years as compared to the first row showing the change over longer periods for which data was available. Figure 2.2 shows total filings in five states from 1999 to 2019. The extent and direction of the change in total filings can vary considerably depending on what time frame is examined.

TABLE 2.1 CHANGE IN COMPARABLE TOTAL FILINGS OVER TIME

	California	Illinois	Minnesota	Ohio	Texas
Change in total filings over the long term	–21% 41 years, FY1978–79 to FY 2018–19	–21% 25 years, 1996 to 2019	–17% 26 years, 1994 to 2018	13% 21 years, 1999 to 2019	61% 16 years, 2004 to 2019
Change in total state population	70% over 41 years	5% over 25 years	22% over 26 years	3% over 21 years	30% over 16 years
Change since most recent peak	–30% since peak in FY 2008-09	–40% since peak in 2010	–31% since peak in 2008	–36% since peak in 2008	21% since peak in 2007
Change from 1999 to 2018	–14%	–23%	–7%	8%	N/A

FIGURE 2.2 TOTAL COMPARABLE CIVIL FILINGS—1999 TO 2019

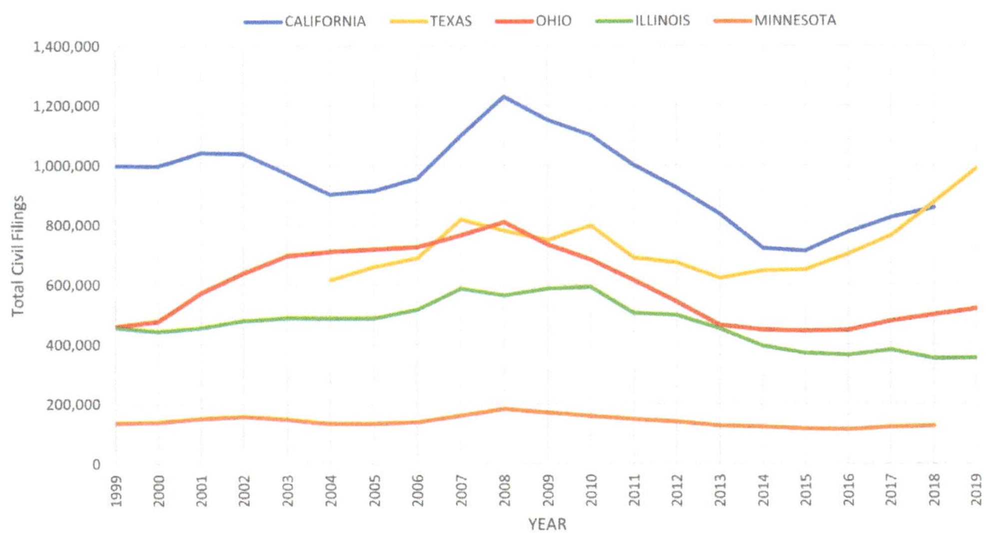

2.2 Per Capita Filings in the Five States

More direct comparison of filing levels across all five states can be done by converting total filings to per capita filings—filings per 100,000 population. The result was a significant finding of similarity of per capita filing levels across very diverse states. In three of the five states, California, Minnesota, and Texas, the per capita filing pattern was remarkably similar, both in terms of filing levels and the pattern over time (see

Figure 2.3 and Table 2.2). The pattern was similar despite very diverse populations, economies, cultures, and laws in the three states. Illinois and Ohio experienced much higher per capita filing levels, and had very different filing patterns. Ohio had a much higher per capita filing level since 1999 and also had a much more prominent surge up to 2008. All five states experienced a peak in or near 2008, associated with the Great Recession, discussed in Chapter 9.

All five states had an increase in per capita filing levels beginning in 2015. Texas tracks California and Minnesota until 2015, at which point per capita filings in Texas began to increase more rapidly than in the other two states. Ohio's increase in the last few years tracks the increase in Texas.

FIGURE 2.3 COMPARABLE TOTAL CIVIL FILINGS PER 100K POPULATION

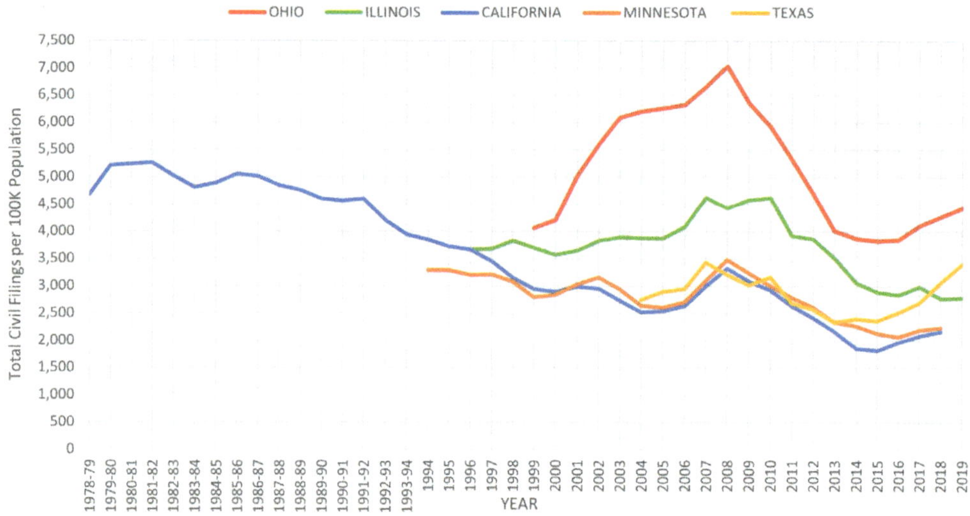

TABLE 2.2 CHANGE IN PER CAPITA COMPARABLE CIVIL FILINGS OVER TIME

	California	Illinois	Minnesota	Ohio	Texas
Change from 1999 to 2018	−26%	−25%	−20%	5%	N/A
Change over longer time frame	−54% over 41 years since FY 1978–79	−24% over 25 years since 1996	−32% over 26 years since 2004	9% over 21 years since 1999	24% over 16 years since 2004
Change since most recent peak	−35% since peak in FY 2008–09	−40% since peak in 2010	−36% since peak in 2008	−37% since peak in 2008	−0.7% since peak in 2007

2.3 Year-to-Year Fluctuations in Total and Per Capita Filing Levels

Another striking feature of both total filing levels and per capita filing levels was the significant fluctuations in filing levels from year-to-year. Looking across all five states since 2000, the maximum and minimum total filing changes year-to-year were similar in magnitude and frequency (see Table 2.3). The greatest year-to-year increases occurred during the first decade of the 21st century. In three of the five states, the largest increase was in 2007. In Ohio, the largest increase was in 2001. The largest year-to-year increases ranged from 13 to 20 percent, a substantial increase. The largest year-to-year decreases were in the years after the Great Recession in 2008–09. Again, the change was substantial, from minus 10 percent to minus 15 percent. In the years since 2000, three of four states had more years with decreases than increases, but Ohio had more years when filings increased than decreased. Looking at a longer time frame, California, Illinois, and Minnesota had more years with decreases than increases in total civil filings. Total filings were declining more often than rising, despite increases in population during the last couple of decades.

TABLE 2.3 FLUCTUATIONS IN TOTAL COMPARABLE CIVIL FILINGS

STATE	Largest One-Year Increase (years of change)	Largest One-Year Decrease (years of change)	Number of Years with Filing Declines since 2000	Number of Years with Filing Declines
California	15% FY 2006–07 to FY 2007–08	–14% FY 2013–14 to FY 2014–15	12 of 20	22 of 40
Illinois	14% 2006 to 2007	–15% 2010 to 2011	11 of 20	12 of 23
Minnesota	16% 2006 to 2007	–10% 2012 to 2013	11 of 20	14 of 24
Ohio	20% 2000 to 2001	–15% 2012 to 2013	7 of 20	7 of 20
Texas	19% 2006 to 2007	–14% 2010 to 2011	N/A	5 of 15

2.4 The Relationship between Filing Levels and Population

One significant finding is that the relationship between total filings and population was very weak. Population was not a good predictor of filing levels, either across states, within states, or over time. In three of the five states, filings levels have declined in most years since the turn of the century, notwithstanding population growth. In Ohio, filings levels have fluctuated dramatically, while population growth was very slow.

There did appear to be a relationship between per capita filing levels and population growth, but the inverse of what might have been expected. Slower growing states had higher per capita filing levels. Two states had relatively slow population growth from 1990 to 2019—Ohio (3 percent) and Illinois (2 percent). The other three states had much higher population growth over 30 years—Minnesota (15 percent), California (16 percent), and Texas (38 percent). Figure 2.4 displays the population growth in the five states since 1990. Comparing per capita filing levels, slower growing states appeared to have higher per capita filing levels (dotted lines in Figure 2.5) than the faster growing states (dashed lines in Figure 2.5). Filings data from more states would be needed to identify what, if anything, about which demographic, economic, or societal factors of a state might explain the per capita civil filing patterns exhibited by these two sets of states.

FIGURE 2.4 GROWTH IN TOTAL STATE POPULATION SINCE 1990

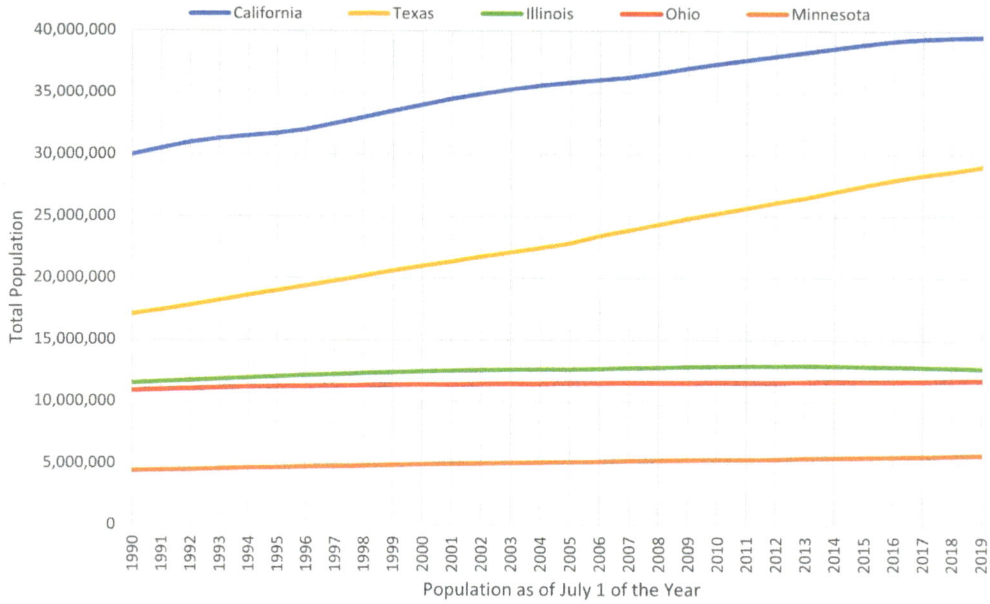

FIGURE 2.5 COMPARABLE CIVIL FILINGS PER 100K POPULATION: SLOW POPULATION GROWTH (OH, IL) AND FAST POPULATION GROWTH (MN, CA, TX)

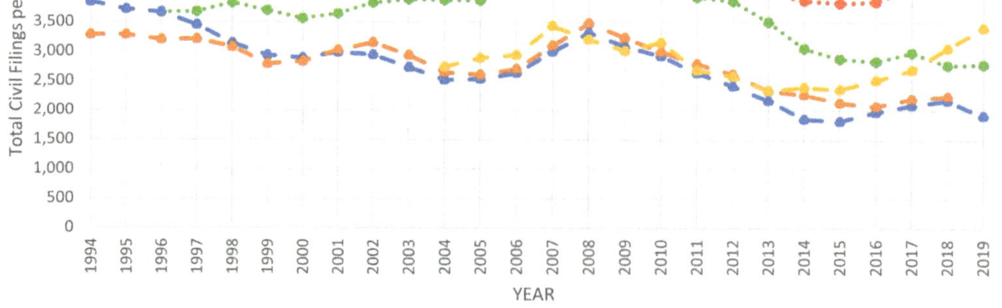

Population was also not a strong predictor of per capita filing levels across counties within a state. In California, larger counties, as a group, had higher per capita filing levels than smaller counties, but there was substantial variation of filing levels within each size group. Similarly, in Minnesota, per capita filing levels varied by county population but not consistently. Although the pattern of per capita filing levels over time were similar, the fluctuations within the pattern varied significantly. Per capita filing levels were likely affected more by other factors, such as the "local legal culture" and differences in demographics and economics, than population.

2.5 Using Total Filings for Resource Allocation

One impact of the significant year-to-year fluctuations in filing levels is that it wreaks havoc in states where judgeship needs or trial court funding is based on total annual filings. There are four problems. First is the lag between when filings increase and when additional resources become available. Second is the reluctance and near impossibility of courts' reducing judges or staff when filings decline. Third is a possible shift in the mix of filings not adequately tracked in the funding methodology that affects the amount and allocation of judicial resources needed for these cases. Fourth are changes in substantive or procedural law, or implementation of new case management programs in response to increases in filings that affect judicial need for particular case categories.

A significant increase in total filings from one year to the next would result in a sudden increase in the number of judges and staff, and the amount of funding, needed to resolve the new cases. Government budget processes and judicial appointment processes do not move this quickly. Budgets are adopted one year in advance, two in some states. Therefore, increases in funding in response to an increase in filings would lag the filings by up to a year, even assuming more resources are appropriated. Moreover, if additional judge or staff positions are approved for the next budget year, it often takes months to fill new positions. In the meantime a significant increase in total filings could overwhelm a trial court, creating backlogs and delay.

A significant decrease in filings is equally problematic. Reductions in judgeships rarely occur. Moreover, reducing the number of judgeships is problematic when judges serve a guaranteed four- to six-year term. Reductions in staff occur when budgets are cut in response to a recession when some categories of filings likely have increased based on the analysis here.

More sophisticated measures of judge and budget needs have been developed, although they suffer from the same problem of the lag between filings changes and budget changes. They also suffer from a lag between changes in the judicial need for a particular case category and corresponding adjustments to the measure of the need.

Because different case categories require different amounts of judge time to be resolved, a method known as weighted caseload was developed in the 1960s. It provides a more sensitive measure than raw filings for estimating judgeship needs and court funding. The method starts with a time study to calculate the average amount of judge time a particular case category requires to be resolved, referred to as the case weight for that case category. Multiplying the annual filings for each case category by its case weight and adding the totals for all case categories produces a measure of the total time required to resolve all the cases filed in a year. The amount of time a judge could reasonably provide in a year to resolve cases is also calculated, referred to as the judge-year value. Dividing the total time estimate by the judge-year value results in a figure of the number of judges needed to resolve the cases filed that year.

One critical factor in the weighted caseload method is the estimate of the time needed to resolve each particular category of case—its case weight. Several factors can affect the case weight. If the pattern of resolution of a particular category of cases changes, more, or less, judge time is required to resolve those cases. For example, if the trial rate increases or there are more or longer-lasting appearances in cases, more judge time is needed to resolve cases. The change could be the result of changes in statutes or case law that affect procedures. Unfortunately, revisions of the case weights to reflect these types of changes never occur on an annual basis, and may only occur once every five to ten years. The consequence is that trial courts can have insufficient resources to address changes in the case weight of filings in a timely manner.

Another factor that could alter case weights would be increases in assistance provided to unrepresented litigants. As described later, this often occurs in response to a surge in filings, for example in eviction or foreclosure cases during recessions. New or expanded programs can either increase or decrease filings. Programs that are made available pre-filing, for example, intervention to assist potential litigants, can reduce filings as more cases are resolved without a court filing. Post-filing programs may decrease the amount of court time needed to resolve cases because of pre-trial resolutions. If post-filing programs add appearances or lengthen hearings, court time to resolve cases would increase. Again, there will be a lag from when changes are implemented and the case weights are revised, again leading to a mismatch of need and resources.

There is a widespread belief among trial judges that the existence of a self-represented litigant in a case will increase the time and resources required to resolve it. The empirical studies that we are aware of do not bear this out. An internal California assessment in the early 2000s made available to one of the authors found that cases with self-represented litigants were resolved in less time than cases with lawyers on both sides in ten of the 18 case types examined. In particular, family law matters with lawyers took 30 percent longer to resolve than those with a self-represented litigant. All the judges in a 2008 study of communications among judges and litigants in cases with two self-represented litigants in four courts disagreed with the statement: "Self-represented persons generally take more of my time than represented persons in similar cases"[6]

Although the weighted caseload method results in a more accurate estimate of need than raw filings, it fails to address the issue of the lag between filing changes and resource changes. The calculation of need generally occurs no sooner than the year after filing levels have changed. If there are changes in the processing of some types of cases that affect case weights, the infrequency of recalculating case weights exacerbates the delay problem. And court systems will find it increasingly difficult to use weighted

---

6. Greacen Associates, LLC, *Effectiveness in Courtroom Communication in Hearings Involving Two Self-Represented Litigants*, NAT'L CTR. FOR STATE COURTS ON BEHALF OF THE SELF-REPRESENTED LITIGATION NETWORK (Apr. 2008), https://www.srln.org/node/349/report-effectiveness-courtroom-communications-hearings-involving-two-self-represented.

caseload studies to justify level or increasing budgets when court filings are decreasing because the studies will necessarily show that judges are needing ever more resources to handle each case.

In California, the weighted caseload methodology is used to estimate trial court judgeship needs, staffing, and trial court funding. In response to significant year-to-year fluctuations in filing levels, California adopted a three-year moving average of filings to "smooth out" calculations of judgeship need, staffing need, and funding. While this better matched the funding and judicial appointment streams, it further delayed needed resources when filings rose, in particular when filings rose significantly. Minnesota also uses the weighted caseload methodology for determining judgeship needs.

2.6 California—Total and Per Capita Filing Levels

Total filings of all civil cases in California displayed considerable fluctuation over the 41-year period (blue columns in Figure 2.6). Filings rose from FY 1978–79 to a peak in FY 1981–82, dropped for a few years, then rose to the highest level during the 41-year period in FY 1991–92. This was followed by a steady decline ending in FY 2004–05. Filings then began a roller coaster pattern that peaked in FY 2008–09, followed by a steep decline until FY 2015–16. Total filings rose in the last three years of the period. The decline from the peak in FY 1991–92 to FY 2018–19 was almost 40 percent. The year-to-year fluctuations were considerable (Figure 2.7). Total filings dropped in 22 years and rose in 18 years. The largest year-to-year increase was almost 15 percent. The greatest drop was almost 14 percent. The 41-year decline in total civil filings was 21 percent. The decline since 2000 was 14 percent.

FIGURE 2.6 CALIFORNIA FILINGS FOR ALL CIVIL CASE CATEGORIES

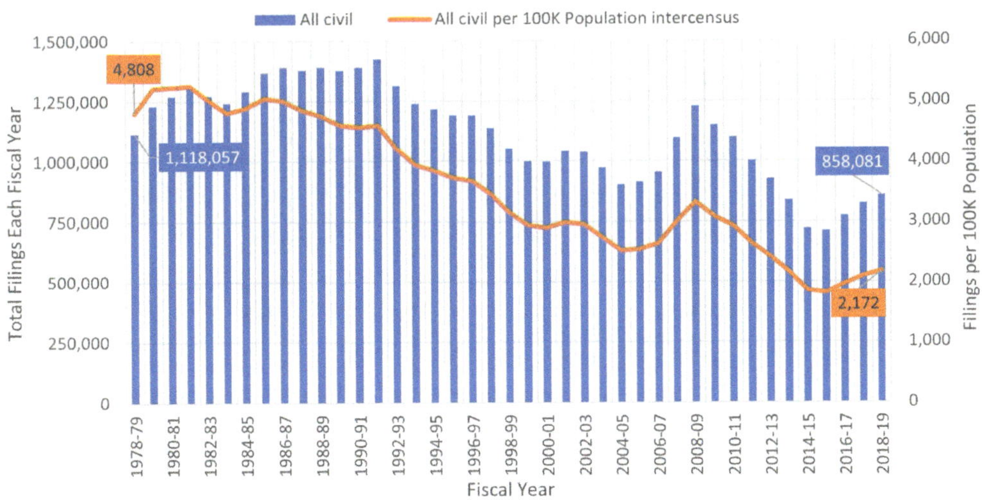

FIGURE 2.7 CALIFORNIA YEAR-TO-YEAR CHANGE IN TOTAL FILINGS

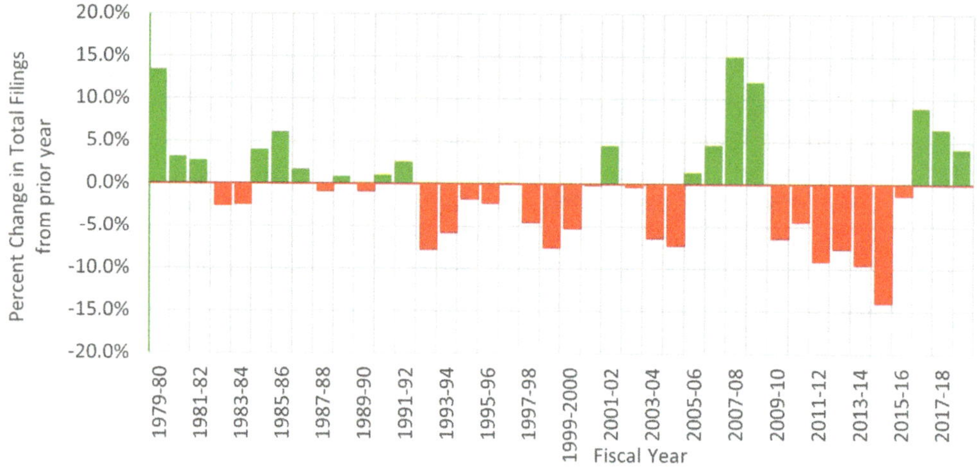

In 1993, the Commission on the Future of California Courts published a report that looked at total civil filings over the 30 years prior to 1993. The report included a display of total civil filings from FY 1961–62 to FY 1991–92 (Figure 2.8). The Commission reported a massive increase in civil filings during this time period.[7] The analysis here involved civil filings data for a 41-year period from FY 1978–79 to FY 2018–19. There was a 14-year overlap of the current study with the Commission study (gray area in Figure 2.9). While the total filings numbers did not include the same case categories,[8] the pattern of filing levels for the overlap period was very similar.

FIGURE 2.8 CALIFORNIA TRIAL COURTS, TOTAL CIVIL FILINGS, FISCAL YEARS 1960–61 TO 1991–92

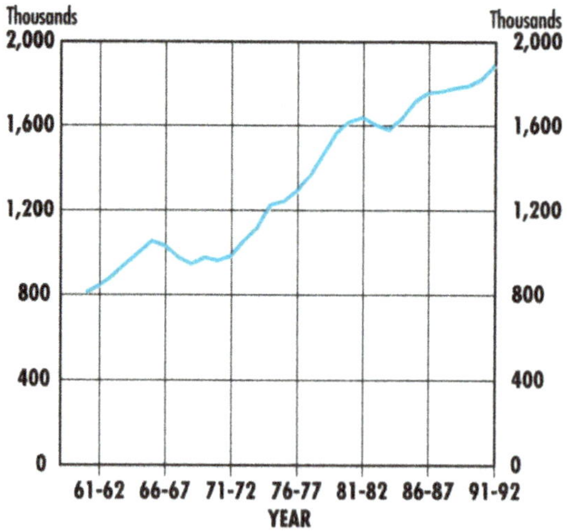

Source: Commission on the Future of the California Courts

7. Justice in the Balance 2020, *supra* note 1, fig. 8.1, p. 133.

8. The Commission Report's definition of a civil case included family law, probate, and mental health filings, which were excluded in the current study.

FIGURE 2.9 CALIFORNIA FILINGS: ALL CIVIL CASE TYPES

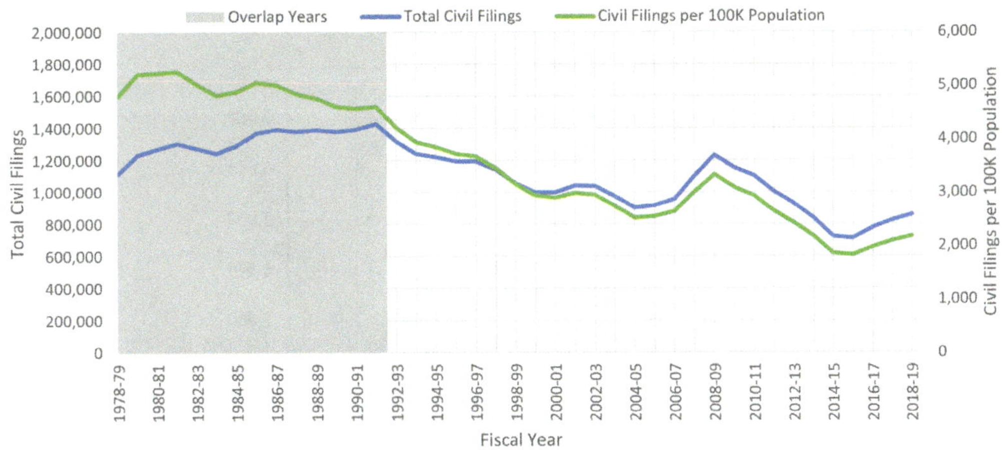

Looking across the 60-year period, California did experience a steady increase in total civil filings for the first 30 years, peaking in FY 1991–92. However, this was followed by a steady decline in total filings for the next 28 years, with the exception of the roller coaster from FY 1989–90 to FY 2015–16. Total civil filings were almost as low in FY 2018–19 as they were in FY 1960–61. Whatever factors were causing the increase at the end of the last century were no longer impacting filings in the same way in the 21st century.

Of the five states, California had the most continuous decline in per capita filings. Per capita filings (orange line in Figure 2.6) declined faster than total filings because of the steady increase in population. The population growth in California over this time frame was significant. It was almost 70 percent since FY 1978–79 and 16 percent since 2000. The peak in per capita filings was in FY 1981–82, ten years earlier than the peak in total filings. Although there were numerous later small upticks in per capita filing levels, none rose above the FY 1981–82 peak. The decline over 41 years from FY 1978–79 to FY 2018–19 was 54 percent. The decline was 59 percent from the peak in FY 1981–82. The drop was 30 percent from the peak in FY 2008–09, and 25 percent from FY 2000–01.

The California Commission also examined filings on a per capita basis and provided a figure of per capita filings (Figure 2.10).[9] The Commission report stated: "What is not as well known is that the growth in civil dockets had closely tracked that of the population. On a per capita basis Californians were only marginally more litigious today than they were in 1960."[10] However, from 1960 to 2020, the population of California more than doubled, and the per capita filing level dropped by more than half (orange line in Figure 2.6). Per capita filing levels no longer tracked the increase in population; rather, they continued to drop while the population continued to increase. Californians were now considerably less likely to file court cases than they were in the 1960s.

9. Justice in the Balance 2020, *supra* note 1, at 134.
10. *Id.* at 133.

FIGURE 2.10 CALIFORNIA TRIAL COURTS, CIVIL FILINGS PER 100,000 TOTAL POPULATION, FISCAL YEARS 1960–61 TO 1991–92

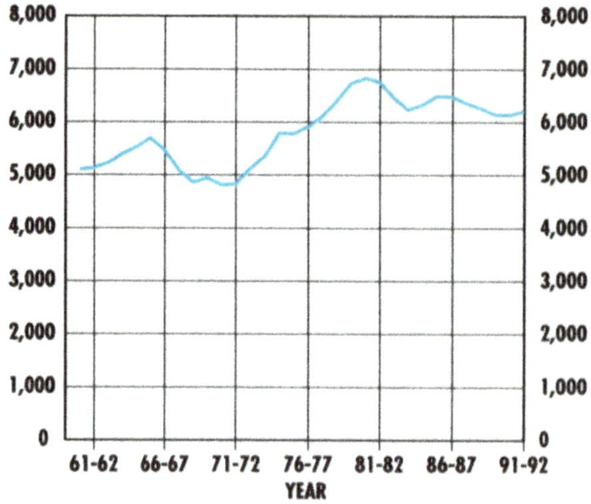

Source: California Futures Commission report; California State Department of Finance

Although the shape of the filing pattern over a 20-year period was similar, per capita filing levels varied significantly by population. Figure 2.11 displays the average per capita filing levels for the lower-value Limited Civil cases for groups of counties based on population. The shape of the pattern over time for all groups was very similar.

FIGURE 2.11 CALIFORNIA AVERAGE PER CAPITA LIMITED CIVIL FILINGS BY GROUPS OF COUNTIES BASED ON POPULATION

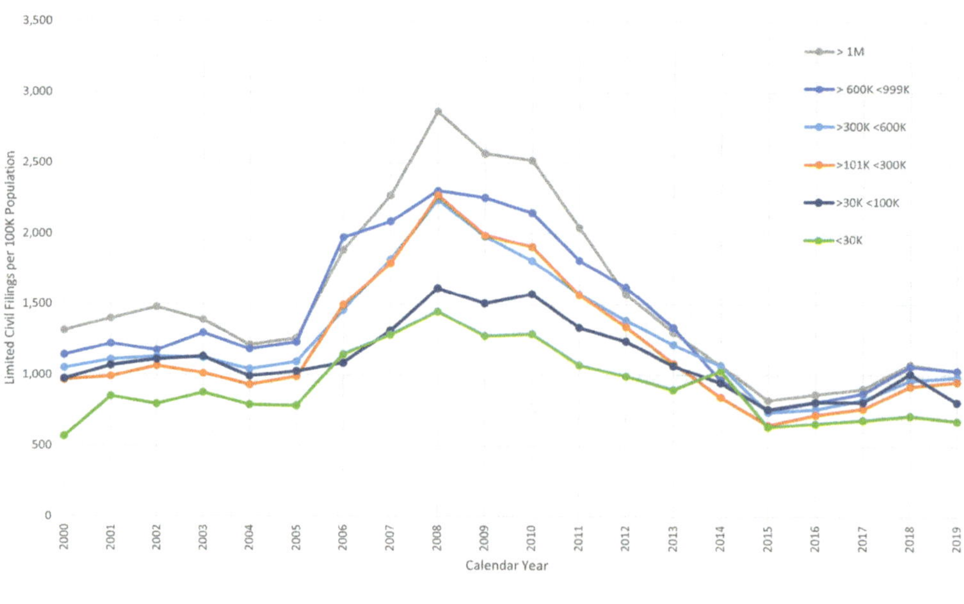

However, the variance was striking. The largest counties (gray line) generally had the highest average filing levels over the 20-year period. The smallest counties (green line) had the lowest average level and smaller fluctuations. At the beginning of the period, and at the end, the spread of the average filing levels was smaller. From 2005 to 2015, around the Great Recession, there was a wider spread of average filing levels, with the higher population counties having higher per capita filings of lower value civil cases.

While the average per capita filing levels of the groups tracked their population, within each population group there was considerable variance by county. Figure 2.12 displays the per capita filing levels of Limited Civil cases for the nine largest counties by population.[11] Again, the shape of the pattern was similar. However, the spread of filing levels increased substantially from 2005 to 2015, but was unrelated to population. The highest levels were in Riverside County, the fourth largest by population. Santa Clara County consistently had the lowest levels, and it ranked sixth in population. The spread of filing levels at the beginning and the end of the period was approximately 2 to 1. In 2009, the year of the widest spread, it was almost 4 to 1. The fourth largest county had almost four times as many per capita Limited Civil filings as the sixth largest county. Factors other than population were driving the filing levels.

FIGURE 2.12 CALIFORNIA PER CAPITA LIMITED CIVIL FILINGS, NINE LARGEST COUNTIES BY 2019 POPULATION

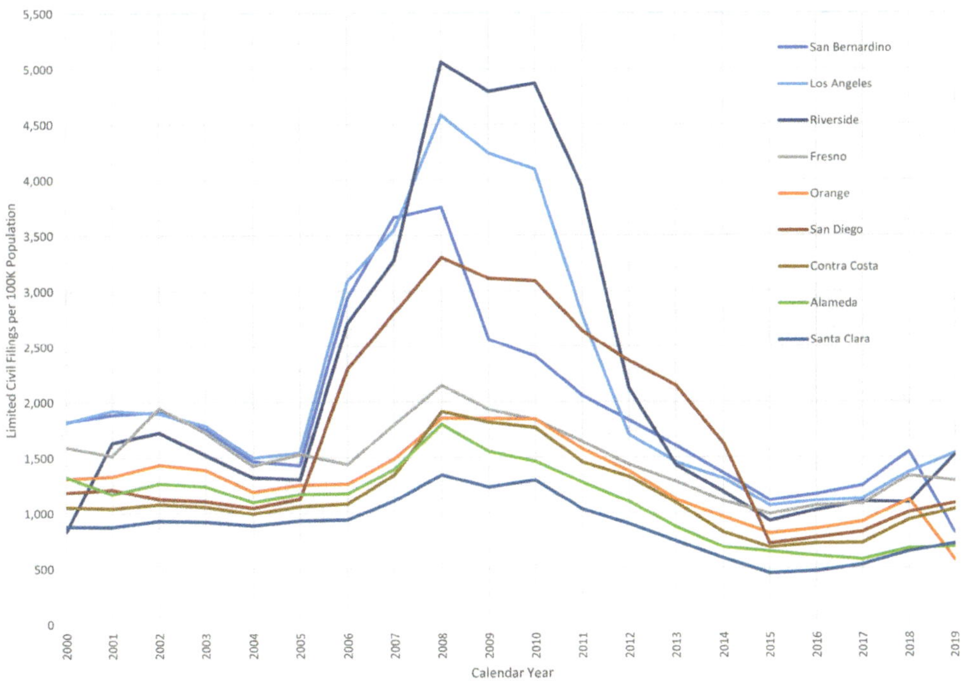

11. Sacramento County was not included because of one category of civil cases that could only be filed in Sacramento, rendering per capita filing levels incomparable.

2.7 Illinois—Total and Per Capita Filing Levels

Total filings of all comparable civil case categories[12] in Illinois displayed several fluctuations over the 25-year period (blue columns in Figure 2.13). Filings rose from 1996 to a peak in 1998, then dropped for a few years. Beginning in 2001, filings slowly rose to a peak in 2007. This was followed by brief dip, then another peak in 2010. A steady decline then continued until 2016. This double peak, associated with the Great Recession, also appeared in Texas and is discussed in Chapter 9. Filings jumped in 2017, but fell in 2018 and in 2019 to the lowest levels in 25 years. The decline over the 25 years was 16 percent. The decline from the peak in 2010 was 40 percent.

FIGURE 2.13 ILLINOIS TOTAL AND PER CAPITA CIVIL FILINGS

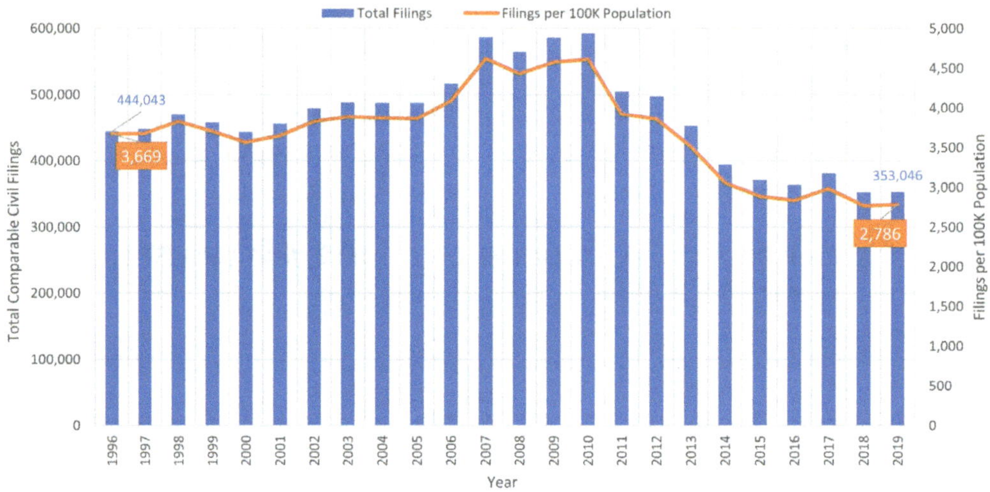

The pattern of per capita filings (green line in Figure 2.13) closely followed that for total filings, as the population grew very slowly over this period. Illinois population growth was less than 5 percent since 1996 and less than 2 percent since 2000. The decline in per capita filings over 25 years was 20 percent. The drop from the peak in 2010 was over 40 percent. During the 25-year period, the year-to-year fluctuations were considerable (Figure 2.14). Total filings dropped in ten years and rose in 14 years. The largest year-to-year increase was more than 13 percent. The greatest drop was more than 14 percent.

12. The filings for Illinois were limited to case categories comparable to filings in other states. See discussion in the Methodology Appendix about what was excluded.

FIGURE 2.14 ILLINOIS: YEAR-TO-YEAR CHANGE IN TOTAL FILINGS

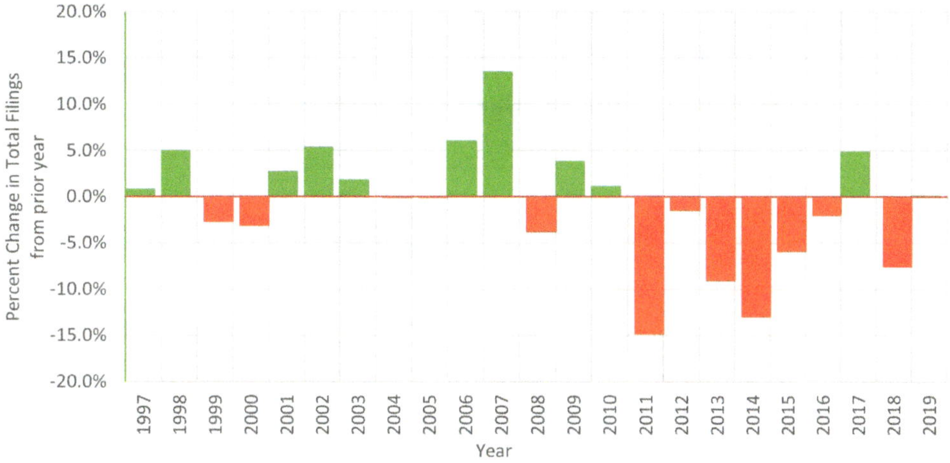

2.8 Minnesota—Total and Per Capita Filing Level

Total civil filings of comparable civil case categories[13] in Minnesota followed a roller coaster pattern over the 26-year period, but trended downward (blue columns in Figure 2.15). From 1994 to 1998 filings were generally stable. There was a valley in 1999 and 2000, a peak in 2002, and another valley from 2004 to 2006. Filings then rose sharply to a peak in 2008. This was followed by a long decline until 2016 to the lowest level in the 26-year period. Filings rose from 2017 to 2019. The decline over the 26-year period was 12 percent. The drop since 2000 was 5 percent. The drop from the peak in 2008 to the lowest level in 2016 was 37 percent.

FIGURE 2.15 MINNESOTA TOTAL COMPARABLE CIVIL FILINGS

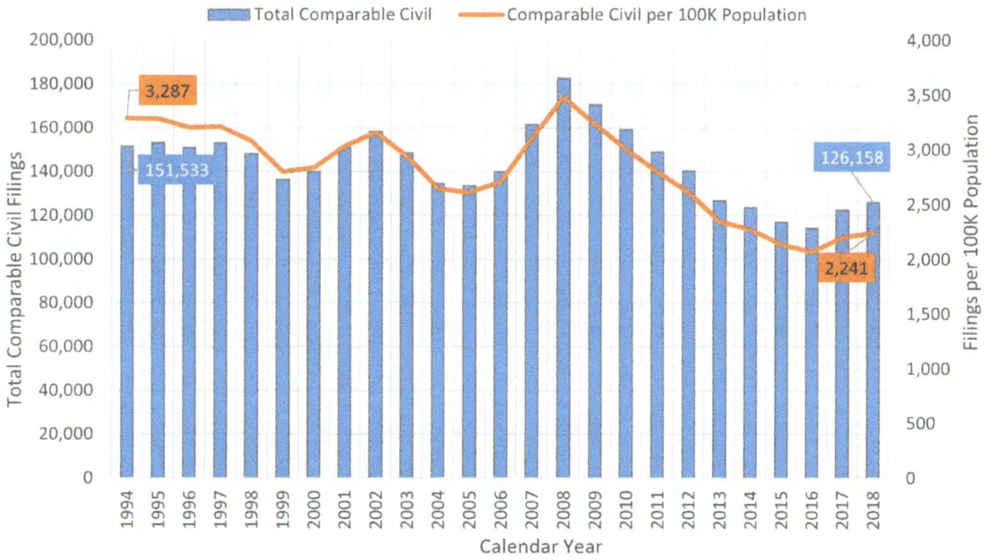

13. The filings for Minnesota were limited to case categories comparable to filings in other states. See discussion in the Methodology Appendix about what was excluded.

During the 26 years, the year-to-year fluctuations were considerable (Figure 2.16). Total filings dropped in 14 years and rose in ten years. The largest year-to-year increase was almost 16 percent. The greatest drop was almost 10 percent.

FIGURE 2.16 MINNESOTA YEAR-TO-YEAR CHANGE IN TOTAL FILINGS

The pattern of Minnesota's per capita filing levels was very similar to California's. The pattern of per capita filings (orange line in Figure 2.15) tracked the total filings pattern, dropping faster because of the gradual increase in population. Minnesota experienced a slow and steady growth in population since 1994. The total population grew 24 percent since 1994 and 15 percent since 2000. From 1994 to 2018, per capita filings shrank 32 percent. The drop from the peak in 2008 was more than 35 percent. The drop from 2000 was 21 percent.

2.9 Ohio—Total and Per Capita Filing Levels

Total civil filings of all trial courts[14] in Ohio steadily rose from 1999 to a peak in 2008 (blue columns in Figure 2.17). Filings then dropped sharply until 2015, after which they rose very slowly through 2019. In contrast to the other four states, the rise to the peak in 2008 was more gradual and started earlier. The drop after the peak was steep, as occurred in the other states. In contrast to three of the other states where total filings declined over the long term, total filings rose 13 percent over the 21-year period. Total filings grew almost 9 percent since 2000. However, the drop from the peak in 2008 to the lowest level in 2015 was 45 percent.

14. Court of claims and certain court of common pleas probate division filings were included with court of common pleas general division and municipal and county court filings to be more comparable to filing data from the other states in the study. See discussion in the Methodology Appendix about what was included.

FIGURE 2.17 OHIO CIVIL FILINGS IN COMMON PLEAS, COURT OF CLAIMS, MUNICIPAL, AND COUNTY COURTS

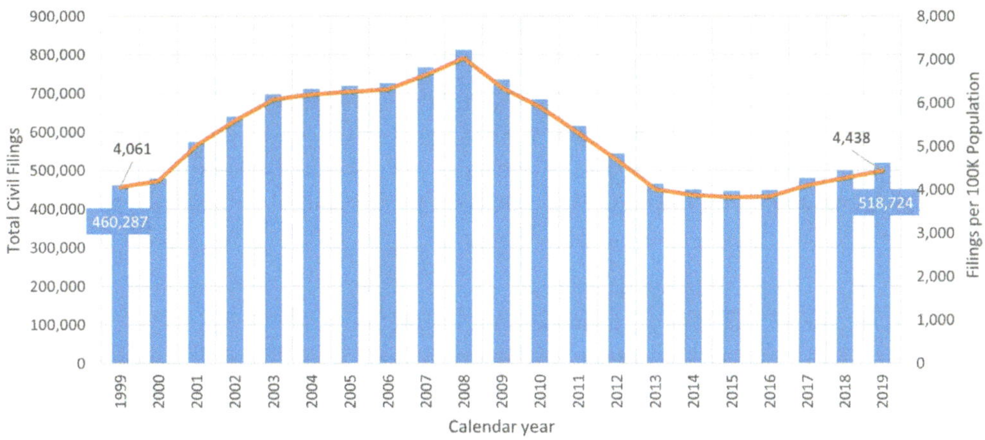

Ohio's per capita filing pattern (orange line in Figure 2.17) was very different from the other three states. Ohio experienced a slow and steady growth in population during the study period, totaling only 3 percent from 2000 to 2019. In contrast, per capita filing levels were much more volatile. Per capita filing levels rose continuously from 1999 to 2008 and then dropped sharply until 2013. Over the 21-year period, per capita filings grew about 9 percent. From 2000 to 2019, per capita filings grew almost 5 percent. However, the drop in the per capita filing level from the peak in 2008 to 2019 was almost 38 percent.

During the 21-year period, the year-to-year fluctuations were considerable (Figure 2.18). Total filings dropped in seven years and rose in 13 years. The largest year-to-year increase was almost 20 percent. The greatest year-to-year drop was almost 15 percent.

FIGURE 2.18 OHIO YEAR-TO-YEAR CHANGE IN TOTAL FILINGS

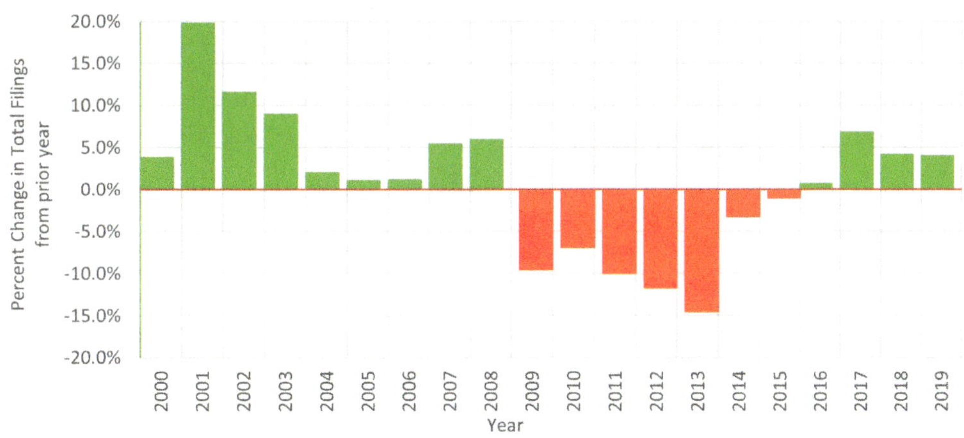

2.10 Texas—Total and Per Capita Filing Levels

Over the 16-year period beginning in 2004, total civil filings in all trial courts in Texas fluctuated some but trended upward, especially during the most recent five years of our study (blue columns in Figure 2.19). Beginning in 2004, total civil filings rose to a peak in 2007, then dropped in 2009, then rose to another, lower, peak in 2010. This double peak pattern, associated with the Great Recession, was similar to the pattern in Illinois. By 2013, filings had dropped to almost the same level as in 2004. Filings then began a steady rise that continued until 2019. From 2004 to 2019, total filings increased almost 61 percent.

FIGURE 2.19 TEXAS TOTAL CIVIL FILINGS—ALL COURTS

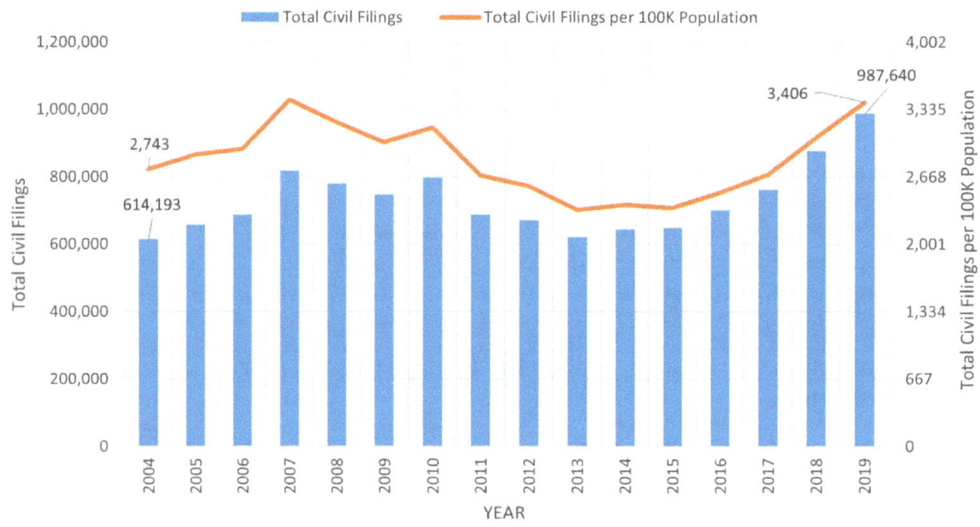

Per capita filings (orange line in Figure 2.19) changed more slowly than total filings, because the population had increased almost 30 percent over the 16 years. The per capita filing pattern for Texas was similar to Illinois, with two peaks in filing levels, in 2007 and in 2010. At the end of the study period, the per capita filing level started rising earlier and faster than the rise in California or Minnesota. Over the 16-year period, per capita filings rose almost 25 percent. From the peak in 2007 to the lowest year 2013, the drop was almost 32 percent. However from 2007 to 2019, per capita filings dropped less than 1 percent.

During these 16 years, the year-to-year fluctuations were considerable (Figure 2.20). Total filings rose in ten years and dropped in five years, in contrast to California, Minnesota, and Illinois where filings dropped in more years than they rose. The largest year-to-year increase was 19 percent. The greatest year-to-year drop was almost 14 percent.

FIGURE 2.20 TEXAS: YEAR-TO-YEAR CHANGE IN TOTAL FILINGS

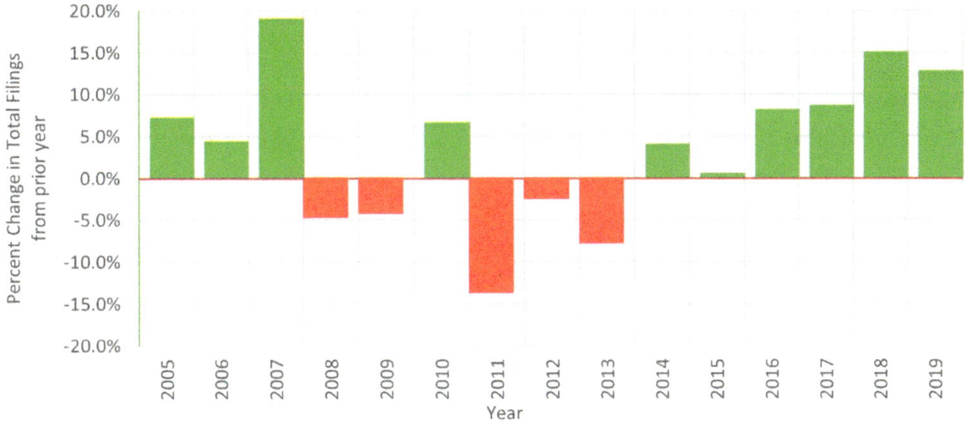

2.11 Conclusions

The observation of the Futures Commission in California, which turned out to have been conducted during an atypical filings period, cautions us against pronouncing "eternal" truths based on data from even the relatively long time frames of our study. The example also shows the need for regular, continuing research on filings issues. However, our experience shows that such research is difficult. Few states have filings data that is sufficiently consistent from year to year, even court to court within the state, to make reliably accurate generalizations.

Large-scale natural or man-made events make the study of filings even more problematic. For example, the pandemic that began in the year after the study period here will result in filing levels during the years of that event that are not typical compared to prior years. The Great Recession of 2008 had a similar, significant impact on civil filings in all five states. The effect differed from state to state in terms of the timing of the onset of the effect, the extent of the pre-recession filings increase, whether there were one or two peaks, and how fast filings declined after the peaks. This issue is explored at length in Chapter 9.

The pandemic will create a discontinuity in filings data, making it difficult to simply add additional years to the filings data used in our study. Researchers will have to wait and see whether filings return to some new equilibrium level after the effects of the pandemic dissipate, and then determine whether it is possible to compare pre- and post-pandemic data and, if so, with what sorts of adjustments.

With that cautionary note in mind, we offer the following generalizations from the summary data set forth in this chapter.

At least during the first two decades of this century (and if the experience in other states was similar to California's, during the last two decades of the 20th century) there has certainly been no "litigation explosion" in civil cases.

The assumption that the workload of courts will consistently expand appears to be mistaken. Even though there was a short trend of higher filings at the end of the study period, the data shows a drop in total filings and filings per capita over the extended period we analyzed in three of the five states. Texas showed a significant filings increase recently, but we had only 16 years of data. The observation that filings do not continue to increase is bolstered by the nationwide per capita filings data showing a generalized decrease over the past eight years, summarized in the Introduction.

The data also shows that civil filings do not exhibit a steady pattern over time—either from state to state, for a state as a whole, or for individual courts within the state. Filings can also fluctuate considerably over time, up or down as much as 15 to 20 percent in one year.

As subsequent chapters will explain, the data shows that filings of small dollar value cases vary more over time, and show a greater long time reduction, than higher value cases. This is particularly apparent regarding Small Claims filings. Overall, this phenomenon suggests a declining use of the state courts by ordinary people.

3

Variation of Filing Levels within a State

3.1 Overview

Why would civil filing levels vary across counties within a state? The laws governing civil liability and civil procedure are the same statewide. Consequently, filing levels within a state would not be expected to vary as much as they might when comparing filing levels across states with different liability and procedural laws. However, the analysis here reveals there can be a wide variance in filing levels in a state.

What might account for this variance? Differences in the type and level of economic activity and the culture—political and legal—might produce differences in civil filing levels across counties. Generally, lawyers and judges practice in a region of the state, and not statewide, allowing development of differing "local legal cultures" regarding filing practices. Economic considerations regarding the filing of a lawsuit will vary across counties with different income levels and wealth. Finally, population levels and population demographics might affect filing practices.

In three of the states analyzed here, California, Illinois, and Minnesota, total filing data was provided at both the county level and the state level. Filing data in these three states was collected at the county level because the trial courts were organized at the county level. County level data readily allows analysis of filing levels based on geographic, population, and demographic factors, although it may not be decisive for several reasons. Subpopulations with similar demographics may spread across county lines into adjacent counties, for example, suburbs of a larger city. However, the demographics of these suburbs might not be reflective of the rest of the county. In addition, there may be one or more cities or suburbs in a county that was otherwise relatively rural or had a low population density. Finally, counties vary considerably in number, geographic size, and population in the five states examined here. California had 58 counties with populations that ranged from less than 1,500 to more than ten million. Illinois had 102 counties with populations that ranged from about 3,800 to more than five million. Minnesota had 87 counties with populations that ranged from less than 3,300 to almost 1.3 million. Ohio had 88 counties with populations that ranged from about 13,000 to more than 1.3 million. Texas had 258 counties with populations that ranged from less than 200 to more than 4.7 million. The findings here suggest that the relationships between civil filing levels and county characteristics and demographics are quite complicated.

3.1.1 Population

Population, which one might expect to be a factor, turns out not to be a significant predictor of filing levels. A greater population does not necessarily mean more filings or fewer filings. Although the average per capita filings in larger counties were generally higher than the average in smaller counties, there can be considerable variation—large counties with per capita filing levels lower than smaller counties and vice versa.

3.1.2 Statewide Variation in Per Capita Filing Levels

The spread of per capita filing levels across California's 58 counties was quite dramatic. In 2000, the spread of per capita filing levels was 12 to 1. It rose to a peak of 21 to 1 in 2008. It dropped to a spread of 4 to 1 in 2019. For counties with more than 100,000 population, the spread was smaller, but still large. It was almost 9 to 1 in 2000, down to 5 to 1 in 2008, and 3 to 1 in 2019.

The variance in per capita filing levels across the 20 Illinois counties examined was not as wide as in California. The spread was the highest in 2001 at 5.4 to 1, and the lowest in 2017 at 2.9 to 1. Cook County, with the largest population, had a higher per capita filing level than the other 19 counties examined for the entire 25-year period, almost twice as high in ten years and dropping to a low of 1.6 to 1 in 2014 and 2018. Excluding Cook County, the spread ranged from a high of 4.5 to 1 in 2001 to a low of 2.3 to 1 in 2007 and 2016.

Per capita filing levels across the 18 counties examined in Minnesota showed different patterns over time than those in California or Illinois, but exhibited a similar divergence. The per capita filing level pattern had two small surges, one in the 2000 to 2004 period and one in the 2006 to 2015 period. The spread of per capita filing levels was similar to Illinois and not as wide as in California. In 1994 and 1995, the variance was 5 to 1. From 1999 to 2014, the variance was consistently between 1.8 to 1 and 2.1 to 1. It started rising in 2016 and ended at 3 to 1 in 2018. In only six of the 25 years was Hennepin County, the county with the largest population, also the county with the highest per capita filing level. From 1994 to 1998, the county with the smallest population was the county with the highest per capita filing level. However, in four of the subsequent 20 years, this county had the lowest per capita filing level.

3.1.3 Regions within a State

Three regions were examined in California based on geography. The Southern California counties had larger populations, a diverse industrial base, and were comparatively more conservative politically and socially. The Bay Area counties, the second largest region in population, had a high-tech industrial base, and were comparatively more liberal. The third region in the southern Central Valley was a mostly rural and agricultural region with two large cities and was comparatively conservative, politically and socially.

The higher-value Unlimited Civil per capita filing level averages of the counties in the three regions varied widely over 20 years, both relative to the other regions and relative to the statewide average. The Bay Area counties had the highest average filing level in 2000 and 2010, but dropped below Southern California and the statewide average in 2019. The Central Valley region filing average was higher than Southern California in 2000, but lower than the other two regions in 2010 and 2019. The filing average in the Central Valley region started the period above the statewide average in 2000, but fell below the statewide average in 2010 and 2019. Unlimited Civil per capita filing levels were lowest in 2019 in all three regions.

Focusing on the counties within each of these three regions also revealed widely varying Unlimited Civil per capita filing levels. Although the filing pattern over time was often similar, in terms of peaks and long-term trends, there was considerable variation within each region, both as to filing levels and the spread of filing levels. The general pattern of per capita filing levels in all three regions was fairly closely grouped through 2005. Beginning in 2006, per capita filing levels diverged. Although counties experienced a surge in filing levels, the height and duration of the surge varied significantly. The surge generally peaked in the 2008 to 2010 period. Filing levels in some counties then dropped, but the surge continued as late as 2015 in some counties. From 2016 forward, the per capita filing levels were again closely grouped, as they had been at the beginning of the period.

Looking at lower-value Limited Civil cases, per capita filing levels in the three regions were very similar through 2005. In 2006, a surge began, peaking in the 2008–10 period. Per capita filing levels had dropped back to pre-surge levels by 2015. After 2015, the per capita filing levels were closely grouped, as they were before 2006. The differences between the regions were the timing, height, and sharpness of each county's surge. In the southern Central Valley counties, the pattern for Limited Civil per capita filings was slightly different from other regions. Three showed more of a sharp peak followed by a sharp drop than the more rounded surge in the other regions. The peaks for several counties were earlier than for counties in the other regions.

Three regions were also examined in Illinois. One group included Cook County and the five geographically adjacent and larger population counties. The second group consisted of the nine counties in one judicial circuit in the center of the state. The third group was comprised of the five smallest population counties. The pattern and spread of per capita filing levels were different than in California and Minnesota. Per capita filings in the largest counties, not including Cook, exhibited a very similar pattern, with a peak in 2010, and were tightly grouped. Cook County's level was much higher, and its surge began earlier, was much broader, and exhibited two peaks. The spread in the smallest counties was similar to that in the other two regions, but year-to-year filing levels fluctuated widely. The geographically adjacent counties in the single judicial circuit also had varying levels, year-to-year, but the levels were in a smaller range. Neither the small county region nor the single circuit region exhibited the surge that was seen in the larger courts.

Three regions were also examined in Minnesota. One region was the Twin Cities region, which consisted of the nine urban and suburban counties and included the two largest population cities of Minneapolis and St. Paul. The second region consisted of the four counties in the Sixth Judicial District in the northeast corner of the state. The third region consisted of five adjacent counties in the south-central part of the state.

The per capita filing pattern of the Twin Cities counties was similar over time, and more tightly grouped than in the California regions. Filing levels in all the counties were dropping from 1994 until 1999. There was then a small surge around 2002, followed by a drop to 2005. All filing levels then rose to a higher peak in 2008. Filing levels then dropped, with all nine counties at a lower level in 2018 than in 1994.

The per capita filing pattern in Minnesota's Sixth District was different than the patterns in the other regions examined in Minnesota. There were two surges, one from 2000 to 2005, and another from 2006 to 2013. The surges were later than the surges in the Twin Cities region. The peak level in each county was not in the same year during the surge.

The five south-central counties were mostly rural, farming counties. The per capita filing level pattern in this region showed two surges, both more pronounced than in the other two regions in Minnesota. Thereafter, all but one of the county's filing levels dropped. However, the per capita filing levels in 2018 were higher than in 1994 in all but one county.

In the Twin Cities region, the two largest counties, Hennepin County and Ramsey County, were consistently above the state average for the entire period. Two other counties in the region rose above the state average in 2018. The remaining counties were below the state average for most of the period.

In the Sixth District, three of the four counties were below the state average in 1994. The largest county, St. Louis County, rose above the state average in 1997, and stayed above for the rest of the period. Cook County, the smallest county in population, was considerably above the state average in 1994, but fell below the state average in 1999, and stayed below for the rest of the period. By 2019, St. Louis County and Carleton County were well above the state average, Lake County was at the state average, and Cook County was below the state average.

All five counties in the southern region were below the state average from 1994 until 2001. For the rest of the period, the counties stayed near, but generally below, the state average. The county with the largest population in this group rose slightly above the state average in five different years, beginning in 2007.

Over the 25-year period, per capita filing levels in the counties in the Twin Cities region slowly converged to more similar levels. For both the Twin Cities region and the Sixth District, the spread of filing levels was largest at the beginning and end of the period. In the southern region, the spread of per capita filings was quite small over the 25-year period. This group had the tightest grouping of any of the regions studied in either Minnesota, California, or Illinois.

3.1.4 Adjacent Similarly Sized Counties

A comparison of geographically adjacent counties of similar population in California revealed different filing levels and patterns for higher-value Unlimited Civil cases. Orange County and San Diego County, two large counties in southern California had about the same population, but different filing patterns. Beginning in 2006, San Diego

County's per capita filing level experienced a surge that lasted until 2017, when its per capita filing level was almost twice the level in Orange County. Orange County experienced a much shallower surge and for a shorter duration. At the end of the period, Orange County's filing level was half its level in 2000. San Diego County's filing level in 2019 was above the levels in 2000, but it had been dropping sharply since 2017.

Two similarly sized counties in the southern Central Valley, Fresno County and Kern County, also showed very different per capita filing patterns for higher-value Unlimited Civil cases. Fresno County was consistently higher than Kern County. Both showed a surge beginning in 2006. Kern County peaked in 2008. Fresno County peaked in 2010. At the widest spread, Fresno County's filing level was almost twice Kern County's level, but in 2019 the spread had dropped to less than 1.4 to 1. In 2019, the per capita filing levels in both counties were higher than they had been at the beginning of the period.

The patterns for lower-value Limited Civil cases were quite different in the two sets of adjacent counties. San Diego County experienced a strong surge from 2006 to 2015. Orange County had a much shallower surge. Both peaked in the 2008–10 period. In contrast, Fresno County and Kern County had very similar patterns, staying very close in filing levels, with a much smaller peak in 2008. All four counties returned to similar filing levels beginning in 2015. The Limited Civil filing levels in 2019 were lower than the filing levels in 2000 in all four counties.

Per capita filing levels in the two geographically adjacent Minnesota counties of Hennepin County and Ramsey County varied significantly. Hennepin County's population was more than twice that of Ramsey County. Hennepin County's per capita filing level was slightly larger than Ramsey County's in 1994 and then dropped to lower levels. Ramsey County's per capita filing level surpassed Hennepin County's in six of the years from 2007 to 2018.

The variance in per capita filing levels was also present in adjacent counties in the south-central rural counties. The two smallest population-adjacent counties were Waseca County and Faribault County. The spread of per capita filing levels was almost 2 to 1 in 1995. In 2018, the ratio was 0.9 to 1, but the order had flipped, with Faribault County's filing levels exceeding Waseca County's in 2015.

Two similarly sized counties in population in the rural group also exhibited significant variances. Steele County's per capita filing level was lower than Freeborn County's in 14 of the 25 years, while Steele County's population was larger and growing. From 2016 to 2018, the ratio was less than 1 to 1, even though Steele County's population was 20 percent larger. The county with a steadily growing population had lower per capita filings levels than the adjacent county whose population was shrinking.

3.2 California—Variation in Filing Levels

The large size and diversity of California allowed analysis by regions that had distinct differences in demographics, industrial base, and culture. The analysis examined the two broad categories of civil cases—higher-value Unlimited Civil and lower-value Limited Civil—for which county-level data was available. Three regions were selected based on geography and similarity of demographics. Southern California was the most heavily populated region. It included five of the ten largest counties and 57 percent of the state's total population, had a diverse industrial base, and was generally more conservative politically and socially. The Bay Area[1] was also large. It included three of the ten largest counties and 17 percent of the state's population, had a high-tech industrial base, and was generally more liberal. The third region was composed of the counties in the southern Central Valley, a mostly rural and agricultural region with two large cities, encompassing less than 8 percent of the state's population, and generally more conservative.

3.2.1 Regional Differences in Higher-Value Unlimited Civil Filing Levels

The average Unlimited Civil per capita filing level of the counties in the three regions varied widely from 2000 to 2019 (see Table 3.1). The Bay area counties had the highest filing levels in 2000 and 2010, but dropped below Southern California and the statewide average in 2019. The southern Central Valley area filing average was higher than Southern California in 2000, but lower than the other two regions in 2010 and 2019. The region was above the statewide average in 2000, then below the statewide average in 2010 and 2019. Per capita filing levels in most counties in all three regions reached a peak between 2008 and 2010.

Average Unlimited Civil per capita filing levels were lowest in 2019 in all three regions, and all were below the statewide average. Statewide, the average filing level dropped 12 percent from the 2000 average, and 28 percent if LA was excluded (reflecting the large impact of LA's higher filing levels as noted further in Section 3.6.1 in the discussion about the impact of the large counties in a state).

Looking across all California counties from 2000 to 2019, 38 counties reported a drop in per capita filing levels and 17 reported an increase.[2] The percentage change varied widely. Increases ranged from 3 percent to 114 percent. Drops ranged from 5 percent to 89 percent. There did not appear to be any obvious relationship between changes in Unlimited Civil per capita filing levels and region.

TABLE 3.1 CALIFORNIA UNLIMITED CIVIL PER CAPITA FILINGS (AVERAGE OF THE COUNTIES IN EACH REGION)

Year → Region ↓	2000	2010	2019	Percent Change 2000 to 2019
Southern California	590	819	479	–19 %
Bay Area	708	983	452	–36 %
Southern Central Valley	633	559	417	–34 %
Statewide	605	934	532	–12 %
Statewide without LA	612	790	442	–28 %

1. San Francisco was included in this figure notwithstanding its unique demography—the daytime population was estimated to be twice the nighttime (census) population because of the very large number of commuters and its small geographic size. If you halve the SF filing levels to account for the daytime population being approximately twice as big as the census population, the unlimited civil filing levels per capita are more comparable to the other Bay Area counties.

2. Three small counties did not report filing data for one or more years during this period.

3.2.2 Variation within Regions

The following figures show per capita civil filing levels for each county in each of the three regions: Southern California, Figure 3.1; the Bay Area, Figure 3.2; and the southern Central Valley, Figure 3.3. All three figures have the same scale and include a line of the statewide per capita filing average (the red line).

FIGURE 3.1 SOUTHERN CALIFORNIA UNLIMITED CIVIL FILINGS PER 100K POPULATION

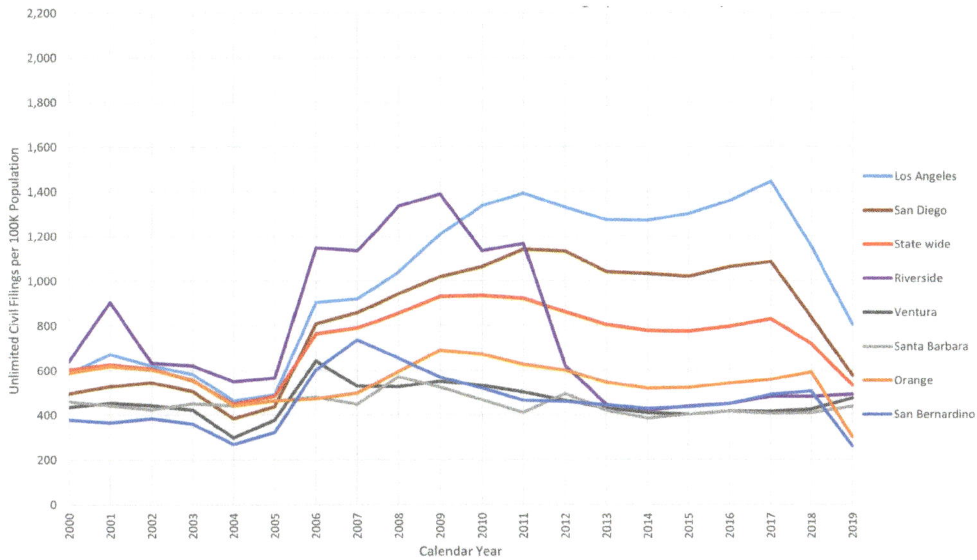

FIGURE 3.2 CALIFORNIA BAY AREA UNLIMITED CIVIL FILINGS PER 100K POPULATION

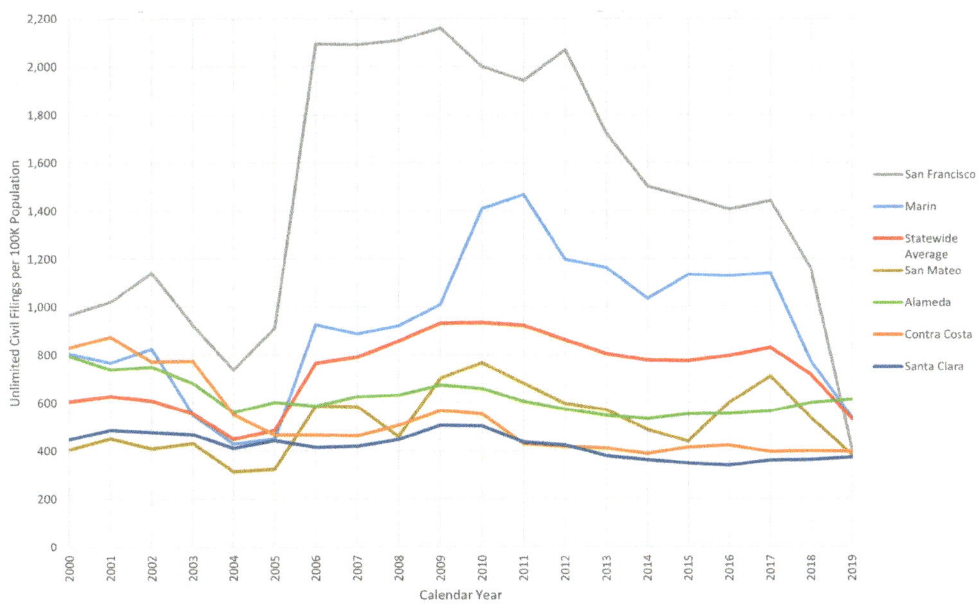

FIGURE 3.3 CALIFORNIA LOWER CENTRAL VALLEY UNLIMITED CIVIL FILINGS PER 100K POPULATION

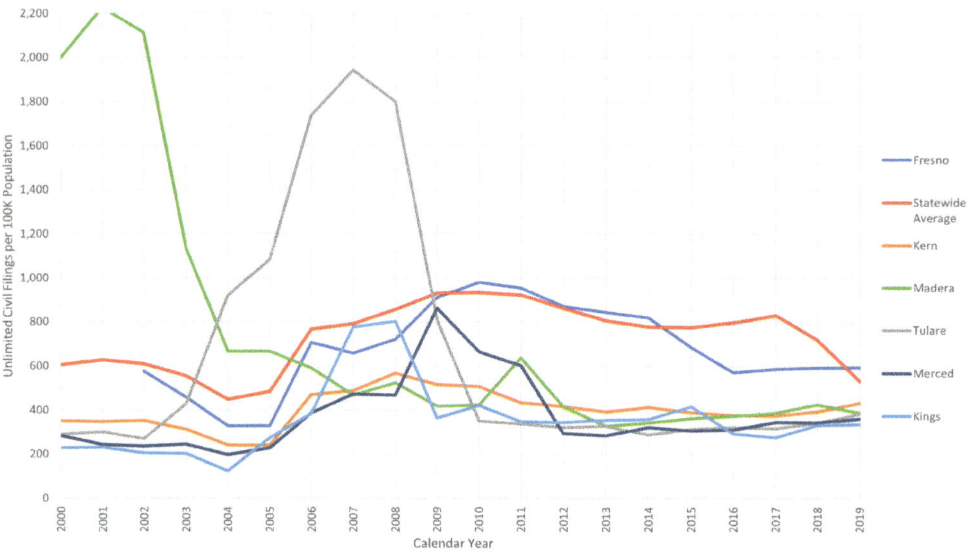

All three regions exhibited a similar pattern of Unlimited Civil per capita filings despite significant variation across counties within the region. Each region showed relatively similar per capita filing levels from 2000 until 2005. After 2005, the filing levels of the counties in each region diverged. A few counties experienced a surge in filing levels, beginning in 2006, while others were comparatively stable. Between 2005 and 2019, the patterns in each region were quite different, especially in the Central Valley region. By 2019, filings levels once again became more closely grouped in all three regions.

Another significant aspect of each region was the significant spread of per capita filing levels across counties within a region and over time. For Southern California, the spread of filing levels in 2005 was about a 2 to 1, and in 2019 it had increased to 4 to 1. For the Bay Area counties, the spread in 2005 was about a 2 to 1, and in 2019, it had dropped to 1.6 to 1. For the southern Central Valley area counties, the spread in 2005 was about a 1.5 to 1, and it had increased to about 2.5 to 1 in 2019.

Despite the range of per capita filing levels within each region, the counties in each region did not have noticeably different high and low filing levels. Most of the counties fell within the range of 400 to 1,000 per capita filings for most of the period. Only two or three counties were outside this range, and usually not for the whole period.

The spread of per capita filing levels across all California counties was much greater. For all 58 counites, the spread of per capita filings was 12 to 1 in 2000. It rose to a peak of 21 to 1 in 2008. It dropped to a spread of 4 to 1 in 2019. For counties with more than 100,000 people, the spread was smaller, but still large. It was almost 9 to 1 in 2000, down to 5 to 1 in 2008, and 3 to 1 in 2019.

3.2.3 Adjacent Counties

Two geographically adjacent and similarly sized counties were examined in two regions. In southern California, Orange County and San Diego County displayed very different Unlimited Civil per capita filing patterns over the 20-year period. Both had just over three million residents and had similar demographics. Figure 3.4 displays the per capita filing levels for the two counties from 2000 to 2019. The filing levels were close from 2000 to 2005. Beginning in 2006, San Diego County's per capita filing level experienced a surge that lasted until 2017. At its peak in 2011 and 2012, San Diego County's filing level was 2.4 times its filing level in 2006. San Diego County's lowest level was 384 in 2004, and the high level was 1,142 in 2011. And at the end of its surge in 2017 the San Diego County per capita filing level was almost twice the level in Orange County. San Diego County's filing level in 2019 was above the level in 2004, but it had been dropping sharply since 2017. In contrast, Orange County's filing level was comparatively stable. Orange County's surge did not begin until 2007, peaked in 2009 at 690, and then dropped slowly until 2014. Filings then rose through 2018 to the same level as in 2000, followed by a sharp drop in 2019 to 302, half the level in 2000.

FIGURE 3.4 UNLIMITED CIVIL FILINGS PER 100K POPULATION IN SAN DIEGO AND ORANGE COUNTIES

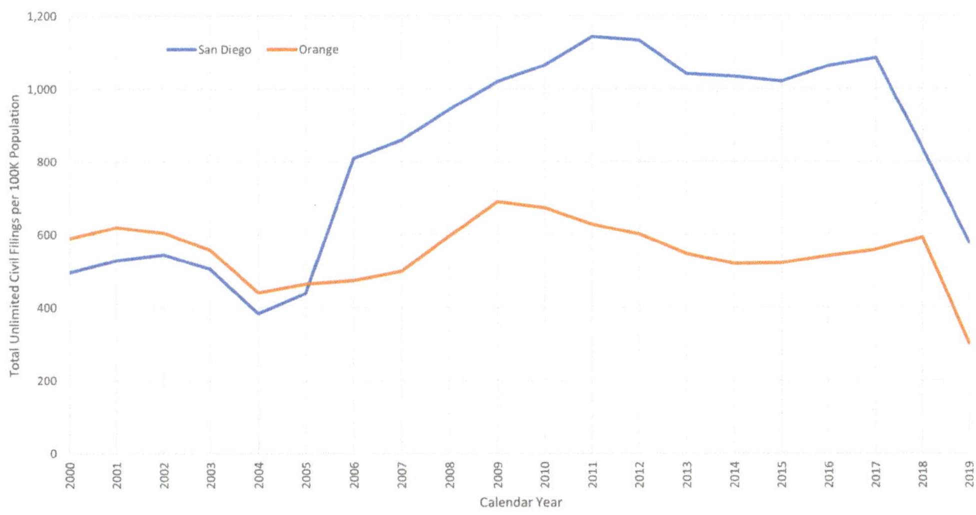

An examination of the filing subcategories of Unlimited Civil cases in these two courts after FY 2005–06 reveals that the surge in filings was mostly Other Civil Complaints and Petitions[3] filings. In Orange County, at the peak in FY 2009–10, the total number of Other Civil filings was 1.9 times the level in FY 2005–06. In San Diego County, at the peak in FY 2008–09, the total number of Other Civil filings was 1.3 times the number in FY 2005–06. During this time period, total higher value Injury/damage filing levels were comparatively flat in both counties.

3. Examples of this case category include contract (including debt collection), real property (including foreclosure), unlawful detainer, employment, and equity cases. It also includes judicial reviews, enforcement of judgment actions, and miscellaneous nonfamily petitions, although these are less common. These types of cases involved a damage claim over $25,000 and did not include tort cases.

In the southern Central Valley, two geographically adjacent and similarly sized counties, Fresno County and Kern County, also showed very different per capita filing patterns for the higher-value Unlimited Civil cases. Figure 3.5 displays the per capita filing levels from 2000 to 2019. Fresno County was consistently higher than Kern County. Both showed a surge beginning in 2006. Kern County peaked in 2008, then settled to a more stable level by 2011. In contrast, Fresno County kept rising; it peaked in 2010, stayed relatively high, then dropped slowly through 2015. From 2016 to 2019, Fresno County's filing levels were almost flat. At the widest spread, Fresno's filing level was almost twice Kern County's level. In 2019, the spread was less than 1.4. In 2019, the per capita filing levels in both counties were higher than they were in 2000.

FIGURE 3.5 UNLIMITED CIVIL FILINGS PER 100K POPULATION IN FRESNO AND KERN COUNTIES

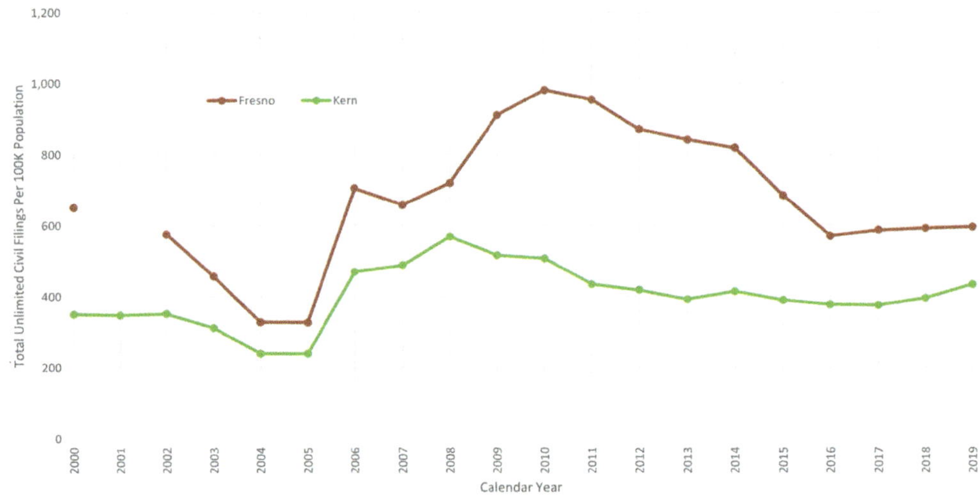

As was found in the two adjacent southern California counties, the surge in Fresno County and Kern County was Other Civil Complaints and Petitions. In Fresno County, at the peak in FY 2009–10, more than twice as many Other Civil cases were filed than in FY 2005–06. In Kern County, at the peak in FY 2008–09, Other Civil filings were only 1.5 times higher than in FY 2005–06. During this period, total higher value Injury/damage filing levels were comparatively flat in both counties.

3.2.4 Variation in Lower-Value Limited Civil Filing Levels by Region

Figures 3.6, 3.7, and 3.8 display lower-value Limited Civil per capita filing levels for the same preceding three regions. All three figures have the same scale and include a line of the statewide per capita filing average (the red line) for comparison purposes.

Notwithstanding the diversity of population, industrial base, and political and social leanings, all of the figures showed a similar per capita filing pattern. Filing levels are very similar through 2005. In 2006, a surge began, peaking in the 2008–10 period. Per capita filing levels had dropped back to pre-surge levels by 2015. After 2015, the filings

FIGURE 3.6 SOUTHERN CALIFORNIA LIMITED CIVIL FILINGS PER 100K POPULATION, SOUTHERN CALIFORNIA COUNTIES

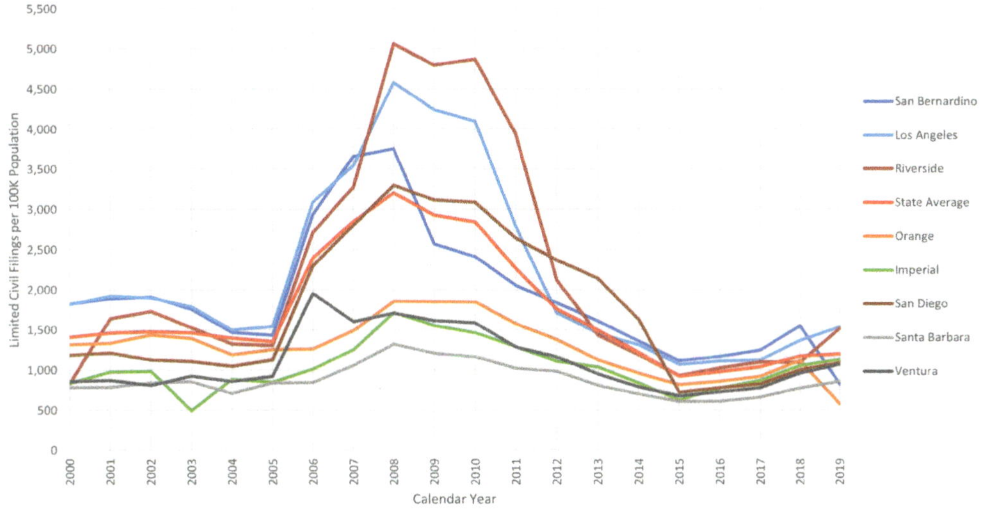

FIGURE 3.7 CALIFORNIA LIMITED CIVIL FILINGS PER 100K POPULATION, BAY AREA COUNTIES

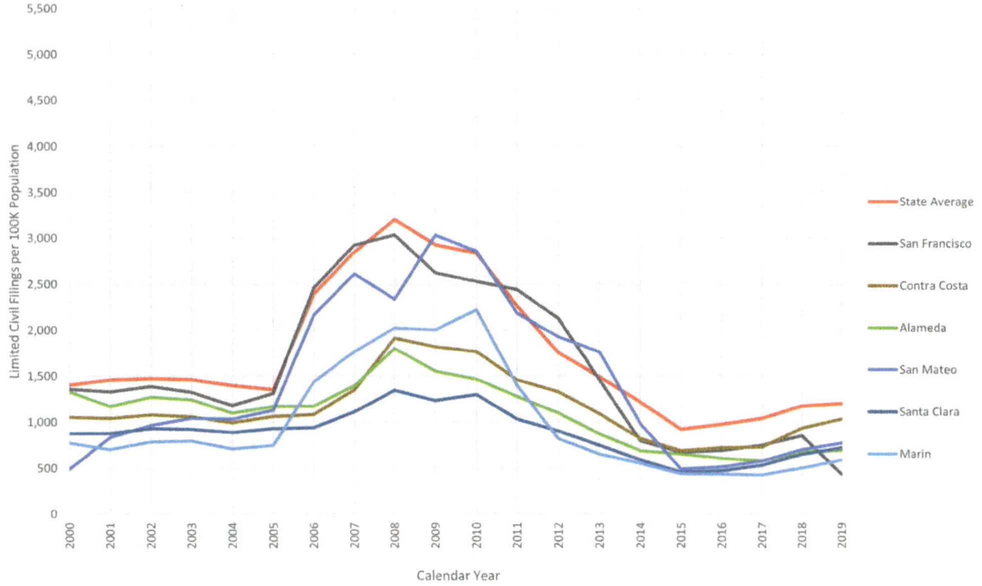

were closely grouped, as they were before 2006. The differences between the regions were the timing, height, and sharpness of each county's surge.

Per capita Limited Civil filings in the Southern California counties are shown in Figure 3.6. At the beginning of the period, three of the counties were above the state average, and the rest were at or below the state average. The spread in per capita filing levels was about 2 to 1. The surge from 2006 until 2015 was present in most of these

FIGURE 3.8 CALIFORNIA SOUTHERN CENTRAL VALLEY LIMITED CIVIL FILINGS PER 100K POPULATION, LOWER CENTRAL VALLEY COUNTIES

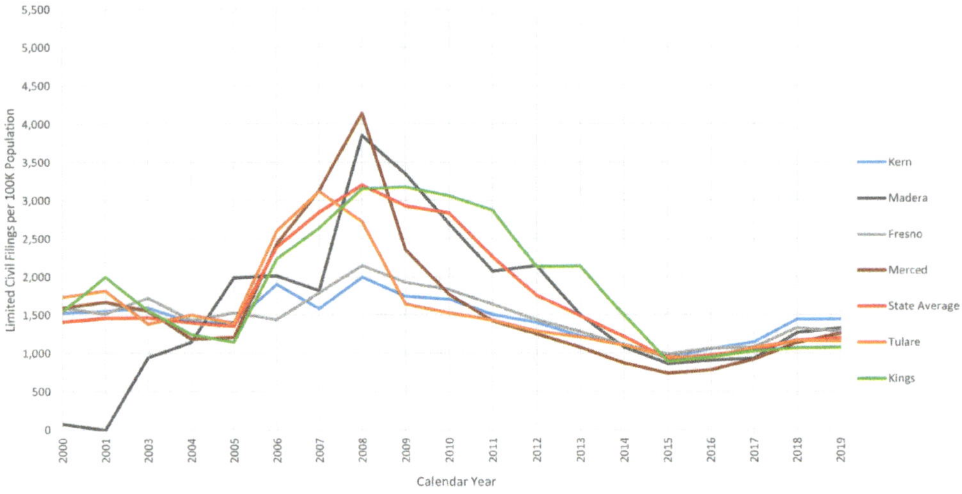

counties, although of different heights and with peaks in different years. Four had pronounced surges, the rest were more subdued. This surge was associated with both the aerospace industry collapse and the Great Recession, as discussed in Chapter 9. At the peak of filing levels in 2008, the spread was almost 4 to 1. Four of the counties were consistently above the state average during the period of the surge.

Beginning in 2015, the Southern California county filing levels became more closely grouped, as they had been prior to 2006. In 2019, only two of the three counties that were above the statewide average in 2000 were still above the state average. The rest of the Southern California counties were below the state average. The spread in 2019 was almost 3 to 1, still a significant spread.

Per capita Limited Civil filings in the San Francisco Bay Area counties are shown in Figure 3.7. Significantly, only two of the counties were above the statewide average in only some of the years during the period. The spread of filing levels was close from 2000 to 2005. It then diverged, but less widely than the Southern California counties. Filing levels returned to earlier levels by 2015, and stayed closely grouped through 2019. In 2000, the spread was about 3 to 1. During the 2006 to 2016 surge, the widest spread was 2.5 to 1, much smaller than in the Southern California region. The spread dropped to less than 2 to 1 in 2019. The surge from 2005 to 2016 was present in all of these counties, although of different heights and years. During the surge, most of the county filing levels were below the statewide average. Most peaked in 2008, but the two smallest in population, San Mateo County and Marin County, both relatively wealthy counties, peaked later. The two counties with the largest fluctuations were San Francisco County and San Mateo County. San Mateo County, the home of Silicon Valley (along with Santa Clara County), had the lowest surge during the period. All of the counties, except San Mateo County, ended the period in 2019 with filing levels below each county's level at the beginning of the period in 2000. All six counties were below the state average in 2019.

Per capita Limited Civil filings in the southern Central Valley counties are shown in Figure 3.8. The pattern for these counties was slightly different from other regions. All but one had filing levels above the statewide average in 2000, but two dropped below the statewide average in 2019. Three showed more of a sharp peak followed by a sharp drop than a rounded surge starting in 2006. The peaks for several counties were earlier than for counties in the other regions. Only one county, Kings County, displayed a rounded surge similar to that found elsewhere in the state. The two largest counties by population, Fresno County and Kern County, showed a comparatively small surge. The spread of filing levels in 2000 was only 1.1 to 1 (excluding Madera County[4]), increased to 1.9 to 1 in 2008, and dropped to 1.3 to 1 in 2019. Beginning in 2015, the filing levels for these counties were tightly grouped. Excluding Madera County, all had per capita filing levels in 2019 below levels in 2000.

Looking across all 58 counties in California, the spread of per capita filing levels for Limited Civil cases was more dramatic. In 2000 the spread was 24 to 1 for all counties and 5 to 1 for counties with a population of more than 100,000 people. The widest spread was in 2007, 30 to 1 for all counties and almost 11 to 1 for counties with a population of greater than 100,000 people. In 2019, the spread had dropped to 13 to 1 for all counties and 5 to 1 for counties with a population of more than 100,000 people. Unfortunately, there was no data allowing an identification of which Limited Civil case subcategories surged between 2006 and 2015.

3.2.5 Adjacent Counties

Examination of the per capita Limited Civil filings in the two sets of adjacent counties revealed very different patterns. San Diego County experienced a much steeper and higher surge than Orange County beginning in 2006 (Figure 3.9). Both peaked from 2008 to 2010, although San Diego's filing level was 1.8 times higher. Filing levels in both counties began dropping in 2011 to a low point in 2015. The filing levels were then once again very similar. The filing levels in 2019 were lower than the filing levels in 2000 in both courts.

In contrast, the filing patterns in Fresno County and Kern County were very similar for the entire period (Figure 3.10). Kern County had two peaks, one in 2006 and one in 2008. Fresno County's peaks were in 2003 and in 2008. Both experienced a long, slow drop in filing levels from 2009 to 2015. Filing levels then began to rise in both courts until 2018. The filing levels in 2019 were slightly lower than the filing levels in 2000 in both courts.

4. Madera only reported 95 total filings in 2000, none in 2001, 552 in 2002, and 914 in 2003. It is likely the 2000 and 2001 numbers represented incomplete reports.

FIGURE 3.9 CALIFORNIA PER CAPITA LIMITED CIVIL FILINGS PER 100K POPULATION IN ORANGE AND SAN DIEGO COUNTIES

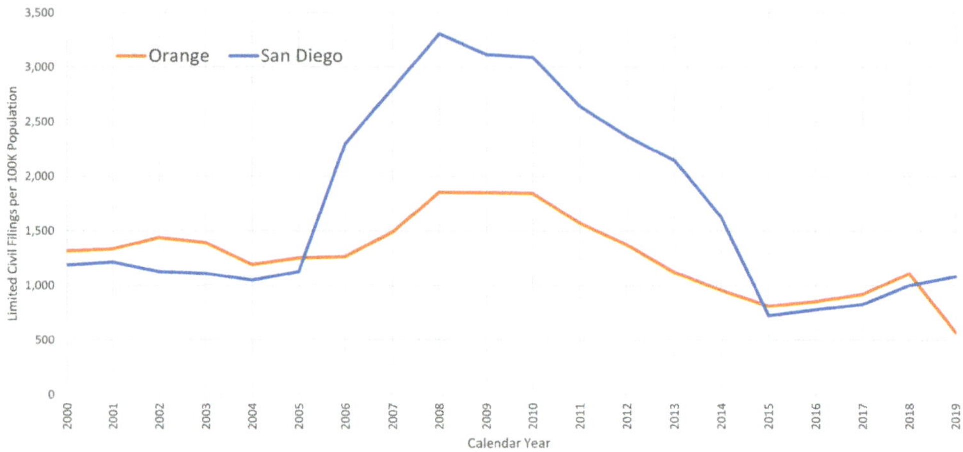

FIGURE 3.10 CALIFORNIA LIMITED CIVIL FILINGS PER 100K POPULATION IN FRESNO AND KERN COUNTIES

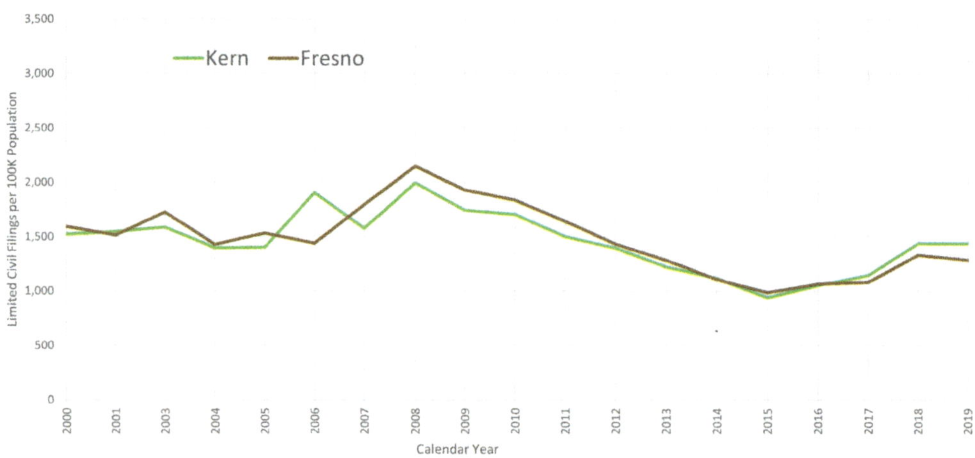

3.3 Illinois—Variation in Filing Levels

The counties in Illinois with the largest populations were Cook County and the five geographically adjacent counties. Unlike the analysis of the California data, the civil filings data for Illinois counties is not subdivided into subcategories of civil filings. The five adjacent counties had per capita filing patterns and levels that were quite similar to each other (Figure 3.11). The filing pattern in Cook County was similar, although it peaked earlier, in 2007, whereas the adjacent counties all peaked in 2010. The spread of filing levels in these five counties was small; it ranged from a low of 1.3 to 1 to a high of 1.5 to 1. The filing levels for Cook and three of the adjacent counties were lower in 2019 than in 2016.

FIGURE 3.11 ILLINOIS LARGEST POPULATION COUNTIES

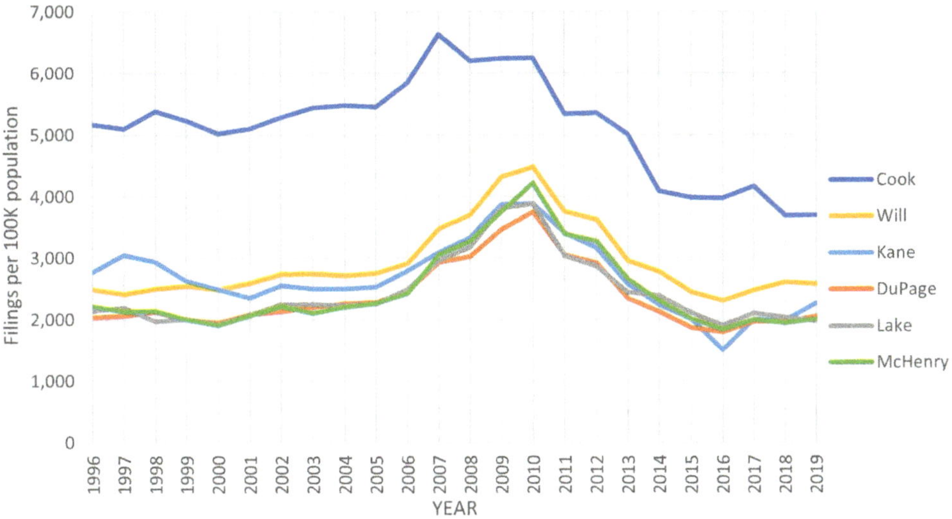

The per capita filing level in Cook County was significantly higher, more than double the average of the adjacent counties from 1996 to 2007, but smaller for most years thereafter. Cook's population was eight to ten times the average of the five counties for these 25 years. All of the adjacent counties had grown in population, four substantially, over the 25 years, but Cook County's population shrank. As noted previously, slow-growing counties tended to have higher per capita filing levels.

The Fourth Judicial Circuit is located in the lower center of the state geographically. The circuit contains nine counties that are geographically contiguous. In 2019, the population ranged from 9,610 to 37,562, with four having a population of more than 30,000. Despite being contiguous and several of similar size, the per capita filing pattern and levels varied widely (Figure 3.12). The per capita filing levels in Clinton, the largest county, and Jasper, the smallest county, were the lowest for most of the 25-year

FIGURE 3.12 ILLINOIS FOURTH JUDICIAL CIRCUIT COURTS

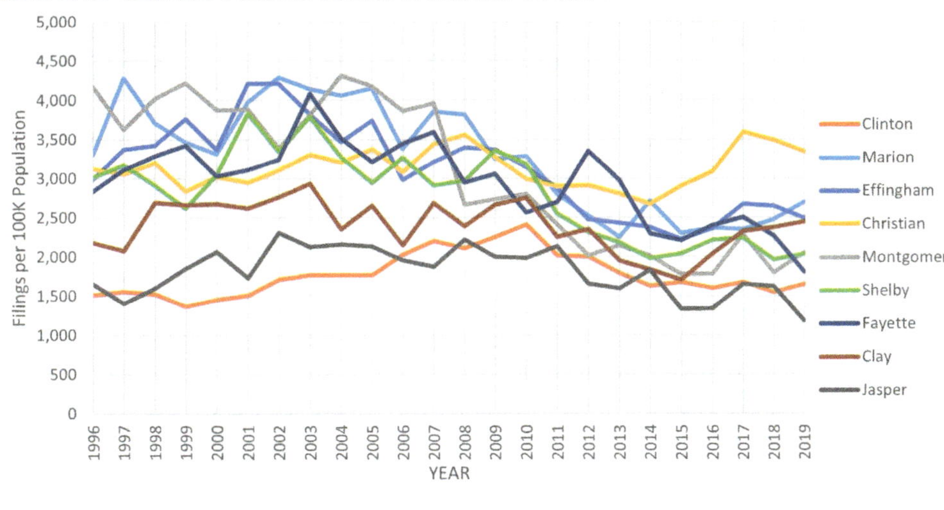

period. The spread of filing levels was highest at 3 to 1 in 1997 and 1999. The spread tightened during and after the Great Recession, with a low of 1.4 to 1 in 2011, but widened again by 2019. From 1996 to 2007, the range of filing levels in the Fourth Circuit was similar to the range for the five largest counties. Five of the nine had lower per capita filing levels in 2019 than in 1996.

The filing patterns and levels in the five smallest counties were more varied than for either the large counties or the Fourth Circuit counties (Figure 3.13). The year-to-year filing levels fluctuated significantly. The highest filing levels in each county were in different years, and only two were associated with the Great Recession. The spread of filing levels ranged from 1.4 to 1 to 4.3 to 1, but were below 2 to 1 in most years. Only two of the five had filing levels lower in 2019 than in 1996. There was no common pattern to the filing levels compared to the other two groups.

FIGURE 3.13 ILLINOIS SMALLEST POPULATION COUNTIES

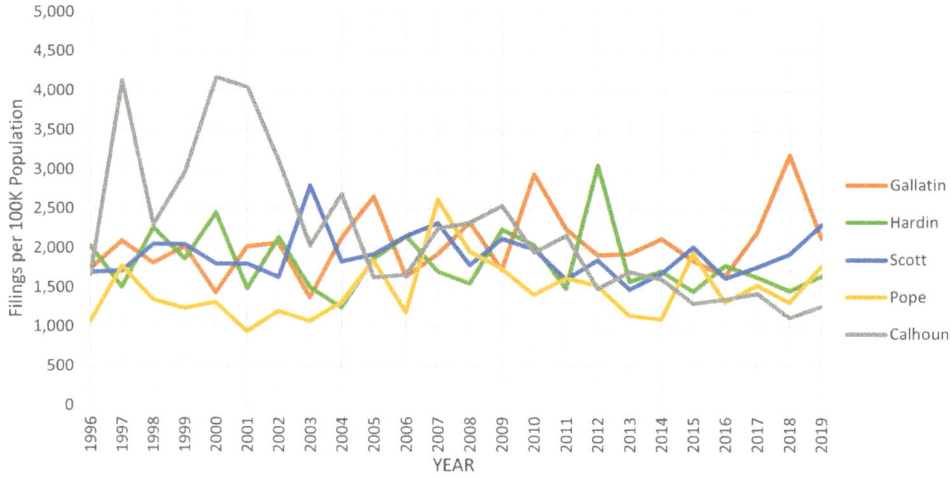

3.4 Minnesota—Variation in Filing Levels

The per capita filing patterns and levels in the five smallest counties were more varied than for either the large counties or the Fourth Circuit counties (Figure 3.13). In contrast to the other states, the per capita filing patterns had two small surges, one in the 2000 to 2004 period and one in the 2006 to 2015 period, which was associated with the Great Recession. As with the civil filings data for Illinois, the data for Minnesota is not subdivided into subcategories of civil filings for this review of filings levels by county.

Per capita filings fluctuated widely across Minnesota counties and over time. Figure 3.14 displays the per capita filings from 1994 to 2018 for the ten largest counties by population and, for comparison, the statewide per capita filing average (the red line). The list of counties in the legend are ordered by population. From 1994 to 2001, Hennepin County, the largest county, had the highest filing level. Starting in 2002, the sixth largest county, St. Louis County, had the highest per capita filing level for several years. St. Louis County also had the highest level for the last nine years of the period. For the first 25 years of the period, Olmstead County, the seventh largest, and Washington

County, the fifth largest, had the lowest filing levels. The spread of filing levels was larger at the beginning of the period, 2.4 to 1 in 1994, but narrowed by 2004 to 1.8 to 1 or lower.

FIGURE 3.14 MINNESOTA COMPARABLE CIVIL FILINGS PER 100K POPULATION, TEN LARGEST COUNTIES BY POPULATION

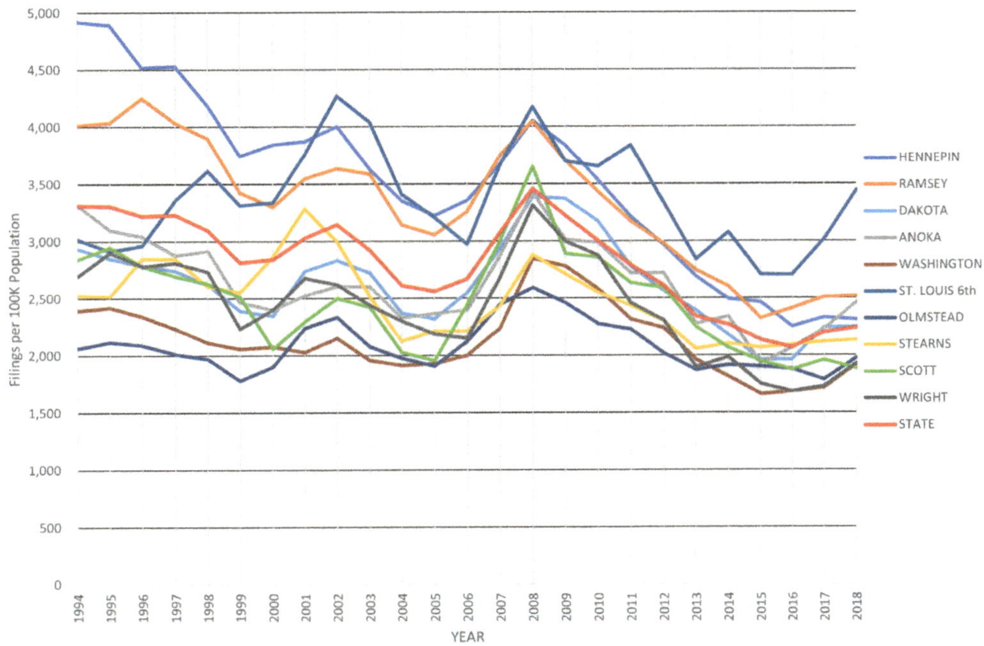

Figures 3.15, 3.16, and 3.17 display the per capita filings over 25 years for three groups of geographically adjacent counties in different parts of Minnesota. All three figures have the same scale and include a line of the statewide per capita filing average (the red line) for comparison. Figure 3.15 includes data for the nine urban and suburban counties, including the twin cities of Minneapolis and St. Paul. Figure 3.16 includes the four counties in the Sixth Judicial District in the northeast corner of the state. Figure 3.17 includes five counties in the south-central part of the state.

The twin cities region includes Hennepin County (the largest county by population, including the city of Minneapolis), Ramsey County (the second largest in population, including the city of St. Paul, the state capitol), and the seven adjacent suburban counties. Together these nine counties included almost 60 percent of the state's population in 2019. Five of the counties were among the six fastest growing counties in population over the last 25 years.

The per capita filing pattern of the Twin Cities region was similar over time, and more tightly grouped than for any of the California or Illinois regions. Filing levels in all the counties were dropping from 1994 until 1999. There was then a small surge around 2002, followed by a drop to 2005. All filing levels then rose to a peak in 2008. Filing levels then dropped, with all nine counties at a lower level in 2018 than in 1994.

FIGURE 3.15 MINNESOTA COMPARABLE CIVIL FILINGS PER 100K POPULATION, TWIN CITIES REGION

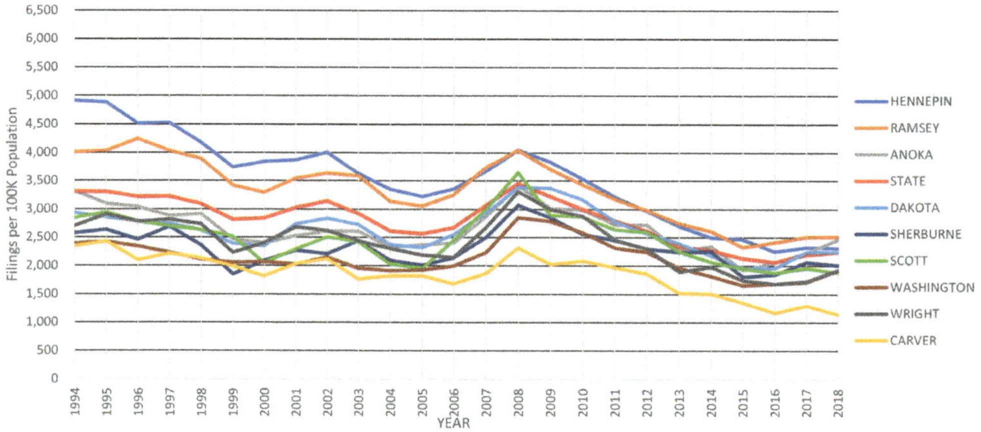

FIGURE 3.16 MINNESOTA COMPARABLE CIVIL FILINGS PER 100K POPULATION, SIXTH JUDICIAL DISTRICT

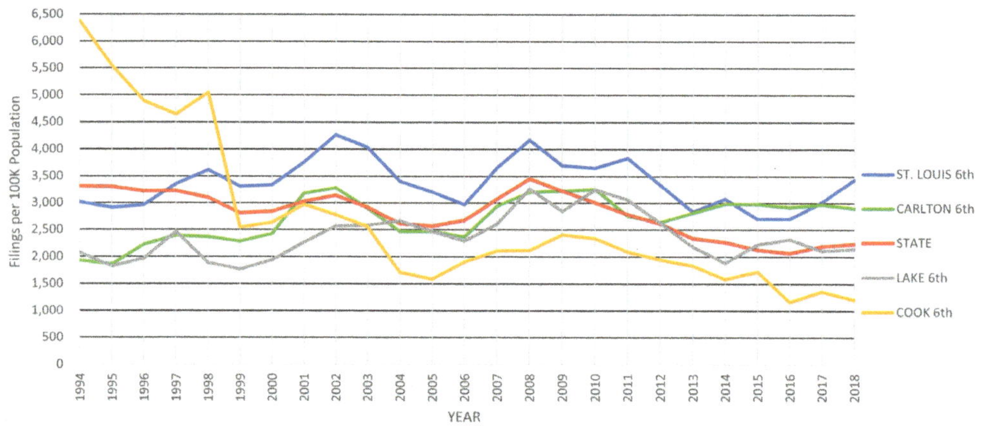

FIGURE 3.17 MINNESOTA COMPARABLE CIVIL FILINGS PER 100K POPULATION, SOUTH-CENTRAL COUNTIES

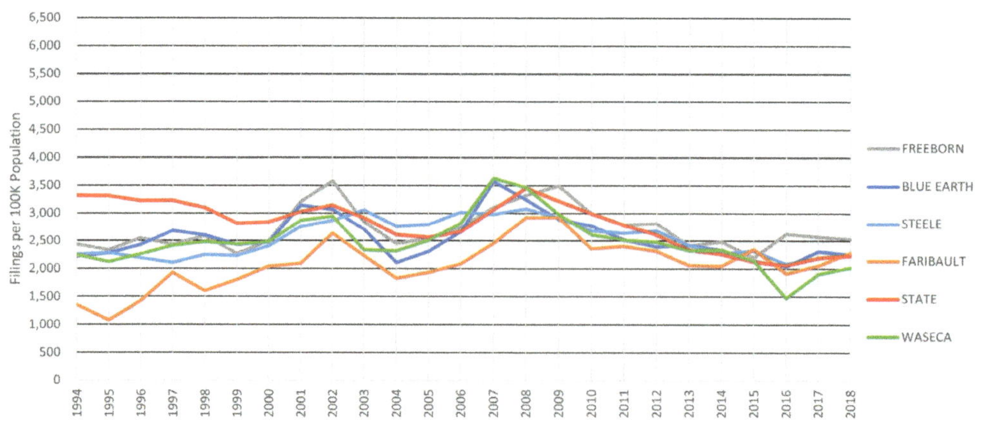

The drop in filing levels ranged from 20 percent to 53 percent, as compared to the state average, which dropped about 32 percent.

The two largest counties were consistently above the state average for the entire period. Two other counties, Anoka County and Dakota County, rose above the state average in 2018. The remaining counties were below the state average for most of the period, although three counties exceeded the state average in at least one year after 2008. Carver County had the lowest filing level of this group in 21 of the 25 years, and every year from 2002 to 2018.

Over the 25-year period the per capita filing levels in the Twin Cities region slowly converged to more similar levels. The spread of filing levels was largest at the beginning of the period. In 1994, the spread was 2.1 to 1 from Hennepin County to Carver County. It had compressed to 1.6 to 1 in 2011 and 2012. In 2018, the spread had increased to 2.2 to 1, although, without Carver County, the spread was only 1.3 to 1.

Per capita filing levels in the two largest geographically adjacent counties of Hennepin and Ramsey varied significantly. The ratio of Hennepin County's population to Ramsey County's increased slightly, from 2.1 to 1 to 2.3 to 1 over the 25-year period. Hennepin County's population grew 19 percent and Ramsey County's population grew 12 percent. In contrast, the ratio of Hennepin County's per capita filing level to Ramsey County's declined from 1.2 to 1 in 1994 to 0.9 to 1 in 2018. Ramsey County's per capita filing level surpassed Hennepin County's in 2007 and every year from 2013 to 2018, except for 2015. The smaller, slower growing county ended the period with a higher per capita filing ratio.

The Sixth District included four counties in the northeast corner of the state. The area is rural with mining, timber, and tourist economic sectors. It included St. Louis County, the sixth largest county in population, with the city of Duluth, and geographically the largest county in the state. The other three counties were quite small, although two, Carlton County and Cook County, were also among the fastest growing in the state over the last 25 years. The total population of the Sixth District was a little more than 4 percent of the state population in 2019.

The per capita filing pattern in the Sixth District was different from other regions. There were two surges, one from 2000 to 2005 and another from 2006 to 2013. The surges were later than the surges in the Twin Cities region. The peak levels in each county were not in the same years during the surges. St. Louis County peaked in 2002 and again 2008. Carlton County peaked in 2002 and 2010. Lake County had peaks in 2004, 2008, and 2010.

Three of the four counties were below the state per capita filing average in 1994. St. Louis County rose above the state average in 1997, and stayed above the state average for the rest of the period. Cook County, the smallest county in population, was considerably above the state average in 1994, but fell below the state average in 1999, and stayed below for the rest of the period. Carleton County was below the state average until 2001, followed the state average until 2012, and then was consistently above the state average. Lake County was below the state average until 2004, then followed the state average for the rest of the period. By 2019, St. Louis County and Carleton County were well above the state average, Lake was at the state average, and Cook was below the state average. The pattern of faster growing counties having lower per capita filing levels did not hold in the Sixth District.

The spread of filing levels was wide but relatively consistent over most of the 25 years. In 1994, the spread was 1.6 to 1 without Cook County, and 3.3 to 1 including Cook County. From 1996 to 2017, the spread oscillated, with a high of 2.7 to 1 in 1998 and a low of 1.5 to 1 in 2013. In 2018 the spread was 2.9 to 1.

The five south-central counties were mostly rural, farming counties. Two counties had small populations, two were comparatively mid-sized, and one was larger. Over the 25-year period, two counties had shrinking populations (Faribault County and Freeborn County), one grew slowly (Waseca County), and two grew modestly (Steele County and Blue Earth County). The total population of the five counties was 3 percent of the state's total population in 2019.

The per capita filing level pattern in this region showed two surges, both slightly more pronounced than in the other regions in the state. The first surge peaked in 2002, and the second surge was from 2007 to 2009. Thereafter, each of the county's filing levels dropped except Freeborn County. In all of the counties except Waseca County, the per capita filing levels in 2018 were higher than in 1994. Freeborn County's levels fluctuated the most, and the level was almost 70 percent higher in 2018 than in 1994.

All five counties were below the state per capita filing average from 1994 until 2001. For the rest of the period the counties stayed near, but generally below, the state average. Blue Earth County, the county with the largest population in this group, rose slightly above the state average in five different years, beginning in 2007. Freeborn County, midsize in population of this group, was above the state average from 2012 until 2018.

The spread of per capita filings was quite small over the 25-year period. This group had the tightest grouping of any of the regions studied. The range of filing levels fluctuated from a high of 2.2 to 1 in 1995 to a low of 1.2 to 1 in 2015. The spread narrowed beginning in 2008, varying between 1.1 to 1 and 1.3 to 1, except for a peak of 1.8 to 1 in 2016 because of a jump in Freeborn County, and a drop in Waseca County.

For the last 11 years of this period, the ratio of per capita filing levels, Blue Earth County to Faribault County, ranged from 0.9 to 1 to more than 2 to 1 even though Blue Earth County's population was five times larger than Faribault County's in 2018.

The variance in per capita filing levels in adjacent counties was also present in the South Central region over the 25-year period. The two smallest population-adjacent counties were Waseca County and Faribault County. Waseca County's population was slightly larger and rose almost 5 percent, whereas Faribault County's dropped 18 percent. The population spread ranged from a low of 1.1 to 1 in 1994 to a high of 1.4 to 1 in 2018. The ratio of per capita filing levels exhibited a higher variance in 1995; it was almost 2 to 1. The ratio dropped, with Faribault County passing Waseca County in 2015. In 2018 the ratio was 0.9 to 1.

Two other similarly sized counties in population in the group, Freeborn County and Steele County, also exhibited significant variances. Both had similar populations, between 31,000 and 34,000 from 1994 to 2000. After 2000, Steele County's population grew, and had increased almost 17 percent by 2018. Although Freeborn County had a slightly higher population in 1994, its population peaked in 2000 and dropped almost 8 percent by 2018. The ratio of Steele County's population to Freeborn County's rose from less than 1 to 1 in 1994 to 1.2 to 1 in 2018. The per capita filing ratio did not show the same pattern. Steele County's per capita filing level was lower than Freeborn

County's in 19 of the 25 years. It was only greater than 1 to 1 from 2003 to 2005, and in 2013 and 2015. From 2016 to 2018, the ratio was less than 0.9 to 1. The county with a steadily growing population had per capita filings levels lower than a similarly sized adjacent county whose population was shrinking.

3.5 Conclusions

Chapter 1 shows the wide variation in per capita filings from state to state across the five states studied here. This chapter shows that this variation exists to the same extent *within* each of the states for which we have county-level data. Looking across regions and counties within the five states, there is no consistency of per capita filing levels or pattern based on population or region. Rather, per capita filing levels vary widely across counties and fluctuate considerably, year-to-year. Even geographically adjacent counties with similar populations have different per capita filing levels. Per capita filing levels also vary widely over time and in different patterns. Although not always the case, generally the faster-growing counties had lower per capita filing levels than the slower-growing counties.

The search for a causal pattern for observed fluctuations in civil filings is confounded not only by wide differences in filing patterns from state to state but also within states. While one might suggest that the lower per capita civil filings fluctuations within Minnesota suggest that the population of that state is more culturally and socially homogeneous than that of the other two states, the data as a whole, analyzed to test exactly that hypothesis by focusing on like and adjoining counties, shows the opposite—that like communities have very different civil filings patterns.

3.6 Impact of Largest Courts in the State on Filing Levels

The five states studied here each had at least one county, if not several counties, where the population was much larger than was typical for the other counties in the state. In these states, there were 19 counties with a population of more than one million people. Table 3.2 displays the population and civil filing levels for the large counties, each state as a whole, and each state not including the large counties. Several findings were apparent from this data.

The civil filings in these large counties were generally higher than that for the rest of the state, both in terms of the share of total state filings and per capita filing levels. However, in the three states with more than one large county, there was considerable variation in the per capita filing levels across the larger counties. This suggests caution when comparing filing levels across states with widely different population center patterns. It also suggests that using filing data from the large counties in a state as representative of a state or to compare states is problematic.

Per capita filing levels varied significantly across the large counties. In Illinois, Minnesota, Ohio, and Texas all of the large counties had per capita civil filing levels significantly higher than the level for the state not including the large counties. In

California, seven of the ten large counties had per capita filing levels higher than the rest of the state. In 2019, the ratio of per capita filing levels from the largest court in the state to the state average, not including the large courts, ranged from 1.80 in Los Angles to 1.04 in Hennepin, with the ratio in the other three states greater than 1.40. Thus, per capita levels for the whole state were significantly impacted by the per capita filing levels in the large courts in the state.

In many of the large counties, the total civil filings were disproportionate to their population. In three of the five states, the largest county's share of total statewide civil filings significantly exceeded their share of the state population. In the other two states, the share of total filings was higher than their population share, but only by a few percentage points. In five of the 19 counties, all in California, the percentage of statewide filings was a few percentage points less than their population share.

Figure 3.18 displays the per capita filing levels in 2019, or 2019 relative to county population for the 19 largest counties. The color of a dot indicates the state in which the county is located. The dots along the left axis indicate the per capita filing level in each state, not including the large counties. The county with the largest per capita filing level in each state is labeled with the county name. From the figure it is clear that counties with larger populations do not have consistently higher, or lower, per capita filing levels than smaller population counties. There was a 5.2 to 1 spread between the highest per capita filing level (Cuyahoga County, Cleveland, Ohio) and the lowest per capita filing level (Orange County, Santa Ana, California). In addition the per capita civil filings levels for counties with similar populations are not similar.

TABLE 3.2 PER CAPITA FILING LEVELS FOR LARGE COUNTIES IN 2019

County (largest city)	Population	Comparable civil filings per capita	Share of total state population	Share of total civil filings
CALIFORNIA*	39,512,223	2,172		
CA w/o Los Angeles	29,327,845	1,799	74%	64%
CA w/o the ten largest	10,876,703	1,613	28%	22%
Los Angeles	10,184,378	2,909	26%	36%
San Diego	3,340,312	1,983	8%	8%
Orange (Santa Ana)	3,192,987	1,147	8%	4%
Riverside	2,422,146	2,322	6%	7%
San Bernardino	2,168,964	1,333	5%	4%
Santa Clara (San Jose)	1,954,833	1,345	5%	3%
Alameda (Oakland)	1,664,783	1,637	4%	3%
Sacramento	1,541,301	4,551	4%	8%
Contra Costa (Concord)	1,150,621	1,667	3%	2%
Fresno	1,015,195	2,173	3%	3%

County (largest city)	Population	Comparable civil filings per capita	Share of total state population	Share of total civil filings
ILLINOIS	12,671,821	2,786		
IL without Cook	7,521,588	2,350	59%	50%
Cook (Chicago)	5,150,233	3,357	41%	50%
MINNESOTA**	5,680,337	2,241		
MN without Hennepin	4,368,312	2,220	77%	77%
Hennepin (Minneapolis)	1,261,104	2,313	22%	23%
OHIO**	11,689,100	4,438		
OH without the two largest***	9,137,272	3,875	78%	73%
Franklin (Columbus)***	1,316,756	4,535	11%	12%
Cuyahoga (Cleveland)***	1,235,072	6,007	11%	15%
TEXAS	28,995,881	3,406		
TX without the five largest	16,267,017	2,847	56%	47%
Harris (Houston)	4,713,325	4,549	16%	22%
Dallas	2,635,516	4,068	9%	11%
Tarrant (Forth Worth)	2,102,515	3,995	7%	8%
Bexar (San Antonio)	2,003,554	3,846	7%	8%
Travis (Austin)	1,273,954	3,282	4%	4%

* California county population estimates are from the California Department of Finance, not U.S. intercensal data.

** Figures for Minnesota and Ohio data are for 2018.

*** Ohio county filings do not include civil cases in the Probate Division of the Court of Common Pleas.

In Chapter 2 we noted that states that had experienced slower population growth had higher per capita filing levels than states with higher population growth rates. Looking at the large courts from 2000 to 2019, in four of these five states the same pattern appears, but not as strongly. In California, the two slowest growing large courts had higher per capita filing levels than all but one of the courts in faster growing counties and higher than the rest of the state. However, Sacramento County had a high growth rate and had a per capita level almost 150 percent higher than the average of other large California counties. In Illinois, Cook County declined in population and had a per capita filing level much higher than the rest of the state, which grew nominally. In Minnesota, Ramsey County had a lower growth rate and a higher per capita level than either Hennepin County or the rest of the state. In Ohio, Cuyahoga County, which had fewer people, had a higher per capita level than Franklin County, which had a high growth rate, and a higher level than the rest of the counties. The pattern did not hold in Texas. All five

FIGURE 3.18 COMPARABLE CIVIL FILINGS PER 100K POPULATION IN 2019 IN COURTS WITH MORE THAN ONE MILLION POPULATION

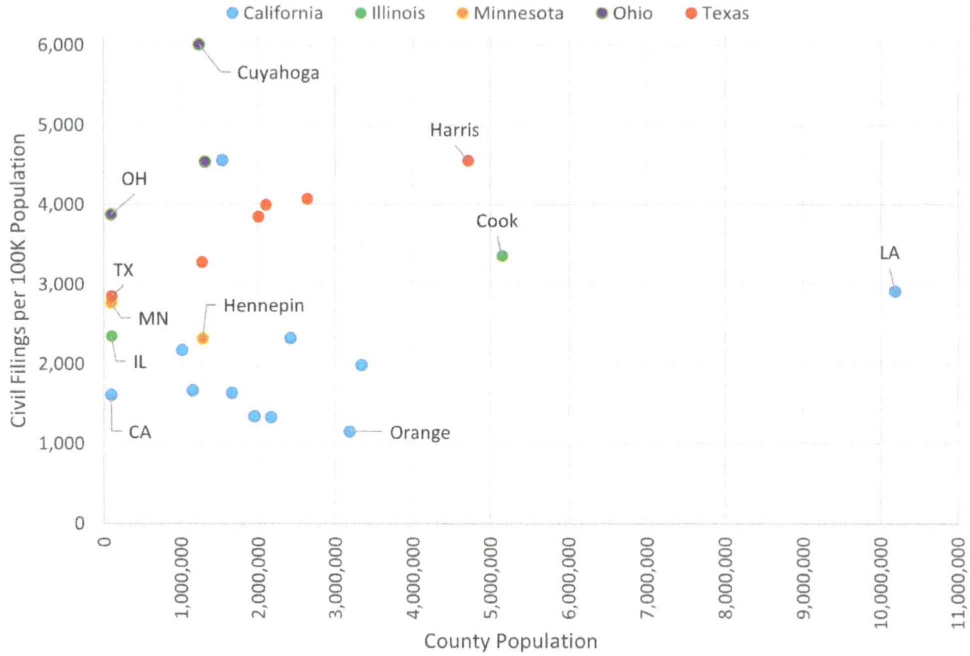

of the largest counties had per capita levels higher than the rest of the state, but all had high growth rates, as did the rest of the counties.

Another interesting finding concerns the filing levels in state capitols. In all five states, the county in which the state capitol is located has a higher per capita filing level than the counties in the rest of the state, not including the largest counties. In California, Illinois, and Minnesota, the county with the state capitol also has a higher per capita filing level than all the largest counties in the state. Only California (Employment Development Department actions), Ohio (actions against the state), and Minnesota (noncriminal tax cases) have case categories that can only be filed in the county where the state capitol is located, and all are low volume, so this would not explain the difference.

The filing characteristics of the largest counties in each of the five states are discussed in greater detail in the following sections.

3.6.1 California

There was one very large county in California, Los Angeles County, and nine other counties with a population of more than one million people. Looking at total civil filings, Los Angeles County's share of total filings was disproportionate to its population share and the share was increasing. The population of Los Angeles County on January 1, 2019, was 10,172,951,[5] or about 26 percent of the state's population. Total civil

5. California Department of Finance population estimates, http://dof.ca.gov/Forecasting/Demographics/Estimates/e-4-population-estimates-for-cities-counties-and-the-state-2011-2020-with-2010-census-benchmark-new/.

filings in Los Angeles County were a disproportionate 36 percent of total state filings. Los Angeles County's higher-value Unlimited Civil filings were 27 percent of statewide Unlimited Civil filings in 2000, peaked at 45 percent in 2017, then dropped to 39 percent in 2019. Its proportion of lower-value Limited Civil filings was 36 percent in 2000, peaked at 38 percent in 2009, then dropped to 33 percent in 2019. Its proportion of Small Claims filings was 33 percent in 2000, stayed in the 33–36 percent range until 2015, then rose to 41 percent in 2019. During this period, the population in Los Angeles County grew much more slowly than statewide growth. Since 2000, statewide population, not including Los Angeles County, grew 22 percent, whereas Los Angeles County's population only grew by 7 percent. The slower-growing county had a disproportionate share of total filings.

Focusing on per capita filing levels, Los Angeles County's levels were higher than the state, not including Los Angeles County. Per capita filing levels also changed in different ways than the rest of the state.[6] Table 3.3 compares Los Angeles County's per capita filing levels with statewide levels and those for the state not including Los Angeles in 2000 and 2019. Unlimited Civil per capita filing levels in Los Angeles County were over 80 percent higher than the state level, not including Los Angeles. Limited Civil per capita filing levels were 40 percent higher than the level for the rest of the state. Small Claims per capita filing levels were double the level in the rest of the state. From 2000 to 2019, per capita Unlimited Civil filing levels increased in Los Angeles County whereas per capita filing levels fell in the rest of the state. Limited Civil per capita filing levels decreased faster in Los Angeles County, and Small Claims per capita filing levels decreased at a much slower rate than the rest of the state. Both the levels and patterns of filing levels in Los Angeles County were very different than for the rest of the state.

The patterns were also different for the other nine large counties in California (see Table 3.2). Only one large county, Sacramento, had a higher share of state filings than their state population share. Interestingly, Sacramento is the state capitol. The other eight had a share of statewide filings similar to their share of population. As seen from the distribution of large California counties, blue dots in Figure 3.18, there was no apparent relationship between population and per capita filing levels. Five of the ten had per capita filing levels higher than the level for the rest of the state. Three had a lower level. The spread from the highest per capita filing level to the lowest was 4 to 1, a very large spread.

6. This was noted in Alexander B. Aikman & Karen A. Viscia, *Exploring the Work of the California Trial Courts: A 20-Year Retrospective*, ADMIN. OFF. OF THE COURTS, CTR. FOR CT. RSCH., INNOVATION, & PLAN., at iv, 3–4, 100 (2003), and the JUDICIAL COUNCIL OF CALIFORNIA, 2004 ANNUAL REPORT, PRESERVING EQUAL ACCESS 20–21.

TABLE 3.3 COMPARING LOS ANGELES PER CAPITA FILING LEVELS WITH FILING LEVELS IN THE REST OF THE STATE OF CALIFORNIA

Case category	Statewide	Statewide w/o Los Angeles	Los Angeles
All Civil Filings per capita in 2000	2,939	2,716	3,509
All Civil Filings per capita in 2019	2,082	1,799	2,909
Unlimited Civil filings per capita in 2019	532	442	805
Unlimited Civil filings per capita change from 2000 to 2019	–12%	–28%	+37%
Limited Civil filings per capita in 2019	1,199	1,092	1,533
Limited Civil filings per capita change from 2000 to 2019	–15%	–12%	–16%
Small Claims filing per capita in 2019	352	279	571
Small Claims filings per capita change from 2000 to 2019	–62%	–68%	–48%

3.6.2 Illinois

The disparity between Cook County (Chicago) and the rest of Illinois was similar to that between Los Angeles and the rest of California. Table 3.4 displays the filing levels and population share in Cook County and the rest of the state over 24 years. Cook County's share of total state civil filings dropped from 57 percent in 1996 to 50 percent in 2019. During that period, Cook County's share of total state population dropped from 45 percent to 41 percent. From 1996 to 2019, Cook County's population shrank 3 percent, whereas the rest of the state had grown by almost 11 percent.

The per capita filing levels also changed over time. In 1996, the per capita filing level in Cook County was 89 percent higher than the per capita filing level for the rest of the state. In 2019, it was still 57 percent higher than the rest of the state. Per capita filings in Cook County peaked in 2007. The rest of the state peaked in 2010. In 2019, Cook County's per capita level had dropped almost 29 percent since 1996. In 2019, the per capita filing level for the rest of the state was down only 14 percent. As with Los Angeles in California, the largest county in the state had very different filing levels than the rest of the state.

TABLE 3.4 COMPARING FILING LEVELS IN COOK COUNTY WITH THE REST OF THE STATE OF ILLINOIS

Case Category	State	State without Cook County	Cook County
1996—Civil filings per capita	3,669	2,734	5,170
1996—Share of total state civil filings		43%	57%
1996—Share of total state population		55%	45%
Peak per capita filing level	4,620 in 2007; 4,613 in 2010	3,650 in 2010	6,632 in 2007
2019—Civil filings per capita	2,786	2,350	3,691
2019—Share of total state civil filings		50%	50%
2019—Share of total state population		59%	41%
Population growth 1996 to 2019	5%	11%	−3%

Looking at the major case categories, the proportion of Law case filings heard in Cook County far exceeded its share of population. Cook County's share of Law cases valued at $50,000 or less was more than 80 percent in 1996, peaked at 84 percent in 2007, and ended at 72 percent in 2019. Law cases over $50,000 started at 56 percent, peaked at 65 percent in 2007, and ended at 56 percent in 2019. In contrast, Cook County's share of small claims cases rose from 12 percent in 1996 to 29 percent in 2019, with most of the increase occurring after 2013.

3.6.3 Minnesota

There is only one comparatively large county in Minnesota—Hennepin County (constituting the Fourth Judicial District). Unlike Los Angeles County in California and Cook County in Illinois, Hennepin County did not have a disproportionate share of statewide filings relative to state population. In 2018, Hennepin County accounted for 23 percent of all statewide filings and 22 percent of the state's population. In addition, Hennepin County's per capita filing levels were very similar to the rest of the state. Notably, Hennepin County's population growth was also similar to the rest of the state, 25 percent versus 21 percent. The district court in Hennepin County did not disproportionately affect statewide filing levels as much as the largest county did in the other states.

Table 3.5 compares the per capita filings in 2018 for the state, the state without Hennepin County, and Hennepin County for the three high-level case categories. Hennepin County's filing levels were marginally higher than the statewide levels for Major Civil and Minor Civil (not including Conciliation cases). Hennepin County's level for Conciliation cases was slightly lower than the rest of the state. The spread was much smaller than for the large courts in the other states.

TABLE 3.5 COMPARING PER CAPITA HENNEPIN COUNTY FILING LEVELS WITH THE REST OF THE STATE OF MINNESOTA IN 2018

Case Category	Statewide	Statewide without Hennepin County	Hennepin County
Total Per capita civil filings	2,241	2,220	2,313
Per capita Major Civil filings	526	519	550
Per capita Minor Civil filings without Conciliation	817	801	875
Per capita Conciliation Court Filings	897	900	888

The following figures display per capita filings in Hennepin County (Figure 3.19) and the rest of the state (Figure 3.20) for all civil cases and for the three high-level case categories. The roller coaster pattern of per capita filing levels is quite similar for Hennepin County and the rest of the state. However, Hennepin County shows a steeper decline, both as to all case categories and Conciliation case per capita filing levels, over the period. Both groups had peak filing levels in 2002 and 2008 for all cases and Minor Civil cases. Major Civil per capita filing levels in both groups surged in 2008 and 2009, although the surge was greater in Hennepin County. By 2018, the per capita filing levels were comparable in both groups.

FIGURE 3.19 MINNESOTA COMPARABLE CIVIL FILINGS PER 100K POPULATION, HENNEPIN COUNTY

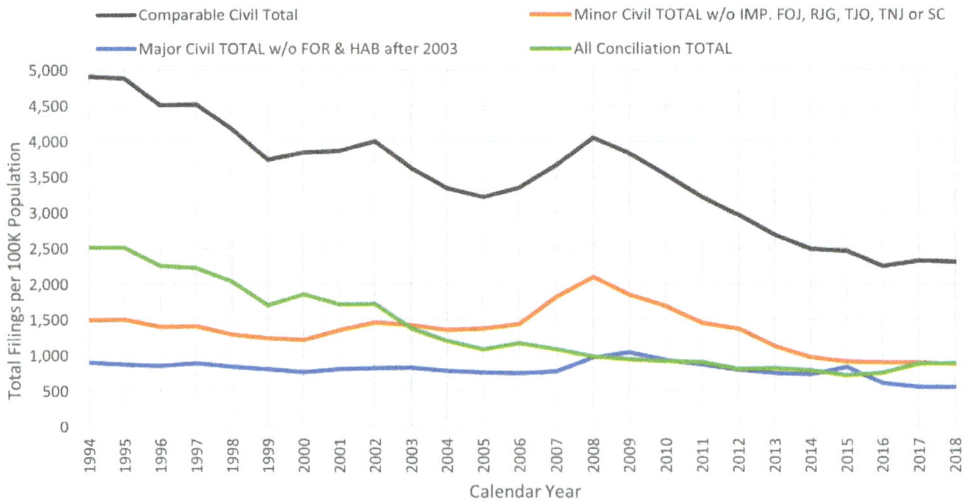

FIGURE 3.20 MINNESOTA COMPARABLE CIVIL FILINGS PER 100K POPULATION, NOT INCLUDING HENNEPIN COUNTY

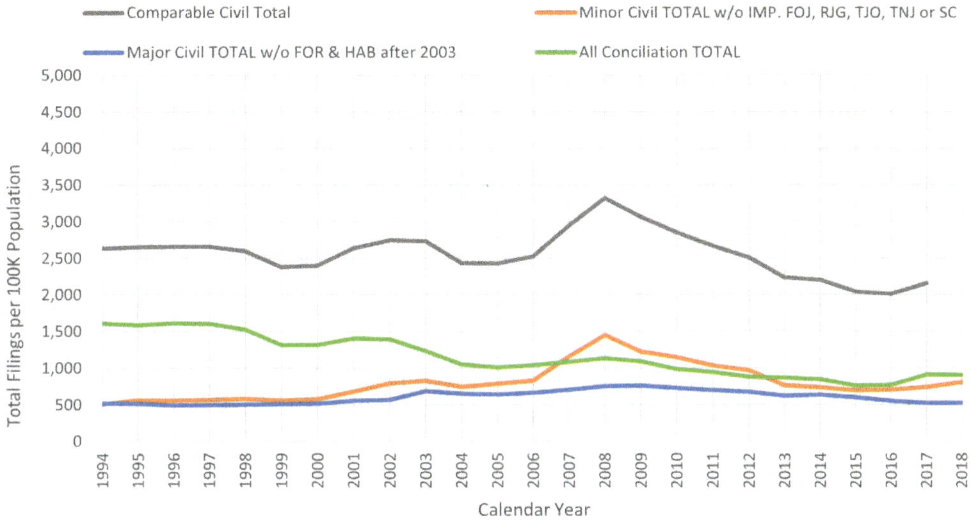

3.6.4 Ohio

There are three comparatively large counties in Ohio. Two counties had similar populations, Franklin County (Columbus, the state capitol) and Cuyahoga County (Cleveland). The next largest county was Hamilton County (Cincinnati) whose population was less than one million. Table 3.6 shows each of these large county's share of statewide total new civil filings for 1999, 2009, and 2018, and the share of total state population in 2018. There was no obvious pattern relating the population of a county to its share of total filings. The three large counties' share of the total statewide civil filings did not change as much as their populations did over the 20 years from 1999 to 2018. Cuyahoga County's share of all new filings was larger than its share of total population in all three years, although the share declined with its decline in population.

TABLE 3.6 OHIO LARGEST COUNTIES SHARE OF TOTAL NEW CIVIL FILINGS IN ALL COURTS IN A COUNTY AND STATEWIDE

County	Cuyahoga County	Franklin County	Hamilton County	Statewide without three largest counties	Statewide
Share of Filings 1999	18%	12%	9%	62%	
Share of Filings 2009	14%	10%	*		
Share of Filings 2018	15%	12%	8%	72%	
Change in filings, 1999 to 2018	−6%	11%	−3%	13%	8%
Share of population in 2018	10.8%	11.2%	7%	71%	
Population change 1999 to 2018	−11%	23%	−4%	4%	3%

* From 2003 to 2009, Hamilton county reported a significantly disproportionate number of Other Civil Terminations, which would skew the interpretation of the data for the total period covered by this table.

Hamilton also had a higher share of filings than population in 1999 and 2018, although the share declined slightly. Although Franklin County's population grew substantially, its share of the total statewide caseload did not grow at the same rate, and actually dipped in 2009.

Table 3.7 displays the per capita civil filing levels for the three counties, the rest of the state, and statewide in 1999 and 2018. The per capita civil filing levels for all three large counties were substantially higher than for the rest of the state in both years. The two counites that had lost population, Cuyahoga and Hamilton, both showed increases in per capita filing levels over time. Franklin, which had grown, had a lower per capita filing level in 2018, whereas the level in the rest of the state had grown.

TABLE 3.7 OHIO PER CAPITA CIVIL FILINGS IN THE LARGEST COUNTIES AND STATEWIDE

County	Cuyahoga County	Franklin County	Hamilton County	Statewide without three largest counties	Statewide
Per Capita Filing Levels 1999	5,679	5,038	4,841	3,463	3,987
Per Capita Filing Levels 2018	6,007	4,535	4,886	3,776	4,176
Change in per capita filings, 1999 to 2018	6%	−10%	1%	9%	5%

Looking at each type of trial court, the per capita filing levels in the larger courts were always higher than the levels for the rest of the state. In addition, changes in the levels over time did not correspond to changes in population.

Table 3.8 provides information about per capita civil filing levels in the court of common pleas general division where higher-value cases are heard. The table compares the three largest counties, the rest of the state, and statewide, in 1999, 2009, and 2018. The year 2009 was chosen not only as the midpoint of the 20-year period but also was the year total filings peaked in Ohio.

In 1999, Cuyahoga County's per capita filing level was more than 50 percent higher than the level in either Franklin County or Hamilton County and almost twice the level of the smaller counties in the state. This disparity was repeated in 2009 and in 2018 when Cuyahoga County's level was again almost twice the other county levels, although now below its level in 1999. In 2009, Hamilton County's filing level was lower than the level in Franklin County, but it was higher than in 2018. In 2018, both Franklin County and Cuyahoga County had lower levels than they experienced in 1999, whereas the Hamilton County and smaller county filing levels were higher. Again, there appears to be no relationship to changes in population.

TABLE 3.8 OHIO LARGE COUNTY PER CAPITA FILING LEVELS IN THE COURT OF COMMON PLEAS GENERAL DIVISION

County	Per capita filing levels in 1999	Per capita filing levels in 2009	Per capita filing levels in 2018	Change in per capita filings, 1999 to 2018
Cuyahoga	1,508	2,601	1,445	–4%
Franklin	1,030	1,718	898	–13%
Hamilton	945	1,734	1,055	12%
Statewide without the three largest counties	764	1,446	778	2%
Statewide	895	1,622	881	–2%

The share of the lower-value civil cases filed in municipal and county courts revealed a similar pattern. Table 3.9 shows the share of statewide municipal and county court civil caseload in 1999 and 2018. Total filings statewide grew almost 10 percent over the 20-year period. Franklin County's filing growth was slightly greater than the statewide growth, and its share of municipal and county court filings was slightly more than its share of population in both years. Cuyahoga municipal and county court total filings dropped 3 percent from 1999 to 2018, but its share of statewide filings was above its share of state population in both years. Hamilton County's share of municipal and county court filings dropped over the study period, but its share was still greater than its share of population in 2018. Total filings in Hamilton County dropped almost 6 percent, whereas total statewide filings had increased almost 10 percent. Again, there was no relation between changes in population and share of total state filings or per capita filing levels.

TABLE 3.9 OHIO'S LARGEST COUNTIES MUNICIPAL AND COUNTY COURTS' SHARE OF NEW CIVIL CASES

County	Share of New Filings 1999	Share of New Filings 2018	Change in total filings, 1999 to 2018	Share of statewide population in 2018
Cuyahoga	17%	15%	–3%	11%
Franklin	12%	12%	12%	11%
Hamilton	9%	8%	–6%	7%
Statewide			10%	

The pattern of per capita filing levels for municipal and county courts in the three largest counties was different than the pattern for court of common pleas per capita filing levels. Table 3.10 displays the per capita filing levels for municipal and county courts in the three largest counties, the rest of the state, and statewide. Per capita filing levels in the three large courts were significantly higher than the levels in the rest of the state in 1999 and 2018. Cuyahoga County again had higher levels of filings than either of the other two large counties. Cuyahoga County experienced a 10 percent increase in per capita filing levels from 1999 to 2018, whereas per capita filing levels in the court of common pleas had dropped. The per capita filing levels for Franklin County dropped over the two-decade period, but less than the drop for court of common pleas filing levels. The Hamilton County level dropped slightly, whereas its court of common pleas per capita filings had increased. The per capita filing levels in the rest of the state increased 6 percent over the 20-year period compared to a 2 percent increase in court of common pleas per capita filing levels.

TABLE 3.10 OHIO MUNICIPAL AND COUNTY COURT PER CAPITA FILING LEVELS

County	1999	2018	Change in per capita filings, 1999 to 2018
Cuyahoga	4,171	4,562	9%
Franklin	4,008	3,637	−9%
Hamilton	3,896	3,831	−2%
Statewide without the three largest counties	2,699	2,999	11%
Statewide	3,093	3,294	6%

3.6.5 Texas

Texas had one very large county with a population of more than four million (Harris County) and three large counties with a population of more than two million (Dallas, Tarrant, and Bexar Counties) as of July 1, 2019. A fifth county with a population of less than one million (Travis County) was also considered a large county. Texas has experienced significant population growth since 2004, especially in the larger counties. In 2019, the five largest counties included almost half of the total state population. The populations in Bexar, Tarrant, and Travis Counties grew faster than the overall state population. Harris County grew at the same rate as the overall state. Dallas County grew more slowly. Each large county's share of the statewide population stayed approximately the same over the 15-year period.

Table 3.11 compares the share of total filings and the per capita filing levels statewide in the largest counties in 2004 and 2019. Together, the five largest counties received 53 percent of statewide civil filings in 2019, but included only 44 percent of the statewide population. The disproportionate share of civil filings in the largest counties was noted in several annual reports.[7] Harris, Tarrant, and Bexar Counties' share of the total filings grew marginally over the 15-year period. Dallas and Travis Counties' shares shrank. In 2019, Harris County's share of total filings was much greater than its share of total state population. Dallas, Tarrant, and Bexar Counties' share of total filings was only slightly greater than each counties' share or the total state population. Travis County's shares was about the same.

Focusing on per capita filings in 2004 and in 2019, all five large counties had per capita filing levels much higher than the level for the smaller counties in the state in both years. Harris, Dallas, and Tarrant Counties' shares were significantly higher. In Texas, large counties appeared to be driving statewide per capita filing levels more than large courts did in the other states.

7. For example, Annual Report of the Texas Judiciary for Fiscal Year 2007, at 36, 42, 50.

TABLE 3.11 RELATIONSHIP OF TOTAL AND PER CAPITA FILINGS FOR ALL COURTS STATEWIDE VERSUS FIVE MOST POPULOUS COUNTIES

State/County (largest city)	Share of Total Statewide Civil Filings in 2004	Share of Total Statewide Civil Filings 2019	Share of State Total 2019 Population	Total Civil Per Capita Filings in 2004	Total Civil Per Capita Filings in 2019
Statewide				2,743	3,396
Statewide without the five largest counties	46%	47%	56%	2,269	2,829
Harris (Houston)	21%	22%	16%	3,502	4,549
Dallas (Dallas)	14%	11%	9%	3,858	4,068
Tarrant (Forth Worth)	7%	8%	7%	2,786	3,995
Bexar (San Antonio)	7%	8%	7%	2,713	3,282
Travis (Austin)	5%	4%	4%	3,508	3,282

3.6.6 Conclusion

The patterns of per capita civil case filings in large counties are not representative of statewide filings patterns in these five states. Moreover, the relationship between large (or largest) county filings and statewide filings is not consistent from state to state. As with most of the other findings from this study, variation—even dramatic variation—from state to state and place to place within a state is the norm.

Jurisdictions with rapid population growth tend to have slower civil filings growth (or more rapid filings declines) than jurisdictions with more stable populations. But even this finding does not hold for all five states and for all their major cities.

4

Composition of Civil Caseload

4.1 All Civil Case Types

4.1.1 Overview

What broad categories of civil cases were most common? The five states we examined had different trial court structures, case categories, and monetary jurisdictional boundaries. In order to compare case mix across the five states, we grouped the case categories in each state into three broad categories of cases: higher-value/more serious cases, lower-value/less serious cases, and small claims cases. Overall, lower-value civil cases constituted the greatest proportion of civil cases, often more than 50 percent, and the share grew over time. Higher-value civil cases were generally in the 20–30 percent range, and the share fluctuated less than that of the lower-value cases. Small claims cases declined steadily from a significant share of the caseload to a minor share.

The subcategories of higher-value and lower-value civil cases were similar in the five states, although the monetary jurisdiction boundaries were different. In three states, California, Illinois, and Minnesota, there is only one type of trial court. However, these three states distinguished civil cases slightly differently. California categorized civil cases based on the amount of damages claimed—Unlimited Civil for any category of civil case where the damage claim was more than $25,000, and Limited Civil for the balance of the cases. In Illinois, personal injury and contract cases were divided into cases seeking more than $50,000 and cases seeking $50,000 or less, with some other types of civil cases in their own categories. Minnesota categorizes cases as Major Civil or Minor Civil based on the subject matter of the case, as opposed to the amount of damages claimed. However, the case categories counted as Minor Civil generally do not involve damage claims as large as those in Major Civil cases.

Ohio and Texas each have more than one type of trial court. The monetary jurisdiction boundaries between the two types of trial courts in Ohio essentially split civil cases into higher value and lower value cases at $15,000. Trial court jurisdictions in Texas are very complicated, with overlapping jurisdictions between the courts, with the higher value cases generally heard in the district and county courts.

All five states have a category of small claims cases, although the dollar threshold varies, both across states and, over time, within each state.

The lower-value/minor civil cases, not including small claims cases, represented the largest portion of the caseload in all five states, particularly at the end of the study period. Figure 4.1 displays the percentage over time of total comparable civil case filings in each state that were in the lower-value case category. Lower-value cases were the greatest proportion of total filings in California beginning in FY 1985–86, in Illinois since at least 1996, in Minnesota since 2002, in Ohio since at least 1999, and Texas since 2007. In Ohio, the share of municipal and county court cases (those with a value below $15,000) rose from almost 60 percent of the caseload in 1999 to almost 70 percent in 2019. Lower-value/minor cases were over 50 percent in California and Illinois by 2002, and in Texas beginning in 2008. This pattern of the greatest proportion of cases being in lower courts was also found by the National Center for State Courts (NCSC) in its study of the civil dispositions in FY 2012–13 in ten large urban counties in state trial courts.[1] The lower-value case share was trending upward during the period for which data was made available in all states except Illinois, where the trend was the opposite.

FIGURE 4.1 LOWER-VALUE CIVIL FILINGS AS PERCENT OF ALL CIVIL FILINGS

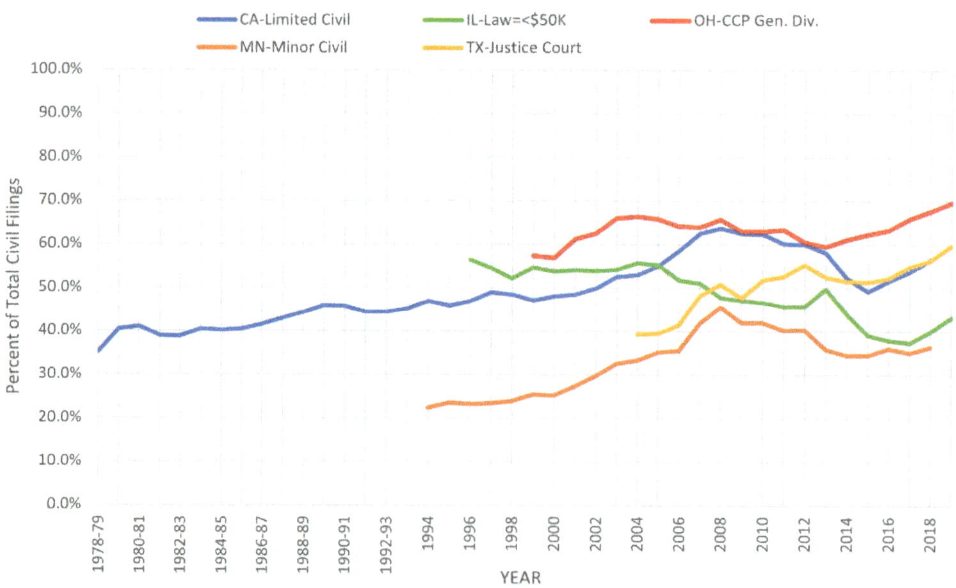

Four of the five states show a clearly perceptible rise and fall for the percentage of lower value civil cases, although the years of the rise and fall do not always coincide.

1. Nat'l Ctr. for State Courts, The Landscape of Civil Litigation in State Courts 35 (2016).

California's was from 2000 to 2015, with the peak in 2008. Ohio's was from 2000 to 2013, with an earlier peak between 2003 and 2005. Minnesota's was from 2000 to 2014, with the peak in 2008. The rise and fall in Texas was from 2006 to 2015, with two peaks, one in 2008 and one in 2012. Illinois was trending down, but there were high levels in 2004–05 and a peak in 2013. This roller coaster pattern was associated with the Great Recession, although the pattern varied somewhat over time across the states.

Generally, the second most common case category in the five states was Small Claims cases, which are generally trending down in four of the five states, discussed in more detail in Chapter 5.

The higher-value/major civil cases generally constituted less than 30 percent of the caseload in Illinois, Minnesota, and Ohio over the long term (Figure 4.2). In California, the share was under 20 percent from FY 1978–79 to FY 2009–10, then rose to almost 28 percent in FY 2015–16. The pattern was different in Texas. The district and county court share of the caseload (which represents the higher-value cases) started much higher, at 50 percent in 2004, then dropped steadily to 33 percent in 2019.

FIGURE 4.2 HIGHER-VALUE CIVIL FILINGS AS PERCENT OF ALL CIVIL FILINGS

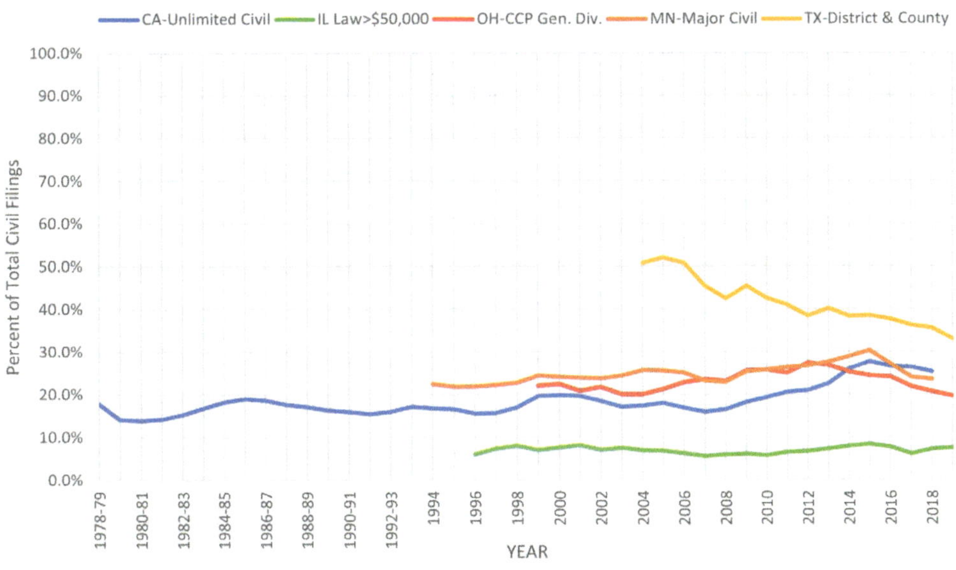

The proportion of higher-value civil cases in the total civil caseload was weakly related to the jurisdictional floor of the courts hearing higher-value cases in four states.[2] Table 4.1 displays the jurisdictional floor and share of total higher-value civil case filings for these four states in 2004 and 2019. As would be expected, a lower jurisdictional floor was associated with a greater proportion of total civil filings in 2004. On the other hand, Ohio's monetary floor was only 60 percent of California's ($15,000 compared to $25,000), but the percentage share of all civil cases was marginally lower, not higher, as

2. Minnesota was not included in the following discussion, as the Minor Civil cases in Minnesota are defined by case category, not dollar jurisdiction, as in the other four states.

might be expected. By 2019, Texas had doubled its floor, but the percentage had only dropped by 16 percent.

TABLE 4.1 RELATIONSHIP OF JURISDICTIONAL FLOOR OF HIGHER-VALUE CASES TO SHARE OF TOTAL CIVIL CASELOAD

	TEXAS District and County Courts	OHIO Court of Common Pleas	CALIFORNIA Superior Court, Unlimited Civil	ILLINOIS Law cases >$50,000
Jurisdictional floor in 2004	$5,000 (prior to 2004)	$15,000 (as of July 1997)	$25,000 (as of Jan. 1986)	$50,000 (as of Jan. 1996)
2004 share of total civil caseload	51%	20%	17% (in FY 2004–05)	7%
Jurisdictional floor in 2019	$10,000 (as of Sept. 2007)	$15,000 (as of July 1997)	$25,000 (as of Jan. 1986)	$50,000 (as of Jan. 1996)
2019 share of total civil caseload	43%	20%	25%	8%

Three states had one additional single subject trial court hearing cases involving the state. Illinois and Ohio each had a statewide court that exclusively handled actions against the state, both called the Court of Claims. Court of Claims cases were 0.9 percent of the total civil caseload in Illinois, and 0.2 percent in Ohio. No data was available to compare the proportion of civil cases filed against the state in the trial courts in California, Minnesota, and Texas. Minnesota had a statewide court that heard all noncriminal tax cases, but data on the statewide number of tax cases was not available. In Texas, tax cases from all levels of government, not just state level, constituted about 8 percent of all civil cases over a 16-year period. Tax cases in Illinois were a little more than 3 percent of all civil cases for the 25-year period. No data was available on the number of tax cases in California or Ohio.

4.1.2 California

The distribution of the broad categories of civil cases in California changed significantly over the 41-year period for which we have data. Figure 4.3 shows the percentage of the total civil caseload for each of the three broad civil case subcategories: Unlimited Civil, Limited Civil, and Small Claims.[3] At the beginning of the period, Small Claims cases were the dominant filings. In FY 1985–86 the percentage of Limited Civil filings exceeded that of Small Claims cases, and became the dominant case category for the rest of the period. The Unlimited Civil portion of cases fluctuated below 20 percent until FY 2011–12 when it began to rise, peaking in FY 2015–16 at almost 28 percent due in large part to the decline in Limited Civil filings after 2008–09.

3. Appeals from Small Claims and Limited Civil cases were not displayed, as each represented less than 1.5 percent of the total caseload in any given year.

FIGURE 4.3 CALIFORNIA MIX OF TOTAL CIVIL FILINGS BY BROAD CASE CATEGORY

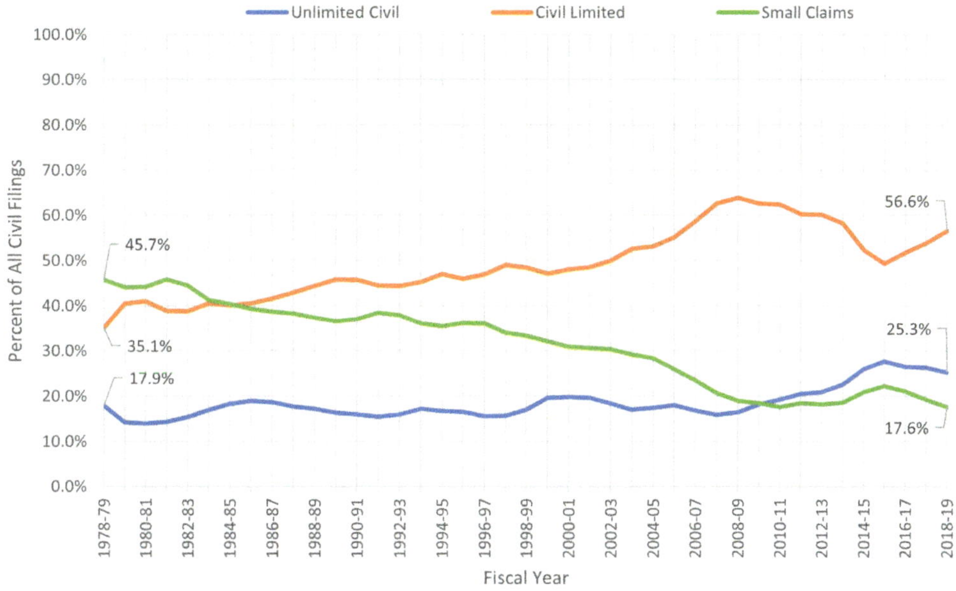

Small Claims filings were the largest category of filings in FY 1978–79 at almost 46 percent of all cases. After a peak in FY 1981–82, Small Claims filings fell steadily, and in FY 2018–19, they were the least common case category, at 18 percent of the total caseload. This decrease occurred despite four increases in the jurisdictional cap for small claims cases over this 41-year period. Over this period, the upper limit was increased from $750 to $10,000, yet the total number of small claims filings dropped almost 70 percent. This is discussed further in Chapter 5.

Limited Civil filings eventually became the most common category of filing during the 41-year period, rising from 35 percent of all civil filings to almost 57 percent. The portion of Limited Civil filings exceeded the portion of Small Claims filings in FY 1985–86. The portion exceeded 50 percent beginning in FY 2002–03. They surged during and after the Great Recession, exceeding 60 percent of the total caseload for several years. An observation in a state court system report regarding the growth of the lower value civil cases, which combined Limited Civil and Small Claims cases, overlooked the significant drop in small claims cases.[4] The Limited Civil share dipped in FY 2016–17, but was almost 57 percent in FY 2018–19.

Unlimited Civil cases (the high-value cases) were the lowest share of civil cases for most of the period. The share rose from the smallest share, about 18 percent in FY 1978–79, to 25 percent in FY 2018–19. Unlimited civil cases were less than 20 percent of the total caseload until FY 2011–12. The Unlimited civil share of filings exceeded the share of small claims filings beginning in FY 2010–11. The share rose to a peak at almost 28 percent in FY 2015–16 when Limited Civil filings declined post 2008–09 and then dropped through FY 2018–19 to 25 percent.

---

4. *See* REPORT TO THE CHIEF JUSTICE OF THE COMMISSION ON THE FUTURE OF CALIFORNIA'S COURT SYSTEM 17 (2017).

4.1.3 Illinois

In Illinois law, cases involving $50,000 or less were the dominant case category for almost all of the 25-year period for which we have data. Small Claims were the next largest share, followed by Chancery cases and law cases involving more than $50,000. Figure 4.4 shows the proportion of each of the major case categories[5] among the total civil filings.

FIGURE 4.4 ILLINOIS—COMPOSITION OF TOTAL CIVIL FILINGS

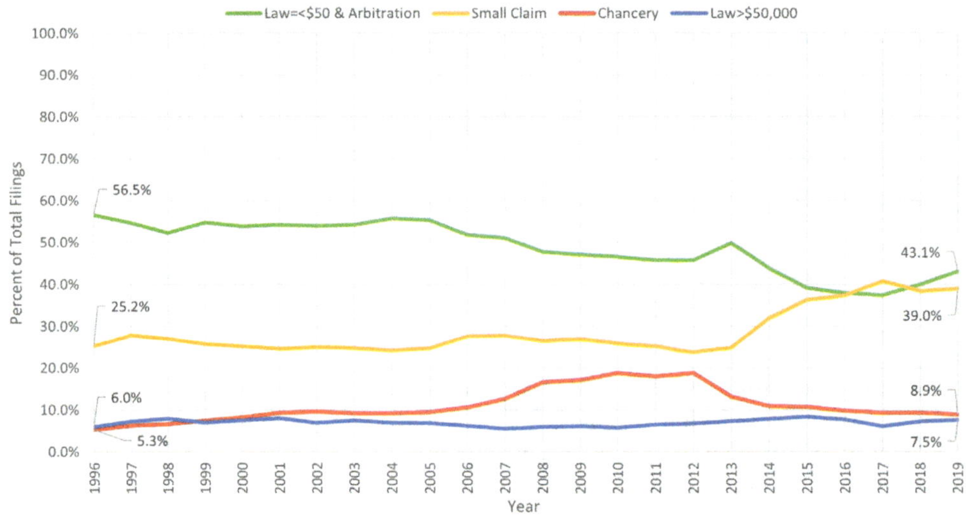

For almost the entire period, the combined group of lower-value Law and Arbitration cases seeking $50,000 or less comprised the largest portion of the caseload. Arbitration cases were combined because the mandatory arbitration program only existed in 16 counties, and the eligible cases were law cases with a value less than $50,000.[6] From 1996 to 2007, this group represented 51–56 percent of all civil cases. Beginning in 2008, the proportion began dropping, initially slowly, then more quickly beginning in 2014. In 2017, these low-value cases were only 37 percent of the caseload, but rose to about 43 percent in 2019. The share of this group was only exceeded for one year, in 2017, by Small Claims cases.

The second largest share of total cases were Small Claims cases. In 1996, these cases were 25 percent of the total caseload. They constituted that same proportion until 2013, notwithstanding a doubling of the jurisdictional limit of Small Claims cases as of January 1, 2006, discussed further in Chapter 5. In 2014, Small Claims rose significantly, reaching 41 percent in 2017, and ending the period at 39 percent in 2019. Small Claims filings grew almost 23 percent from 1996 to 2019. The growth beginning in 2014 was almost entirely due to growth in Cook County Small Claims filings.

---

5. Tax, Miscellaneous Remedy, and Court of Claim cases were not presented in the chart because of their relatively low share of filing. Tax cases were 5 percent or less for the period, and Court of Claim and Miscellaneous Remedy cases less than 1 percent.

6. In Cook County, arbitration cases, by Rule, involved less than $30,000.

The Chancery case category included real estate mortgage foreclosure, foreclosure of security interest in personal property, and mechanic's lien cases, as well as a few other subcategories. Chancery cases showed a roller coaster pattern beginning in 2006, peaking between 2010 and 2012, and dropping back in 2014 to pre-2006 levels, suggesting an association with the Great Recession. Chancery cases began the period at 9 percent of the caseload, peaked at 19 percent in 2010 and 2012, and ended at 9 percent in 2019.

The high-value civil cases seeking more than $50,000 share of total case filings was more stable than the categories just discussed. Their share fluctuated between 6 and 8 percent of the total civil caseload over the 25-year period. Oddly, there was no roller coaster associated with the Great Recession as in other case categories; the number of higher-value cases was quite stable over this period.

4.1.4 Minnesota

The pattern of the change in case mix in Minnesota was similar to the pattern in California, although the case categorization was different. Minnesota had three broad categories of civil cases—Major, Minor, and Conciliation (small claims). The categories reflected, to some extent, the prior two-tier trial court structure where higher-value cases were heard in the district court and lower-value cases were heard in county courts. After unification of the district and county courts, the distinction between Major Civil and Minor Civil cases was based on case category rather than the amount of alleged damages as in the other four states.

FIGURE 4.5 MINNESOTA—COMPARABLE CIVIL FILINGS CASE MIX

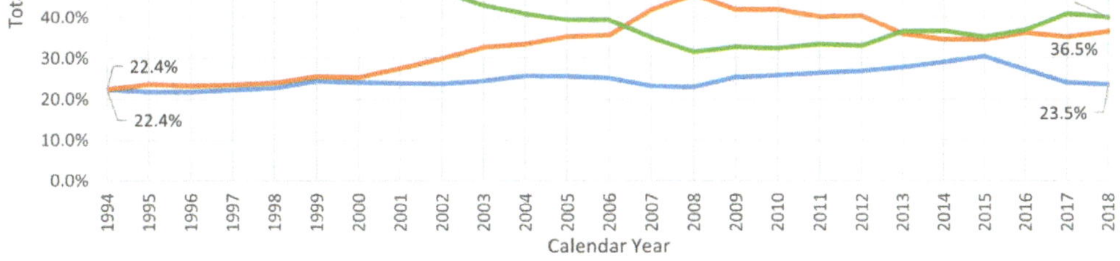

Figure 4.5 displays the three broad case categories comparable to the other states as a percentage of total civil filings. The change in proportions was significant. Conciliation cases started as the largest proportion, but dropped considerably. After 2006, Minor Civil filings became the most common category for several years. Major civil cases were the smallest share for the entire period.

The Minor Civil filings share of total caseload was 22.4 percent in 1994. The share exceeded Conciliation Court (small claims) filings beginning in 2007. Thereafter, the

Minor Civil share was the most common category through 2013. Minor Civil and Conciliation shares were about equal until 2107 when Conciliation cases rose to a higher share. The Minor Civil share peaked in 2008 at almost 46 percent, ending the study period at 36.5 percent in 2018. Only the Minor Civil case share exhibited a roller coaster pattern associated with the Great Recession.

In 1994, Conciliation Court filings were the greatest share of the total civil caseload, at about 55 percent. The share dropped steadily from 1994 to 2008, then leveled off through 2012. It rose slightly in 2013 when the jurisdictional cap was raised. The cap was raised again in 2015 and the share increased in 2016. This is discussed further in Chapter 5. The Conciliation share was 40 percent of the total caseload at the end of the study period in 2018.

Major Civil filings began at 22.4 percent of the total caseload in 1994. The share fluctuated between 22 percent and 27 percent from 1997 to 2012. The share rose, peaking at just over 30 percent in 2015. The share then dropped to less than 24 percent in 2018, due in large part to the increase in the share of both Minor Civil and Conciliation filings.

4.1.5 Ohio

Overall, the Ohio filings distribution showed less shifting of the mix of civil caseload among trial courts over the 21-year study period than was seen in the other states. Figure 4.6 displays the percentage of the total civil caseload for the two levels of trial courts, with small claims cases separated from other municipal and county court civil cases.[7] The proportion of municipal and county court civil cases other than small claim

FIGURE 4.6 OHIO—COURTS SHARE OF TOTAL CIVIL FILINGS

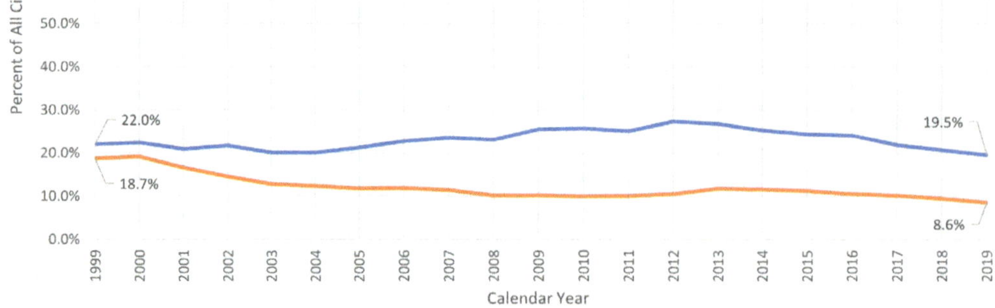

7. Court of common pleas probate division and court of claims cases were not included in the figure, as they represented a small portion of the total caseload. Probate cases represented 1.3 percent over the 21 years, and Court of Claims cases were less than 0.3 percent.

cases was the most common case category, and a larger share than in the other states over the entire period. Unlike in the other states, the share of small claims cases was less than the court of common pleas cases over the entire period, although the share of small claims cases dropped continuously during the period.

The proportion of lower-value municipal and county court civil cases, other than Small Claims cases, rose from almost 58 percent in 1999 to almost 70 percent in 2019. The proportion ranged between 60 percent and 67 percent from 2001 to 2018. In contrast to other states, the Great Recession roller coaster of these cases started in 2001 and extended to 2013, and was less pronounced. The share of these cases started a rise in 2014 that continued to 2019.

The proportion of Small Claims cases fell from a high of almost 19 percent of cases in 2000 to less than 9 percent in 2019. It was not a steady drop. The share dropped through 2008, leveled off until 2012, rose for three years, then drifted down to 2019. The upper monetary jurisdiction of Small Claims cases was doubled in 2016, but the proportion of Small Claims cases did not noticeably change. This is discussed further in Chapter 5.

The proportion of higher-value civil cases heard by the general division of the court of common pleas fluctuated over a small range for the 21 years of our Ohio data. Their proportion began at 22 percent in 1999 and ended at 19.5 percent, its lowest level, in 2019. During the 21-year period, the share fluctuated from 20 percent in 2003 and 2004 to about 27 percent in 2012 and 2013. The Great Recession roller coaster pattern began in 2006 and dropped to pre-2006 levels in 2017. This pattern was later than for lesser-value cases in municipal and county courts noted earlier.

4.1.6 Texas

The pattern in Texas was not as easily compared to the patterns in the other states because of the number of trial courts and their varied and overlapping jurisdiction. The filings in the district and county courts were combined, as they generally heard the higher-value civil cases. Figure 4.7 displays the share of the total caseload for three categories: district and county courts (generally higher-value civil cases), justice courts (generally lower-value civil cases), and Small Claims. In Texas, the district and county court civil cases were the highest share in 2004. However, the justice court cases became a larger share of the caseload beginning in 2007. Their proportion continued to increase over 16 years, and the proportion of higher-value cases fell concomitantly. The share of Small Claims cases was the smallest proportion, at less than 10 percent for the entire 16 years.

Justice court filings, not including small claims cases, rose from almost 40 percent of the total civil caseload in 2004 to 60 percent in 2019. They surpassed the combined district and county court share in 2007. There was a double roller coaster pattern in justice court cases from 2006 to 2013, although the proportion was trending upward for the entire period. The share was more than 50 percent every year from 2008 to 2019, except in 2009.

Combined district and county court shares declined from almost 51 percent to 33 percent over the 16 years. The peak share was in 2005. The share then dropped every year except for blips in 2009 and 2013.

FIGURE 4.7 TEXAS—COURTS SHARE OF TOTAL CIVIL FILINGS

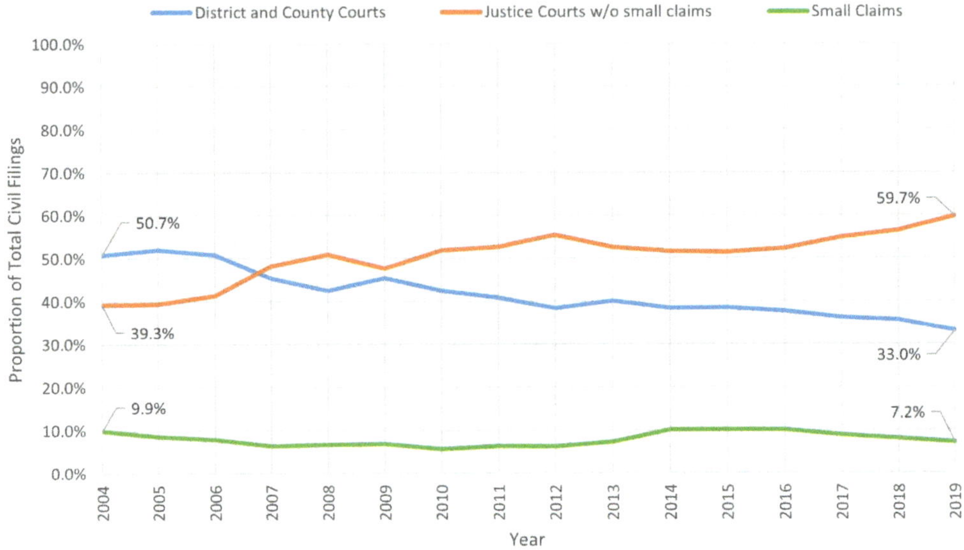

Overall, Small Claims cases dropped from 10 percent in 2004 to 7 percent in 2019, notwithstanding an expansion of their subject matter jurisdiction in late 2013, discussed in Chapter 5. The share had been dropping from 2004 to 2012. After an expansion of the small claims jurisdiction in 2013 there was a step up, peaking at about 10 percent from 2014 to 2016, then the share began declining again.

4.1.7 Summary Observation

The general trend we observed in these five states was that lower-value civil cases generally constituted the largest proportion and an increasing percentage of civil filings, mostly at the expense of ever-falling percentage of small claims filings. The proportion of higher-value civil cases remained relatively stable, except in Texas, where it fell steadily over the period of the study.

4.2 Injury/Damage Suits

4.2.1 Overview

Despite the long-standing attention focused on tort reform by the bar, legislatures, courts, businesses, and by the media, Injury/damage cases were not a significant share of total civil filings in the states studied here. Four of the five states (all but Illinois) provided case filing data that allowed analysis of filing patterns of Injury/damage cases in all trial courts over time. Looking at the changes in Injury/damage filings over time in these four states also provides an interesting perspective on the apparent effect of some tort reform efforts.[8]

---

8. Our study did not gather the data that would be required to address the different question of the impact of these cases on judicial resources.

In order to minimize use of English Common Law or Latin terms, the term "Injury/damage" is used here instead of the term "torts."

In the four states the Injury/damage share of all civil cases dropped over time. In Ohio the Injury/damage share of all civil filings in all trial courts dropped from less than 10 percent in 1999 to a little more than 4 percent in 2019. In Texas the Injury/damage share of all civil filings dropped slightly, from 8 percent in 1994 to a little less than 7 percent in 2019. Injury/damage share of total civil filings in Minnesota was the lowest of the three states. The Injury/damage share of civil cases dropped from less than 5 percent in 1994 to less than 3 percent in 2018. California only separately reported filings for higher-value Injury/damage cases. Lower-value Injury/damage cases were counted in the Limited Civil case category along with a variety of other case categories. In California, the higher-value Injury/damage share of all civil filings dropped from less than 9 percent to less than 8 percent over 41 years. In its comparison of civil dispositions in fiscal year 2012–13 in ten urban counties, the NCSC found that Injury/damage cases were 7 percent of all civil cases.[9]

In sum, in these four states, Injury/damage cases were not a significant proportion of total civil case filings. The shrinking role of these cases is even more apparent from the standpoint of per capita filings.

In three of the four states, the per capita filing levels of Injury/damage cases dropped significantly over time. Figure 4.8 displays the per capita Injury/damage filing levels in the four states beginning in 1994, the earliest year for which comparable data for more than one of the states was available. Per capita filings dropped in three of the four states during the 25-year period shown. The greatest drop was in Ohio where per capita Injury/damage filings in all trial courts dropped almost 53 percent over 20 years. In Minnesota, per capita Injury/damage filings dropped more than 58 percent over 25 years. In

FIGURE 4.8 INJURY/DAMAGE FILINGS PER 100K POPULATION IN FOUR STATES

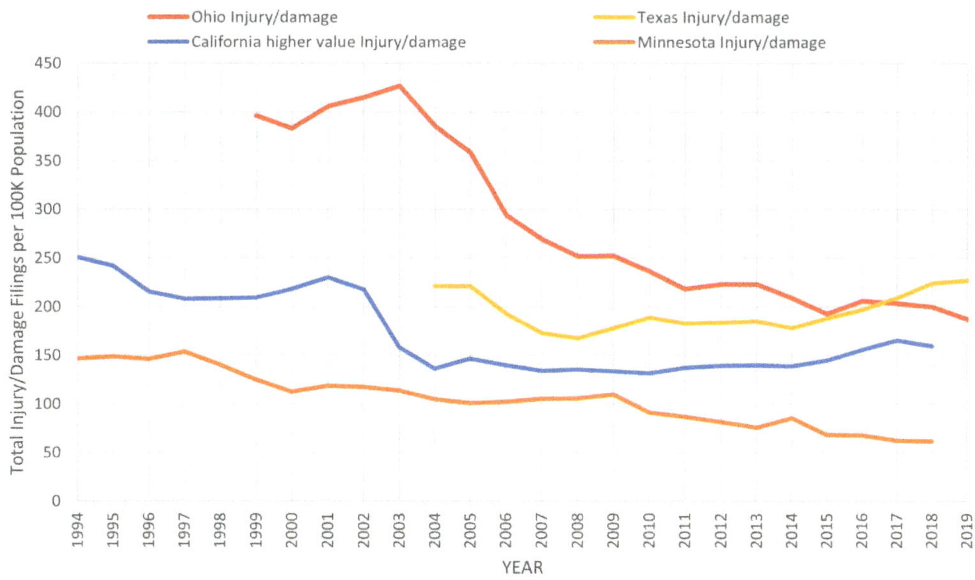

9. Nat'l Ctr. for State Courts, Civil Justice Initiative, The Landscape of Civil Litigation in State Courts 17 (2016).

California, per capita Injury/damage filings for higher-value Injury/damage cases dropped 38 percent over the 25 years depicted in the chart. Over the 41-year period for which we have data from California, its per capita filings in this category dropped by 61 percent. In contrast, Texas experienced an increase over the last 15 years of almost 3 percent, with a dip just before the Great Recession.

Another striking feature is the wide range of per capita Injury/damage filing levels across the four states and over time. In 2000, the per capita filing levels ranged from 113 in Minnesota to 383 in Ohio, a 3.4 to 1 spread. The spread appeared to narrow beginning in 2005 as Ohio's filing levels dropped significantly. In 2010, the range was from 236 in Ohio to 91 in Minnesota, a spread of only 2.6 to 1. However, toward the end of the period, Texas filing levels were increasing and Minnesota's were continuing to drop. As a result, in 2018, the range was from 225 in Texas to 62 in Minnesota, a spread of 3.6 to 1. Per capita Injury/damage filings varied widely across states and over time.

One possible explanation of Minnesota's lower per capita filing levels could be what was known as "hip pocket" filing. In Minnesota, a case could be served on defendants without first filing in court, as required in the other three states. To the extent cases settle without a court filing, Minnesota's filing levels would be expected to be lower. In 2013, Minnesota imposed a one-year limit on hip pocket filing, discussed further in Chapter 7. This caused a one-time blip in filing levels in 2014 (see orange line in Figure 4.8), but not an ongoing impact. Whether the gap between Minnesota's filing levels and the higher filing levels in other states could be attributed to hip pocket filing depends on the number of cases that settled within one year of service (in Minnesota) or of filing (in the other three states). We do not have access to that data.

The filing data from two states indicates that Injury/damage cases involving an auto were the major proportion of Injury/damage cases. California and Texas both collected data for auto Injury/damage cases separately from other Injury/damage cases. In California, the higher value auto Injury/damage cases constituted about two-thirds of all higher value Injury/damage cases from FY 1978–79 to FY 2002–03. Thereafter, the percentage dropped below 60 percent from FY 2003–04 until FY 2014–15. However, by FY 2018–19, the percentage had risen back to more than 65 percent. In Texas, the share of Injury/damage cases involving an auto in all trial courts rose from 62 percent of all Injury/damage cases in 2004 to almost 80 percent in 2019. The ratio in Texas wobbled between 60 percent and 65 percent from 2004 until 2009. A similar figure for auto cases, 60 percent, was reported by the National Center for data from 20 states from 2016.[10]

4.2.2 California

Over the last 41 years, the number of higher-value[11] Injury/damage cases in California dropped, in absolute numbers, on a per capita basis, and as a share of all higher-value

10. Nat'l Ctr. for State Courts, State Court Caseload Digest 2016 Data 6 (2018).

11. In California the only separate count of Injury/damage cases were Unlimited Civil cases involving personal injury, wrongful death, or property damage where the damage claim was more than $25,000. If the damage claim was less than $25,000, Injury/damage case filings were counted together with other case categories in the very broad category of Limited Civil cases.

civil cases. There were two periods when Injury/damage filings surged, but both times Injury/damage filings subsequently dropped to levels before the surge. The surge in the 1980s was generally attributed to two California Supreme Court decisions discussed later. The sudden drop in FY 2003–04 coincided with a legislative change[12] in the statute of limitations in personal injury and wrongful death cases from one year to two, effective January 1, 2003, discussed further in Chapter 7.

The pattern of total filings and per capita filing levels of the higher value Unlimited Civil Injury/damage cases over the last 41 years are displayed in Figures 4.9 and 4.10. Unlimited Civil Injury/damage total filings began at 92,948 cases in FY 1978–79, peaked at 137,458 in FY 1986–87, and ended at 63,138 cases in FY 2018–19. The drop in total Unlimited Civil Injury/damage filings over 40 years was more than 32 percent. Per capita Unlimited Civil Injury/damage filing levels began at 403 cases per 100,000 population in FY 1978–79, peaked at 514 in FY 1986–87, and ended at 159 cases in FY 2018–19. The drop in per capita Unlimited Civil Injury/damage filing levels over 40 years was more than 61 percent.

Injury/damage cases as a percentage of all Unlimited Civil cases also dropped over the last 41 years. In FY 1978–89 the percentage was 48 percent. The percentage peaked in FY 1989–90 at more than 55 percent. It then dropped steadily, ending at 30 percent in FY 2018–19.

FIGURE 4.9 CALIFORNIA TOTAL UNLIMITED CIVIL INJURY/DAMAGE FILINGS

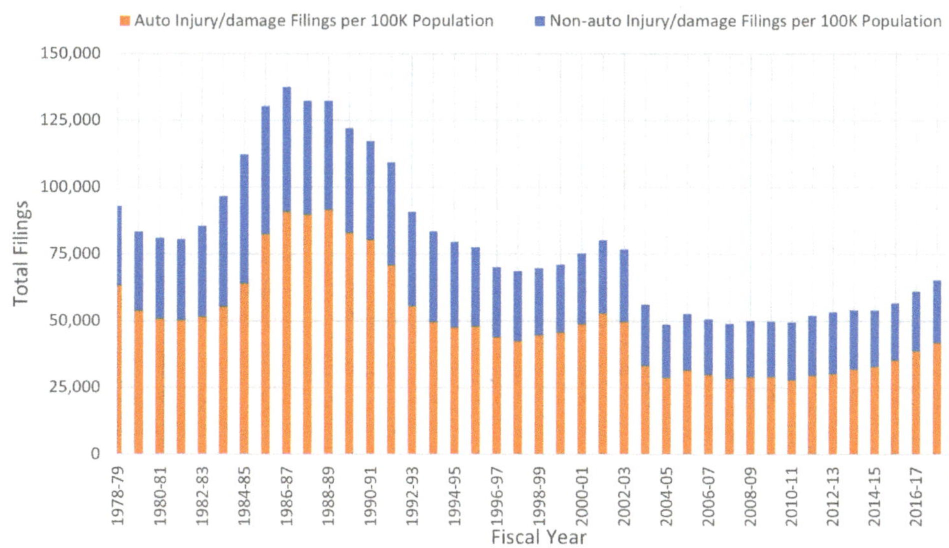

12. 2002 CAL. STAT. ch. 448, § 2, adding CAL. CODE OF CIV. PROC. § 335. 1.

FIGURE 4.10 CALIFORNIA UNLIMITED CIVIL INJURY/DAMAGE FILINGS PER 100K POPULATION

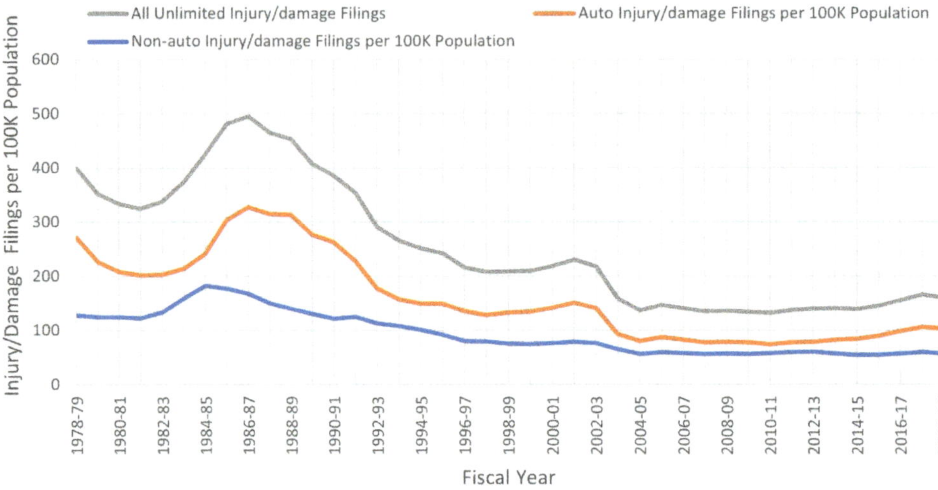

The bump in filing levels in the 1980s was attributed to two California Supreme Court decisions. This was extensively described in the 20-Year Retrospective Report.[13] In 1979, the California Supreme Court ruled that the insurance statute prohibiting insurance companies from engaging in unfair practices, such as not making good-faith effort to reach prompt and fair settlement of a claim, created an additional cause of action for the insured or a third-party claimant in an Injury/damage case.[14] The decision was reversed by the California Supreme Court in 1988.[15]

When the first decision came down, the new risk of a bad faith claim changed the behavior of insurance companies and policy holders. Citing a study by the Rand Institute of Justice,[16] the 20-Year Retrospective Report stated:

> The increased payouts made smaller claims feasible, not only for plaintiffs, but more important, for attorneys. The greater payouts meant that the attorneys' one-third contingency fee became large enough to warrant taking on such cases.[17]

This could explain the increase in filings in the years after the decision. The reversal of the case in 1988 caused the economics in these cases, for insurance companies, lawyers, and litigants, to revert to their previous state—resulting in the decline in filings of this case type beginning in FY 1989–90.

---

13. Alexander Aikman & Karen Viscia, *Exploring the Work of the California Trial Courts: A 20-Year Retrospective*, 2003, CAL., ADMIN. OFF. OF THE COURTS, at vii, 44–46 (2003), https://www.courts.ca.gov/7808.htm [hereinafter *20-Year Retrospective* report].

14. Royal Globe Ins. Co. v. Super. Ct. of Butte Cnty. (1979), 23 Cal. 3d 880, 592 P.2d 329, 153 Cal. Rptr. 842.

15. Shalal v. Fireman's Fund Ins. Cos. (1988) 46 Cal. 3d 287.

16. Angela Hawken, Stephen J. Carroll & Allan Abrahamse, *The Effects of Third-Party, Bad Faith Doctrine on Automobile Insurance Costs and Compensation*, RAND INST. OF CIVIL JUST., MR-1199-ICJ (Jan. 1, 2001), https://www.rand.org/pubs/monograph_reports/MR1199.html.

17. *20-Year Retrospective* report, *supra* note 13, at 45.

Unlimited Civil Auto Injury/damage[18] filings declined even more dramatically than Non-auto Injury/damage cases (Figure 4.11). Over the 41-year period, Auto Injury/damage filings declined by more than 35 percent in total numbers (blue columns and left-side axis in Figure 4.11) and more than 62 percent in per capita filings (orange line and right-side axis in Figure 4.11). There were two distinct humps during this time period. The first was a sharp rise beginning in FY 1983–84, peaking from FY 1986–87 to FY 1988–89—reflecting the insurance bad faith decision and its reversal. The second began slowly in FY 1998–99 and continued until a peak in FY 2002–03. There was a sharp drop in FY 2003–04, followed by a slow rise until FY 2017–18. Notably, there was no hump associated with the Great Recession.

FIGURE 4.11 CALIFORNIA UNLIMITED CIVIL AUTO INJURY/DAMAGE FILINGS

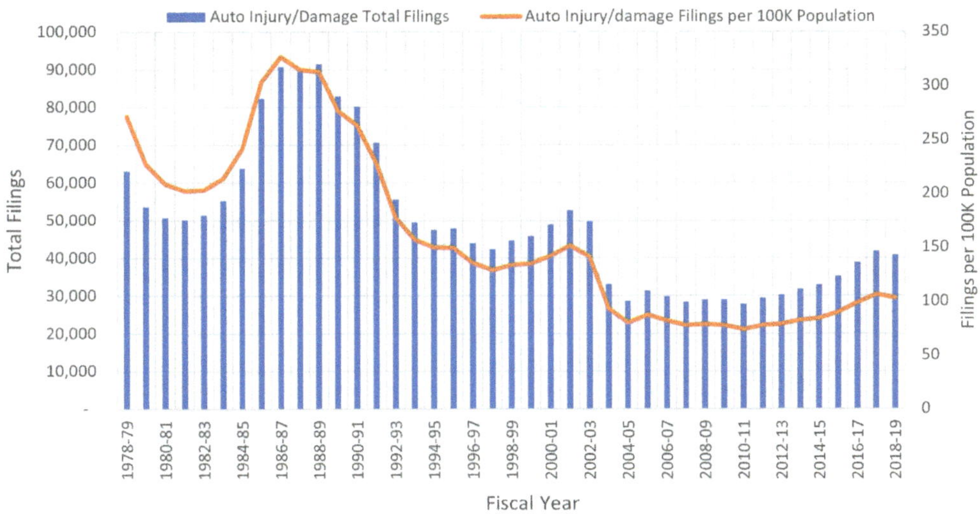

Total Unlimited Civil Auto Injury/damage filings began at 63,105 cases in FY 1978–79, peaked at 91,450 in FY 1988–89, and ended at 40,748 cases in FY 2018–19. The largest year-to-year increase was 22 percent, from FY 1982–83 to FY 1983–84. The largest year-to-year drop was 33 percent from FY 2002–03 to FY 2003–04. Year-to-year total filings dropped in 19 years and increased in 21 years.

Per capita Unlimited Civil Auto Injury/damage filings showed a similar pattern (orange line and right-side axis in Figure 4.11). Per capita filings began at 271 per 100,000 population in FY 1978–79, peaked at 327 in FY 1986–87, dropped to a low of 74 in FY 2010–11, and slowly rose to 103 at the end of the study period. The drop in per capita filings over 40 years was more than 62 percent. The largest year-to-year drop was 34 percent, from FY 2002–03 to FY 2003–04. The largest year-to-year increase was 26 percent ,from FY 1984–85 to FY 1985–86. Year-to-year per capita filing levels dropped in 23 years and increased in 17 years.

18. Unlimited civil—Auto PI/PD/WD cases were personal injury, wrongful death, or property damage cases involving a vehicle with damage claim over $25,000.

Unlimited Civil Non-auto Injury/damage cases were those that did not involve a vehicle. Examples of these types of cases include professional malpractice, product liability, asbestos, premises liability, slip and fall, and so on. From the beginning to the end of the 41-year period, Unlimited Civil Non-auto Injury/damage filings declined by 25 percent in total filings (blue columns, left-side axis in Figure 4.12). Total filings rose from FY 1978–79 to a peak in FY 1984–85, then began a slow steady decline. Since FY 1995–96 the filing levels were below the initial FY 1978–79 level. There were slight increases in total filings from FY 2000–01 to FY 2002–03, from FY 2010–11 to FY 2012–13, and from FY 2015–16 to FY 2018–19. The largest year-to-year drop was 14 percent, from FY 2002–03 to FY 2003–04. The largest year-to-year increase was 22 percent, from FY 1982–83 to FY 1983–84. Year-to-year total filings dropped in 22 years and increased in 18 years. Notably, again there was no hump associated with the Great Recession.

FIGURE 4.12 CALIFORNIA UNLIMITED CIVIL NON-AUTO INJURY/DAMAGE FILINGS

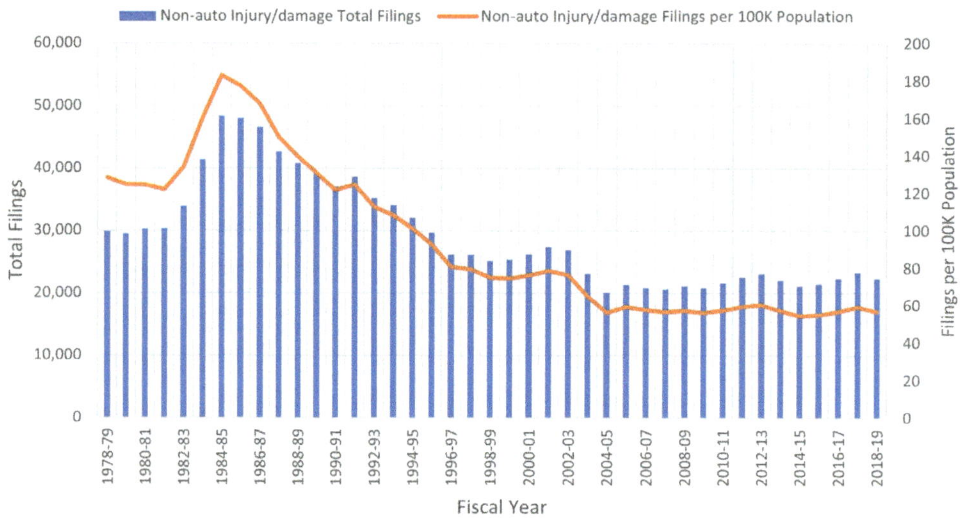

Per capita filings showed a similar pattern (orange line, right-side axis in Figure 4.12). Filing levels peaked in FY 1984–85. Thereafter, per capita filings dropped steadily. Since FY 1991–92 filing levels were below the FY 1978–79 level. Over the 41-year period, per capita filings dropped 55 percent. The largest year-to-year drop was 15 percent, from FY 2002–03 to FY 2003–04. The largest year-to-year increase was almost 20 percent, from FY 1982–83 to FY 1983–84. Year-to-year per capita filing levels dropped in 24 years and increased in 16 years.

4.2.3 Minnesota

The Injury/damage filings share of total civil filings in Minnesota was much lower than in the other three states. Minnesota experienced a steady drop of Injury/damage filings over the 25-year study period. The Injury/damage share of all civil cases dropped from 4.5 percent in 1994 to 2.7 percent in 2018. The drop in total filings over the period was almost 49 percent.

Total filings began in 1994 at 6,750, peaked in 1997, and ended in 2018 at 2,965 (blue columns, left-side axis in Figure 4.13). Year-to-year total filings dropped in 15 of 24 years. Per capita filings dropped 58 percent over 25 years. Per capita filings were 148 per 100,000 population in 1994, also peaked in 1997, and dropped to 62 in 2018 (orange line, right-side axis in Figure 4.13). Year-to-year filing levels declined in 16 of 24 years.

FIGURE 4.13 MINNESOTA INJURY/DAMAGE FILINGS

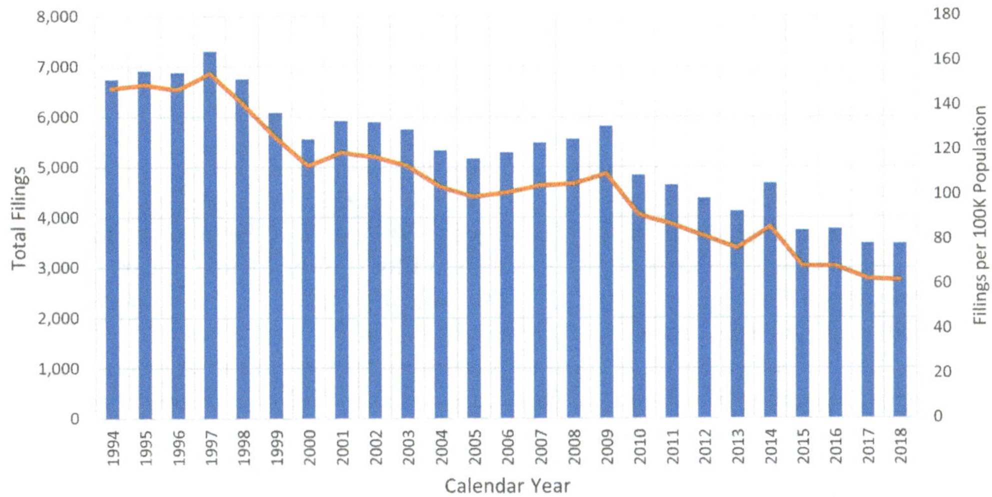

In Minnesota, cases were classified based on the type of injury—personal injury, property damage, or wrongful death. There was no separate category for Injury/damage cases involving a motor vehicle. The total number of filings for all Injury/damage cases and the total filing numbers for each of the subcategories are presented in Figure 4.14. The most frequent subcategory of Injury/damage filings were the Personal Injury filings. All of the other Injury/damage subcategories were relatively few in number.

FIGURE 4.14 MINNESOTA TOTAL INJURY/DAMAGE FILINGS BY SUBCATEGORY

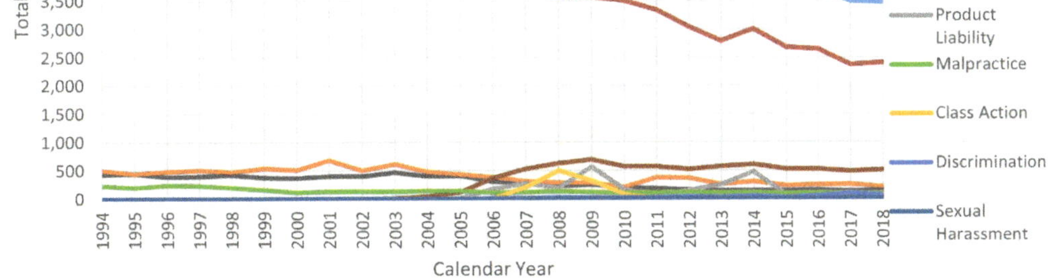

The subcategories in Minnesota are not always comparable to those in the other three states. Injury/damage cases arising in an employment relationship were counted as Employment cases, not Injury/damage cases. A few more subcategories began to be included in Injury/damage filings in 2003. Previously Minor Settlement, Product Liability, and Discrimination cases were classified as Civil Other/Miscellaneous cases. Sexual Harassment cases were classified as Harassment cases. Since the number of cases in these subcategory types were quite small compared with the Personal Injury filings, it did not markedly change the finding of a large drop in Injury/damage filings over this time period.

4.2.4 Ohio

Ohio also experienced an overall drop in Injury/damage filings over the 20-year study period. Total Injury/damage filings began in 1999 at 44,922, peaked in 2003, and ended in 2019 at 21,915 (blue columns, left-side axis in Figure 4.15). The drop in total filings over the period was 51 percent. Year-to-year total filings dropped in 13 years of the 19 years. Per capita filings were 396 per 100,000 population in 1999, also peaked in 2003, and ended at 187 in 2019 (orange line, right-side axis in Figure 4.15). Per capita filings dropped almost 53 percent over 20 years. Year-to-year per capita filing levels declined in 13 of the 19 years. The Injury/damage cases share of all civil cases in all courts dropped from 9.8 percent in 1999 to 4.2 percent in 2019.

Injury/damage cases were heard in four trial courts in Ohio. Higher-value Injury/damage cases were heard in the court of common pleas general division. Lesser-value Injury/damage cases were heard in the municipal and county courts. Injury/damage cases involving the state of Ohio were heard in the Court of Claims. Minor's settlements and some wrongful death cases were heard in the probate division of the court of common pleas. Ohio did not count motor vehicle Injury/damage cases separately from other Injury/damage cases.

FIGURE 4.15 OHIO INJURY/DAMAGE FILINGS—ALL COURTS

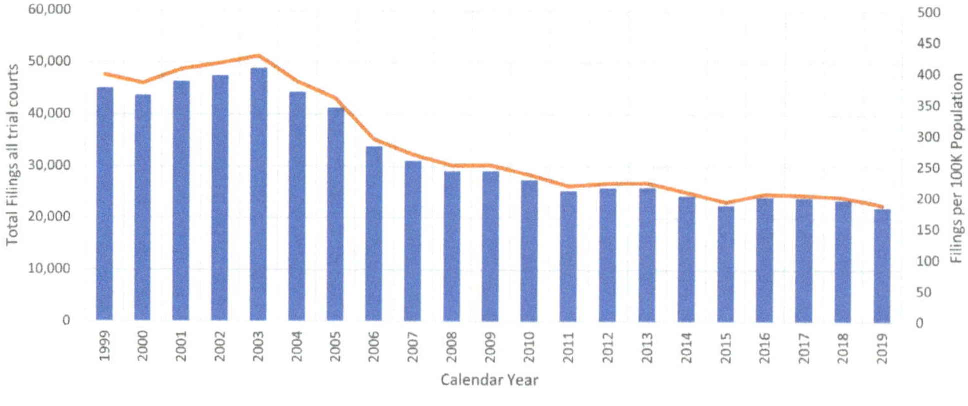

Figure 4.16 displays the level of per capita Injury/damage filings for Injury/damage cases in each of the courts. The bulk of the cases were in the court of common pleas general division and the municipal and county courts. Per capita Injury/damage filing levels were higher in the court of common pleas general division throughout the 21 years. Although filing levels fell in both the court of common pleas general division and the municipal and county courts, the pattern was not exactly the same. There was a slight peak in 2002 for court of common pleas general division Injury/damage filings and in 2003 in municipal and county Injury/damage filings.

FIGURE 4.16 OHIO INJURY/DAMAGE FILINGS PER 100K POPULATION—ALL COURTS

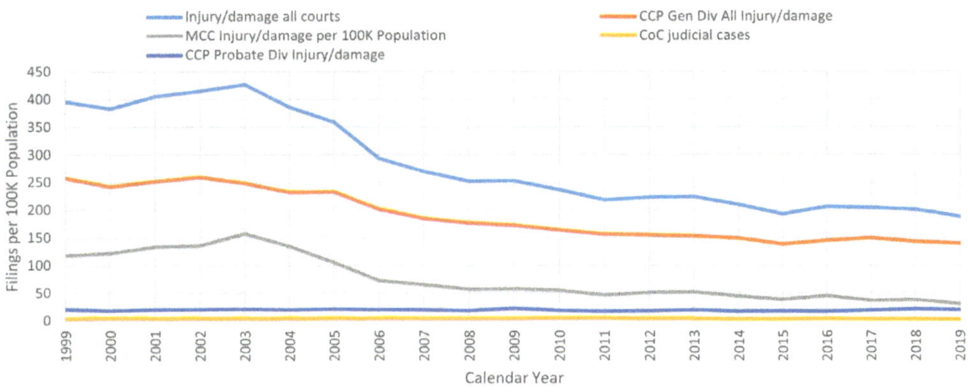

In the court of common pleas general division, the Injury/damage category of cases included three subcategories reported in the monthly statistical reports, defined as follows:[19]

> Professional Injury/damage. Cases that involved allegations of malpractice by a person acting in a professional capacity, such as a doctor, lawyer, or engineer.
>
> Product liability. Cases that involved the alleged responsibility of the manufacturer or seller of an article for injury caused to person or property by a defect in or condition of the article sold, or an alleged breach of duty to provide suitable instructions to prevent injury.
>
> Other Injury/damage cases. Injury/damage cases that could not be classified as Professional Injury/damage or Products Liability. An Injury/damage case was an injury or civil wrong committed either against a person or against a person's property by a party who either did something that he or she was obligated not to do or failed to do something that he or she was obligated to do.

Figure 4.17 displays the total filings levels for all Injury/damage cases and for each of these three subcategories of Injury/damage cases. Total Injury/damage filings experienced a small rise in 2001 and 2002, then began dropping until 2015. The drop was

19. Ohio Instructions for Preparation of Statistical Report Forms, Court of Common Pleas—General Division, Form A, at 2, revised Dec. 6, 2019.

much slower than the drop in municipal and county courts Injury/damage filings. There was a slight rise for two years beginning in 2016, followed by a dip in the last two years of the period. Total Injury/damage filings started the period at 29,128 and ended the period at 16,270, a drop of more than 44 percent. The largest year-to-year drop was 13 percent in 2006. The largest year-to-year rise was 5 percent in 2016.

FIGURE 4.17 OHIO COURT OF COMMON PLEAS GENERAL DIVISION, TOTAL INJURY/DAMAGE FILINGS

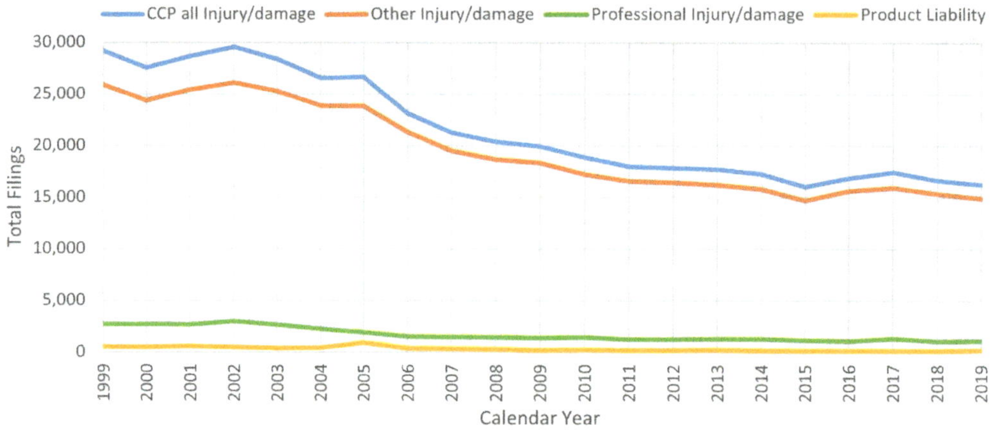

Looking at subcategories of Injury/damage cases in Figure 4.17, the Other Injury/damage subcategory represents the bulk of the Injury/damage cases and sets the filing pattern for all Injury/damage filings. Other Injury/damage filings dropped more than 42 percent over 21 years. Professional Injury/damage filings dropped almost 59 percent over 21 years, but represented only 8 percent of total Injury/damage cases. Product Liability Injury/damage filings dropped more than 61 percent for 21 years, but were only 1.5 percent of total Injury/damage filings.

Looking at per capita Injury/damage filings, the trend was very similar to the total filings curve (Figure 4.18). Per capita Injury/damage filings started at 258 per 100,000 population and ended the period at 139, a 46 percent drop. Beginning in 1999, filing levels dropped in 2000, then rose almost to the starting level in 2002. Filings levels then dropped steadily until 2015. From 2015 to 2019 all Injury/damage per capita filing levels went up and down slightly, ending at the same level as in 2015, well below the levels in 1999.

As noted, the overall filing pattern was again driven by Other Injury/damage. The per capita Other Injury/damage filing level dropped from 229 at the beginning of the period to 128 at the end, a 44 percent drop. After the peak in 2002, the filing level dropped every year, except in 2016 and 2017. Per capita Product Liability filing levels dropped from 5 to 2 over the 20-year period, with a peak at 8 in 2005. The Product Liability filing levels were almost unchanged from 2009 to 2019.

FIGURE 4.18 OHIO COURT OF COMMON PLEAS GENERAL DIVISION, INJURY/DAMAGE FILINGS PER 100K POPULATION

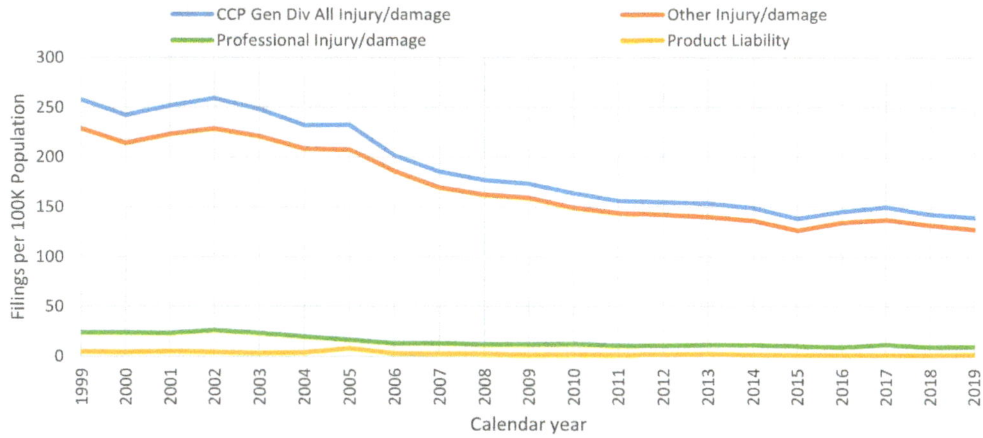

In the municipal and county courts, Injury/damage cases included cases involving personal injury, property damage, or both.[20] There was only one category for all Injury/damage cases in municipal and county courts, as opposed to the three categories in common pleas courts. Total Injury/damage filings in municipal and county courts modestly increased beginning in 1999, then experienced a sharp rise to a peak in 2003 (blue columns, left-side axis in Figure 4.19). Injury/damage filings then dropped sharply until 2006. Their drop was sharper than in common pleas courts Injury/damage cases. The drop then slowed, but continued to 2019. From 2005 forward, total filings were lower than at the start of the period in 1999. Total Injury/damage case filings were down more than 74 percent over the period. The largest one-year increase was 16 percent in 2003, and the largest one-year decrease was almost 31 percent in 2006. From 2006 to 2019, filings dropped in eight of the 13 years.

FIGURE 4.19 OHIO INJURY/DAMAGE FILINGS IN MUNICIPAL AND COUNTY COURTS

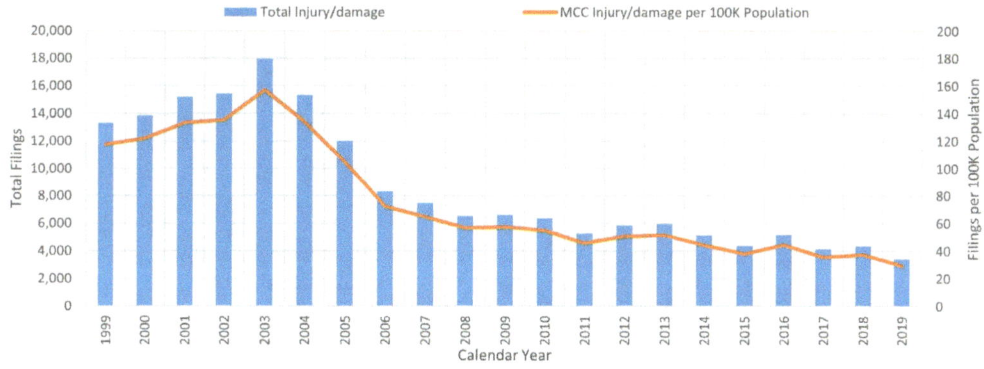

20. Ohio Instructions for Preparation of Statistical Report Forms, Municipal and County Courts—Individual Judge Report, at 3, revised Dec. 6, 2019.

Per capita Injury/damage case filing levels in municipal and county courts experienced a 75 percent decline over the 20-year period (orange line, right-side axis in Figure 4.19). However, the decrease was not steady. Filing levels rose from 1999 to a peak in 2003. Then filing levels dropped faster than they had risen until 2008. For the next 11 years there was a slow, bumpy decline. At the beginning of the period, per capita Injury/damage case filings were 117 per 100,000 population. Filing levels peaked at 157 in 2003, and ended the period at 29.

4.2.5 Texas

The pattern of Injury/damage filings was very different for Texas over the 15-year study period. In contrast to the overall decline, with short-term rises, in the other three states, Texas Injury/damage filings dipped slightly just before the Great Recession, then climbed through 2019.

Total Injury/damage filings in the district and county courts began in 2004 at 49,580, reached a low of 40,785 in 2008, and ended at 65,901 in 2019 (Figure 4.20). The rise in total filings over 15 years was almost 33 percent. Year-to-year total filings rose in ten of the 15 years. Per capita filings were 221 per 100,000 population in 2004, dropped to 168 in 2008, then rose to 227 in 2019. Per capita Injury/damage filings rose almost 3 percent over the 15 years. Year-to-year per capita filing levels rose in nine of the 15 years.

There were two broad subcategories of Injury/damage cases in Texas: Motor Vehicle and Non-motor Vehicle. Both district and county courts used the same definitions for these subcategories. Figure 4.20 displays the total filings for all Injury/damage cases in both courts, and for the subcategories of Motor Vehicle and Non-motor Vehicle cases for the 15-year period.

FIGURE 4.20 TEXAS TOTAL INJURY/DAMAGE FILINGS IN DISTRICT AND COUNTY COURTS

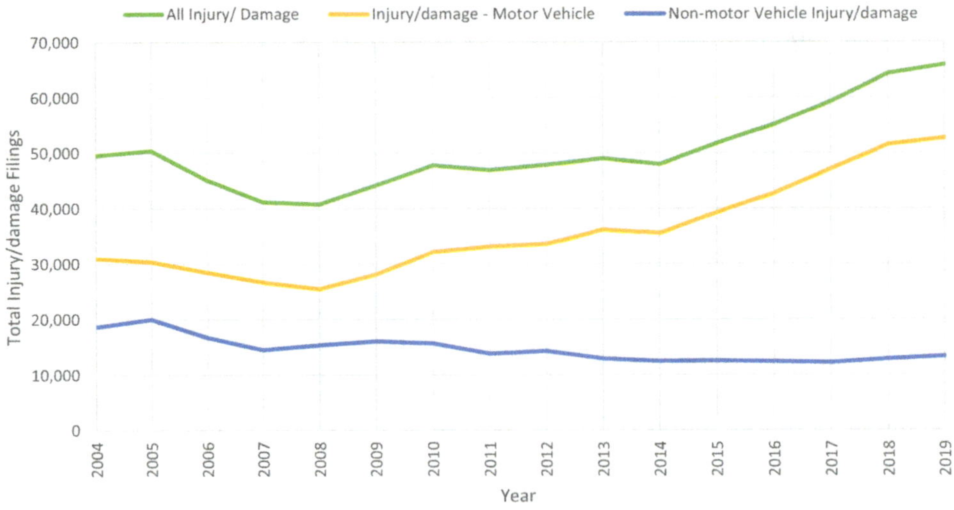

Non-motor vehicle Injury/damage cases in Texas declined over the last 15 years, similar to the decline experienced in the other states. Total Non-motor Vehicle filings fell almost 29 percent. They began at 18,644 in 2004, peaked at 20,022 in 2005, and ended at 13,292 in 2019. Per capita Non-motor Vehicle filings followed a similar pattern. They began at 83 per 100,000 population in 2004, peaked at 88 in 2004, and ended at 46 in 2019, a drop of 45 percent. Per capita filing levels decreased in nine of the 15 years.

A look farther back in time was available from the annual statistical report for 2016 complied by the Texas Administrative Office of the Courts.[21] The report contained a review and discussion of total Injury/damage filings in district and county courts from FY 1980 to FY 2016. A copy of the graph from the report is shown in Figure 4.21. Clearly, Injury/damage cases had fluctuated considerably since FY 1980. And Motor Vehicle cases were driving the increase in total Injury/damage filings.

FIGURE 4.21 TEXAS ALL INJURY/DAMAGE FILINGS IN DISTRICT AND COUNTY COURTS

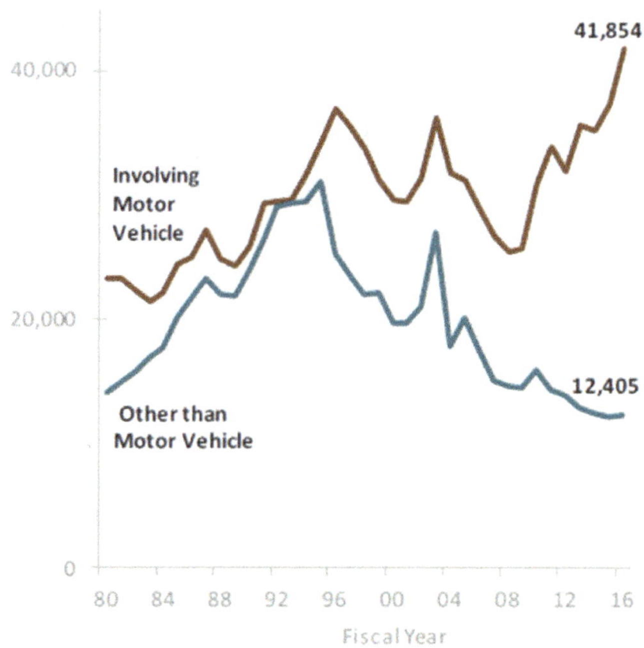

In the discussion in the 2016 annual report, the spike in Injury/damage filings in FY 2003 was attributed to Injury/damage reform legislation that became effective on September 1, 2003.[22] The spike in 2003 were cases filed before the new legislation took effect, causing a dip in filings in 2004. The legislation was described as reforming:

21. Annual Statistical Report for the Texas Judiciary for Fiscal Year 2016, at Statewide-3.

22. The Medical Malpractice and Injury/Damage Reform Act of 2003, 2003 Texas Acts 78th Reg. Sess. Ch. 204 (HB. 4), which amended the Civil Practice and Remedies Code and the Medical Liability and Insurance Improvement Act of Texas.

> certain procedures and remedies in civil actions. It contained elements addressing class action lawsuits, offers of settlement, venue and forum non conveniens, proportionate responsibility, products liability, pre-judgment and post-judgment interest, appeal bonds, seat belts and child safety seats, medical malpractice, charitable volunteer immunity and liability, admissibility of evidence regarding nursing homes, and liability relating to asbestos claims.[23]

Looking at Figure 4.21, total filings dropped to pre-spike levels after 2003, and, in FY 2006, the number of filings fell to the lowest level since 1985. The 2016 report noted that over the past decade, approximately 77 percent of all new Injury/damage cases were filed in the 20 most populous counties.

The pattern of Injury/damage filings was similar from FY 1980 through FY 2008 for both Motor Vehicle and Non-motor Vehicle filings. In FY 1992 and FY 1993, each of the two case subcategories accounted for half of the total Injury/damage cases filed. In FY 2009 the patterns began to diverge. Non-motor Vehicle filings continued to fall, and Motor Vehicle filings began to rise. In 2014, Motor Vehicle filings accounted for 74 percent of all Injury/damage filings—the highest percentage in the previous 35 years.[24] In FY 2017, after reaching the lowest level of filings since 1980, the non-motor vehicle Injury/damage filings increased 6 percent in FY 2018 and 8 percent in FY 2019.[25]

While the pattern of filings for Motor Vehicle and Non-motor Vehicle cases was very similar prior to FY 2009, the rate of change was different. For example, between 1988 and 2007, Motor Vehicle filings increased 8 percent, while filings of cases not involving a motor vehicle declined 31 percent.[26] From FY 2009 to FY 2014 Motor Vehicle filings increased 37 percent, whereas Non-motor Vehicle filings declined 15 percent, to the lowest number since at least 1980. Motor Vehicle cases increased 9 percent in FY 2019 to an all-time high,[27] having increased 79 percent from a low of just over 32,000 in 2010 to almost 53,000 in 2019.[28]

4.3 Summary Observations

Injury/damage cases were the subject of the most intensive public scrutiny and debate of all civil cases over the period of this study. It was these cases most frequently called out as evidence of a "litigation explosion" and of a "flood of frivolous lawsuits" wasting the resources of the courts and unnecessarily raising the insurance rates for the public at large. The data for three of the four states shows that if such phenomena ever existed, they have long since disappeared. Like other civil cases, their number is dwindling both in the actual number of filings and in the per capita rates of filing. Texas is the exception within our study sites. We have no way of knowing whether—if our study had been a 50-state affair—Texas would have remained an exception or would be representative

23. Annual Statistical Report for the Texas Judiciary for Fiscal Year 2006, at 31.
24. Annual Statistical Report for the Texas Judiciary for Fiscal Year 2014, at 42.
25. Annual Statistical Report for the Texas Judiciary for Fiscal Year 2019, at Statewide 5.
26. Annual Statistical Report for the Texas Judiciary for Fiscal Year 2007, at 32.
27. Annual Statistical Report for the Texas Judiciary for Fiscal Year 2019, at iii.
28. *Id.* at ii.

of a category containing numerous states with like experiences counter to the general national trend. We doubt that it represents a national majority.

The lack of any impact of the Great Recession on cases in this category strongly suggests that the filing levels of these personal injury cases is not affected by the business cycle—responding instead to incentives and disincentives related to their own milieu and the carrying capacity of the legal environment for these cases. The distinctive use of billboard and television advertising by personal injury law firms supports this observation that these cases operate within their own distinctive economic as well as professional bubbles.

5

Whither Small Claims

5.1 Overview

When people have a legal problem and they consider "going to court," they may quickly become overwhelmed by the process. Most people do not know a lawyer and may assume they cannot afford to hire a lawyer to litigate on their behalf, especially when a relatively small dollar amount is at stake. Small claims court is intended to address this situation. Not only are court procedures simplified and less formal, but the process is intended to be quick and inexpensive, providing a forum for quick resolution of straightforward disputes. Because small claims is both a case category and a case management practice, small claims filing levels are discussed separately here.

Examples of types of cases most commonly permitted in small claims court in the five states in this study are: claims by people for personal injuries or damage to property sustained in an accident, claims by buyers for defective merchandise or repairs, and claims by stores and service providers for unpaid bills. Some of the states also allow claims for collection of unpaid debts, claims by tenants to recover security deposits, and by landlords for unpaid rent or damage to their property. Some of the states exclude certain case types from small claims court, for example, debt collection by collection agencies, libel, and medical malpractice. Some also exclude remedies other than actual monetary damages, for example, exemplary or punitive damages, or equitable relief.

The discussion of these cases in legislative and court reports characterize them as the everyday disputes between private citizens—such as the matters raised in the TV shows featuring Judge Wapner, Judge Judy, Judge Brown, and others. The data provided does not identify the specific types of cases actually filed—simply the number of cases in the small claims subcategory. Researchers at the National Center for State Courts (NCSC) have conducted two major national studies of small claims courts—one based on data from 15 courts published in 1978[1] and the second based on data from 12 courts in 1992.[2] Both studies found that businesses filed the majority of small claims cases. Eight of the 15 courts in the 1978 study prohibited collection agencies from using small claims courts. In five of those jurisdictions, individual plaintiffs filed more cases than businesses did, from 46 percent to 93 percent of all small claims filings. In the other ten, businesses were the predominant filers, from 62 percent to 85 percent of all small claims filings. In the 1992 study, 63 percent of the cases were initiated by businesses.

Both studies found that allowing collection agencies to use small claims court did not impede the use of those courts by individuals for other types of cases. Per capita filing rates by individuals were higher, on average, in jurisdictions that allowed debt collection cases. The 1992 study found that a majority of the trials held in small claims court were in cases initiated by individual plaintiffs, because a high percentage of debt collection cases were concluded by default. Both studies found that debtors in these cases potentially benefit from having their cases filed in small claims court, where it should be easier for them to raise defenses that may be available to them. Both reports recommended not banning debt collection actions from small claims court.

5.1.1 Findings

In four of the five states, total small claims filings dropped, steadily and by significant percentages, over the period for which data was made available. The drop from 2000 to 2019 ranged from 29 percent in Minnesota to 53 percent in California. Total filings in Illinois rose 23 percent since 2000, but the rise was largely attributable to a dramatic increase in small claims filings in Cook County beginning the 2013. There were roller coaster filing patterns in all five states of varying height and length from the period 2000 to 2015 associated with the Great Recession. Not all peaked in the same years, although most peaks were between 2007 and 2009.

Counterintuitively, the change in total filing levels was the opposite of changes in population. Since 2000, California's population increased 16 percent, but small claims filings dropped 53 percent. Minnesota's population grew by 15 percent, but conciliation filings dropped 29 percent. Illinois's population grew only 2 percent, but their small claims filings increased 23 percent. California's filings were down 75 percent from the peak in FY 1981–82, whereas the population had increased by 56 percent. It was as if the more people there were in the state, or the faster the population grew, the fewer total small claims cases there were. Per capita small claims filing levels varied widely across the five states. In 2019, the range was from 246 to 1,086, a spread of 4.4 to 1. Per capita filing levels dropped at a faster rate than total filings in states where the population grew more quickly.

Total small claims filings declined faster than other civil case categories. As a result, the small claims share of the total civil caseload declined significantly. In California, the share dropped from 44 percent to 18 percent over 41 years. In Ohio, it declined from

1. John C. Ruhnka & Steven Weller with John A. Martin, *Small Claims Courts: A National Examination*, NAT'L CTR. FOR STATE COURTS, Publication No. ROO39 (1978).

2. John A. Goerdt, *Small Claims and Traffic Courts: Case Management Procedures, Case Characteristics and Outcomes in 12 Urban Jurisdictions*, NAT'L CTR. FOR STATE COURTS, Publication No. R-140 (1992).

19 percent to 9 percent over 19 years. In 2018, the share of small claims cases varied widely across the five states, from 7 percent to 40 percent of the total civil caseload. By 2019, the category of small claims cases was the smallest proportion of all civil cases in California, Ohio, and Texas.

The monetary cap for small claims cases was not always a predictor of total filings. In the states with higher monetary caps, the small claims case proportion of all civil cases was higher in 2000. In 2019, the relationship was weaker. California, Illinois, and Texas each had a $10,000 cap, but the small claims share of all civil cases ranged from 7 percent to 39 percent. The proportion was almost the same in Illinois and Minnesota although the cap was 50 percent higher in Minnesota. In 2019, Minnesota's monetary cap was $15,000; in California, Illinois, and Texas the cap was $10,000; and in Ohio $6,000. However, the per capita filing level in Illinois was higher than that in Minnesota, and Texas was the lowest.

Small claims filing levels varied widely not only across states but within states. The filing levels bore little relationship to the population of a county. Filing levels in less-populated counties were neither consistently higher, nor lower, than in more populous counties. Neither geographical location of a county nor socioeconomic basis appeared to be associated with particular small claims filing levels.

Small claims per capita filing levels also varied across counties within a state. In California, the more populous counties generally had higher per capita filing levels than less populous counties. In contrast, the smaller multi-county circuits in Illinois collectively had higher per capita filing levels than the single-county circuits with large populations.

In California, the variance in per capita small claims filing levels relative to population across counties was striking. In 2019, the range across the 58 counties was from 29 to 571, a ratio of almost 20 to 1. Filing levels tended to be higher in the larger counties, but not consistently. Over the study period, counties with larger populations experienced percentage drops in per capita filing levels greater than the statewide drop. The drop in courts with smaller populations varied much more than other courts, but the largest percentage drops tended to be in smaller courts. Pairs of geographically adjacent counties similar in population had different per capita filing levels in 2019.

There were also noticeable differences in small claims filing patterns across groups of circuit courts in Illinois. From 1996 to 2015, the bulk of total filings were in the multi-county circuits, whereas the bulk of the population was in the single-county circuits. The multi-county circuits collectively had higher per capita filing levels than the single-county circuits, in contrast to the pattern observed in California.

An increase in the monetary jurisdictional cap for small claims cases did not have the expected result of increasing total filings. The small claims jurisdictional cap was raised 13 times in the five states during the period for which data was made available. The cap increases ranged from 25 percent to 100 percent. Rather than resulting in filing increases commensurate with the change in the monetary cap, the change in total filings, if any, was modest and transient, lasting only one to two years. Filing levels often reverted to pre-increase levels within a few years. In many instances, when filings had been declining before an increase, they continued to decline during and after the year of the increase. Whatever factors were contributing to the long-term decline in per capita small claims filing levels overrode any impact of an increase in the monetary jurisdiction cap.

The expansion of the subject matter jurisdiction of small claims cases would be expected to increase small claims filing levels because more types of cases could be filed as small claims cases. The subject matter jurisdiction was expanded twice in Minnesota. Neither expansion resulted in a noticeable increase in filing levels. Texas made significant changes to its small claims court in 2013, shifting whole categories of miscellaneous proceedings formerly heard in the justice court to now be heard in small claims court. Total filings increased 44 percent in the first full year after the change, and continued at this higher level through 2019. Initially, the count of small claims cases included all cases now heard in small claims court; there was no separate count of Miscellaneous Proceedings and Small Claims Suits using the pre-change category. As a result, it was not possible to analyze which case subcategory, small claims cases or Miscellaneous Proceedings, contributed to the increase in total filings after the change.

One of the most disappointing findings of this study was the apparent lack of a significant impact on filings from a significant expansion of assistance provided to small claims litigants. The stated intent of the assistance was to improve access and make the process easier, simpler, and less costly. Presumably, this would increase small claims filings, although this was not an explicitly stated goal. Despite the expanded range and nature of assistance available to small claims litigants, in particular using technology, per capita filing levels in four of the five states dropped significantly over the period for which data was made available.

The range of services expanded was significant. Information about small claims court and how it worked was increased, and often was available from several government agencies and nongovernmental organizations, in addition to the courts. Court forms to start and defend a case were simplified and made available as savable forms that could be e-filed. Direct assistance was added and expanded statewide. The assistance took many forms—one-on-one, in classes, remotely over the phone or internet, form filling interview software—and in many languages. Unfortunately, the most that might be attributed to the expansion of assistance was that it may have slowed the decline in filings.

The problem appeared to be that potential small claims litigants often did not understand how their problems could be resolved in small claims court, or did not understand how to use small claims court to resolve their problems. A report of the results of a phone survey of small claims litigants in California stated:

> Many parties to small claims cases in the study appear unable to identify their legal disputes with much specificity. This may have important implications for the effectiveness with which these litigants prepare their cases including identifying and gathering pertinent evidence, as well as for the arguments they will need to develop and make in court.[3]

A public trust and confidence survey conducted by the California Judicial Council in 2005 revealed that the public's perception of small claims court was less positive than for the courts generally.[4] A report on follow-up interviews and focus groups suggested

---

3. David A. Smith, *Procedural Fairness and Effective Court Practices in Small Claims Cases Study Overview*, Cal. Admin. Off. of the Courts, Off. of Ct. Rsch. 6 (Oct. 2012).

4. Judicial Council of California, Trust and Confidence in the California Courts, A Survey of the Public and Attorneys, Part I: Findings and Recommendations 17 (Sept. 2005).

people did not understand the small claims court process, and the confusion and stress reduced their use of the court.[5] This observation provides one explanation of why the efforts to assist litigants have been less successful than anticipated.

5.1.2 Other Factors That Might Affect Small Claims Filing Levels

There were a number of other factors that may have explained differences in small claims filing levels over time or across states. Unfortunately, the small sample size of only five states made it impossible to attribute any difference in filing levels to particular characteristics of small claims cases in the five states. For example, it was not possible to analyze the impact on filings of differences in the subject matter jurisdiction, statute of limitations, whether lawyers were permitted to appear, whether the hearing officer had to be a lawyer, how the hearings were conducted, or whether a jury trial was allowed.[6]

The subject matter jurisdiction of the small claims courts in the five states varied widely. Some only allowed monetary claims for Injury/damage suits, and some excluded certain Injury/damage suits such as libel or malpractice. Only two of the five states allow debt collection cases. The other states expressly excluded these cases or limited the amount claimed or who could sue. Only one allowed eviction cases, but two others allowed suits related to rent and security deposits. Some allowed only monetary damages, whereas others allowed other types of remedies. In order to assess the impact of allowed case types, considerable detail about the types of cases filed and the litigant would be needed and none of these five states reported such detail.

Four states allowed lawyers to appear for a litigant. Lawyers were not allowed in California, except to represent a corporation. Four states required the hearing officer to be law trained, but most justice court judges in Texas were not. Filing data from a much larger set of states would be needed to assess the impact of these differences.

In three states, the hearing was prescribed as a court trial. In Illinois, a party could demand a jury trial, and in Texas a litigant was required to waive a right to a jury trial to have a judge decide a small claims case. Generally, hearings were to be conducted informally. Only Texas permitted discovery by the parties.

The remainder of this chapter analyzes in more detail the filing data across the five states and in each state individually.

5.2 Change in Small Claims Filing Levels over Time

5.2.1 Total Filings

Total Small Claims filings dropped steadily and significantly in four of the five states during the period for which data was made available. Figure 5.1 displays the total filings for the five states. Total filings in California dropped 65 percent from 1976–77

5. Judicial Council of California, Trust and Confidence in the California Courts, Public Court Users and Judicial Branch Members Talk About the California Courts, Phase II: Focus Groups and Interviews 5 (Dec. 2006).

6. All of these matters are discussed at length in Ruhnka, Weller, & Martin, *supra* note 1, and Goerdt, *supra* note 2.

to 2018–19, and 53 percent since FY 1999–2000. Total filings in Ohio dropped 49 percent from 1995 to 2019, and 51 percent since 2000. Total filings in Minnesota dropped 40 percent from 1994 to 2018, and 29 percent since 2000. Total filings in Texas dropped 31 percent from 2004 to 2012, then increased when the subject matter jurisdiction was expanded. Illinois was the only state where total filings rose, 23 percent, from 1996 to 2019.

There were roller coaster patterns in four states of varying height and length. In particular, the states showed increases and then decreases from 2001–02 to 2015 associated with the Great Recession. Not all peaked in the same years. California and Minnesota peaked in 2008, Illinois in 2007 and 2009, and Ohio in 2001 and 2007.

FIGURE 5.1 TOTAL SMALL CLAIMS FILINGS

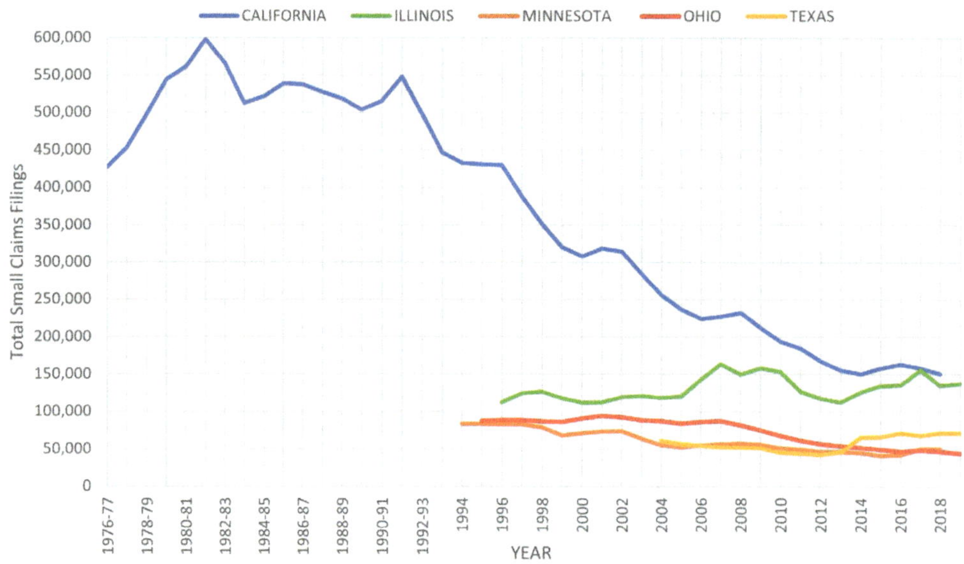

Per capita Small Claims filing levels also decreased in four of the states. Figure 5.2 displays the per capita filing levels for the five states for the same time period. Interestingly, the per capita filing levels dropped at a faster rate in states where the population grew quickly—in California, Minnesota, and Texas. The per capita filing changes more closely tracked the total filings changes where population grew slowly, in Illinois and Ohio. Per capita filing levels dropped 80 percent in California since 1976–77, and 60 percent since 2000. Minnesota per capita filing levels dropped 51 percent since 1994, and 38 percent since 2000. In Ohio, they dropped 51 percent since 1995, and 53 percent since 2000. In Texas, per capita filing levels dropped 41 percent from 2004 to 2012, after which the subject matter jurisdiction was increased. In contrast, per capita filing levels in Illinois increased 17 percent since 1996, and 21 percent since 2000, but dropped somewhat from 2017 to 2019 as Cook County's increase became a decline.

FIGURE 5.2 SMALL CLAIMS FILINGS PER 100K POPULATION

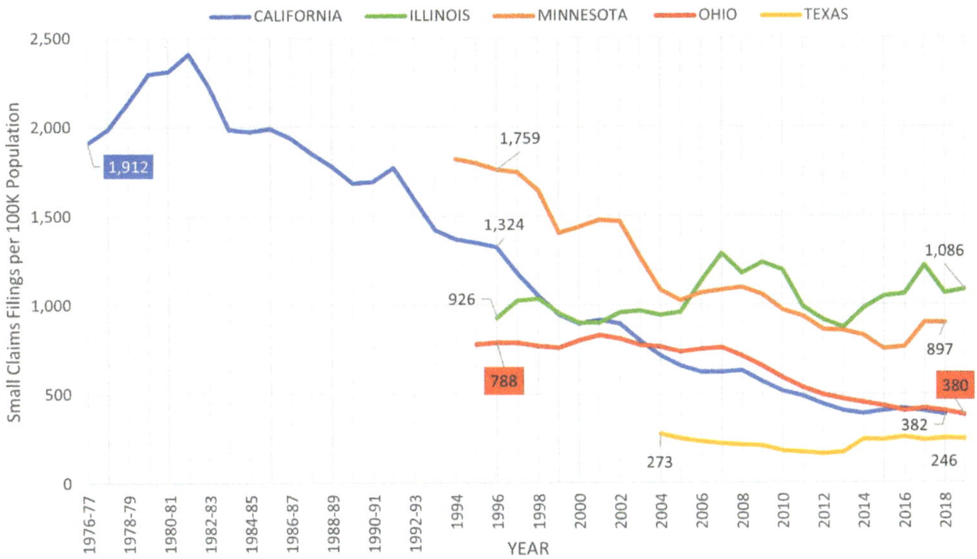

5.2.2 Small Claims Proportion of Total Civil Filings

Small Claims cases were a declining proportion of the total civil caseload in four of the five states. At the same time, the proportions varied considerably from state to state. Figure 5.3 displays the Small Claims case proportion of total civil caseload over time. Small Claims cases were the largest share of all civil cases in California and Minnesota at the beginning of the study period for each state. In 2000, the Small Claims share of the civil caseload varied from 51 percent in Minnesota to 19 percent in Ohio. In 2004, the range was from 41 percent in Minnesota to 9 percent in Texas. By 2019, Small Claims cases were the smallest proportion of all civil cases, less than 20 percent in California, and less than 10 percent in Ohio and Texas.

FIGURE 5.3 SMALL CLAIMS FILINGS AS PERCENT OF ALL CIVIL FILINGS

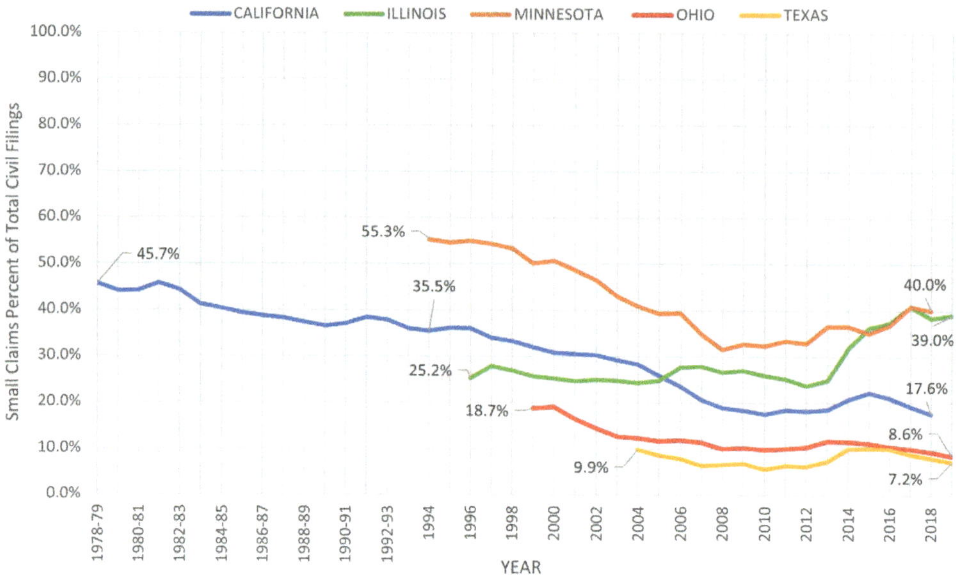

The relationship of the proportion of Small Claims cases in the total civil caseload to the jurisdictional cap in the five states is cataloged in Table 5.1. The table contains information for the start of the study period for each state, which varied, and comparable figures for 2000 and 2019. The relationship in 2000 was consistent; the states with higher caps had a higher proportion of Small Claims cases, as would be expected. However, by 2019, the relationship was weaker. California, Illinois, and Texas all had a $10,000 cap, but the proportion ranged from 7 percent to 39 percent. The proportion was almost the same in Illinois and Minnesota, although the cap was 50 percent higher in Minnesota.

TABLE 5.1 RELATIONSHIP OF SMALL CLAIMS JURISDICTIONAL CAP AND PROPORTION OF TOTAL CIVIL CASELOAD

STATE	California	Illinois	Minnesota	Ohio	Texas
Jurisdictional cap at start of period for each state	$750 as of Jan. 1977	$5,000 as of Jan. 1997	$7,500 as of July 1994	$3,000 as of July 1997	
Share of total civil caseload at start of period	46% in FY 1978–79	28% in 1997	55% in 1994	19% in 1999	
Jurisdictional cap in 2000	$5,000 as of Jan. 1991	$5,000	$7,500	$3,000	
Share of total civil caseload in 2000	32% in FY 1999–2000	25%	51%	19%	No data provided prior to 2004
Jurisdictional cap in 2019	$10,000 as of Jan. 2012	$10,000 as of Jan. 2006	$15,000 as of Aug. 2014	$6,000 as of Sept. 2016	$10,000 as of Sept. 2007
Share of total civil caseload in 2019	18% in FY 2018–19	39%	40% in 2018	9%	7%

5.3 Change in Small Claims Filing Levels by State

5.3.1 California

From 1976 to 2019, California's population grew 80 percent. One might expect the total number of Small Claims filings to have increased by a similar percentage. Quite to the contrary, total filings decreased, and the decline was quite dramatic. Figure 5.4 displays the total number of Small Claim filings (blue columns and left side axis) and per capita Small Claim filing levels (orange line and right-side axis) for the 43-year period. Total filings were down 65 percent from FY 1976–77 to FY 2018–19, and down 75 percent from the peak of filings in FY 1981–82. The lowest level was in FY 2014–15. The largest year-to-year drop in total filings was 10 percent, which happened in four years: FY 1993–94, FY 1997–98, FY 2003–04, and FY 2004–05. On a per capita basis, filings were down more than 80 percent over 43 years. Per capita filing levels dropped from 1,912 to 382, a five-fold decrease. For the last six fiscal years, per capita filing levels were comparatively steady, varying between 382 and 415. The population grew more than 3 percent in this time frame. Counterintuitively, continuous and large population growth was associated with fewer small claims filings.

FIGURE 5.4 CALIFORNIA TOTAL SMALL CLAIMS FILINGS

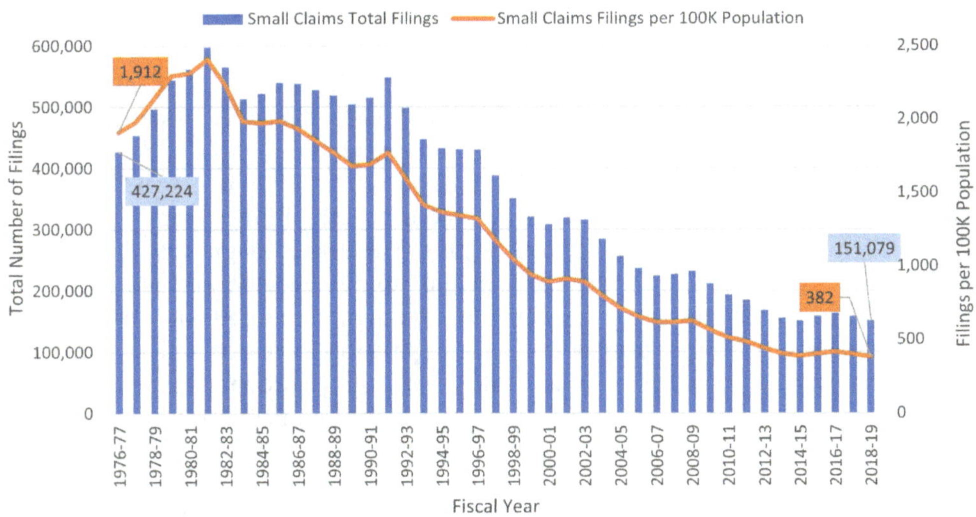

5.3.2 Minnesota

Conciliation case filings in Minnesota also exhibited a significant drop over the 25-year period. Total filings dropped almost 40 percent (blue columns, left-side axis in Figure 5.5), whereas the state population increased 23 percent. Total filings dropped slowly from 1994 to 1997, then dropped sharply until 1999. Filings then rose slowly through 2002, followed by a sharp drop until 2005. Filings then exhibited another roller coaster pattern beginning in 2005, peaking in 2008, followed by a long slow drop until 2015. Filings jumped in 2017, then leveled off in 2018. The largest year-to-year drop in total filings was more than 13 percent, which happened in 1999, 2003, and 2004. Per capita Conciliation filing levels followed a very similar pattern, but with a steeper overall decline of 51 percent (orange line, right-side axis in Figure 5.5). As in California and Ohio, Conciliation case filing levels were not associated with population levels or growth.

FIGURE 5.5 MINNESOTA CONCILIATION FILINGS

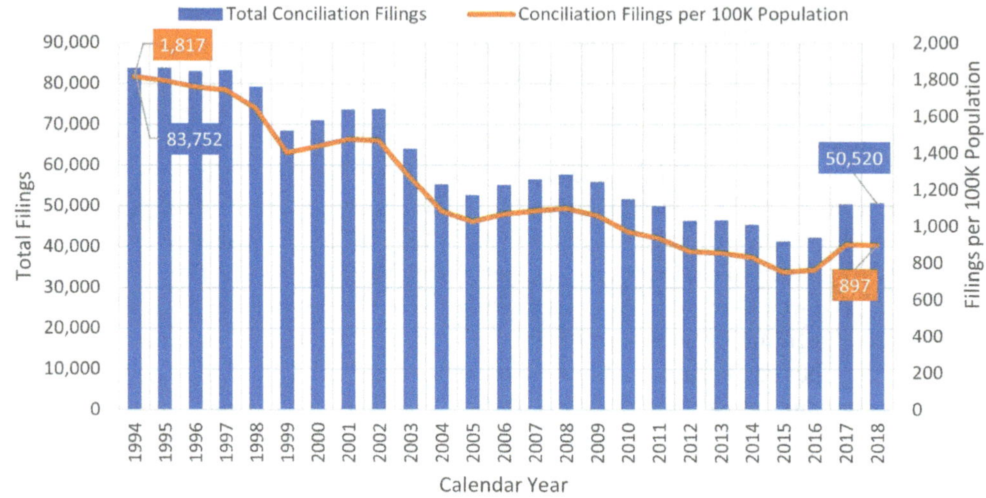

5.3.3 Ohio

Total Small Claims filings in Ohio also dropped significantly, 49 percent, over the 25-year period for which data was made available (blue columns, left-side axis in Figure 5.6). In contrast, the population of Ohio grew 4 percent during this period. Total filings were essentially flat from 1995 to 1999, then rose from 1999 to a peak in 2001. A slow drop began, followed by an increase in 2006 and 2007. Filings then began a long decline though 2019, with a small increase in 2017. The largest single year drop was 10 percent in 2010. The drop from the subpeak in 2007 to 2019 was 49 percent.

Per capita Small Claims filing levels in Ohio (orange line, right-side axis in Figure 5.6) showed a slightly steeper drop because the population increased while total filings fell. Over the 25-year period, per capita Small Claims filings dropped 51 percent. As in California and Minnesota, there was no apparent relationship between filing levels and population totals or growth.

FIGURE 5.6 OHIO SMALL CLAIMS FILINGS IN MUNICIPAL AND COUNTY COURTS

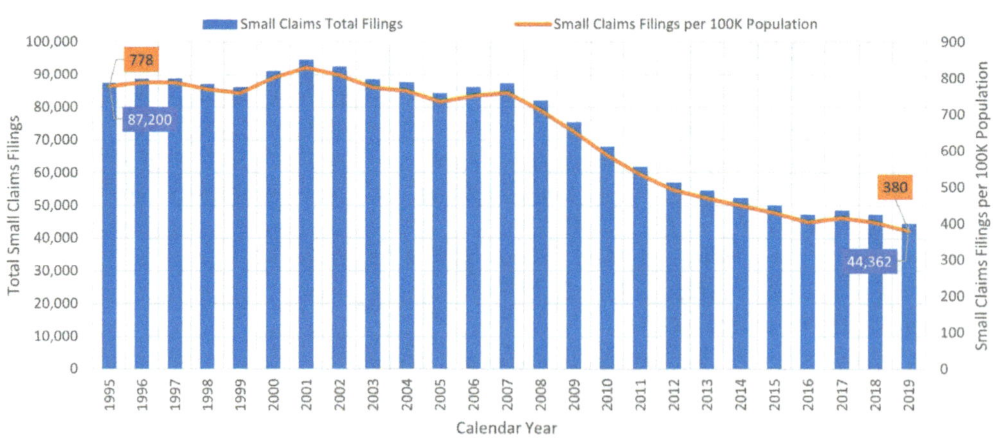

5.3.4 Illinois

In contrast to three of the other states, Small Claims filing in Illinois increased over the 25-year study period. Overall total filings increased almost 23 percent from 1996 to 2019 (blue columns, left-side axis in Figure 5.7). There were several ups and downs in the filing levels. Filings peaked in 2007 and again in 2017. There was a noticeable roller coaster from 2005 to 2013. The largest one-year increase was more than 18 percent in 2006, and the largest drop was more than 17 percent in 2011. Increases in the jurisdictional dollar limit, discussed later, may explain the increases in some years.

Per capita filing levels (orange line, right-side axis in Figure 5.7) showed a similar increase, rising a little more than 17 percent in 25 years. The pattern of per capita filing levels closely followed the pattern of total filings because the growth in population was slow and relatively steady during the 25-year period. Total state population growth was about 5 percent over the last 25 years, but it actually shrank 1 percent during the last decade of the period. In contrast to the other states, total Small Claims filings grew faster than population, and grew even when the population was shrinking.

FIGURE 5.7 ILLINOIS SMALL CLAIMS FILINGS

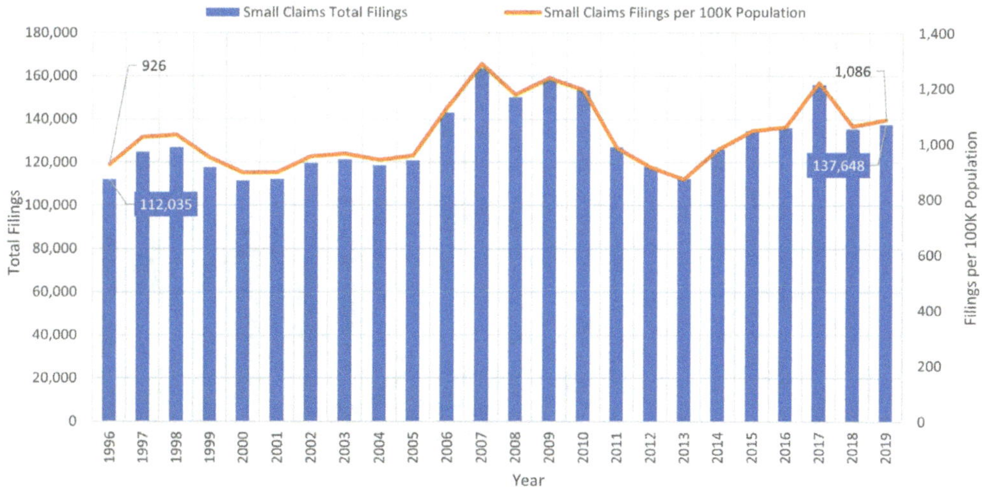

5.3.5 Texas

Comparing Small Claims filings in Texas to the other four states was complicated by a significant change in the subject matter jurisdiction and in the operation of small claims court during the 16-year period for which data was available. In 2011, the legislature passed a law significantly reorganizing the small claims court. In response, the Supreme Court appointed a Task Force for Rules in Small Claims Cases and Justice Court Proceedings to propose new court rules for Small Claims cases. Based on the Task Force proposals and a number of public meetings, the Supreme Court adopted new court rules effective May 1, 2013. The new court rules included significant changes in the subject matter jurisdiction of Small Claims cases, discussed in greater detail later. Because of the legislative and court rule changes in 2013, the periods before the changes and after the changes are examined separately.

Prior to the change, Texas Small Claims filings were declining, as they had in the other four states. The pattern of total Small Claims case filings from 2004 through 2012 is displayed in Figure 5.8 (blue columns and left-side axis). Total filings dropped 31 percent from 2004 to 2012. In contrast, the Texas population grew more than 16 percent during this period. On a per capita basis (gray line and right-side axis in Figure 5.8), the pattern was very similar, with a steeper decline because of the growth in population. Per capita Small Claims filing levels dropped almost 41 percent over the nine-year period.

After the changes, which added more types of cases that were counted as Small Claims cases, the pattern of filings reversed, growing for the next seven years. The pattern of Small Claims filings beginning in 2013 is also displayed in Figure 5.8 (total filings as green columns and per capita filing levels by an orange line). Total filings and per capita filing levels both increased beginning in 2013, but leveled off from 2015 to 2019. From 2014, the first full year after the change, total filings increased 9 percent, per capita filing levels increased almost 2 percent, and the population increased almost 8 percent.

Without more detail of filing levels for subcategories within this larger category, it was unclear whether Small Claims filings, as defined before 2013, increased or decreased as a result of the legislative and rule changes, or whether the increase was from new types of cases that were now counted as Small Claims.

FIGURE 5.8 TEXAS SMALL CLAIMS FILINGS

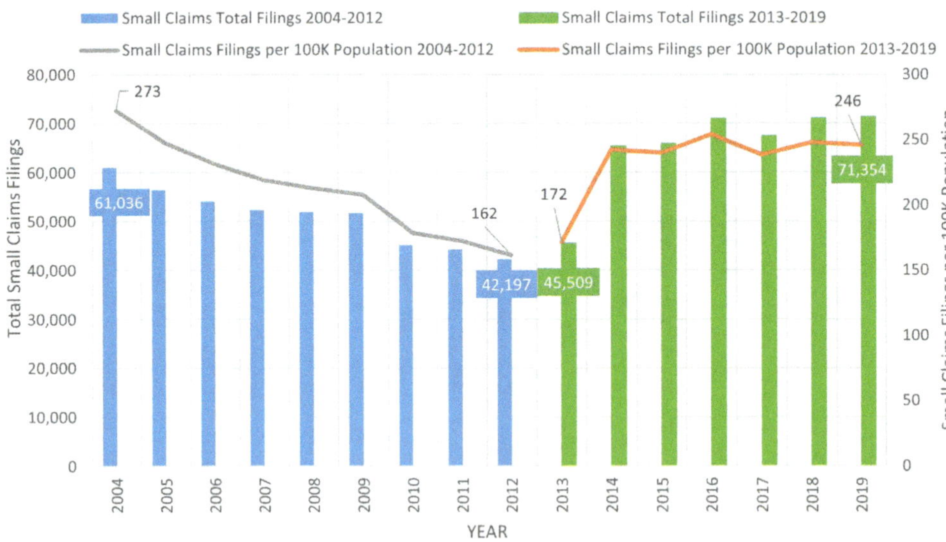

5.4 Variation of Small Claims Filings by Population and Region

Per capita filing levels of Small Claims cases in courts in these five states varied widely over time, geographically, and by population. The filing levels of Small Claims cases bore little relationship to the population of a county. Filing levels in less-populated counties were neither consistently higher, nor lower, than in more populous counties.

The geographical location of a county and its associated socioeconomic characteristics were also not a determining factor in Small Claims filing levels.

5.4.1 California

Neither the population in a county nor the geographical region in which it was located appeared to be a factor associated with Small Claims filing levels. In addition, the drop in filing levels over 20 years occurred in all of the California counties. No county had an increase in Small Claims filings. The drops were not uniform and were weakly related to the population of a county and unrelated to geographical region.

The variance in per capita Small Claims filing levels relative to population across counties was striking. In 2019, the statewide per capita small claim filing level was 352 per 100,000 population, with a range across counties from 29 to 571, a ratio of almost 20 to 1. Filing levels tended to be higher in the larger counties, but not uniformly. In 2019, Los Angeles, the largest county, had the highest per capita filing level at 571. The state per capita filing level without LA was 279. Only six counties had per capita filing levels above the statewide level, two were among the ten largest in population, two were large courts, and two were mid-sized courts. There were 23 counties with per capita filing levels less than 200. One was a large court. Nine of ten counties with less than 30,000 population had filing levels below 200.

Pairs of geographically adjacent counties similar in population had different per capita filing levels in 2019. In Southern California, adjacent counties similar in population and economies had varying filing levels. San Bernardino's filing level was 253 and Riverside's was 311. Orange's filing level was 272 and San Diego's was 320. In the Central Valley, Fresno's filing level was 292 and Kern's was 387. Farther north, Yuba's filing level was 137 and Sutter's was 78.

The change in per capita filing levels over a 20-year period, both across and within courts, showed a wide variance. The statewide per capita filing level was 929 in 2000 and 352 in 2019. The range in 2000 was from 225 to 1,706, a 7.5 to 1 ratio. In 2019, the range was from 29 to 571, both much lower levels than in 2000, but the spread was larger, almost a 20 to 1 ratio. Forty-nine of 58 courts were above 500 in 2000, but only one court was above 500 in 2019.

The significant collapse in Small Claim filing levels was weakly related to size and historical filing levels. Courts with larger populations experienced greater percentage drops in per capita filing levels than the statewide drop. The drop in courts with smaller populations varied much more than other courts, but the largest percentage drops tended to be in smaller courts.

Statewide, the 20-year drop in total Small Claims filings was 50 percent. It was 53 percent, not including LA, the largest county in the state. Across the counties, the drop in total filings ranged from 15 percent to 83 percent. In LA, the drop was 43 percent and the drop in the ten largest counties (each with more than a million in population) ranged from 37 percent to 63 percent. In the smallest 11 counties (with population less than 30,000) the drops ranged from 50 percent to 83 percent. Generally, the drop for the smaller counties was higher than the statewide drop, but there were several large- and medium-sized counties with drops over 60 percent, including two with more than 800,000 in population.

When measured by per capita filing levels, the decline in Small Claim filing levels showed a similar wide range, and weak relationship to population as was found for total filings. The percentage drop in per capita filing levels statewide was 62 percent over 20 years. Excluding Los Angeles, the statewide drop was 68 percent. The drop in individual counties ranged from 27 percent to 93 percent. It was 48 percent in Los Angeles. The counties with the largest percentage drops (more than 80 percent) were mostly small, but included one large county. The group of counties with the drops less than that for the state included counties with a wide range of total population and from all regions of the state.

Looking at two sets of counties over 20 years, the drops were not consistent, over time or within a county, although the overall downward pattern was similar. Two figures display changes in per capita Small Claim filing levels for two groups of counties. The statewide level (red line) is included in each figure. The first group was the ten largest courts (Figure 5.9). All show a long-term decline over the period. In 2000, six of the ten were above the statewide level. In 2019, only one, LA, was above the statewide level and it had been above the statewide level for the entire period. The four courts below the statewide level at the beginning of the period were below the statewide level for the whole period. Several had increases in filing levels in one or more years, usually in different years. Several had small surges in the 2007 to 2010 period, associated with the Great Recession, but not in the same years.

FIGURE 5.9 CALIFORNIA SMALL CLAIMS FILINGS PER 100K POPULATION IN TEN LARGEST COUNTIES BY 2019 POPULATION

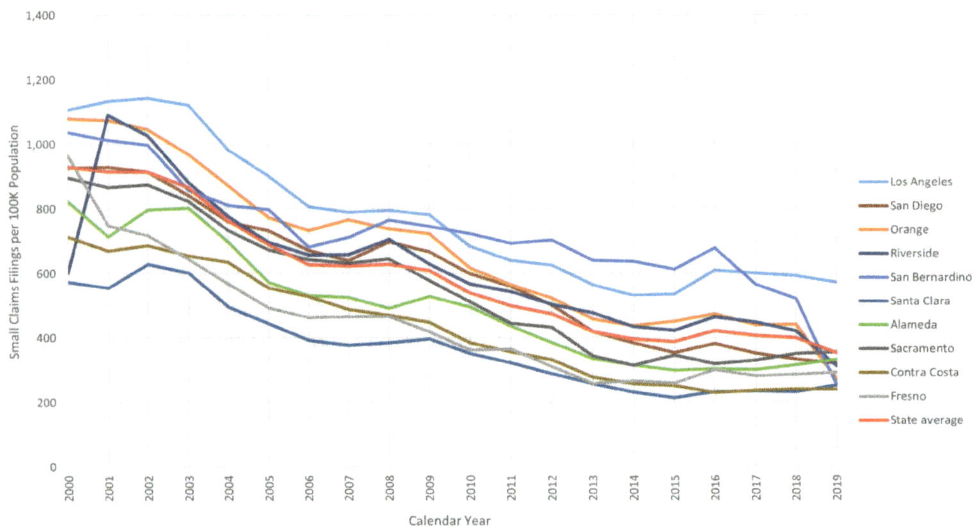

The second figure is of the eight courts in the southern end of California's Central Valley, a primarily agricultural area and more conservative socially and politically (Figure 5.10). This group included two large courts (Fresno and Kern). The rest were mid-sized. All of the courts showed a similar long-term decline in Small Claim filing levels. Four were below the statewide level for the whole period. The two that started above the statewide level dropped below the statewide level in 2002 and 2004 and remained below the statewide level at the end of the period. Two other courts rose above the statewide level, but only in 2019. As with the ten largest courts, each court experienced surges in filings at different years during the long decline. The spread of filing levels was relatively large in 2000, 2.5 to 1, but narrowed in 2019.

FIGURE 5.10 CALIFORNIA SMALL CLAIMS FILINGS PER 100K POPULATION IN LOWER CENTRAL VALLEY COUNTIES

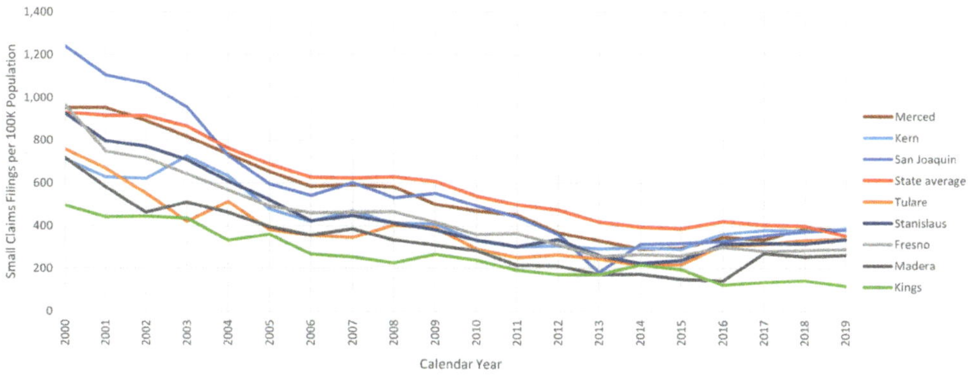

5.4.2 Illinois

There were some noticeable differences in Small Claims filing patterns across groups of circuit courts in Illinois over a 24-year period. Figure 5.11 displays the total filing patterns for the state as a whole, four of the single-county circuits combined (DuPage, Lake, Will, and Kane Counties), Cook County, and the rest of the state. Table 5.2 indicates the share of statewide population and Small Claims filings in 1996 and 2019 for these groups. From 1996 to 2015, the bulk of total filings were in the smaller multi-county circuits, whereas the bulk of the population was in the single-county circuits. The multi-county circuits involved a disproportionate share of Small Claims filings in 1996, but the proportion dropped beginning in 2013 due to a notable increase in the Cook County filings.

Looking at total filings, there were similar roller coaster patterns for the multi-circuit counties and the single-county circuits (Figure 5.11). For the multi-county circuits and the combined four single-county circuits, not including Cook County, the roller coaster began in 2006, when there was a change in jurisdictional monetary cap (discussed later), and ended in 2013. However, the timing of the peaks was different. It was in 2007 for the multi-county circuits, and in 2009–10 for the four single-county circuits. Cook County's filings showed an almost undiscernible roller coaster pattern during this period. Cook County did have a roller coaster pattern that started in 2013 and peaked in 2017, which both rose and fell more sharply than the earlier roller coaster patterns.

Per capita Small Claims filing levels also exhibited variance over time and across the state. In contrast to the other states, the smaller multi-county circuits collectively had higher per capita filing levels. Statewide per capita filing levels were 926 per 100,000 population in 1996, and rose to 1,086 in 2019. In Cook County, the per capita rate rose from 247 to 783. In the other four single-county circuits, all geographically adjacent to Cook County, the per capita level of the combined counties rose from 759 to 1,071. The per capita levels in each of these four circuits ranged from 626 to 927 in 1996 and from 922 to 1,273 in 2019. In the multi-county circuits, the per capita level fell from 1,803 to 1,429, but was still greater than that of any of the single-county circuits. In Illinois, per capita filing levels were related to population and changed similarly over time. In contrast to California, the smaller counties in Illinois had higher per capita filing levels.

FIGURE 5.11 ILLINOIS SMALL CLAIMS FILINGS

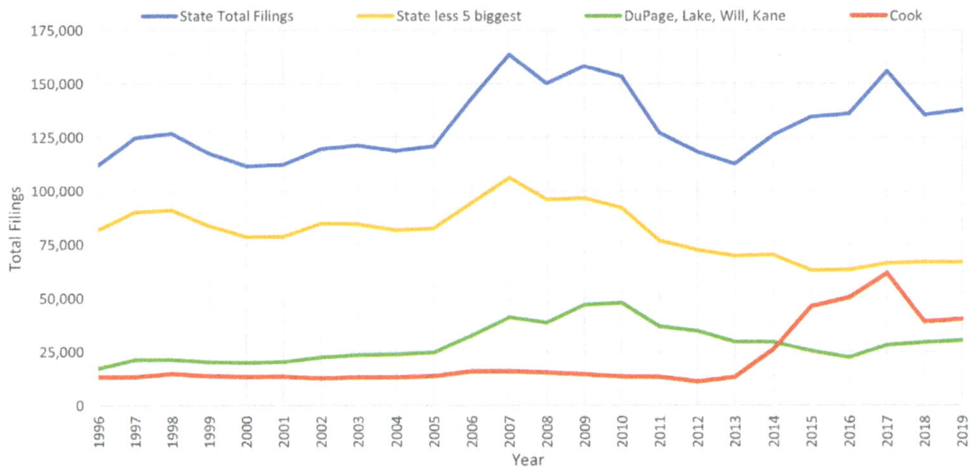

TABLE 5.2 ILLINOIS COMPARISON OF POPULATION AND TOTAL SMALL CLAIMS FILINGS

	In 1996		In 2019	
Circuit	Percent of state population	Percent of total small claims filings	Percent of state population	Percent of total small claims filings
Cook	44%	12%	41%	29%
Other four single-county circuits*	19%	15%	22%	22%
All multi-county circuits	37%	73%	37%	47%

*Single-county circuits other than Cook were DuPage, Lake, Will, and Kane counties.

5.5 Impact of an Increase in Monetary Jurisdiction Cap for Small Claims

5.5.1 Overview

There were several possible scenarios for the impact of an increase in the monetary jurisdictional cap on Small Claims filings. Because the jurisdictional cap is fixed, and the value of a dollar depreciates over time, each year fewer potential cases fall within the monetary jurisdictional cap. Raising the jurisdictional cap would theoretically increase filings, as more cases would now be within the jurisdiction. The simpler procedures and quicker time frame of small claims court might encourage more filings of cases that were not prosecuted because of the more complicated procedural requirements of the court where the cases would previously had to have been filed. Another factor might be how long ago the jurisdictional limit was increased and the magnitude of the increase. The longer it had been, or the greater the increase, more filings would be expected after the increase.

The magnitude of the filings increase, if any, would be hard to predict. Any increase would occur only if litigants with a claim knew about the increase when considering filing a Small Claims case. The increase might be less than expected if litigants, before the increase, were filing Small Claims cases even though their damages were above the limit, accepting that any damages awarded would be capped. Another possible explanation of little or no increase would be that it was still not practical or economical to pursue even a Small Claims case because of perceived costs, barriers, or lost time. Some potential litigants may not have even been aware that their problem was a legal dispute that could be taken to small claims court. Finally, it may be that potential litigants did not even consider filing a case, foregoing any potential recovery, regardless of the jurisdictional limit.

5.5.2 Findings

Increases in the small claims monetary jurisdictional cap occurred 13 times in the five states during the period for which data was made available. The increases ranged from a 25 percent increase to a doubling of the cap. The number of years between increases ranged from two years to 19 years, with an average of 9.4 years. As of 2018, the cap was $15,000 in Minnesota; $10,000 in California, Illinois, and Texas; and $6,000 in Ohio.

Typically, an increase, if any, in total filings in the years immediately after the monetary increase were short-lived, lasting one to two years. After many of the monetary increases, filings did not rise, but continued to fall. Rarely did a monetary increase result in an ongoing step-up in filing levels. After several of the increases, the filing level returned to a pre-increase level after a few years. In California, for three of the five monetary increases, filings dropped in the year of the monetary increase and for several years after.

Looking at per capita filing levels and jurisdictional cap levels, the findings were unexpected. Figure 5.12 displays the per capita filing levels in each state in the first full year after each jurisdictional cap increase. Raising the jurisdictional cap would be expected to increase per capita filing levels. However, in four of the five states, lower per capita filing levels were associated with a higher jurisdictional cap. Only Illinois consistently experienced higher filing levels after raising the cap. Oddly, there were steeper drops when the cap was doubled. Whatever factors were causing the long-term decline in per capita Small Claims filing levels overrode any impact of an increase in the cap.

FIGURE 5.12 PER CAPITA SMALL CLAIMS FILING LEVELS VERSUS JURISDICTIONAL CAP

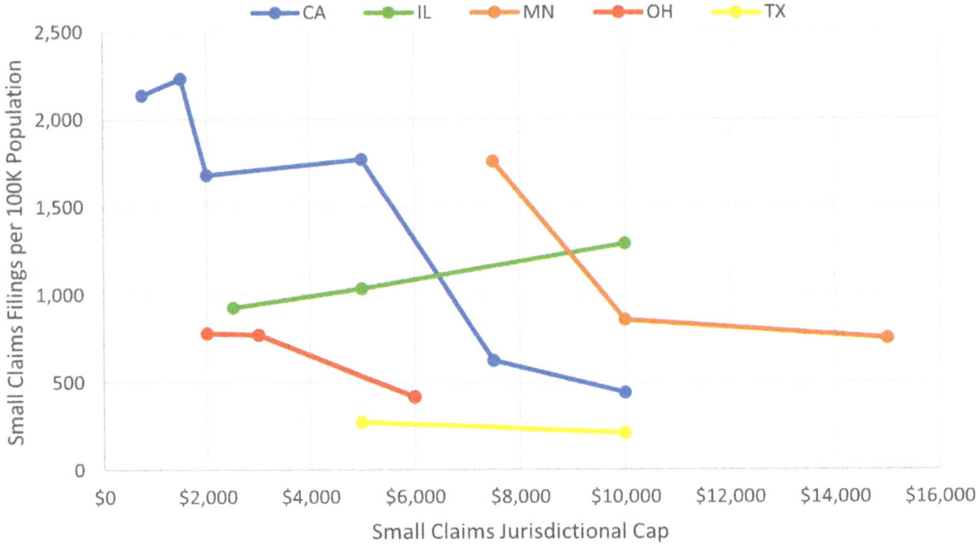

The ongoing decline in Small Claims filings, notwithstanding increases in the cap, also meant that the Small Claims share of total filings did not increase. Figure 5.13 displays the Small Claims share of total civil filings. Again, except in Illinois and one time in California, the Small Claims case share of total civil filings declined despite an increase in the cap, which, presumably, would have shifted some cases to the Small Claims total or increased the total number.

FIGURE 5.13 SMALL CLAIMS SHARE OF ALL CIVIL CASES VERSUS JURISDICTIONAL CAP

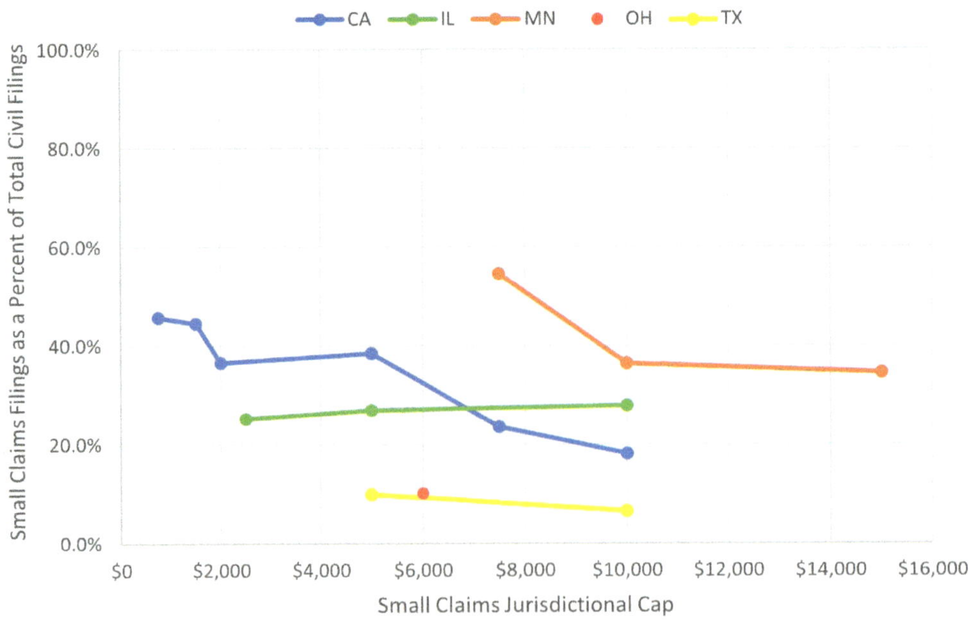

The lack of any significant increase in filing levels, let alone a sustained impact, is curious. Perhaps there were not that many cases near the jurisdictional limit, or litigants waived any damages above the limit when filing a case in the years before the cap was raised. An analysis of damages sought, and award amounts, would have to be done to address these questions. Another explanation might be that potential small claims litigants were not aware of a jurisdictional increase, or were not even aware that their problem was a legal dispute that could be taken to small claims court.

5.5.2.1 California

The monetary jurisdiction of the Small Claims court in California was increased six times in 43 years. Figure 5.14 and Table 5.3 indicate when the jurisdictional cap was increased, what the new amount was, and what the increase in per capita filing level was before, during, and immediately after the year of increase. Per capita filing levels only rose in two of the years with cap increases. Nor was there a sustained increase in total filings in subsequent years that might be attributable to a cap increase. California's 20-Year Retrospective Report noted filing increases, especially in individual courts, in the years the jurisdictional cap increased significantly, in FY 1981–82 and FY 1990–92.[7] However, there was no similar increase when the amount was increased in other years. Most increases in per capita filing levels during the 43-year period were not associated with a jurisdictional cap increase.

FIGURE 5.14 CALIFORNIA SMALL CLAIMS TOTAL FILINGS WHEN THE JURISDICTIONAL LIMIT WAS INCREASED

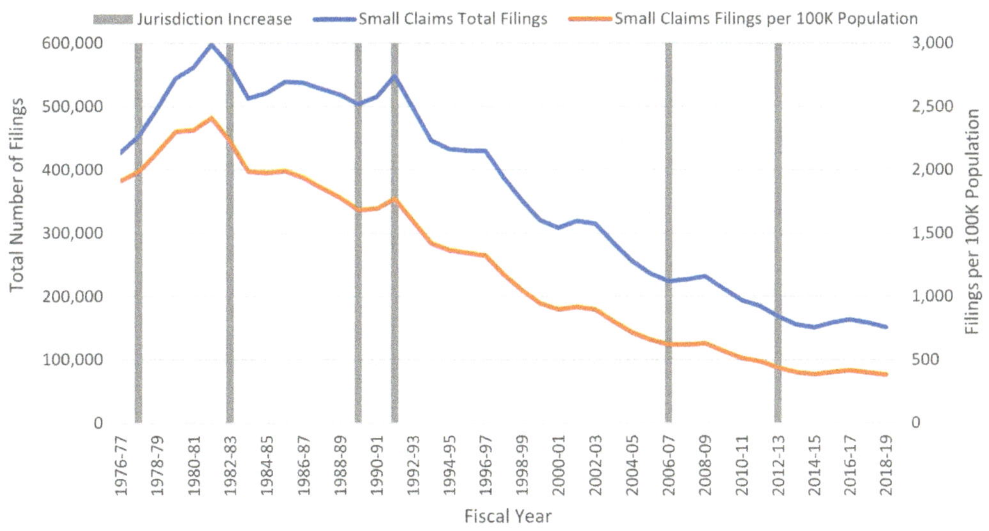

7. Alexander Aikman & Karen Viscia, *Exploring the Work of the California Trial Courts: A 20-Year Retrospective*, California, Administrative Office of the Courts 71 (2003) https://www.courts.cagov /7808.htm.

TABLE 5.3 CALIFORNIA: IMPACT OF INCREASE IN SMALL CLAIMS MONETARY JURISDICTION

Date of increase	Jurisdictional amount	Subsequent change in total filings
Effective January 1, 1977[8]	$750	Filings increased in the first year after the change and for the next six fiscal years.
Effective January 1, 1982[9]	$1,500	Filings had been increasing in the prior fiscal years and rose again in FY 1981–82. However, filings dropped in the next two fiscal years.
Effective January 1, 1989[10]	$2,000	Filings dropped in FY 1988–89 from prior year and dropped again in FY 1989–90.
Effective January 1, 1991[11]	$5,000	Filings rose slightly in FY 1990–91, rose the next fiscal year, then began a drop that continued for 23 fiscal years.
Effective January 1, 2006[12]	$7,500	Filings dropped in the prior five years, including in the year of the increase, rose slightly in the two full years after the increase, then dropped steadily.
Effective January 1, 2012[13]	$10,000 for natural persons	Filings dropped in the prior three fiscal years, dropped in the fiscal year of the increase, then continued dropping for the next two fiscal years.

5.5.2.2 Illinois

The jurisdictional cap of Small Claims filings was raised twice during the 25-year period, in 1997 and 2006. Both times the total filings and per capita filing levels increased for the next two years, then fell to pre-increase levels. Figures 5.15 and 5.16 display the total filings and per capita filing levels of Small Claims cases for 25 years. The years in which a jurisdictional increase took effect are identified by gray columns.

The jurisdictional cap of Small Claims cases in Illinois is established by Supreme Court rule.[14] In 1981, the jurisdictional cap was increased from $1,000 to $2,500. Sixteen years later the cap was doubled, from $2,500 to $5,000, effective January 1, 1997.

8. 1976 Cal. Stat. ch. 1289, § 2, amending Cal. Code of Civ. Proc. § 116.2(a).
9. 1981 Cal. Stat. ch. 958, § 2, amending Cal. Code of Civ. Proc. § 116.2(a).
10. 1988 Cal. Stat. ch. 481, § 1, amending Cal. Code of Civ. Proc. § 116.2(a).
11. 1990 Cal. Stat. ch. 1683, § 1, amending Cal. Code of Civ. Proc. § 116.2(a); renumbered as § 116.220 by 1990 Cal. Stat. ch. 1305, § 3.
12. 2005 Cal. Stat. ch. 600 (SB 422), § 2, amending Cal. Code of Civ. Proc. § 116.221.
13. 2011 Cal. Stat. ch. 64 (SB 221), § 1, amending Cal. Code of Civ. Proc. § 116.221.
14. Ill. Supreme Court Rules, r. 281.

Total filings rose more than 11 percent in 1997 and were slightly higher in 1998. Total filings dropped in 1999 and 2000 to pre-increase levels and stayed at those levels until the next increase. Per capita filing levels showed a similar pattern.

The cap was doubled again nine years later, from $5,000 to $10,000, effective January 1, 2006. Total filings increased more than 18 percent in 2006, the first full year the increase took effect. Filings rose another 14 percent in 2007. Filings dropped in 2008, but rose again in 2009, almost to the level of 2007. Beginning in 2010, filings dropped every year through 2013. Per capita filing levels followed a similar pattern. Note that the roller coaster pattern apparent in the Figures 5.15 and 5.16 coincides with the Great Recession, so both factors may have affected filing levels. At the end of the 25-year period, both total filings and per capita filing levels were slightly higher than they were in 1996.

FIGURE 5.15 ILLINOIS SMALL CLAIMS TOTAL FILINGS WHEN THE JURISDICTIONAL LIMIT WAS INCREASED

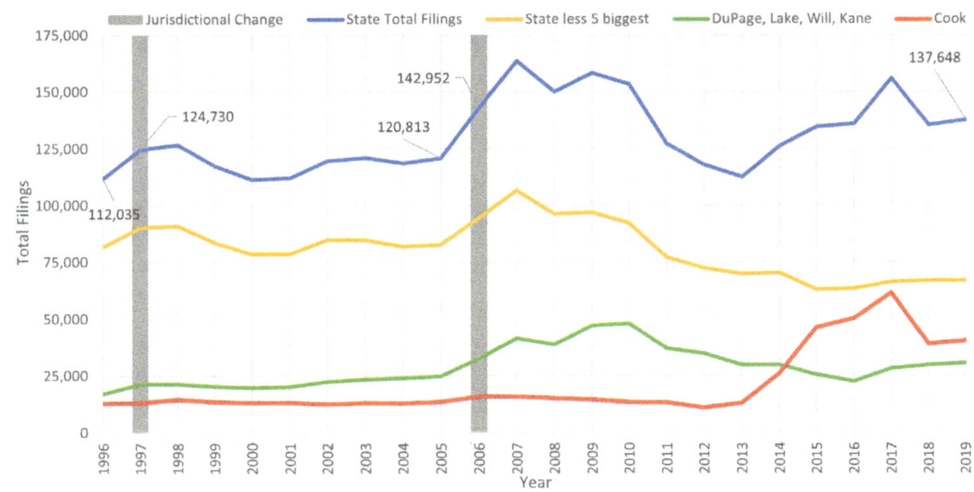

The change in filing levels was not consistent across the state. Figure 5.15 displays total filing levels for the state, for the state without the five single-county circuits, for Cook County, and for the other four one-county circuits. Total filing fluctuations from 1996 to 2005 were mostly due to the multi-county circuits. The single-county circuits were relatively stable. The patterns changed after 2005. The roller coaster pattern spanned from 2006 to 2015–16 for the multi-county circuits and the four single-county circuits, not including Cook County. During this same period, the roller coaster for Cook County was much less pronounced. However, Cook County experienced a surge beginning in 2014 that was not present in the other circuits, bringing it up to roughly the per capita filing rate of the rest of the state. It is not apparent from the filing data alone why it was so low before or why it grew almost to the statewide level by 2017 before falling back somewhat in 2018–19.

FIGURE 5.16 ILLINOIS SMALL CLAIMS FILINGS PER 100K POPULATION WHEN THE JURISDICTIONAL LIMIT WAS INCREASED

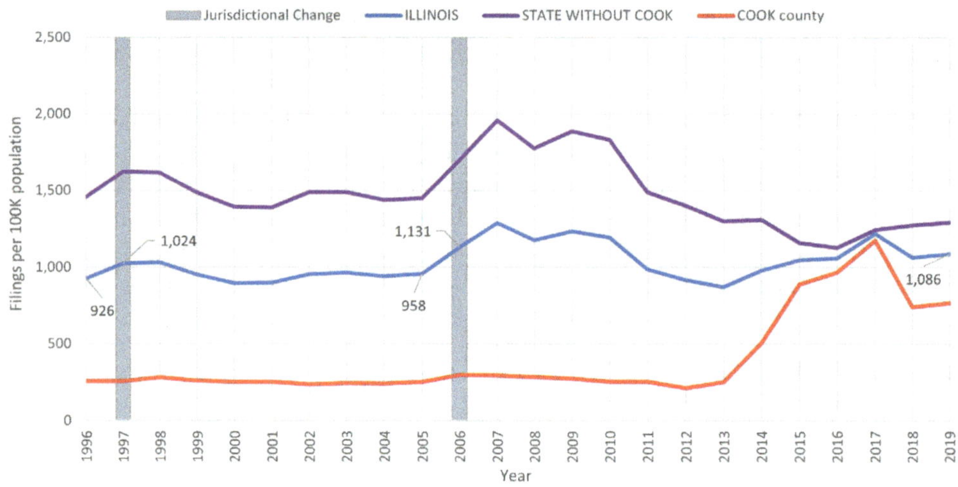

5.5.2.3 Minnesota

During 25 years for which data was made available, two types of changes occurred regarding Conciliation Court jurisdiction: increases in the monetary cap and changes in subject matter jurisdiction. The monetary cap was increased three times over 25 years. Effective July 1, 1994,[15] the dollar cap was changed from $6,000 to $7,500, with a lower cap of $4,000 if the claim involved a consumer credit transaction. The dollar cap was raised to $10,000 effective August 1, 2012,[16] and to $15,000, effective August 1, 2014.[17] The $4,000 cap on consumer credit transaction cases was not changed. Figure 5.17 displays the total filings (blue line) and per capita filing levels (orange line) from 1994 to 2018. The first full year after each increase is noted with gray columns.

After the increase in 1994, total filings were flat for several years, but per capita filings dropped. After the 2012 increase, total filings and per capita filing levels were flat for one year, then dropped the next year. Concerns expressed by several groups about a potential increase in caseloads from raising the limit[18] appear to have been unwarranted. After the 2014 increase, total filings and per capita filing levels dropped in 2015, then rose in each of the next two years. Increases in the monetary cap of Conciliation cases may have slowed the decline in filing levels in the near term, but filings continued to drop over the long term.

---

15. 1993 Minn. Laws ch. 321, § 2, amending 2020 MINN. STAT. § 491A.01 subdiv. 3.

16. 2012 Minn. Laws ch. 283, § 1, amending 2020 MINN. STAT. § 491A.01 subdiv. 3.

17. 2012 Minn. Laws ch. 283, § 2, amending 2020 MINN. STAT. § 491A.01 subdiv. 3a.

18. RECOMMENDATIONS OF THE MINNESOTA SUPREME COURT CIVIL JUSTICE REFORM TASK FORCE, FINAL REPORT 31–33 (Dec. 23, 2011).

FIGURE 5.17 MINNESOTA CONCILIATION FILINGS WHEN THE JURISDICTIONAL LIMIT WAS INCREASED

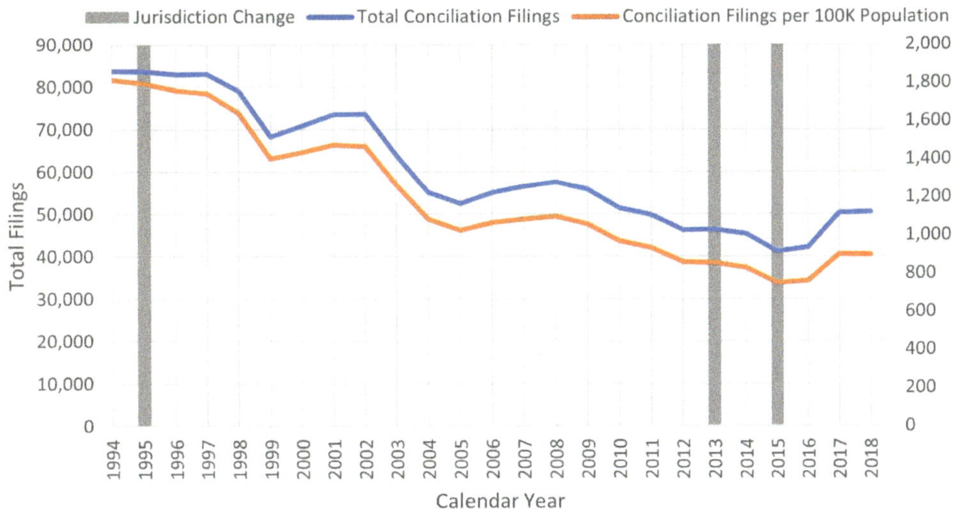

5.5.2.4 Ohio

In Ohio, the jurisdictional ceiling of Small Claims cases was raised twice during the 25 years examined. The ceiling was raised from $2,000 to $3,000, effective July 1, 1997.[19] Looking at Figure 5.18, filings rose slightly the two years before the increase, then dropped in the next two years despite the 50 percent increase in the jurisdictional limit.[20] Filings did start to rise in 2000, and then started a slow and steady decline with a small surge from 2006 to 2008 associated with the Great Recession.

The General Assembly doubled the monetary jurisdiction from $3,000 to $6,000, effective September 28, 2016.[21] There was a small increase in filings of 3 percent in 2017. However, filings then declined for the next two consecutive years, continuing the long-term downward trend in Small Claims filings that began in 2002. Doubling the jurisdictional ceiling of Small Claims did not have a significant or sustained impact on filing levels. It may have slowed the decline for a few years.

19. 121st General Assembly, H.B. 438, §§ 1 and 3; codified in OHIO REV. CODE § 1925.02(A)(1).

20. Data for small claims new filings from 1995 to 1998 were gathered from THE OHIO COURTS SUMMARY 1999, at 215, 246.

21. 131st General Assembly, H.B. 387, § 1; codified in OHIO REV. CODE § 1925.02(A)(1).

FIGURE 5.18 OHIO SMALL CLAIMS FILINGS IN MUNICIPAL AND COUNTY COURTS WHEN THE JURISDICTIONAL LIMIT WAS INCREASED

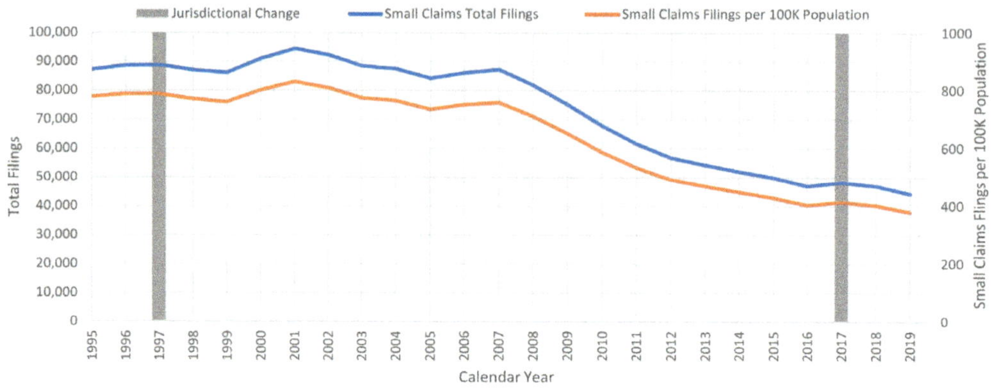

5.5.2.5 Texas

There was one increase in the monetary jurisdiction of Small Claims cases in Texas during the 15 years examined. The monetary cap was raised from $5,000 to $10,000, effective September 1, 2007.[22] Looking at Figure 5.19, total filing levels (blue columns, left-side axis) dropped from 2006 to 2007, were level in 2008 and 2009, then dropped steadily from 2010 to 2012. Per capita filing levels (orange line, right-side axis) exhibited a slow decline that began before 2004, and became steeper in 2010. Doubling the monetary jurisdiction of the Small Claims court did not increase the per capita filing levels of Small Claims cases, but appeared to have slowed the decline for a few years.

FIGURE 5.19 TEXAS SMALL CLAIMS SUITS 2004 TO 2013, JURISDICTIONAL CHANGE SEPTEMBER 1, 2007

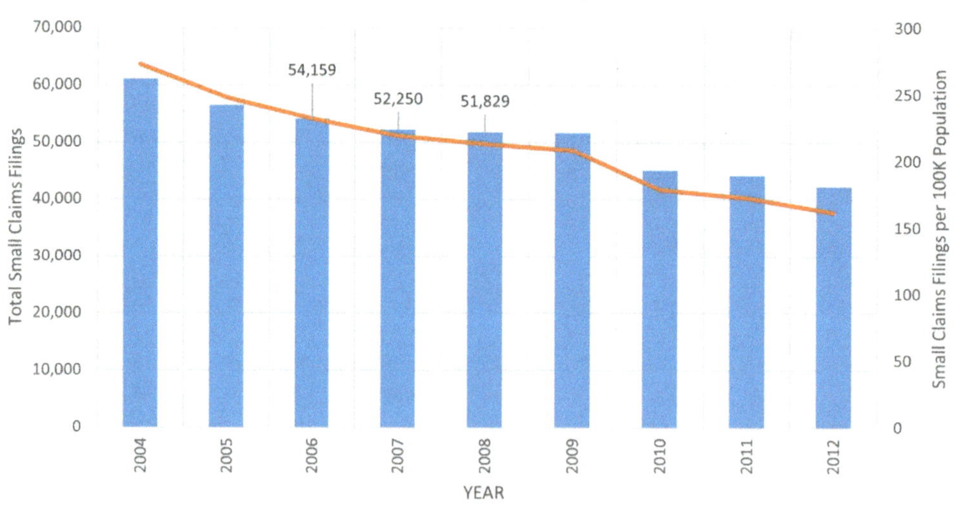

22. 2007 TEX. ACTS 80th Reg. Sess. ch. 383 § 3 (SB 618), amending TEX. GOV'T CODE § 28.003.

The jurisdictional cap was doubled again to $20,000, effective September 1, 2020.[23] A legislative committee analysis of the bill that raised the cap stated: "Increasing the jurisdictional limits for justice courts on matters with no more than $10,000 in dispute to matters with no more than $20,000 would make these speedy, efficient courts available for more Texans."[24] The expectation was that filings would increase. However, any increase appears to have been mooted by the pandemic in 2020—Small Claims filings dropped 18 percent from FY 2019 to FY 2020.

5.6 Changes in Subject Matter Jurisdiction

A change in the subject matter jurisdiction of Small Claims would be expected to change filing levels. An expansion of the types of cases that could be filed as Small Claims matters should increase filing levels, depending on the frequency of these types of cases. Unfortunately, a count of total Small Claims cases without counts of subcategories of cases, makes it difficult to measure the impact of adding another category of cases to small claims courts.

5.6.1 Minnesota

In Minnesota there were two changes in the subject matter jurisdiction of Conciliation Court during the study period. In 2010, the jurisdiction of the Conciliation Court was amended to explicitly include certain types of forfeiture cases and the monetary cap for these cases was set at $15,000.[25] In 2012, the law was amended to add additional types of forfeiture cases.[26] The list of specific forfeiture statutes was removed effective August 1, 2014,[27] as the forfeiture statutes already specified Conciliation Court jurisdiction.[28] Looking at Figure 5.17, filing levels went down in 2011, increased very slightly in 2013, and dropped in 2014 and 2015. Without more detail on changes in filings by nature of action, it does not appear the expansion of jurisdiction to include forfeiture cases increased filing levels.

The second change was the addition of jurisdiction over cases involving a debt owed by a resident to the county.[29] The change became effective in 2016, the year after an increase in the monetary jurisdiction. Without greater detail as to filing number for case subcategories, it was not possible to identify the impact of the expanded subject matter jurisdiction on filing levels versus the increase in the monetary cap. Since filing levels did not change significantly in 2015 or 2106, the impact appeared to have been minimal.

---

23. In the Supreme Court of Texas, Misc. Docket No. 20-9070, amending TEX. R. CIV. PROC. r. 500.3.
24. House Research Organization Bill Analysis, Tex. S.B. 2342, 86th Leg., Reg. Sess. (2019), p. 3, https://hro.house.texas.gov/pdf/ba86r/sb2342.pdf#navpanes=0.
25. 2010 MINN. LAWS ch. 391, § 6.
26. *Id.* at ch. 128, § 15.
27. *Id.* at ch. 283, § 2.
28. For example, in 2020 MINN. STATS. § 609.5314, subdiv. 3(a).
29. 2015 MINN. LAWS ch. 27, § 2, adding § 491A.01, subdiv. 11, https://www.revisor.mn.gov/statutes/cite/491A.01.

5.6.2 Texas

In 1985, the Texas legislature established a separate small claims court in each county,[30] with the cases heard by the justice court judges in the county.[31] In 2011, in response to a proposed reduction in the judiciary budget, the legislature passed a law significantly reorganizing the small claims court.[32] The legislation repealed the old small claims court law as of May 1, 2013,[33] and transferred Small Claims cases to a docket in the justice courts.[34] The Supreme Court was directed to adopt court rules governing the small claims court, including its subject matter jurisdiction.[35]

On September 7, 2011, the Supreme Court appointed a Task Force for Rules in Small Claims cases and justice court proceedings to propose rules as required by the legislation.[36] The Task Force met several times and focused on drafting rules that would maintain existing procedural aspects of the small claims court, in particular, the informality of the proceedings and the ability of the judge to develop a case. In drafting proposed rules, the Task Force considered comments from several outside groups, including the Texas Creditor's Bar Association and Texas Rio Grande Legal Aid. The Task Force submitted its proposed rules in March 2012. The proposals were referred to a Supreme Court Advisory Committee, which met on four days to consider the proposals. The meetings included a public forum where members of the public and representatives of interested organizations could comment on the proposed rules. Based on the proposals and the public meetings, the Supreme Court revised the proposals and adopted court rules effective May 1, 2013.[37]

The changes in the Small Claims Court law and rules resulted in significant changes to the subject matter jurisdiction of Small Claims cases. Prior to September 1, 2013, the subject matter jurisdiction of small claims court included:

> actions by any person for the recovery of money in which the amount involved, exclusive of costs, did not exceed $10,000.[38]

Effective September 1, 2013, several subcategories were added:[39]

> Small Claims Suits filed on or after September 1, 2013 for the recovery of money damages, civil penalties, personal property, or other relief allowed by law. The claim cannot exceed $10,000, excluding statutory interest and court

30. Tex. Gov't Code § 28.001, repealed by 2011 Texas Acts, 82d Leg., 1st C. S., ch. 3, HB 79, § 5.06, effective May 1, 2013 (§ 5.09).

31. Tex. Gov't Code § 28.002, repealed by 2011 Texas Acts, 82d Leg., 1st C. S., ch. 3, HB 79, § 5.06.

32. 2011 Tex. Acts, 82d Leg., 1st C. S., ch. 3, HB 79.

33. 2011 Tex. Acts, 82d Leg., 1st C. S., ch. 3, HB 79, § 5.09.

34. 2011 Tex. Acts, 82d Leg., 1st C. S., ch. 3, HB 79, § 5.02, adding Tex. Gov't Code § 27.060 and § 5.08.

35. 2011 Tex. Acts, 82d Leg., 1st C. S., ch. 3, HB 79, § 5.02, adding Tex. Gov't Code § 27.060 and § 5.07.

36. In the Supreme Court of Texas, Misc. Docket No. 11-9180.

37. In the Supreme Court of Texas, Misc. Docket No. 13-9023. Adoption of Rules for Justice Court Cases.

38. Tex. Gov't Code § 28.003(a), repealed by 2011 Texas Acts, 82d Leg., 1st C. S., ch. 3, HB 79, § 5.06, effective May 1, 2013 per § 5.09.

39. Office of Court Administration, Texas Judicial Council, Official Justice of the Peace Monthly Report Instructions 13, effective Sept. 1, 2013, *rev'd*, Aug. 21, 2014.

costs but including attorney fees, if any. Also included were cases involving occupational licenses, writs of re-entry, tax cases, tax warrants, dangerous dog cases (in which no criminal charges had been filed), tow hearings, habitual toll violator hearings, junk vehicle, deed restriction cases, and bond forfeiture proceedings, but not property hearings heard by magistrates.

And,

Other Civil Suits filed prior to September 1, 2013, that were within the civil jurisdiction of the justice court, including those for recovery of money damages or debt up to $10,000 and for foreclosure of mortgages and enforcement of liens on personal property.

The new categories included several types of cases that were not previously heard in small claims court, including cases that were formerly filed and counted as Other Civil cases in the justice courts.

In 2018, the subcategories were restated as follows:[40]

1. **Small Claims Suits.** Cases filed for the recovery of money damages, civil penalties, personal property, or other relief allowed by law. The claim cannot exceed $10,000, excluding statutory interest and court costs but including attorney fees, if any.

2. **Miscellaneous proceedings** including occupational licenses, bond forfeitures, writs of re-entry, writs of restoration, writs of retrieval, tax cases, tax warrants, dangerous dog cases (in which no criminal charges had been filed), tow hearings, habitual toll violator hearings, junk vehicle, and deed restriction cases.

Because of the significant changes made in 2013, the analysis of Small Claims cases here was bifurcated as of that year. As would be expected, the addition of new case subcategories to the small claims jurisdiction noticeably increased Small Claims filings. Figure 5.20 displays the total filings (green columns) and per capita filing levels (orange line) after the 2013 change. Total filings jumped 44 percent from 2013 to 2014. Total filings then trended slowly upward for the next several years. In 2019, total filings were 57 percent higher than in 2013. Unfortunately, from 2014 to 2018, the annual statistical reports only reported one number for all subcategories of Small Claims cases. Because there was no separate filing numbers for Miscellaneous Proceedings and Small Claims Suits subcategories prior to 2014,[41] it not possible to analyze which case subcategories contributed to the increases noted.

---

40. Annual Statistical Report for the Texas Judiciary for Fiscal Year 2018, Appendix, at ix.
41. Annual Statistical Report for the Texas Judiciary for Fiscal Year 2014, at 116.

FIGURE 5.20 TEXAS SMALL CLAIMS FILINGS

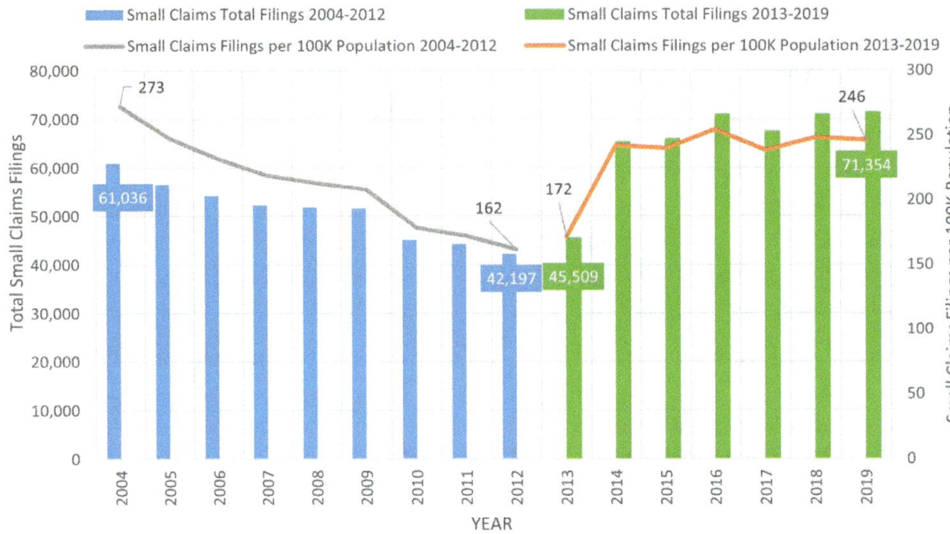

5.7 Impact of Self-Help Services on Small Claims Filing Levels

One of the most disappointing findings of this study was the apparent lack of a significant effect of the expansion of a wide range of self-help assistance provided to small claims litigants on filings. The stated intent of the assistance was to improve access and make the process easier and simpler, and less costly. Presumably, this would increase Small Claims filings, although this was never explicitly stated as a goal.

Despite the expanded range and nature of assistance provided to small claims litigants, per capita filing levels in four of the five states dropped significantly. Only Illinois reported an increase in Small Claims filings. At best, the expansion of assistance may have slowed the decline in four states. However, the variety of potential factors impacting filings and the lack of information about these factors make it difficult to sort out the impact, if any, of the expanded assistance to litigants.

The five states examined here had developed a range of assistance to unrepresented parties, including small claims litigants. There were significant barriers to providing assistance, including limited funding, unauthorized practice of law provisions constraining self-help programs, and the unavailability of lawyers willing to assist in small value cases. Working within these barriers, the five states developed several types of assistance, as follows:

- **Information about Court Processes:** websites (court level and statewide) containing written explanations of court processes and terminology, instructional videos, and referrals to community resources and legal services;
- **Court Forms:** creation of uniform statewide forms, development of plain English forms with minimal "legalese," availability of forms online, fillable PDF forms, savable PDF forms, and e-filing of completed forms;

- **One-On-One Assistance:** help regarding navigating court procedures, review of court forms before filing, court annexed self-help centers, and legal services providers such as legal aid societies, bar associations, volunteer attorneys, law school clinics, public librarians, and private providers;
- **More Modes of Assistance:** step-by-step instructions for completing forms, phone assistance, remote access to forms, information, and assistance, live online chat help, classes providing information or assistance to a group of people, assistance in languages other than English, and workstations at the court or in public libraries that people could use to find information, print court forms, or obtain remote assistance.

The following subsections summarize the extensive programs developed in each of the five states. Despite the range and nature of assistance made available, the most that could be said was that the expanded assistance may have slowed the decline in filings.

5.7.1 California

Over time considerable energy was directed to improving the assistance provided to self-represented litigants, particularly in Small Claims cases. The efforts involved the legislature, Judicial Council and courts, and the state Department of Consumer Affairs. It is not apparent that any of these efforts has been effective in slowing or reversing the long-term decline of Small Claims filings that began in FY 1981–82, especially on a per capita basis.

In 1976 the legislature provided for experimental projects regarding the operations of small claims courts.[42] The intent of the projects was to:

> (a) Establish procedures and programs in the small claims courts . . . to stimulate use of the courts by, and reduce the number of defaults by, untrained individual litigants unfamiliar with the judicial system who might previously considered small claims courts an inconvenient or unnecessary forum for the resolution of disputes; and
>
> (b) Establish systems for data collection and evaluation of these programs and procedures with recommendations for future action.[43]

Legislation in 1978 provided further direction to the Judicial Council and the Department of Consumer Affairs regarding the conduct of the experiments.[44] Five courts were given additional funding to establish or expand self-help centers and to develop materials that could be used by self-help programs in other courts in the state.

A Small Claims Advisor program to assist litigants in Small Claims cases was established in 1978.[45] The law required each county to have a small claims legal advisor who was a lawyer, paralegal, or law student. The advisor was to assist small claims litigants in navigating the small claims process and completing necessary forms to file and prosecute a case at no charge, but the advisor could not appear in court on behalf

42. 1976 Cal. Stats. ch. 1287.
43. Cal. Code of Civ. Proc. § 118, since repealed.
44. 1978 Cal. Stats. ch. 723, §§ 8–14.
45. Cal. Code of Civ. Proc. § 117.18 added by 1978 Cal. Stats. ch. 723, § 4.

of any litigant. Over time the Department of Consumer Affairs,[46] Judicial Council, and local courts increased the type and level of assistance provided to small claims litigants as part of the advisor program.[47]

Legislation in 1991 required the Judicial Council to adopt standard forms for use statewide in Small Claims cases.[48] In 2001, the Judicial Council established a statewide Self Help Center page on its statewide website.[49] All superior courts also developed pages on their websites for self-help specific to that court.[50] By 2003 52 of the 58 courts had developed strategies and tools to better assist self-represented litigants, for example, form completion tools, e-filing of completed forms, written materials explaining court processes, training of court staff to assist litigants, self-help kiosks, and partnering with various organizations to assist litigants.[51]

In 2001, a Judicial Council task force was appointed to develop a statewide action plan to expand court access for self-represented litigants. The Task Force members represented the judiciary, the State Bar of California, trial court administration, court-based self-help centers, county governments, local bar associations, legal services, law libraries, and the public. The task force delivered a report containing an action plan in 2004,[52] which was adopted by the Judicial Council. The action plan recommended that court-based programs collaborate with pro bono programs, local bar associations, public law libraries, law schools, social services agencies, and other legal service providers to provide the types of assistance self-represented litigants needed. The court self-help centers would have staff supervised by an attorney to provide court users information about the applicable laws and court processes, procedures, and operations. The action plan also recommended a state-level system of support of court self-help centers to include resources, training of judges and court staff, and technical assistance. The action plan recommended assistance for all case types, not just Small Claims cases.

The 2001 legislature provided funding to establish five pilot court-based self-help centers to test the effectiveness of different models of providing assistance to self-represented litigants. The five pilot models included (1) providing services to more rural courts using a regional approach, (2) providing services to a Spanish speaking population, (3) providing services in other languages, (4) use of technology to provide

46. *See* California Department of Consumer Affairs, Basic Considerations and Questions, What Is Small Claims Court?, https://www.dca.ca.gov/publications/small_claims/basic_info.shtml.

47. Significant changes were made in amendments to Cal. Code of Civ. Proc. § 117.18 by 1981 Cal. Stats. ch. 958, § 8, and by 1991 Cal. Stats. ch. 1305, § 3, which split the provisions into Cal. Code of Civ. Proc. §§ 116.260 and 116.940. *See also* Cal. R. Ct., r. 3.2120 on small claims advisor assistance.

48. 1991 Cal. Stats. ch 915, § 35, codified at Cal. Code of Civ. Proc. § 116.920.

49. Site with links to all case types https://www.courts.ca.gov/selfhelp.htm, small claims page https://www.courts.ca.gov/selfhelp-smallclaims.htm.

50. Webpage with link to each superior court's small claims legal advisor is located at: https://www.courts.ca.gov/selfhelp-advisors.htm.

51. See, for example, discussions in the California 2004 Annual Report, Preserving Equal Access 7–8 and 22–23; California 2005 Annual Report, Corner Stones of Democracy 14–17; and California 2006 Annual Report, Progress Through Unity 13.

52. Judicial Council of California, Task Force on Self-Represented Litigants, Statewide Action Plan for Serving Self-Represented Litigants, Feb. 2004, www.courtinfo.ca.gov/reference/documents/selfreplitsrept.pdf.

assistance, and (5) coordination of support services in a large urban area. The pilot programs began operations in 2002.

The pilot project program required a comprehensive evaluation of the effectiveness of the programs in order to inform future program and funding decisions. In 2005, an evaluation report was submitted to the legislature covering the model pilot programs.[53] The report documented the effectiveness of the approaches and techniques tested in the pilots. Court proceedings were more efficient and effective and reduced court costs, and litigants were more satisfied with the results. However, a review of the annual Small Claims filings of the seven courts involved in the pilot programs found that all continued to experience drops of both total filings and per capita filing levels during the program period.

A public trust and confidence survey conducted by the Judicial Council in 2005 revealed that the public's perception of small claims court was less positive than for the courts generally.[54] A report on follow-up interviews and focus groups stated: "Defendants in traffic court and small claims litigants complained about long lines and delays in court, overcrowding with other court users, parking cost, and inconvenient court hours."[55] Responses of those interviewed suggested people did not understand the small claims court process, and the confusion and stress reduced their use of the court.

The FY 2005–06 state budget provided additional funding and directed the Judicial Council to allocate the funding to support self-help centers.[56] As required by the legislation, the Judicial Council submitted a report evaluating the Self-Help Centers in 2007.[57] The report concluded that the funding support had "significantly expanded the resources and services available to self-represented litigants throughout the state. All 58 counties in the state now had a basic level of attorney-supervised self-help services, while courts work closely with legal services partners and local resources to develop a true continuum of services for their residents to have meaningful access to the court system."[58] The reports and evaluations did not directly address the issue of Small Claims filing levels in courts.

In 2007, the Judicial Council called for a further study of both the public's sense of procedural justice and for the development of more effective case-processing practices in high-volume cases, including Small Claims.[59] Unfortunately, the study was not completed because of funding cuts made in response to the Great Recession. An interim

---

53. Judicial Council of California, Administrative Office of the Courts, Model Self-Help Pilot Program, A Report to the Legislature, Mar. 2005, https://www.courts.ca.gov/documents/Model-Self-Help-Pilot-Program-March-2005.pdf.

54. Trust and Confidence in the California Courts, Part I: Findings and Recommendations, A Survey of the Public and Attorneys, 2005, at 17.

55. Trust and Confidence in the California Courts, Phase II: Focus Groups and Interviews, Public Court Users and Judicial Branch Members Talk About the California Courts, 2006, at 17–18.

56. Budget Act for FY 2005-2006, 2005 Cal. Stats. ch. 38, at 32, provision 7 of item 0250-101-0932.

57. Judicial Council of California, California Self-help Centers, Report to the California Legislature, June 2007, https://www.courts.ca.gov/documents/LegRpt2007Self-Help.pdf.

58. *Id.* at 8.

59. Judicial Council of California, FACT SHEET, Research Study of Procedural Justice and Effective Court Practices in Small Claims Cases, Aug. 2007, https://www.courts.ca.gov/documents/rspjsm.pdf.

report was issued in 2012.[60] It reported the results of a phone survey of 900 litigants in three large urban courts in Northern California. The report focused mostly on the demographics of the respondents. However, it included the following observation:

> Many parties to small claims cases in the study appear unable to identify their legal disputes with much specificity. This may have important implications for the effectiveness with which these litigants prepare their cases including identifying and gathering pertinent evidence, as well as for the arguments they will need to develop and make in court.[61]

This observation provides one explanation of why the efforts to assist litigants had been less successful than anticipated.

In the 2018–19 fiscal year the legislature almost tripled the amount of funding for self-help centers. The budget also required the Judicial Council to conduct a cost-benefit analysis of self-help services and report to the legislature on its findings by November 2020.[62] The report was to "assess the costs and benefits of each method by which self-help services are provided and . . . also include the impacts of self-help services on trial court operations."[63] The funding was used to open new self-help centers, increase hours of service in other centers, add both attorney and non-attorney staff and bilingual staff in self-help centers, and improve technology infrastructure, including video conferencing. The additional funding was also used to expand services to more case types, especially in eviction and consumer credit matters, and not just in Small Claims cases.

A report to the legislature was submitted in January of 2021.[64] The report described a wide range of services that were added or expanded and several pilot programs to test new delivery approaches. There was also significant expansion of remote services, both because of their demonstrated effectiveness and in response to the pandemic. The number of people served, documents prepared, and assistance provided increased significantly. The report did not discuss the impact of the expansions on case filings specifically. The increase in activities only began in the fall of 2018, so any impact on filings would appear in the later part of FY 2018–19. Although statewide Small Claims filings were down slightly in FY 2018–19, it was too early to assess the impact of the changes on filings. A review of filings in subsequent years would be needed to determine any impact on filings. Unfortunately, the pandemic probably would have suppressed any positive impact.

The impact of all of these efforts to assist litigants in Small Claims cases was disappointing from the perspective of seeking to expand use of the small claims court. As seen in Figure 5.4 since the peak in FY 1981–82, total Small Claims filings had dropped significantly. Statewide per capita filing levels had dropped precipitously, from 2,488 at the peak in FY 1981–82 to 380 in FY 2018–19. As was often the case with changes in procedures and case management practices for other case types, the initial support

---

60. David A. Smith, *Procedural Fairness and Effective Court Practices in Small Claims Cases Study Overview*, OFF. OF COURT RSCH., CAL. ADMIN. OFF. OF THE COURTS, Oct. 2012.

61. *Id.* at 5–6.

62. Budget Act of 2018, 2018 CAL. STATS. ch. 29, item 0250-101-0932, provision 17.

63. *Id.*

64. JUDICIAL COUNCIL OF CALIFORNIA, REPORT TO THE CALIFORNIA LEGISLATURE, IMPACT OF SELF-HELP CENTER EXPANSION IN CALIFORNIA COURTS, Jan. 2021.

of self-represented litigants was increased incrementally, and not uniformly across the state. The more recent efforts involved increases in fiscal support for programs in all courts, although recessions and budget reductions limited the increases. The actions and efforts may yet reverse the decrease in filings. Notwithstanding all of the efforts just noted to improve the experience of small claims litigants and to provide assistance to navigate the process, and the documented success of the efforts, substantially fewer Small Claims cases are being filed now than 40 years ago.

5.7.2 Illinois

Illinois also made considerable efforts similar to those in the other four states to assist litigants in Small Claims cases. Development of these efforts intensified beginning in 2013. Programs and services provided include:[65]

- A statewide small claims website[66] and another website of resources for self-represented litigants[67] with guides and instructions on how to navigate the court system;[68]
- Legal self-help centers located inside courthouses;[69]
- Development of a policy to assist court clerks and court staff on the types of guidance that they were able to offer to self-represented litigants;[70]
- A statewide network of self-represented litigant coordinators launched in December 2017;[71]
- Legal self-help centers located inside courthouses; and
- A small claims mediation program.[72]

Beginning in 2013, standardized statewide small claims forms[73] using plain language were developed through the joint efforts of the Supreme Court Commission on Access to Justice Forms Committee, the Illinois Supreme Court Commission on Access to Justice, and the Access to Justice Division of the Administrative Office of the Illinois Courts. Litigants were required to use these forms. A guided interview process

65. *See* Illinois Annual Report 2020, at 23 and Illinois Courts Annual Report 2019, at 52 & 80.

66. https://www.illinoiscourts.gov/small-claims.

67. For example, *How to File & Serve a Small Claims Complaint & Small Claims Summons*, https://ilcourtsaudio.blob.core.windows.net/antilles-resources/resources/8f0f79db-5797-4fb3-a1ca-cf9c8602a2a0/SMC%20Instructions.pdf. *See also* https://www.illinoiscourts.gov/self-help/.

68. *See* https://www.ilcourthelp.gov/hc/en-us.

69. For example, Cook County's site at: https://www.cookcountycourt.org/FOR-PEOPLE-WITHOUT-LAWYERS/Help-Desks-in-the-Courthouse/cid/237/Fourth-Municipal-District-Maywood.

70. *What Information Can I Provide to Court Patrons?*, https://ilcourtsaudio.blob.core.windows.net/antilles-resources/resources/ac9f2fcf-00dd-483d-9d28-1615f80e72d4/Deskcard-Info_to_Patrons.pdf.

71. Illinois Supreme Court Commission on Access to Justice, Quarterly Newsletter, July 2022, https://ilcourtsaudio.blob.core.windows.net/antilles-resources/resources/b3b5aa0b-0ccc-412d-9f1d-7803a707934a/July%202022%20ATJ%20Newsletter.pdf.

72. Illinois Annual Report 2018, at 58.

73. Standardized small claims complaint forms: https://www.illinoiscourts.gov/documents-and-forms/approved-forms/forms/approved-forms/forms-approved-forms-circuit-court/small-claims-complaint.

for completing the forms was also developed.[74] Finally, the completed forms could be e-filed.[75]

Other state agencies[76] and nongovernmental entities and providers[77] also provided assistance to potential small claims litigants.

Most of these efforts were instituted after 2013. Total Small Claims filings did begin a rise in 2013. However, the steep growth in Small Claims filings in Cook County that began at that time may account for more of the increase than the increased assistance provided to litigants.

5.7.3 Minnesota

Minnesota engaged in several initiatives to assist self-represented litigants in all types of cases, not just civil cases. Instructional videos were created for different case types beginning in 2000.[78] Court forms were made available through a public website beginning in 2002,[79] along with step-by-step instructions for completing the forms. A Forms and Procedures Task Force edited court forms to be legalese-free and in plain English that were introduced in 2004.[80] Conversion of court forms into a fillable, savable Portable Document Format (PDF) format began in 2017.[81] During 2017 development was begun of a 'guide & file interview' tool for initiation of Conciliation Court cases,[82] which became available in 2018.[83]

Self-help centers providing assistance were established in most counties.[84] The services provided by the centers included: videos on how to represent yourself in court, online tools for filling out forms, brief legal advice from volunteer attorneys, one-on-one help to learn court procedures, one-on-one review of court forms, and referrals to community resources and legal services.[85] Some judicial districts also implemented remote access to self-help services in addition to in-person services.[86] Beginning in 2008, courts made available self-help workstations people could use to find court information, print court forms, and talk over the phone with statewide self-help center staff about forms,

---

74. https://www.illinoislegalaid.org/legal-information/small-claims-complaint.

75. https://www.illinoiscourts.gov/eservices/efileil/. Over the past two years the Illinois Administrative Office of the Courts has been collecting information on "pain points" associated with the e-filing process.

76. For example, the Illinois Attorney General, https://ag.state.il.us/consumers/smlclaims.html.

77. For example, Illinois Legal Aid Online, https://www.illinoislegalaid.org/, and other providers, such as https://www.lawyers.com/legal-info/research/illinois/illinois-small-claim.html, and https://www.freeadvice.com/legal/illinois-small-claims-court/, and https://www.smallclaimsfiling.com/illinois/.

78. Minnesota Judicial Branch Annual Report, 1999–2000, at 17.

79. Minnesota State Courts 2001–2002 Annual Report, at 9.

80. Minnesota Judicial Branch 2004 Annual Report, at 18.

81. Minnesota Judicial Branch, A Report to the Community, The 2017 Annual Report, at 11.

82. *Id.* at 11–12.

83. Minnesota Judicial Branch, A Report to the Community, The 2018 Annual Report, at 9.

84. Authorized by Minn. Gen. R. Prac., r. 110, eff. Jan. 1, 2004. See, for example, discussion in Minnesota State Courts 2001–2002 Annual Report, at 7, and feature of Hennepin's Self Help Center in the Minnesota Judicial Branch 2005 Annual Report, at 11.

85. Minnesota Judicial Branch, A Report to the Community, The 2009 Annual Report, at 10.

86. Sheldon Clark, *Evaluating Remote Technology Options to Increase Self-Help Center Access*, 2019 Trends in State Courts, NCSC, at 54–59.

procedures, and legal resources. These workstations were available in 89 courthouse and library locations across Minnesota by 2017.[87]

A new statewide web page for the judicial branch[88] was introduced in 2006 that included a new self-help center with information and links to legal resources to assist those who chose to represent themselves in court.[89] A statewide virtual self-help center was established in 2008, including a self-help website that included an option to get one-on-one help via telephone or email from specially trained court staff.[90] By 2009, public service computer terminals with a phone connection to the statewide self-help center had been installed in all courthouses.[91] Assistance through the statewide website was also provided in English, Spanish, Hmong, and Somali.[92] Availability of e-filing and access to electronic documents was expanded beginning in 2013.[93]

Several organizations not affiliated with the judicial branch also provided assistance to people. Some agencies offered help for specific types of problems, for example, housing.[94] There was also an interactive website at LawHelpMN.org[95] that assisted people to find resources that addressed a variety of legal problems on a statewide basis. The site provided explanatory summaries of how to deal with certain legal problems. The site also walked the user through the process of completing some simple forms. Additionally, the website offered live online chat with an agency employee to assist in navigating the system.

Minnesota was one of seven states to receive funding from the Public Welfare Foundation to develop a Justice for All strategic action plan for providing everyone access to effective assistance regarding their essential civil legal needs. A Justice for All Steering Committee was established that issued a strategic plan in December 2017 with five strategic goals.[96] Since implementation was only beginning in 2018, it was too early to assess any impact of this initiative on filing levels.

In addition to the statewide assistance to self-represented litigants described earlier, each district court was required to provide certain types of assistance to conciliation court litigants as follows:

> Under the supervision of the conciliation court judges, the court administrator shall explain to litigants the procedure and functions of the conciliation court and shall on request assist them in filling out all forms and pleading necessary for the presentation of their claims or counterclaims to the court. . . .[97]

---

87. Minnesota Judicial Branch, Report to the Community Spring 2017, at 12.

88. www.mncourts.gov/selfhelp.

89. Minnesota Judicial Branch, *supra* note 87, at 7–8 and 12.

90. Minnesota Judicial Branch, A Report to the Community, The 2008 Annual Report, at 8.

91. Minnesota Judicial Branch, A Report to the Community, The 2009 Annual Report, at 10.

92. Minnesota Judicial Branch, A Report to the Community, The 2010 Annual Report, at 10.

93. Minnesota Judicial Branch, A Report to the Community, The 2013 Annual Report, at 5–6.

94. *See* Call for Justice, LLC, *Legal Resources Cheat Sheet*, updated Feb. 12, 2015.

95. The website was managed by Legal Services State Support, a project of the Minnesota Legal Services Coalition, a group of seven legal aid programs that help low-income residents with a variety of legal matters, https://www.lawhelpmn.org/about-us.

96. Minnesota Judicial Branch, Minnesota State Bar Association, and Minnesota Legal Services Corporation, Strategic Action Plan, Minnesota Justice for All Project, Dec. 2017.

97. 2020 Minn. Stats. §491A.02 subdiv. 2. *See also* Minn. Gen. R. Prac., tit. VI, r. 504(b).

A Uniform Statement of Claim form has been available at least since 1993,[98] although claimants were not required to use the form.[99] In 2008, Turbo Court, a private vendor, offered a web portal for conciliation court litigants that included document preparation and assembly and an e-filing capability. However, usage was reported to be low.[100]

As was seen in California, the extensive self-help assistance developed in Minnesota did not appear to increase conciliation filings. Both total filings and per capita filing levels had steadily dropped since 1994. There was a 19 percent increase in 2017, but filings were still below the level of 2010. There was a negligible increase in 2018. Self-help assistance did not appear to have driven, or sustained, an increase in use of conciliation court in terms of filings.

5.7.4 Ohio

In 2004, a Task Force on Pro Se and Indigent Litigants was established to examine how Ohio courts could better serve those who could not afford an attorney or chose to represent themselves. The Task Force submitted its final report in 2006.[101] The recommendations in the final report regarding civil cases sought to: increase pro bono representation by private attorneys; improve access to the court system by litigants who chose to represent themselves; and increase resources for legal aid, pro bono, and court-based pro se assistance.[102] Recommendations to improve access included development of standard forms useable in any court in the state, plain language instructions for use with the forms, and providing access to these documents through the state judiciary website.[103] The report noted that the Futures Commission had made similar recommendations in its 2000 report.[104]

The 2006 Task Force report also recommended the development of self-help centers in courts to assist litigants and development of other information to better inform litigants about courts.[105] It also recommended that lawyers be allowed to provide "unbundled" services or limited representation to self-represented litigants.[106] The Task Force also noted the need to increase funding for legal aid services for civil litigants and proposed sources of funding.[107]

A Task Force on Access to Justice was established in July 2014 and issued a final report in March 2015. The Task Force was formed in response to the drastic decline in

---

98. Minn. Gen. R. Prac., tit. VI, r. 507(b).

99. Minn. Gen. R. Prac., tit. VI, r. 507(a).

100. Access and Service Delivery 2 Committee, Report to Minnesota Judicial Council, December 14, 2009, Appendix P.

101. Report and Recommendations of the Supreme Court of Ohio Task Force on Pro Se & Indigent Litigants, Apr. 2006 [hereinafter 2006 Task Force].

102. 2006 Task Force 9–25.

103. 2006 Task Force, Recommendations 21–30, at 15–20.

104. Ohio Courts Future Commission, at 20–21, 25, 38–41, and 57–61.

105. 2006 Task Force, Recommendation 31, at 21.

106. 2006 Task Force, Recommendation 39, at 25–36.

107. 2006 Task Force, Recommendations 40 and 46–51, at 36 and 42–44.

funding for civil legal services and the continuing need for legal services as a result of the Great Recession. The directives to the task force were to:[108]

(1) Identify gaps in and obstacles to accessing the civil justice system in Ohio;
(2) Review those entities established by other states to address access to justice issues;
(3) Determine whether the creation of a Supreme Court operated or affiliated entity focused upon access to justice would assist in addressing or resolving the gaps in and obstacles to accessing the civil justice system in Ohio;
(4) If the creation of such entity was suggested, present recommendations concerning the organizational structure, membership, and responsibilities of the entity.

The 2015 Task Force recommendations mirrored those of the earlier 2006 Task Force report. They included creation of a statewide website to inform and assist self-represented litigants, creation of self-help centers, more standardized forms, allowing limited scope representation, and increasing pro bono legal help. The 2015 Task Force included a table indicating the extent of implementation of the 2006 Task Force report recommendations.[109] For many of the recommendations there had been only limited implementation and there was no action on several recommendations. In 2017, a "Civil Justice Program Fund" was established to provide legal assistance and increased access to assistance for Ohioans' civil legal needs.[110] In 2018 grants were made to several organizations as part of this program.[111]

The Task Force reports did not provide information about the number or percentage of cases in which pro se or indigent litigants were involved. Nor did either discuss possible impacts of their recommendations on the number of filings.

The 2015 Task Force report resulted in the development of a strategic plan for creation of a new statewide legal information website and reconstituting of the Ohio Legal Assistance Foundation as the Supreme Court's Access to Justice Commission. The website is now in operation and has been an important asset for the judicial branch in its response to the pandemic.

Notwithstanding the Task Force efforts and implementation, Small Claims filings have declined steadily since at least 2007.

5.7.5 Texas

Texas also took a number of steps to assist small claims litigants, but they were more recent and not yet as extensive as in the other states. A statewide website was established by the State Law Library in 2013 that was available to self-represented litigants. There was a web page for information related to small claims court[112] that includes links

108. Report and Recommendations of the Supreme Court of Ohio Task Force on Access to Justice, Mar. 2015, at 1 [hereinafter 2015 Task Force].

109. 2015 Task Force, Appendix F, at 91–97.

110. The Ohio Supreme Court of Ohio, 2017 Annual Report 20.

111. The Ohio Supreme Court of Ohio, 2018 Annual Report 17.

112. How to Sue in Justice Court (Small Claims Court), https://texaslawhelp.org/article/how-to-sue-in-justice-court-small-claims-court.

to a guide about how to sue in justice court,[113] forms,[114] and links to general information about Small Claims cases provided by other providers who had websites to assist.[115] As of 2017, in addition to the statewide assistance, the clerks of all courts were required to provide links on their court's website to the texaslawhelp.org website, the State Law Library's website, and to conspicuously display in the clerk's office in a location frequently accessed by the public a sign with the information about the website and links.[116] Court clerks were also authorized to establish a self-help center to provide resources to county residents representing themselves in legal matters.[117]

In 1997, the legislature authorized the collection of a filing fee by the appellate courts to provide basic civil legal services to indigent litigants.[118] The Supreme Court, assisted by the Texas Equal Access to Justice Foundation, administered the funding for the Basic Civil Legal Services program.[119]

In June 2017, the Texas Judicial Council established a Civil Justice Committee to review the Texas judicial system and recommend necessary reforms to improve access to civil justice. In its June 2018 report, the Committee made a number of recommendations to expand the resources available to self-represented litigants.[120] The report mentioned the creation of the texascourthelp.gov website, but noted that the site contained few forms or services. One recommendation was to work with appropriate stakeholder groups to increase the number of legal forms available on the site for use by self-represented litigants. Other recommendations were to establish a platform to connect self-represented litigants with attorneys, mediators, and other legal services who could assist them and to allow litigants to appear remotely when appropriate. The committee also recommended that the legislature increase funding for civil legal aid services throughout the state to assist litigants who could not afford an attorney.

Most of these changes were recent, and occurred at the same time as other changes in the small claim court jurisdiction and operations. Consequently, it is not yet possible to associate any changes in filing levels with these actions.

5.8 Whither Small Claims?

The decline in Small Claims filings is the most striking and consistent pattern found in our study. It is clearly time for another national study of small claims courts to attempt to identify a cause or causes for the almost universal filings decline shown in our data. This is the place where public trust and confidence in the state courts seems to be most

---

113. How to Sue in Justice Court, https://www.texasbar.com/AM/Template.cfm?Section=Consumer_and_Tenant_Rights1&Template=/CM/ContentDisplay.cfm&ContentID=24859.

114. *See* Civil Procedure forms, https://www.tjctc.org/tjctc-resources/forms.html.

115. For example, Texas State Law Library, https://guides.sll.texas.gov/small-claims. Nolo Press https://www.nolo.com/legal-encyclopedia/texas-small-claims-court-32055.html, and People's Lawyer http://www.peopleslawyer.net/legal-topics/small-claims-court.html.

116. Tex. Gov't Code § 51.808.

117. Tex. Local Gov't Code § 323.023(b)(4).

118. Tex. Gov't Code, ch 51, subch. J. In 1999, the subchapter was re-lettered as Subchapter L.

119. Tex. Gov't Code § 51.943.

120. Texas Judicial Council, Civil Justice Committee, Report and Recommendations, June 2018, recommendation 14.

at risk—where the public has stopped using the procedure most clearly established to meet their needs.

It is hard to attribute the consistent filings decrease to changes in the debt collection process, such as debt buying, since the filings decline is similar for states that allow and states that do not allow the filing of debt collection cases in small claims courts.

It is possible that the gradual adoption of mandatory arbitration clauses in standard banking, credit card, and consumer purchasing agreements has diverted increasing segments of ordinary, small dollar disputes from use of the courts. It is also possible that changes in business practices regarding disputes, particularly online businesses, and the willingness to address problems with sales and automatically accept returns could explain some of the drop in filings. These issues would be worth explicit exploration in a small claims court study.

6

Implementation of New Case Management Programs

6.1 Overview

Another source of possible effects on filing practices were changes in how a court manages its cases, known as case flow management (CFM). Several new CFM programs were implemented in the five states during the time frames studied here, usually in response to criticisms of court delay or the high costs of litigation. Although directed at improving the pace of litigation or reducing costs of litigation, these programs could also result in changes in filing levels. One theory would predict an increase in filings, as cases were now less expensive to prosecute and would proceed more quickly. A contrary theory would predict a reduction in filings, at least initially, because of new procedures and perceived new barriers these programs added.

The CFM programs discussed here had different labels and a variety of characteristics. Descriptions included "delay reduction programs," "expedited litigation," "expedited actions," and "economical litigation project." Four of the five states in this study also established some type of case management program for hearing cases that required unusually high levels of judicial attention, referred to as "complex," "commercial," or "business" courts. The goals of all of these programs included delay reduction, reducing the cost of litigation, improving the efficiency of civil case processing, providing resolutions more relevant to the parties, or expanding access to justice. The program characteristics generally included early and continuous management of cases by the judge to whom the case was assigned, differentiated case management, specialized dockets, and streamlined procedures, for example, limitations on discovery or motions, and so on. Changes in filing levels were not an explicit goal or expectation of the programs.

Evaluations of these new CFM programs often found a positive impact on the pace or cost of litigation. Rarely did the studies observe or comment on any changes in filing levels.

Several aspects of the new CFM programs made it difficult to assess changes in filing levels associated with their implementation. Generally the changes in case management practices were first introduced in a few pilot courts, then expanded to more courts, or all courts, after the efficacy of the change was accepted. Starting with pilot courts then expanding statewide made the impact on statewide filing levels less obvious. Testing in pilot projects, followed by expansion to other courts, sometimes occurred simultaneously with other changes in the law or the justice system environment that made it difficult to assess whether filing level changes were attributable to the new CFM program or to some other factor.

A further complicating factor was whether the program was mandatory for certain cases, or required the consent of all parties. The Minnesota Civil Justice Reform Task Force noted new CFM programs were often ineffective if they required the consent of all parties, which was seldom forthcoming. This was also a factor resulting in the limited success of California's Expedited Jury Trial program. All parties were not willing to agree to the limitations in the allowed length of testimony. The NCSC Landscape study also found that opt-in programs were underused.[1]

Assessing whether filing levels changed when a new CFM program began was also complicated if the program only applied to a specific category of case that was not separately counted in filing reports. Some CFM programs only applied to a specific case category that involved only a small volume of cases, for example, toxic torts. Because there were so few cases, the change in statewide filings might be negligible, even if there was a clear change in filing levels of the specific case subcategory.

Finally, a new CFM program might suffer from a lack of cooperation from some judges concerned about of a negative impact on their individual caseload. This arose in trial courts where judges were randomly assigned new cases at the time of filing for which they were responsible from filing to resolution, referred to as individual or direct calendaring. If a new CFM program reduced the caseload of the judge to whom a case was assigned, the other judges on the court would receive more cases, which some might perceive would impose a greater, possibly unfair, burden on their caseloads.

6.1.1 Summary of Findings

Three of the six states studied here implemented new CFM programs on a statewide basis during the time period we studied. Some began as pilot projects in a few courts and then were implemented on a statewide basis after the benefits were acknowledged. In addition, some trial courts within the states implemented new CFM programs locally. Only one of the evaluations of the programs specifically noted any changes in filing levels. In some instances, there was a short-term increase in filing levels associated with a new CFM program. More often, there was a reduction in preprogram filing levels.

---

1. Nat'l Ctr. for State Courts, The Landscape of Civil Litigation in State Courts 36 (2016).

In California, an increase in filing levels was associated with a new program to improve case processing of lower-value civil cases. New, simpler procedures for lower-value civil cases, referred to as the Economical Litigation Program, took effect in FY 1983–84. In the two fiscal years preceding the new law there was a slight drop in filings. In the fiscal year in which the law took effect, a slow rise in filings began. Filing levels continued to increase for the next several years, although an increase in the monetary jurisdiction cap a few years later may have contributed to the increase in filing levels, as discussed in Chapter 7.

In 1988, California began a pilot program to reduce case processing times and the cost of litigation for high-value civil cases based on legislation referred to as the Trial Court Delay Reduction Act. There were nine mandatory pilot courts and ten volunteer courts. Eight of the nine pilot courts were experiencing declining civil filings before the program began, which continued after the program started. In three of the nine pilot courts there was a significant step down in filing levels during the first year of the program, ranging from a quarter to a third of the previous monthly filing average. Intriguingly, the cases that would have been expected based on past filing levels appeared to have "disappeared." There was no corresponding increase in Limited Civil filings in the municipal and justice courts in the three counties, and filings did not return to pre-pilot levels in subsequent years. A similar pattern of a decline in filings was found in the ten voluntary courts. Eight of the ten voluntary courts experienced a general decline in high-value case filings that continued after the program began. Four of the ten showed a step down in filing levels after the start of the program. In many of the participating courts, civil filings spiked the month before the program started, and dipped in the first month of the program, suggesting some attorneys filed some cases before the program began so as not to be subject to the program. While the programs were successful in reducing case processing times, they did not encourage the filing of high-value civil cases.

In response to the success of the pilot programs, California expanded the provisions of the Trial Court Delay Reduction Act to all superior courts beginning in July 1992. Statewide total civil filings and per capita filings were lower in the fiscal year the program began than in the preceding fiscal year. Filings rose very slightly in the second fiscal year of the program, but then resumed a long-term decline that had begun in FY 1986–87, before the start of the program.

In 2009, at the request of the Minnesota legislature, the Chief Justice convened a Civil Justice Forum to examine civil justice practices in search of new efficiencies and potential cost savings. In 2010, as a result of the Forum's work, the Chief Justice established a Civil Justice Reform Task Force to review civil justice reforms proposed in other states and make recommendations for court changes that would facilitate more effective and efficient case processing in Minnesota. In 2013, the Supreme Court established the Expedited Litigation Track (ELT) pilot program, also referred to as the "rocket docket." The objectives of the program were to improve the efficiency of civil case processing for certain categories of civil cases, reduce costs, and provide resolutions more relevant to the parties. Based on the filing data available in the pilot courts, there was no increase in filings associated with the ELT program. Rather, filings continued to drop, and, in some courts, dropped even faster.

In 2011, the Texas legislature passed a law reforming certain remedies and procedures in civil actions. The law required the Texas Supreme Court to adopt rules to promote the prompt, efficient, and cost-effective resolution of civil actions in which the total amount in controversy did not exceed $100,000. The Supreme Court adopted rules for an Expedited Actions program effective March 1, 2013. An evaluation of cases filed before and after the adoption of the rules in five county courts found an overall positive impact on civil case processing in the courts, but did not address any change in filing levels. A follow-up evaluation suggested the program was not widely adopted by judges and lawyers. Analysis of statewide filings suggested an initial, short-lived, flattening of filing levels of Injury/damage and Contract and Debt case categories.

Evaluations of the complex/commercial/business courts also found that the programs met the goal of managing complex cases more efficiently and effectively. However, the evaluations provided little filing data from which to assess whether the existence of these programs increased filings, or slowed the decline in filings, of complex cases or total civil filings.

In July of 2016, the Conference of Chief Justices and Conference of State Court Administrators adopted a resolution supporting a National Civil Justice Initiative.[2] The initiative was dedicated to developing a national repository of research, implementation tools, and links to state efforts to support civil justice reform.[3] All of the five states here began reform efforts associated with this initiative.[4] Because many of the programs involved only a few pilot courts, or were initiated toward the end of the period for which data was made available, it was not yet possible to assess changes in statewide civil filings associated with the new programs.

6.2 California Trial Court Delay Reduction Act

The most extensive delay reduction program in the five states during the period for which data was made available was in California. The statewide implementation of a trial court delay reduction program initially reduced filings of higher-value civil cases. Filing levels of lower-value civil cases appeared to be unchanged, suggesting many presumably mid-value civil cases previously filed as Unlimited civil cases were not filed. They appear to have disappeared.

In 1986, the California Legislature adopted the Trial Court Delay Reduction Act[5] (TCDRA) to address the delay in resolving civil litigation in the superior courts. The TCDRA directed the Judicial Council of California (JCC) to adopt standards for the timely disposition of civil and criminal cases. It also required the JCC to identify the nine most delayed superior courts in the state regarding civil cases, referred to as

2. See CCJ and COSCA Resolution 8, *In Support of the Call to Action and Recommendations of the Civil Justice Improvements Committee to Improve Civil Justice in State Courts* (adopted at the Annual Meeting, July 27, 2016), HTTPS://CCJ.NCSC.ORG/__DATA/ASSETS/PDF_FILE/0017/23480/07272016-SUPPORT-CALL-ACTION-RECOMMENDATIONS-CJI.PDF.

3. Materials on the national civil justice initiative can be found at https://www.ncsc.org/cji/about-this-project.

4. See each state's description, https://iaals.du.edu/action-ground?project_type=70.

5. Trial Court Delay Reduction Act of 1986 (AB 3300), 1986 Cal. Stat. ch. 1335, codified at Cal. Gov't Code §§ 68600 *et seq.*

the pilot courts. The pilot courts were to implement delay reduction programs on or before January 1, 1988. The legislation authorized all other superior courts to voluntarily implement delay reduction programs, and ten other superior courts chose to do so, referred to as the voluntary courts.

The TCDRA did not mandate any particular form of calendar or case management for the delay reduction programs, leaving it up to each pilot court. However, the TCDRA required the judges in the pilot courts to "actively monitor, supervise and control the movement of all cases assigned to the program from the time of filing of the first document invoking court jurisdiction through final disposition."[6] The pilot courts were to designate at least four judges to participate in the program. The TCDRA did not specify which civil case categories were to be included in the pilot program, again, leaving it up to each pilot court. The pilot courts were required to include both existing cases and new filings in their programs.

The TCDRA required the JCC to collect and publish statistics regarding compliance with the adopted time standards and to report to the legislature on the progress of the programs. The JCC contracted with the National Center for State Courts (NCSC) to analyze the nine pilot courts after the first year of implementation and produce a report on their progress.[7] JCC staff continued to review the results of both the nine pilot courts and the ten voluntary courts and produced a report in July 1991[8] summarizing the results of the pilot and voluntary programs and making recommendations to the legislature. Based on the success of the pilot and voluntary programs, the TCDRA was made permanent by the legislature,[9] and was applicable to all civil cases in all superior courts, effective July 1, 1992.[10]

The focus of the TCDRA was on the pace of civil litigation in Unlimited Civil cases—the higher-value civil cases. The TCDRA made no mention of filings. However, it was unlikely there would be no changes in filing levels. One hypothesis was the increased requirements placed on litigants and lawyers to comply with continuous monitoring by the court would increase the cost of litigation, possibly discouraging filings, or resulting in some cases being filed as Limited Civil cases, which had less burdensome procedures. Another hypothesis was that the improved pace of litigation would speed any recovery and might reduce the cost of litigation, thus encouraging filings, or shift filings from Limited Civil to Unlimited Civil.

Looking at statewide filings, total Unlimited Civil filings and per capita filing levels had been falling for several fiscal years before the TCDRA pilot program began (Figure 6.1). Filings dropped during the pilot program period (1988 to 1991), which also coincided with the Savings and Loan recession discussed in Chapter 9. When delay reduction was implemented in all superior courts in July 1992, total filings and per capita

---

6. Cal. Gov't Code § 68608(a).

7. Alexander B. Aikman, Heidi Schmidt Green & Marilyn Callaway, *Improving the Pace of Litigation in California, The First Year's Results*, Western Reg'l Off., Nat'l Ctr. for State Courts, Mar. 1989.

8. Judicial Council of California, Administrative Office of the Courts, Prompt and Fair Justice in the Trial Courts, Report to the Legislature on Delay Reduction in the Trial Courts, July 1991, 3 vols. [hereinafter Prompt and Fair Justice].

9. Trial Court Delay Reduction Act, 1990 Cal. Stat, ch. 1232, §§ 2–3 (AB 3820), codified at Cal. Gov't Code §§ 68600 *et seq.* and Cal. R. Ct. 3.720 *et seq.* (formerly Cal. R. Ct. 2100 *et seq.*).

10. Cal. Gov't Code § 68605.5.

filing levels were lower in the fiscal year of implementation than in the preceding year. Filings rose very slightly in the next fiscal year of the program, but were still below the filing level the year before statewide implementation. In FY 1994–95, the third year after statewide implementation, the decline in Unlimited Civil filings that had begun in FY 1986–87, before the program was contemplated, resumed, and filings continued to fall for the next four fiscal years.

FIGURE 6.1 CALIFORNIA UNLIMITED CIVIL FILINGS—TRIAL COURT DELAY REDUCTION ACT (TCDRA) PILOT BEGAN JANUARY 1, 1988, EXPANDED STATEWIDE JULY 1, 1992

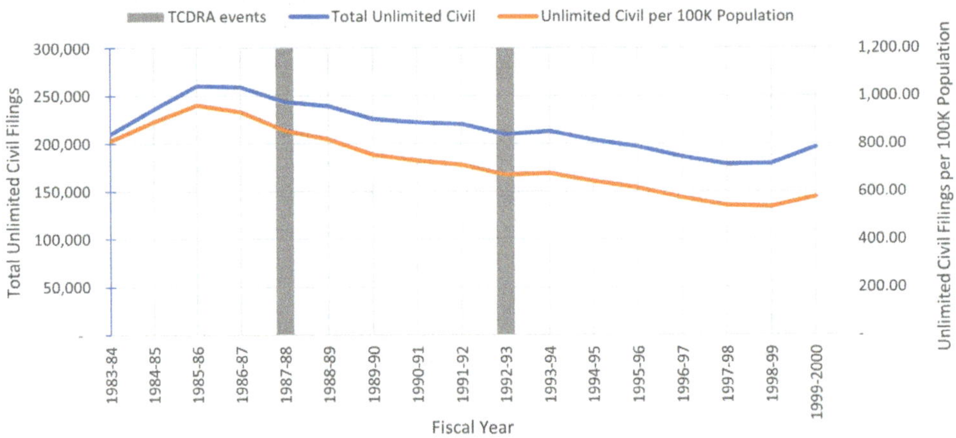

The 1991 JCC report to the legislature reviewed civil filings in both the pilot and voluntary courts. Filings in calendar 1987, the 12 months preceding the start of a delay reduction program, were compared to the first 12 months of the program, calendar 1988.[11] In seven of the nine pilot courts, civil filings spiked the month before the program started, and dipped in the first month of the program, suggesting some attorneys filed some cases before the program began on the erroneous assumption that their cases would not to be subject to the program. Looking more broadly, eight of the nine pilot courts were experiencing declining civil filings before the program began, which continued after the program started. In three of the nine pilot courts there was a significant step down in filing levels during the first year of the program, ranging from a quarter to a third of the previous monthly filing average. Disturbingly, many cases that previously might have been filed appeared to have "disappeared," as there was no corresponding increase in Limited Civil filings in the municipal and justice courts in the counties where the superior court filing levels dropped (Figure 6.2).

11. PROMPT AND FAIR JUSTICE vol. 1, at II-38 to II-43.

FIGURE 6.2 CALIFORNIA LIMITED CIVIL FILINGS, ELP PILOT STARTED JANUARY 1, 1978, MANDATORY JULY 1, 1983; TCDRA APPLICABLE STATEWIDE JULY 1, 1992

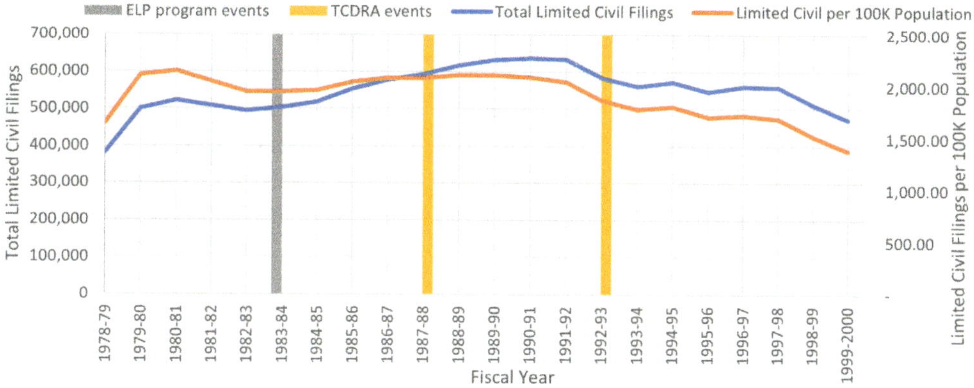

Similar filing patterns were found in the ten voluntary courts, although not as pronounced.[12] Five of the ten voluntary courts showed a spike in filings just before the program and a dip at the start of the program. Four of the ten showed a step down in filing levels after the start of the program. In eight of the ten voluntary courts, the program was instituted in the midst of a general decline in filings that continued after the program began.

Overall, high-value Unlimited Civil filing levels declined, sometimes significantly, when the delay reduction programs involving strong judicial control of the pace of litigation were implemented. Existing declines in filing levels continued. Fewer higher-value case filings did not result in more filings in the court hearing the lesser-value cases. The mid-value civil cases just were not being filed in court anymore.

6.3 California Economical Litigation Project

In 1976, the California legislature adopted legislation establishing a pilot program with simplified civil procedure laws for the lesser-value Limited Civil cases.[13] The law was known as the Economical Litigation Program (ELP). As spelled out in legislative findings, the objective of the pilot program was to experiment with simplified procedural law in order to reduce the cost of litigation.[14] The new procedures simplified pleadings, limited discovery and pre-trial motions, and modified trial proceedings. The legislation required the JCC to adopt rules of court to implement new procedures outlined in the legislation. The pilot program legislation became effective on January 1, 1978. The pilot program began in the superior and municipal courts in Fresno County and one branch court location (Torrance) of the Los Angeles Superior Court.[15]

12. Prompt and Fair Justice, at IV-7 to IV-13.
13. 1976 Cal. Stat. ch. 960, codified in Cal. Code of Civ. Proc. §§ 1823–1833.2.
14. Cal. Code of Civ. Proc.§ 1823.
15. Cal. Code of Civ. Proc. § 1823.1 and Cal. R. Ct. r. 1711(a) and r. 1811(a).

Legislation in 1982 made the procedures developed in the pilots applicable to all Limited Civil cases in all municipal and justice courts.[16] The statewide provisions took effect on July 1, 1983, and did not apply to small claims cases or unlawful detainer cases.

Preliminary results from the pilot projects in Fresno and Los Angeles found very little change in filing levels.[17] In the two fiscal years before the law took effect, statewide filing levels, both total and per capita, dropped slightly (Figure 6.2). In FY 1983–84, the fiscal year in which the law took effect statewide, a slow rise in filings began. The increase continued, buoyed by the increase in jurisdictional limit in FY 1985–86 discussed in Chapter 7. Per capita filings peaked in FY 1988–89, and total filings peaked in FY 1990–91. Filings then declined, although this coincided with the Savings and Loan crisis, discussed in Chapter 9. The increase in Limited Civil filings at the end of the 1980 decade appeared to be associated with the adoption of the simplified procedures for these cases.

6.4 California Expedited Jury Trial Program

In 2010, the California legislature adopted the Expedited Jury Trial Act (EJT),[18] which established a simplified jury trial process for lower-value Limited Civil cases. The expedited procedures involved smaller juries and fewer peremptory challenges. It also limited voir dire and case presentation to three hours for each party. The program had two objectives. One was to improve access for litigants with cases involving smaller dollar amounts that otherwise might not be prosecuted. The second was to make the trials more efficient in order to help courts deal with overloaded dockets. The law went into effect on January 1, 2011, but included a sunset provision of January 1, 2016. Significantly, the law required the consent of all parties to the simplified trial procedures.

In 2015, the JCC conducted a study of EJTs for the first three years and eight months.[19] Thirty-nine of 58 courts responded to the request for data, but only 14 courts had conducted one or more EJTs. Most were larger courts. The total number of EJTs reported in the 14 courts was small, 156, about 15 percent of the 1,070 Limited Civil jury trials held statewide in those three fiscal years.[20] In the 2015 session, the legislature removed the sunset provision, added a requirement that most jury trials in Limited Civil cases were required to follow EJT procedures, and increased the presentation time to five hours.[21] Unlawful and forcible detainer cases were excluded from the requirement.

---

16. 1982 CAL. STAT. ch. 1581, codified at CAL. CODE OF CIV. PROC. §§90 *et seq.*

17. Cheryl E. Seltzer, *California's Pilot Project in Economical Litigation*, 53 S. CAL. L. REV. 1497, 1515 (1980).

18. 2010 CAL. STAT. ch. 674 (AB 2284), codified CAL. CODE OF CIV. PROC. ch. 4.5, §§630.01 *et seq.*

19. Report to the Judicial Council of California, Trial Courts: Report on Expedited Jury Trials, Jan. 30, 2015.

20. *Id.* at App. A.

21. 2015 Cal. Stat. ch. 330, §5 (AB 555) added ch. 4.6, Mandatory Expedited Jury Trials in Limited Civil Cases, codified at CAL. CODE OF CIV. PROC. §§630.20 to 630.29.

The change occurred during an increase in filing levels that began before the change, and continued after, so there was no obvious change in filing levels associated with the new expedited trial requirements.

6.5 Minnesota Civil Justice Reform Task Force

In 2009, at the request of the Minnesota legislature, the Chief Justice convened a Civil Justice Forum to examine civil justice practices in search of new efficiencies and potential cost savings. The Forum examined civil case processing statutes, court rules, and case management practices in an effort to identify changes that would facilitate more cost-effective and efficient civil case processing.[22] In 2010, as a result of the Forum's work, the Chief Justice established a Civil Justice Reform Task Force to review civil justice reforms proposed in other states and make recommendations for court changes that would facilitate more effective and efficient case processing. Task force members were concerned that the existing civil procedure laws and processes took too long and were expensive. The Task Force examined total civil case filings and trial rates over a ten-year period. It noted that filings had increased, but flattened out at the end of the period. This ten-year period included the Great Recession, although this was not noted in the report.

The Task Force submitted a report with a number of recommended changes to the Supreme Court in December 2011.[23] The report noted problems with excessive e-discovery costs, vanishing jury trials, and a high dollar threshold for pursuing a case. It also noted surveys and studies that reported a consensus that litigation costs caused cases to settle for reasons unrelated to the substantive merits of the claims or defenses. A supplemental report was submitted in May of 2012 that contained specific language for proposed changes in rules and statutes to implement the Task Force's recommendations.[24]

Several of the Task Force's recommendations were adopted, including:

- Changes to hip-pocket filing rule, discussed in Chapter 7;
- Adoption of an Expedited Litigation Track program, discussed later in this chapter;
- Establishment of a complex case program, discussed later in this chapter;
- Raising the Conciliation court monetary jurisdiction cap, discussed in Chapter 7; and
- Adoption of a Civil Cover sheet to assist a court in triaging and assigning cases.[25]

---

22. Minn. Civil Justice Forum, Recommendations for Improved Civil case Processing, included as Appendix A to the Civil Justice Reform Task Force Final Report 37–44.

23. Recommendations of the Minn. Supreme Court Civil Justice Reform Task Force, Final Report, Dec. 23, 2011.

24. Recommendations of the Minn. Supreme Court Civil Justice Reform Task Force, Supplemental Report, May 22, 2012.

25. *Id.* at App. A, pp. 15–17.

6.6 Minnesota Expedited Litigation Track

In 2013, the Minnesota Supreme Court established the Expedited Litigation Track (ELT) pilot program based on the recommendation of the Civil Justice Reform Task Force.[26] The objective of the program was:

> to promote efficiency in the processing of certain civil cases, reduce cost to the parties and the court system, maintain a system for resolution of claims that was relevant to the parties, and provide a quick and reduced cost process for obtaining a jury trial when civil actions cannot be resolved by judicial decision (dispositive motions) or by settlement.[27]

This was to be accomplished by providing early and active judicial case management and automatic disclosure of information with a goal of resolving the case in four to six months. The program was referred to as the "rocket docket."

Assignment of a case to the ELT was mandatory for some civil case categories.[28] The civil case categories assigned to the ELT pilot track varied in each pilot court but generally included: Consumer Credit Contract, Other Contract, Personal Injury, Other Civil, and Conciliation Court Appeals.[29] A party could make a motion to opt out,[30] and, where all parties consented, they could elect to have a case assigned to the ELT if it did not fall within one of the mandatory case categories.[31]

The pilot program began in Dakota County and the Duluth court in St. Louis County on July 1, 2013. A 2015 evaluation of the ELT pilots found positive results in Dakota County and the Duluth court in terms of time to disposition and, based on surveys, an overall improvement in the quality of justice and access to the courts.[32] ELT was expanded to Hennepin County, the largest county in the state, on January 1, 2016;[33] Olmsted County on July 1, 2016;[34] and to the courts in the Sixth Judicial District[35] on July 1, 2019.[36]

---

26. Minn. Supreme Court Administrative Order ADM10-8052, ADM09-8009, & ADM04-8001, *Order Relating to the Civil Justice Reform Task Force, Authorizing Expedited Civil Litigation Track Pilot Project, and Adopting Amendments to the Rules of Civil Proc. and the General Rules of Practice*, filed May 8, 2013.

27. Minn., Special Rules for the Pilot Expedited Civil Litigation Track, Preface.

28. Minn., Special Rules for the Pilot Expedited Civil Litigation Track, Rule 1(a).

29. Minn., Special Rules for the Pilot Expedited Civil Litigation Track, Rule 1(b).

30. Minn., Special Rules for the Pilot Expedited Civil Litigation Track, Rules 1(c) and 1(d).

31. Minn., Special Rules for the Pilot Expedited Civil Litigation Track, Rule 1(b)(3). Parties could request assignment to ELT via the Civil Cover Sheet (nonfamily case category), Form 117, question 3 on p. 2-3.

32. Minn. Judicial Branch, Report to the Community, 2016 Annual Report 14–15 and Minn. Judicial Branch, Report to the Community, 2019 Annual Report 9.

33. Minn. Supreme Court Administrative Order ADM10-8051, ADM09-8009 & ADM04-8001, *Order Relating to the Civil Justice Reform Task Force, Authorizing Modifications to Expedited Civil Litigation Track Pilot Project*, filed Nov. 3, 2015.

34. Minn. Supreme Court Administrative Order ADM10-8051, ADM09-8009, & ADM04-8001, *Order Relating to the Civil Justice Reform Task Force, Authorizing Modifications to Expedited Civil Litigation Track Pilot Project*, filed May 26, 2016.

35. The Sixth Judicial District included St. Louis, Lake, Cook, and Carlton Counties.

36. Minn. Supreme Court Administrative Order ADM10-8051, ADM09-8009, & ADM04-8001, *In Re Expedited Civil Litigation Track Pilot Project*, filed Feb. 15, 2019.

Based on the filing data available, there was no increase in filing levels associated with the ELT program. Rather, filings continued to drop, and, in some courts, drop even faster. When ELT was instituted in 2013, the filings of the designated mandatory case categories in Dakota County continued a decline that began in 2008. Olmstead County ELT filings declined steeply in 2016 and 2017 but rose in 2018. In Hennepin, filings of mandatory ELT cases dropped in 2016 and 2017, but not as fast as they had dropped in 2014 and 2015. Hennepin filings of the case categories where inclusion in ELT was at the discretion of the presiding judge rose in 2015, the year before ELT began, but dropped in 2016 and 2017. In general, filings declined when the ELT programs were implemented.

Separate filing data for the Duluth court in St. Louis County was not available to assess whether there were changes in filing levels in that court. Because the implementation of the ELT program in the rest of the Sixth Judicial District began in 2019, after civil filings data was made available to us, it was not possible for us to identify any changes in filing levels in those counties.

6.7 Minnesota Civil Case Management Programs

Prior to the civil justice reform initiative described earlier, a few district courts in Minnesota had implemented civil case management programs directed at reducing delay or the cost of litigation.[37] For example, Ramsey County (St. Paul) introduced a program to reduce the cost of litigation in 2001. Comparable civil filings rose in 2001 and peaked in 2002, then dropped in 2003. It was not clear that the rise was attributable to the pilot program, as this filing pattern was the same for most other Minnesota courts in those years. The Civil Justice Reform Task Force report in 2012 noted these programs were often not effective, as they usually required the consent of all parties, which was seldom forthcoming.[38]

6.8 Texas Expedited Actions

In 2011, the Texas legislature passed H.B. 274,[39] reforming certain remedies and procedures in civil actions and family law matters. Article 2 of the legislation authorized the Texas Supreme Court to adopt rules to promote "the prompt, efficient, and cost-effective resolution of civil actions."[40] The rules were to apply to civil actions in which the amount in controversy did not exceed $100,000.

---

37. A discussion of several programs was included in the MINN. STATE COURTS, 2001–2002 ANNUAL REPORT 6–7.

38. RECOMMENDATIONS OF THE MINN. SUPREME COURT CIVIL JUSTICE REFORM TASK FORCE, FINAL REPORT 4, Dec. 23, 2011.

39. Texas Acts 2011, 82d Reg. Sess. ch. 203 (H.B. 274), art. 2, § 2.01, effective Sept. 1, 2011, http://www.legis.state.tx.us/tlodocs/82R/billtext/html/HB00274F.htm.

40. TEX. GOV'T CODE § 22.004(h).

In September 2011, the Texas Supreme Court appointed a Task Force to advise the court in developing the program.[41] The Task Force issued its final report on January 25, 2012, and presented proposed rules to the Supreme Court Advisory Committee on January 27, 2012.[42] The Task Force focused on the following issues: the scope of discovery, disclosure of documents, proof of medical expenses, time limits on depositions, expedited setting of trial, limits on monetary damages, and alternate dispute resolution. There was considerable debate about whether the expedited procedures would be mandatory for cases under $100,000 or voluntary. Unable to reach a consensus, the Task Force proposed two sets of rules, one for mandatory application and one for voluntary participation. The Task Force's proposal and a proposal from the State Bar of Texas Rules Committee were reviewed by a Supreme Court Advisory Committee, which made recommendations to the Supreme Court.

In November 2012, the Texas Supreme Court issued rules for the expedited handling of cases, effective March 1, 2013.[43] The Supreme Court decided that the rules were mandatory in cases where a party sought "monetary relief of $100,000 or less, including damages of any kind, penalties, costs, expenses, pre-judgment interest, and attorney fees."[44] The changes included a new Rule of Civil Procedure, Rule 169, that established procedures for Expedited Actions. In particular, the new rule restricted a court's ability to require alternative dispute resolution, mandated quick trial settings, and provided for abbreviated trials for expedited cases. There were also amendments to Rule 190 providing for limits on pre-trial discovery and requirements for pre-trial exchange of documents.

An evaluation of the Expedited Actions program was prepared by the National Center for State Courts and a report was released in September 2016.[45] The evaluation was based on a sample of cases filed in 2011 and 2013 in five county courts at law that were disposed by settlement, summary judgment, bench trial, or jury trial. The analysis focused on discovery, alternative dispute resolution, and case processing times, not filing levels. The evaluation found an "overall positive impact on civil case processing in the participating courts,"[46] although it was not clear the impact was due to the implementation of the expedited action rules. While the report commented on the composition of civil filings in the sample courts, it did not assess changes in filing levels associated with the Expedited Actions program.

---

41. In the Supreme Court of Texas, Misc. Docket No. 11-9193, *Appointment of a Task Force for Rules in Expedited Action*, Sept. 26, 2011, as amended In the Supreme Court of Texas, Misc. Docket No. 11-9201, *Amended Appointment of Task Force for Rules in Expedited Actions*, Oct. 5, 2011.

42. The Task Force for Rules in Expedited Actions, Final Report to the Supreme Court of Texas, http://iaals.du.edu/sites/default/files/documents/publications/task_force_for_rules_in_expedited_actions_final_report_to_texas_supreme_court.pdf.

43. In the Supreme Court of Texas, Misc. Docket No. 12-9191, *Adoption of Rules for Dismissals and Expedited Actions*, https://www.txcourts.gov/All_Archived_Documents/SupremeCourt/AdministrativeOrders/miscdocket/12/12919100.pdf.

44. Tex. Rules Civ. Proc. r. 169(a)(1).

45. NCSC, Texas: Impact of the Expedited Actions Rules on the Texas County Courts at Law, Final Report, Sept. 1, 2016, http://www.txcourts.gov/media/1437615/texasimpactoftheexeditedactionsrulespdf.pdf.

46. *Id.* at vi, 31, & 46.

Given events of the ensuing years (hurricanes, the pandemic, turnover of judges, and changes in the rules), a follow-up study was initiated in October 2021, with a report issued in 2023.[47] The new study replicated the methodology of the first study, examining a sample of cases filed in the same five counties during the period July 1, 2018, to June 30, 2019, pre-COVID. The new study included cases in district courts as well as county courts. A comparison of the case mix in the three samples was made, but no analysis of changes in case filings was done.

Assessing possible changes in civil filings associated with the implementation of the program was not possible because of the lack of filing data for just those cases with a claim less than $100,000. Figure 6.3 displays the total filings for all Injury/damage and Contract and Debt cases in both the district and county courts, as the new rules applied to both courts. The gray column is 2013, the year in which the Expedited Actions rules became effective. Contract and Debt filings had been dropping since 2010, and dropped further in 2013 and 2014, although more slowly. Motor Vehicle Injury/damage cases had been rising slowly, but were flat in 2014, then began rising again. Non-motor Vehicle Injury/damage cases appeared to have stabilized in 2014, whereas they had been very gradually falling since 2005. Overall, filing levels changed little, if at all, when the Expedited Actions program was implemented. The absence of an impact may be explained in part by statements in both reports that there was a lack of awareness by attorneys as to whether the rules applied to their case, and that the rules were not consistently enforced by the judges.

The Expedited Actions rules were amended, effective January 1, 2021, to raise the monetary cap from $100,000 to $250,000, now excluding interest, punitive damages, attorneys fees, and costs. As this was after the data made available here, any changes in filing levels cannot be identified.

FIGURE 6.3 TEXAS INJURY/DAMAGE AND CONTRACT FILINGS, DISTRICT AND COUNTY COURTS

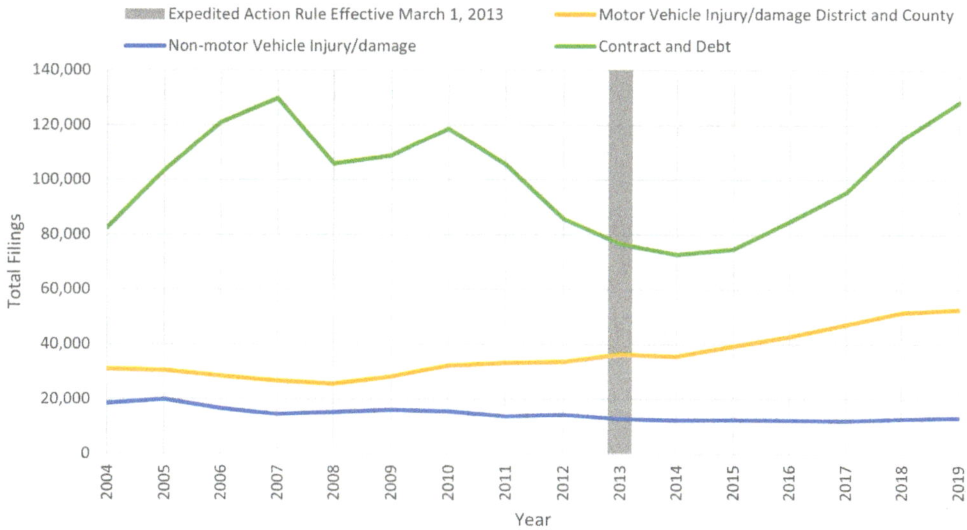

47. Civil Justice Initiative, A Renewed Analysis of the Expedited Actions Rules in Texas Courts, Mar. 28, 2023.

6.9 Complex/Commercial/Business Case Programs

6.9.1 Overview

Four of the five states in the study established some type of case management program for hearing cases that required unusually high levels of judicial attention. California and Minnesota established complex courts. Ohio established commercial dockets and developed procedures for complex cases. Texas established a program for "cases requiring additional resources." Illinois developed manuals for handling complex cases to assist judges assigned these cases, as did all the states, but did not establish a formal program, docket, or division(s) in the trial courts.

There were several arguments for creating a commercial or business court or a court/docket to hear complex cases of any type. Primarily the goal was to identify ways for trial courts to manage these types of cases more efficiently and effectively. There was a sense that these cases were too expensive to prosecute and took too long to resolve. Some states expressed the concern that complex cases were not being filed in the state's courts because of perceived lack of judicial expertise in commercial matters. Another basis explicitly stated in some states was to have a judiciary that attracted, rather than discouraged, companies from doing business in the state, with the intent of improving the business climate of the state.

None of the states explicitly indicated that increasing court filings was a goal of establishing complex/commercial/business courts. It was not obvious how the existence of a complex/commercial/business court would impact total filings. It was unlikely parties would not file a complex/commercial/business case because of the difficulties anticipated in prosecuting such a case where there was no complex/commercial/business court. There may have been some ability to "forum shop," causing parties to choose to file such a case in a particular court in a state, or to move a case to a court they felt would better handle their case. There was also the option of filing in federal district court, if there was diversity or federal question jurisdiction, which there often was. Finally, there was the option of an alternative dispute resolution approach, such as arbitration, mediation, or private judging.

Conversely, there may be a backlash if litigants contemplating filing a non-complex lawsuit forego doing so if they perceive a court to be preoccupied or overburdened with complex cases, or that the court will not devote sufficient judicial resources to their non-complex case.

Evaluations of these programs in each state did find that the programs met the goal of managing complex cases more efficiently and effectively. However, the evaluations provided little filing data from which to assess whether the existence of these programs impacted filing levels. None of the states were identifying and counting such cases before such a court was established, and most did not report the number after the program was established. Reporting would have been even more difficult due to shifts in the definition of what types of cases could be heard by such a court. Finally, parties often had to opt in to participate in the program, so there may have been complex cases filed that were not included in the program and therefore might not have been counted.

6.9.2 California Complex Civil Litigation Courts

The presence of complex cases requiring a disproportionate level of court resources to be resolved was discussed in the 2020 Commission Report issued in 1993.[48] While there was no data on the actual number of complex cases, surveys of judges and lawyers suggested the number was rising and that complex cases represented about 5 percent of filings.

In 1996, the Chief Justice appointed a Business Court Study Task Force to conduct a study of whether or not to create a specialized court program for resolving business disputes.[49] The Task Force recommended against creating a specialized court just for business cases. There were several reasons for the recommendation, including that there were non-business complex cases that should share the resources and expertise for resolving complex business cases and a negative public perception of specialized courts just for business cases. Instead, the recommended approach was to create complex litigation divisions within the superior courts. In response, the Chief Justice appointed a Complex Civil Litigation Task Force in 1997 to identify ways for trial courts to manage complex cases more efficiently and effectively. The Task Force made proposals for implementing a complex litigation program, and the Judicial Council approved a set of recommendations in October 1999.[50]

A Complex Civil Litigation Pilot Program in six superior courts was established in 2000.[51] A complex case was defined as one requiring "exceptional judicial management to avoid placing unnecessary burdens on the court or the litigants and to expedite the case, keep costs reasonable, and promote effective decision making by the court, the parties, and counsel."[52] The decision as to whether a case was complex was ultimately determined by a judge at the request of any party. Examples of complex cases included in the program were antitrust, securities claims, construction defects, toxic torts, mass torts, and class actions. Factors considered in whether a case was complex included:

- Large number of separately represented parties;
- Extensive motion practice raising difficult or novel issues that will be time-consuming to resolve;
- Substantial amounts of documentary evidence;
- Large numbers of witnesses;
- Coordination with related actions pending in one or more courts in other counties, states, or countries, or in a federal court; and
- Substantial post-judgment judicial supervision.[53]

The authorizing legislation required a report on the effectiveness of the complex civil litigation pilot programs.[54] NCSC evaluated the first few years of the pilot programs.[55] The primary purpose of the evaluation was to determine whether the pilot

---

48. COMM'N ON THE FUTURE OF THE CALIFORNIA COURTS, JUSTICE IN THE BALANCE 2020, at 134.
49. FACT SHEET, COMPLEX CIVIL LITIGATION, June 2003.
50. FACT SHEET, COMPLEX CIVIL LITIGATION PROGRAM, July 2008.
51. Authorized by the Budget Act of 1999, 1999 CAL. STATS., ch. 67 (AB 1105).
52. CAL. R. CT. r. 3.400(a), originally r. 1800.
53. These were the factors listed on the Civil Case Cover Sheet, Form CM-010, *rev'd*, July 1, 2007.
54. CAL. GOV'T CODE § 68617.
55. Paula L. Hannaford-Agor, Nicole L. Mott & Timothy F. Fautsko, *Evaluation of the Centers for Complex Civil Litigation Pilot Program, Final Report*, NCSC, June 30, 2003, https://www.courts.ca.gov/documents/compcivlitpub.pdf.

court programs addressed concerns previously expressed about the handling of complex cases, not the impact of the pilot programs on total filings. The evaluation did find complex cases included a variety of case types, not just commercial cases, and that they were handled more effectively in the pilot program courts. The evaluation did collect data on complex cases filed in the pilot programs, but did not relate these to total filings in each pilot program court, in part because some cases pending when the pilot programs began were assigned to the pilot program along with new cases.

In 2017, the Commission on the Future of California's Court System provided some information on complex case filings.[56] The number of filings from FY 2011–12 to FY 2015–16 was extrapolated from filing fees collected, which were significantly higher for complex cases. Complex cases had been filed in 52 of the 58 superior courts. The statewide complex case filings per year fluctuated, from a low of 4,042 to a high of 5,908, and did not appear to be rising or falling. The total number of complex filings for the five fiscal years represented 2.4 percent of all Unlimited Civil filings for the same period. The report estimated courts with between six and 15 judges experienced an average of seven complex case filings per year.

6.9.3 Minnesota Complex Case Program

One of the recommendations of the Civil Justice Forum convened by the Minnesota Supreme Court in 2009 was to develop a complex case program statewide.[57] In its 2011 final report, the Task Force stated "[t]he fact is that complex cases are leaving the state court system and going elsewhere. . . ."[58] In response to the report, the Supreme Court established a Complex Case Program (CCP) in 2013 by court rule.[59] The purpose of the CCP was to "to promote effective and efficient judicial management of complex cases in the district courts, avoid unnecessary burdens on the court, keep costs reasonable for the litigants and to promote effective decision making by the court, the parties and counsel."[60] No reference was made to a possible increase in filing levels.

Any type of case could be designated a complex case. A complex cases was defined as "an action requiring exceptional judicial management to avoid placing unnecessary burdens on the court or the litigants and to expedite the case, keep costs reasonable, and promote effective decision making by the court, the parties, and counsel."[61] The program provided for assignment to a single judge for all purposes[62] and strong case management practices.[63] Designation as a complex case could be requested on the Civil

56. Report to the Chief Justice, Commission on the Future of California's Court System 37–43 (2017).

57. *Id.* at 27–29. Proposed rules for a complex civil program were included in Appendix D of the report, pp. 63–67.

58. *Id.* at 27.

59. Minn. Gen. R. Prac. r. 146.

60. Minn. Gen. R. Prac. r. 146.01.

61. Minn. Gen. R. Prac. r. 146.02(a). A list of factors to be considered in designating a case as complex was included in Rule 146.02(b).

62. Minn. Gen. R. Prac. r. 146.03.

63. Minn. Gen. R. Prac. r. 146.01, 146.04 & 146.05.

Cover Sheet[64] when the case was filed, or by a party filing a CCP election.[65] In addition, there was a list of case types deemed "provisionally complex" by rule.[66]

Cases designated as complex were not separately counted as complex cases. They are counted in the case category based on the nature of the lawsuit—personal injury, contract, and so on. Since no data was available on the number of cases designated complex during the study period, it was not possible to assess the number of complex case filings or the possible impact of the program on case filing levels.

6.9.4 Ohio Court of Common Pleas—Complex Cases

In 1996, new case management procedures were established in Ohio for what were deemed complex cases—a special category reserved for civil cases "involving novel or complicated issues of law and fact that were not likely to be resolved within the time guidelines established for other cases."[67] When a potentially complex case was filed, it was categorized on the basis of the underlying nature of the action—personal injury, contract, employment, and so on. After a new case was filed, the judge to whom it was assigned could re-designate the case as a complex litigation case if it met certain criteria.[68] The case, now re-designated as a complex case, would be counted in the month of re-designation, as a "re-designation," not a new filing.

Cases re-designated as complex represented a small portion of the total civil caseload. During the 21-year study period, the percent of total court of common pleas cases re-designated as complex was less than 0.1 percent in every year, except in 2000 when it was 0.2 percent. For the entire 21-year period, complex cases totaled less than 0.07 percent of total civil filings. Figure 6.4 shows the number of cases re-designated as complex each year. The number varied considerably from year to year. Although the overall trend was declining, there were significant peaks in 2000, 2008, and 2014. Since the total numbers are small, a large number of filings in one court from one incident or pattern of allegedly unlawful behavior could explain at least some of the peaks. Given the low percentage of complex filings and the lack of data from years prior to establishing the program, it is not possible to assess any impact of the program on complex filings or total civil filings.

FIGURE 6.4 OHIO TOTAL COMPLEX CASE FILINGS IN COURT OF COMMON PLEAS

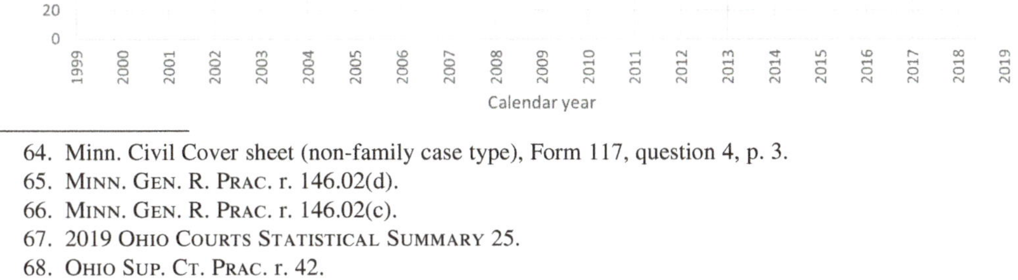

64. Minn. Civil Cover sheet (non-family case type), Form 117, question 4, p. 3.
65. MINN. GEN. R. PRAC. r. 146.02(d).
66. MINN. GEN. R. PRAC. r. 146.02(c).
67. 2019 OHIO COURTS STATISTICAL SUMMARY 25.
68. OHIO SUP. CT. PRAC. r. 42.

6.9.5 Ohio Court of Common Pleas—Commercial Dockets

In June of 2007, the Chief Justice established the Supreme Court Task Force on Commercial Dockets. The Task Force's charge was to determine the best approach for establishing commercial dockets to handle litigation between businesses in the courts of common pleas. In May 2008, temporary rules governing pilot projects proposed by the Task Force were adopted by the Supreme Court.[69] In 2009, commercial docket pilot projects began in Cuyahoga, Franklin, Hamilton, and Lucas Counties.[70] Once the commercial dockets were operational, the Task Force began monitoring the progress of commercial dockets through surveys and communicating with commercial docket judges.[71] In a 2011 interim report, the Task Force noted "the great success of the pilot project at that point in time, but also revealed the biggest challenge to each of the commercial dockets—the burden the docket places on the commercial docket judges." [72] In its final report issued in December 2011, the Task Force recommended establishment of commercial dockets in courts of common pleas on a permanent basis and the creation of a Commission on Commercial Dockets to oversee the program.

In 2012, the Commission on Commercial Dockets was created.[73] Court rules governing the establishment and operation of commercial dockets were adopted in 2013.[74] The rules allowed any court of common pleas with six or more judges or a population of more than 300,000 people to establish (or discontinue) a commercial docket.[75] Only litigation between business entities or a business entity and an owner, sole proprietor, shareholder, partner, or member of a business entity could be assigned to a commercial docket.[76]

The creation of the commercial dockets was driven by a desire to improve the business climate of the state, at least as to the impacts of potential litigation.[77] With the creation of specialized commercial dockets "the efficient resolution of commercial cases is promoted, fewer court resources are required, the administration of justice is enhanced, and ultimately the state's business climate is improved."[78] The benefits contemplated included:[79]

- Providing the commercial docket judges with more concentrated experience in handling business disputes;
- Increasing the number of published commercial litigation decisions, thus providing more guidance to businesses and their legal advisors;
- Promoting predictable outcomes, which were important to business decision-makers;

69. The Supreme Court of Ohio, ANNUAL REPORT 2008, at 31.
70. The Supreme Court of Ohio, ANNUAL REPORT 2009, at 29.
71. The Supreme Court of Ohio, ANNUAL REPORT 2010, at 25.
72. REPORT AND RECOMMENDATIONS OF THE SUPREME COURT OF OHIO TASK FORCE ON COMMERCIAL DOCKETS 3, Dec. 2011.
73. The Supreme Court of Ohio, ANNUAL REPORT 2012, at 11.
74. OHIO SUP. CT. PRAC. r. 49 to 49.12.
75. OHIO SUP. CT. PRAC. r. 49.01.
76. OHIO SUP. CT. PRAC. r. 49.05.
77. REPORT AND RECOMMENDATIONS OF THE SUPREME COURT OF OHIO, *supra* note 72.
78. *Id.*
79. *Id.* at 5.

- Contributing to greater efficiency in the court system; and
- Lessening delays in the court system.

Not every county that was authorized to establish a commercial docket did so. Moreover, some courts initially voted to create a commercial docket, then later voted to discontinue their commercial dockets. The decision not to create a commercial docket, or to discontinue one, reportedly involved concerns about commercial docket judges receiving smaller criminal caseloads, resulting in larger criminal caseloads for other judges, and about which judges were designated commercial docket judges.

Cases assigned to commercial dockets were initially not categorized as commercial cases; they retained their original case type designation.[80] Commercial docket judges were required to submit a supplemental monthly report for cases on their commercial dockets, but data from these reports was not made available for analysis here.

No explicit discussion of the impact of implementing commercial courts on court filings was included in the various reports about the dockets. If the goal was to keep businesses in Ohio, or encourage other businesses to locate in Ohio, the possibility of more business litigation in the courts where there was a commercial docket was implicit. However, determining whether this occurred would be very difficult.

6.9.6 Texas Additional Resources Cases

In 2011, the legislature adopted legislation authorizing "Additional Resources for Certain Cases."[81] The legislation directed the Supreme Court to ask the state bar to form a task force "to consider and make recommendations regarding the rules for determining whether civil cases pending in trial courts require additional resources for efficient judicial management."[82] The Supreme Court adopted rules effective January 1, 2012, and applicable to cases pending or after May 1, 2012.[83]

Any party to a case or the judge to whom the case had been assigned could ask that a case be designated as one requiring additional resources.[84] If the judge decided the case needed additional resources, the presiding judge of the administrative judicial region was notified of the decision. If the presiding judge agreed,[85] a request was made to the Judicial Committee for Additional Resources, which could allocate additional resources.[86]

No data was requested on the number of cases that were designated during the study period as requiring additional resources, nor was there a reporting category on monthly reports for such cases. Therefore, it was not possible to assess the impact of the program on case filing levels.

---

80. Supreme Court of Ohio, Instructions on Form A Supplement for Commercial Dockets, General Division, Court of Common Pleas, ver. Mar. 10, 2009.

81. 2011 Texas Acts 82d 1st C. S., ch. 3, H.B. 79, §7.04, adding subch. J to ch. 74 of Tex. Gov't Code.

82. 2011 Texas Acts 82d 1st C. S., ch. 3, H.B. 79, §7.05(a).

83. Tex. R. Jud. Admin. r. 16, Additional Resources for Certain Cases.

84. Tex. Gov't Code §74.253(a).

85. Tex. Gov't Code §74.253.

86. Tex. Gov't Code §74.254.

7

Changes in Civil Procedure Laws and Rules

Changes in civil procedure laws or rules of court are another possible source of changes in filing levels. This chapter examines two types of changes. The first is a change in the monetary jurisdictional boundary for a category or categories of cases. A change in the jurisdictional cap would be expected to move cases between courts, or change which case management rules and practices apply to cases above or below the new boundary. The second type of change examined is the statute of limitations, the time period within which a case must be filed in court. An extension or reduction of the time limit can affect settlement discussions as well as filing deadlines for cases.

7.1 Impact of Changes in Monetary Jurisdiction Boundaries

7.1.1 Overview

There are several possible scenarios for a change in filing levels associated with a change in the monetary jurisdiction limit.[1] Intuitively, the impact of raising the monetary jurisdiction limit between two tiers of courts would be a decrease in filings in the court whose jurisdiction floor was now higher and an increase in filings of the court whose jurisdiction limit was increased. Cases with value between the old and new limit would now have to be filed in the court hearing cases below the new limit, unless the jurisdiction was concurrent. However, the magnitude of the decrease and increase would

1. The jurisdiction limit between higher and lower value civil cases is generally specified in statute and changes are made by the legislature, not the courts.

not necessarily be equal if the decisions of litigants and lawyers about the cost, benefits, and pace of litigation in the two tiers of courts varied.

A second possible change in filing levels associated with a change in the monetary jurisdiction limit would involve those cases whose claim was above the old limit that were previously not filed in the court because of the perceived barriers or higher cost of litigation in that court. If the procedures in the court hearing lower-value cases were perceived to be simpler or less expensive, a rise in the monetary jurisdiction limit might encourage filing of cases that would otherwise not have been filed. This would result in an increase in filings in the court hearing lower-value cases without a concomitant decrease in filings in the court hearing higher value cases.

A third possible result would be no noticeable impact on filings in either court. There are several possible explanations for no impact. It may be that a party alleged damages within the jurisdiction of the court hearing higher-value cases even if it was unlikely the party would realize damages above the jurisdiction limit. After the change, a party could still allege higher damages to file in the court hearing higher value cases rather than filing in the court hearing lower value cases. Another possible explanation would be that it was not economical, for litigants or lawyers, to pursue litigation in either court because of perceived costs or barriers. These "middling cases" were not previously filed, and might still not be filed after the change in the monetary jurisdiction limit if it did not alter the economic calculus of deciding whether to file.

Other relevant jurisdictional limit factors that might affect filing levels include how long it had been since the jurisdictional limit was last changed and the magnitude of the change. Was the limit recently changed or regularly changed, for example, to adjust for inflation? Was the increase a modest percentage, or was the value of the limit doubled or tripled? Finally, did the change have different impacts for different case types?

7.1.2 Findings

All of the possible scenarios just described were observed when the monetary jurisdiction limit was changed during the time frame of the data made available for this study.[2] Changes in filing levels in both the court hearing higher-value cases and the court hearing the lower-value cases were observed in three of the five states. The change, if any, was often short-lived or generally within the same range as normal year-to-year fluctuations. Moreover, a dramatic increase in the jurisdictional level, even a doubling, did not result in an equivalent shift in filing levels. In general, the change produced more new filings in the court hearing the lower-value cases, not just an equivalent transfer of filings.

In California, the monetary jurisdiction limit between Unlimited Civil (higher-value) and Limited Civil (lower-value) cases was raised twice during the 41 years examined. In 1979, the limit was tripled, from $5,000 to $15,000. The result was fewer Unlimited Civil filings for the next two years. There was a substantial increase in Limited Civil filings in the first year after the change and a smaller increase in the second year. The increase in Limited Civil filings in the first year was greater than the decrease in

2. Only changes involving case categories other than small claims are discussed here. Changes in small claims case monetary jurisdiction limits are discussed in Chapter 5.

Unlimited Civil filings that year. The change in filing levels associated with the change in the jurisdictional limit was noticeable, but short term.

In 1986, the jurisdictional limit was increase by two-thirds, from $15,000 to $25,000. The filing levels for Unlimited Civil cases dropped, but not by as much as after the 1979 change. Unlimited Civil filings had been rising before the change, but dropped for the next 13 years. Limited Civil filings did rise, but by a smaller percentage than in 1979, and not by much more than the year-to-year increases before the change. Moreover, in contrast to the 1979 change, the volume increase was less than the drop in Unlimited Civil filing levels. Limited Civil filing levels continued to increase by a similar percentage for several years after the 1986 change, suggesting the impact of the jurisdictional change was minimal.

The changes in filing levels of the subcategories of higher-value Unlimited Civil cases when the jurisdictional limit changed was very different. After the 1979 change, both Non-Injury/damage cases and Auto Injury/damage cases dropped. Non-Injury/damage filings experienced the largest year-to-year drop in 41 years, but filings began to increase in the second year after the change to levels higher than before the change. Auto Injury/damage cases continued to slump for three years after the change, but then began to rise. Non-auto Injury/damage filings were unchanged.

The impact of the 1986 change was very different. Non-Injury/damage cases had peaked in FY 1985–86, were dropping when the change occurred, and continued to drop for the next three years. Auto Injury/damage case filings were already rising when the change occurred, so it is difficult to say what the change contributed. Filings of Non-auto Injury/damage cases had peaked in FY 1984–85 and were slowly dropping when the change occurred.

In Ohio, there was one increase in the monetary jurisdiction boundary between small claims cases and non-small claims cases heard in the municipal and county courts during the study period. The monetary jurisdiction boundary was doubled from $3,000 to $6,000 in late 2016. The change in filing levels was small compared to the change in the boundary. Small claims filings had been dropping for nine years. The total filings rose only about 3 percent in 2017, then dropped by 3 percent in 2018, and continued to drop thereafter. Although they might have been expected to fall, municipal and county court filings began rising in 2015, before the change, and the rise continued though the end of the study period in 2019.

In Texas, there were two changes in monetary jurisdiction limits as of September 1, 2007. The upper limit of the concurrent jurisdiction of the justice court was doubled, from $5,000 to $10,000. Unexpectedly, the filings in the justice court hearing the lower-value cases dropped, very slightly in the first year after the change took effect and then trended down for the next seven years. Filings in the district and county courts, which heard higher-value cases, did drop, as was expected. Because the jurisdiction of district, county, and justice courts was concurrent from $200 to the jurisdiction limit, the change appears to have only increased the jurisdiction limit of the justice courts. There was no real change in the jurisdiction of the district and county courts. There did not appear to be a change in filing levels associated with a change in the jurisdictional limit.

The upper limit of the concurrent jurisdiction between small claims cases and the justice courts was also doubled from $5,000 to $10,000 in 2007. During the first full year after the change, per capita filings in justice court and small claims cases were essentially unchanged, suggesting this doubling of the concurrent monetary jurisdictional limit had no discernable impact on filing levels.

The Texas legislature adopted significant changes in the subject matter jurisdiction of the justice and small claims cases, effective May 1, 2013. The changes shifted small claims cases to a docket in the justice court and expanded the types of cases that could be heard as small claims cases. In 2014, the first full year after the shift, there was a noticeable increase in both total filings and per capita filing levels for small claims cases. The justice court non-small claims filing levels did not drop, but increased very slightly. After the change, from 2014 through 2019, the small claims per capita filing level was essentially flat. The justice court per capita filing level was flat in 2014 and 2015, then began rising in 2016. Since the two dockets retained concurrent jurisdiction, the increase in small claims filings appears to be additional new cases, not cases shifted from the justice court dockets.

In Illinois and Minnesota there was no change in monetary jurisdiction limits during the time frame covered by the data provided by the states. In Illinois, the monetary jurisdiction distinguishing the category of Law cases was raised from $15,000 to $50,000, effective January 1, 1996. As this was the first year of the data set supplied, no analysis could be done. When Minnesota merged all trial courts in each county into one district court, the concept of a monetary jurisdiction limit between higher-value and lesser-value civil cases was eliminated. Cases were either designated Major Civil or Minor Civil based on the subject matter of the suit, not the dollar value of the claim. During the time frame here, there were no shifts in case types from Minor to Major, or Major to Minor. The impact of changes in the jurisdictional limit for small claims cases is discussed in chapter 5.

7.1.3 California

The monetary jurisdiction limit between Unlimited Civil and Limited Civil cases in California was raised twice over the 41 years for which data was available. The jurisdictional limit was raised from $5,000 to $15,000, effective January 1, 1979.[3] It was raised to $25,000 effective January 1, 1986.[4] It has not been raised since, although there was unsuccessful legislation to raise the limit to $50,000 in the 1995–96 legislative session.[5] A shift of filings from Unlimited Civil to Limited Civil occurred at both changes, although the magnitude varied.

In the first full fiscal year after the threefold 1979 change, Unlimited Civil total filings dropped almost 10 percent and per capita filing levels dropped more than 12 percent (orange line in Figures 7.1 and 7.2). Unlimited Civil filings were stable in the second year, then began to rise in the third year after the change.

3. 1978 Cal. Stat. ch. 146, § 1, amending Cal. Code of Civ. Proc. § 86(a).
4. 1985 Cal. Stat. ch. 1383, § 1, amending Cal. Code of Civ. Proc. § 86(a).
5. AB 3381 (Baugh) in the 1995–96 Cal. Legislative session.

FIGURE 7.1 CALIFORNIA TOTAL CIVIL FILINGS, JURISDICTIONAL INCREASES JANUARY 1, 1979 AND JANUARY 1, 1986

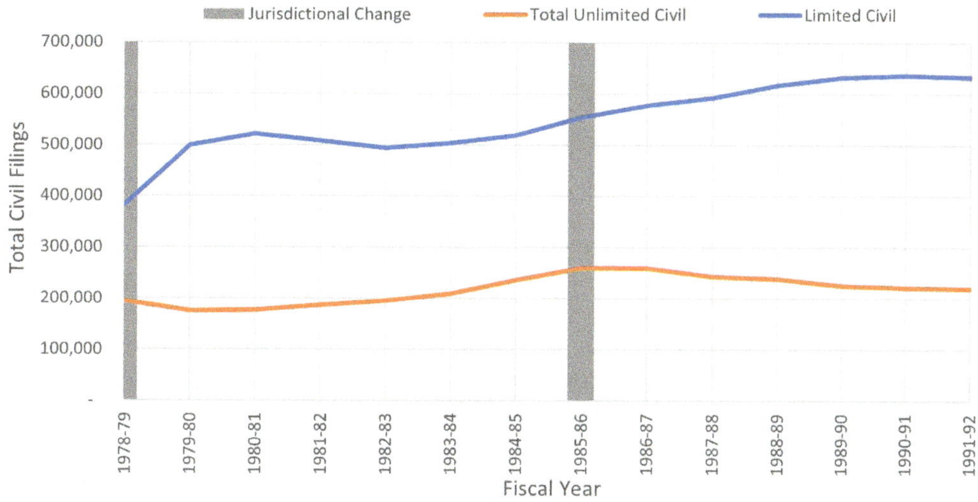

After the threefold increase in 1979, there was initially a sharp increase in Limited Civil filings, both in total filings, 31 percent, and per capita filing levels, 28 percent (blue line in Figures 7.1 and 7.2). There was another small increase in total filings the next fiscal year, 4.4 percent, but there were slightly lower total filings in the next two fiscal years.

The change in the number of total filings after the threefold increase in 1979 was significantly different for the two court tiers. Unlimited Civil filings dropped 19,212 cases in the first full fiscal year after the change. Limited Civil filings increased by 117,133 cases in the first full fiscal year, and another 21,888 cases in the second fiscal year. This was an example of a monetary jurisdiction change that resulted in far more filings in the court hearing lower-value case than the reduction in filings in the court hearing higher-value cases.

FIGURE 7.2 CALIFORNIA CIVIL FILINGS PER 100K POPULATION, JURISDICTIONAL INCREASES JANUARY 1, 1979 AND JANUARY 1, 1986

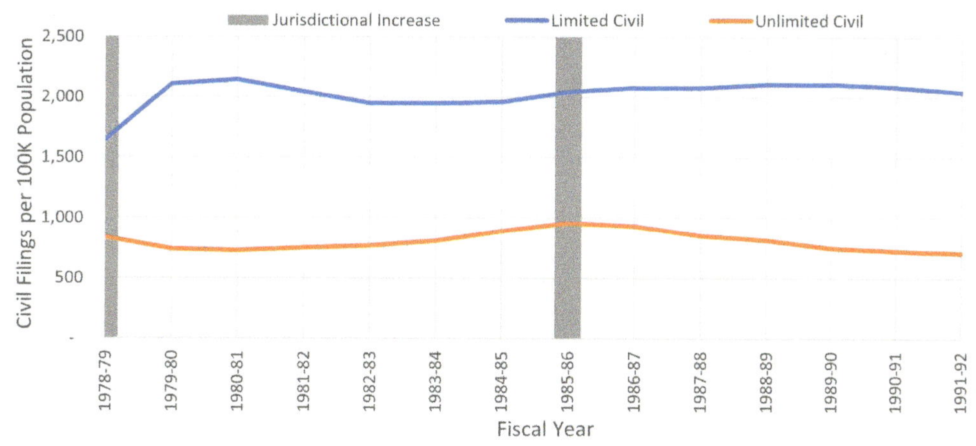

After the two-thirds increase in 1986, Unlimited Civil filing levels, both total and per capita, dropped steadily for the next 13 fiscal years (orange lines in Figures 7.1 and 7.2). The drop in total filings the first full year was less than 1 percent, then 6 percent in the next year. The drop in per capita filings was almost 3 percent in the first year, then more than 8 percent in the next year. When the change occurred, Unlimited Civil filing levels had been rising for several years, so the impact of the change may have been greater if total filing levels had continued their previous rise.

After the 1986 increase, total Limited Civil filings increased, but at a much smaller pace than after the 1979 increase (blue lines in Figures 7.1 and 7.2). Total filings increased almost 7 percent in the year of the increase, and more than 4 percent in the next fiscal year. Total filings increased by fewer cases than the drop in total Unlimited Civil filings. After the 1986 increase, Limited Civil filing levels continued a slow rise that peaked in FY 1990–91 in total filings and in FY 1989–90 in per capita filings. Thereafter, filing levels fluctuated considerably. Total Limited Civil filings were below the FY 1990–91 peak in 22 of the subsequent 27 fiscal years. Limited Civil total filings were only higher during the Great Recession period. Per capita Limited Civil filings were below the peak in 26 of the 27 subsequent years. By FY 2018–19 Limited Civil per capita filings were down 44 percent from the peak in FY 1988–89.

The 1986 change resulted in an increase in Limited Civil filings less than the drop in Unlimited Civil filings, in contrast to the 1979 change. The 1986 change was a 67 percent increase in the limit, whereas the 1979 change was a 300 percent increase in the limit. The elapsed time between the 1979 and 1986 changes was only six years, whereas the change in 1979 was nine years from the increase in the monetary jurisdiction limit in 1970.[6]

The impact of the jurisdictional limit change on the subcategories of higher-value Unlimited Civil cases was more complicated (Figure 7.3). In the first fiscal year after the 1979 change, both Auto Injury/damage (red line) and Non-Injury/damage (green line) filings dropped, but Non-auto Injury/damage cases (yellow line) remained steady. These results suggest the jurisdictional limit changes can be very different for different case subcategories.

6. 1969 CAL. STAT. ch. 773, § 1, raising the limit from $3,000 to $5,000, codified at CAL. CODE OF CIV. PROC. § 89.

FIGURE 7.3 CALIFORNIA UNLIMITED CIVIL FILINGS PER 100K POPULATION, JURISDICTIONAL INCREASES JANUARY 1, 1979 AND JANUARY 1, 1986

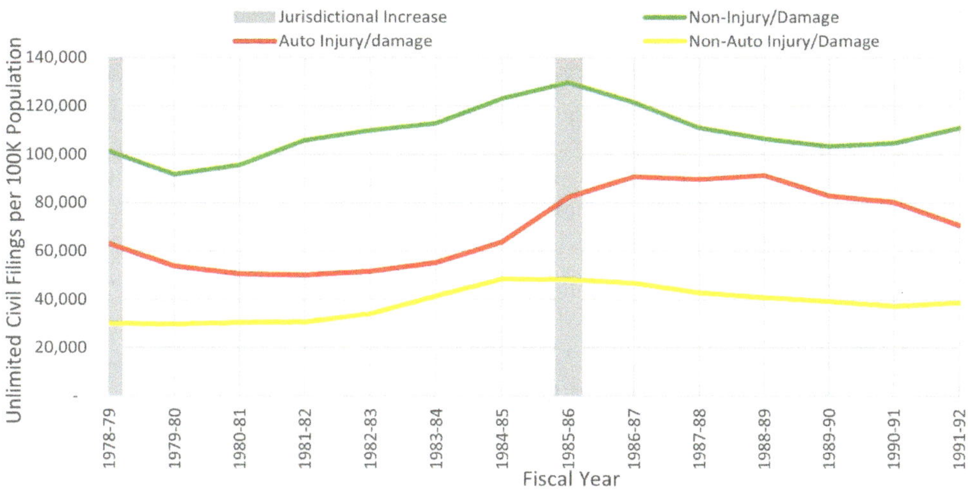

Unlimited Civil Non-Injury/damage filing levels (green line in Figure 7.3) dropped significantly after the 1979 threefold increase, both as to total filings and per capita filings. It was the largest year-to-year drop in 41 years. However, within two years, filing increases resulted in filing levels greater than the pre-change level. Filings then peaked in FY 1985–86. After the 1986 increase, total filings dropped for the next four years, then began to increase. Notably, there were year-to-year drops of a similar size in several other years where there was no change in the jurisdictional limit. Unfortunately, no data was available to examine the corresponding change in Auto Injury/damage case levels in the Limited Civil category.

Unlimited Civil Auto Injury/damage filing levels (red line in Figure 7.3) dropped significantly after the 1979 increase, both total filings and per capita filings, but it was not the largest year-to-year drop in 41 years. Filing levels continued to drop slightly for a few years, then began rising. The 1986 change occurred in the midst of a hump in filing levels, probably attributable to a change in third part liability discussed elsewhere. Again, no data was available to examine the corresponding change in Non-auto Injury/damage case levels in the Limited Civil category.

Unlimited Civil Non-auto Injury/damage filing levels (yellow line in Figure 7.3) were essentially flat after the 1979 change. They began rising in 1982–83 but leveled off just before the 1986 change. After the 1986 increase, filings slowly declined, but maintained a level higher than before the 1986 change. Again, no data was available to examine the corresponding change in Non-Injury/damage case levels in the Limited Civil category.

7.1.4 Ohio

Theoretically, an increase in the monetary jurisdiction cap of the small claims court would be expected to reduce the filings in municipal and county courts to the extent filers shifted cases to small claims court because of simpler procedures. In 2016, the Ohio

General Assembly doubled the monetary jurisdiction in small claims cases from $3,000 to $6,000, effective September 28, 2016.[7] The jurisdiction of the small claims division was not exclusive; a litigant could still file a case claiming less than $6,000 as a non-small claims municipal or county court civil case.

Figure 7.4 displays the total filings levels for several years before and after the increase. Small claims filings (orange line in Figure 7.4), which had dropped every year for the prior nine years, rose almost 3 percent in 2017. However, they dropped almost 3 percent in 2018 and more than 5 percent in 2019. In contrast, municipal and county court (MCC) filings without small claims (blue line in Figure 7.4), which were relatively flat in the prior two years, rose about 1 percent in 2015, more than 2 percent in 2016, the year of the increase, and 11 percent in 2017. The increase did not decrease non-small claims filings in the municipal and county courts.

FIGURE 7.4 OHIO TOTAL FILINGS IN MUNICIPAL AND COUNTY COURTS, JURISDICTIONAL LIMIT INCREASED SEPTEMBER 28, 2016

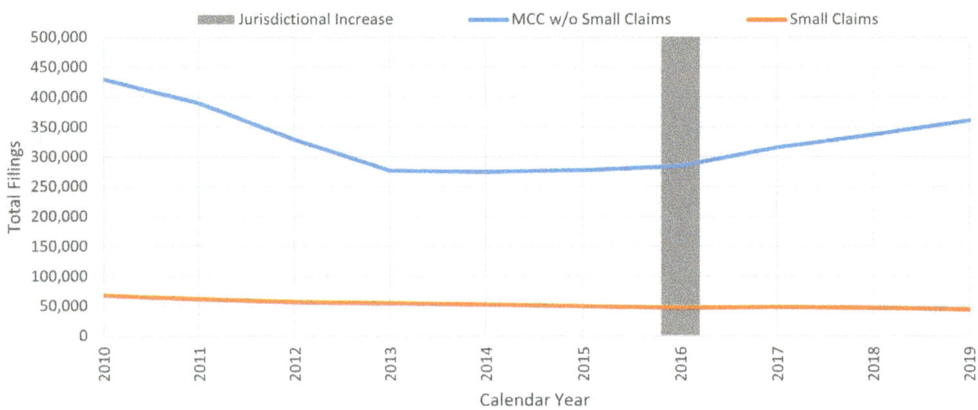

Earlier, on July 1, 1997, the monetary jurisdiction limit of small claims cases heard in municipal and county courts was raised from $2,000 to $3,000.[8] At the same time, the monetary jurisdiction limit between the courts of common pleas and the municipal courts and county courts was increased from $3,000 to $15,000 in county courts[9] and in municipal courts.[10] Unfortunately, the data set made available did not include filings data for this period.

7.1.5 Texas

Because there were several types of trial courts in Texas with significant concurrent jurisdiction, only two shifts in jurisdictional boundaries were examined. The first change was an increase in the jurisdictional limit of the justice court. The second analysis

7. Ohio 131st General Assembly House Bill 387, amending Ohio Rev. Code §§ 1925.02 and 1925.10.

8. Ohio 121st General Assembly, House Bill 438, §§ 1 and 3; codified in Ohio Rev. Code § 1925.02(A)(1).

9. Ohio 121st General Assembly, House Bill 438, §§ 1 and 3, codified in Ohio Rev. Code § 1907.03(A).

10. Ohio 121st General Assembly, House Bill 438, §§ 1 and 3, codified in Ohio Rev. Code § 1901.17.

looked at the changes in justice court filings associated with an increase in the Small Claims case jurisdiction. Figure 7.5 displays the total filings of the combined district and county courts, the justice courts without small claims, and small claims filings when the jurisdictional limits were changed.

FIGURE 7.5 TEXAS TOTAL FILINGS—DISTRICT AND ALL COUNTY COURTS, JUSTICE W/O SMALL CLAIMS, AND SMALL CLAIMS JURISDICTIONAL INCREASES SEPTEMBER 1, 2007 AND SEPTEMBER 1, 2013

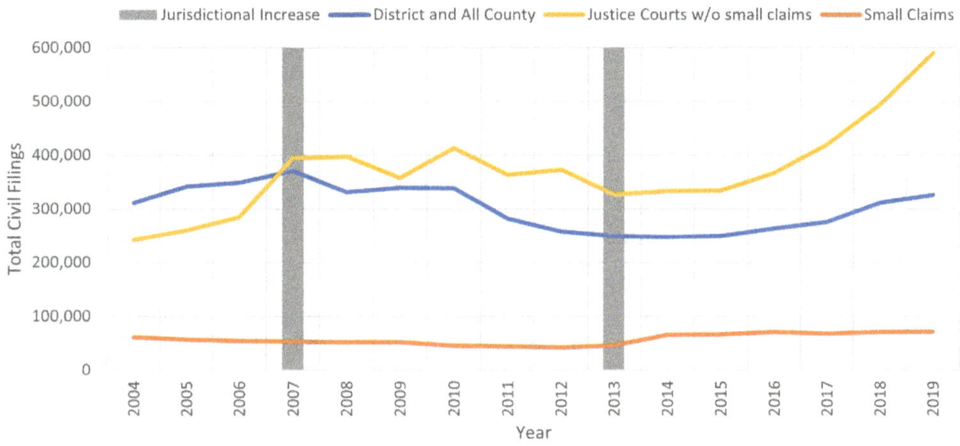

Justice courts have concurrent monetary jurisdiction with district and county courts in civil cases with monetary claims from $200 up to the jurisdictional limit. The legislature increased the upper monetary jurisdiction limit of the justice court from $5,000 to $10,000, effective September 1, 2007.[11] The increase of the limit had a mixed effect on filings. Justice court filings (yellow line) jumped in 2007, although the change only took effect in the last third of the year. Justice court filings rose very slightly in 2008, then wobbled from 2009 through 2012. The change in district and county court filings did not match the change in justice court filings. District and all county court total filings (blue line in Figure 7.5) were rising slowly prior to the change and peaked in 2007. Filings dropped in 2008 by more than the increase in justice court filings that year, but less than the increase in 2007. District and county filings rose very slightly in 2009 and 2010, followed by a drop every year until 2014. The 2008 drop was mostly county court filings, primarily of Other Civil and Suits on Debt cases. This change occurred at the same time as the Great Recession, so this may have contributed as much to the filing changes as the jurisdictional increase did.

The second analysis looked at the impact on filings as a result of changes in both the monetary jurisdiction limit and subject matter jurisdiction of small claims cases. Prior to 2007, the concurrent monetary jurisdiction limit of small claims cases and the justice court was $5,000. As of September 1, 2007, the upper limit of the concurrent

11. 2007 Texas Acts 80th Reg. Sess., ch. 383, SB 618, § 2, amending Tex. Gov't Code § 27.031(a)(1).

jurisdiction was raised to $10,000 in both small claims cases[12] and the justice courts.[13] Unexpectedly, in the first full year after the change, 2008, total filings in justice court rose 0.7 percent and small claims filings dropped 0.8 percent. Small claims filings dropped through 2013 (orange line in Figure 7.5). The doubling of the concurrent monetary jurisdictional limit had a negligible impact on filing levels of both small claims and non-small claims justice court filings, noting that this change happened during the Great Recession.

Legislation in 2011 transferred small claims cases to a docket in justice courts,[14] and required the Supreme Court to adopt rules governing the small claims court, including its subject matter jurisdiction.[15] The rules adopted by the Supreme Court shifted certain case types to the small claims docket, effective May 1, 2013.[16] Prior to the change, small claims cases involved:

> actions by any person for the recovery of money in which the amount involved, exclusive of costs, did not exceed $10,000.[17]

The shift in jurisdiction added the following case types to the small claims docket, which were previously counted as Other Civil cases in the justice courts:[18]

> Cases filed for the recovery of money damages, civil penalties, personal property, or other relief allowed by law. The claim cannot exceed $10,000, excluding statutory interest and court costs but including attorney fees, if any. Also include occupational licenses, writs of re-entry, tax cases, tax warrants, dangerous dog cases (in which no criminal charges have been filed), tow hearings, habitual toll violator hearings, junk vehicle, and deed restriction cases. Also include bond forfeiture (*nisi*) proceedings conducted pursuant to Code of Criminal Procedure, Article 22.02.
>
> and
>
> All other suits filed that were within the civil jurisdiction of the justice court, including those for recovery of money (damages or debt up to $10,000) and for foreclosure of mortgages and enforcement of liens on personal property in cases in which the amount in controversy was otherwise within the justice court's jurisdiction as provided by Section 27.031 of the Government Code.

In 2014, the first full year after the shift in cases, there was a noticeable increase in total filings of small claims cases (orange line in Figure 7.5). Justice court total filings without small claims (yellow line in Figure 7.5) did not drop, as might be expected, but

---

12. Texas Acts 2007, 80th Reg. Sess. ch. 383 (SB 618), § 3, amending Tex. Gov't Code § 28.003(a), repealed effective Aug. 31, 2013.

13. Texas Acts 2007, 80th Reg. Sess. ch. 383 (SB 618), § 2, amending Tex. Gov't Code § 27.031(a)(1).

14. Texas Acts 2011, 82d, 1st Called Session, ch. 3 (HB 79), § 5.02, adding Tex. Gov't Code § 27.060 and § 5.08.

15. Texas Acts 2011, 82d, 1st Called Session, ch. 3 (HB 79), § 5.07.

16. In the Supreme Court of Texas, Misc. Docket No. 13-9023. Adoption of Rules for Justice Court Cases, adopting Rules of Civil Proc. Part V, r. 500–507.

17. Tex. Gov't Code § 28.003(a).

18. Office of Court Administration, Texas Judicial Council, Official Justice of the Peace Monthly Report Instructions, effective Sept. 1, 2013, revised Aug. 21, 2014, at 13.

rose very slightly. Total small claims filings increased by 20,000 cases from 2013 to 2014, and non-small claims justice court filings increased almost 7,000 cases. Since the jurisdiction was concurrent, the increase in filings appears to be new cases, not cases shifted to the small claims docket.

The upper monetary jurisdiction limit of statutory county courts varied across counties according to court-specific statutes. Legislation in 2011[19] raised the upper monetary jurisdiction limit to $200,000 of those statutory county courts whose jurisdiction was less than $200,000. It became effective on January 1, 2012. The legislation did not change the monetary jurisdiction limit of those statutory county courts whose upper limit was already $200,000 or more. The impact of this change was not examined. It would have required an identification of those counties where the legislation increased the upper limit, and a comparison of the total filings before and after January 1, 2012, in those counties. This information was not readily available.

The legislature increased the monetary jurisdiction limit of the justice court from $10,000 to $20,000, concurrent with the monetary jurisdiction limit of county courts, effective September 1, 2020.[20] As this change occurred after the data set was made available, the impact of the change on filings could not be analyzed.

7.2 Impact of Changes in Statute of Limitations

7.2.1 Overview

The statute of limitations is the time period within which a case must be filed in court after the event or injury giving rise to the court case. If a case is not filed within the applicable time period, the litigants are precluded from filing a court case based on that event or injury. The time limitations are generally set by the legislature, and vary by case type.

The impact of a change in the statute of limitations on total case filings depends on the perceptions and reaction of litigants and lawyers to the change. When the time period is extended, litigants and lawyers have more time to resolve a case before incurring the costs and burdens of filing a case. Plaintiff's lawyers often note that it takes time for injuries to stabilize and total damages to be ascertained before meaningful settlement discussions can take place. A longer time period allows more of these uncertainties to be resolved, which can lead to a settlement without a court filing. The effect would be fewer filings than in a state with a longer time period. Conversely, a shorter time period could cause comparatively more cases to be filed to avoid loss of the claim.

If a state increases the time period of a statute of limitations, filings would be expected to drop, to the extent more cases settle during the longer period. Conversely, if the period is reduced, filings would be expected to increase. The impact, whether an increase in filings or a decrease, would be expected to be ongoing, reflecting the new pattern of filing practices. To the extent litigants and lawyers anticipate changes in the time period, they may act earlier, reducing the impact of the change.

---

19. Texas Acts 2011, 82d 1st Called Session, HB 79, art. 4, §§4.14 *et seq.*

20. Texas Acts 2019, 86th Reg. Sess. ch. 696, SB 2342, §32, eff. Sept. 1, 2020, amending TEX. GOV'T CODE §27.031(a)(1).

7.2.2 Findings

Changes in the statute of limitations occurred in two of the states during the periods for which data was made available. California extended the statute of limitations for personal injury and wrongful death cases from one year to two in 2003. In Minnesota, there had been a practice of a complaint being served on defendants without filing a case in court, referred to as "hip pocket filing." In 2013, an amendment to a court rule required that civil cases be filed with the court within one year of the service on defendants, effectively shortening the time period for filing. In both instances, there was a step change in total filings associated with the change in the statute of limitations period. The magnitude of the step change varied for different case categories.

In California, the extension of the statute of limitations caused a step down in higher-value[21] Injury/damage filings, as expected. The magnitude of the reduction was different for Auto and Non-auto Injury/damage cases. The reduction in Auto Injury/damage case filings was dramatic. There were 33 percent fewer filings in the first full year after the change and almost 14 percent fewer in the next year. Filings stabilized in the third year at a level 37 percent lower than in the five full fiscal years before the change took effect. There was also a reduction of total filings of Non-auto Injury/damage cases. However, the drop was smaller. The filings dropped significantly in the first full year after the change took effect, then stabilized at a level almost 20 percent lower in the next five fiscal years. For both types of Injury/damage cases, the impact was one time; filings stabilized at a new, lower level by the third full fiscal year after the change took effect.

The change in Minnesota effectively shortened the time period for filing in all civil cases. Prior to the change, a civil case was served on defendants, but not filed in court until court intervention was initiated by any party. There was no time limit within which the case had to be filed in court. In 2013, the Supreme Court amended a rule of court to require all non-family civil cases to be filed within one year of the commencement of the action by service on defendants. Discussions leading to the change anticipated a one-time spike in filings of cases that had been served but were already more than a year old and, on an ongoing basis, a step-up in total filings from cases that did not settle within one year, but might have settled more than one year after service without filing a case in court.

The actual changes in total filings were not quite as expected. At the aggregate level, total filings of Major Civil cases had been falling for several years before the change. The expected spike in filings from cases more than one-year old since service appeared not in the year of the change, but in the first full year after the change. Total filings dropped more than 6 percent the year the change took effect, then rose almost 2 percent in the first full year after the change. The expected step-up in total filings of cases that now had to be filed within one year of service did not appear. After the spike, total filings resumed the decline that was occurring prior to the change.

The subcategories of Major Civil cases experienced a similar pattern. The subcategory of Contract cases had a spike in filings in the first full year after the change. Filings then steadily declined for the next several years; there was no step-up in filings.

21. No filing data was available for lower value injury/damage cases, as they were aggregated with all other case types in the category of Limited Civil cases.

The spike was mostly Consumer Credit cases, as predicted, and, at a lower level, Contract cases other than Consumer Credit. Injury/damage filings also spiked in 2014. The largest increases were product liability cases (largest increase in percentage) and personal injury cases (largest increase in terms of number of cases). Other types of Injury/damage cases also exhibited spikes in 2014, but the volume was generally small and there had been fluctuations of similar magnitude, in both number and percentage, in the years before and after the change. These subcategories then continued the long-term decline, with no step-up in total filings.

The change in total filings of Minor Civil cases was not as expected. Filings dropped almost 20 percent in 2013, the largest year-to-year drop in 25 years. The drop was primarily in Default and Confession of Judgment filings, which dropped 32 percent in 2013. Total filings dropped another 5 to 6 percent in each of the next two years. The other Minor Civil subcategories dropped much less, or barely at all, after the change. There was no spike after the change and no step-up in total filings for any Minor Civil case subcategory.

7.2.3 California—Extension of Statute of Limitations in Personal Injury and Wrongful Death Cases

Effective January 1, 2003, the California legislature extended the statute of limitations in personal injury and wrongful death cases from one year to two.[22] The limitation was one of the most stringent in the country, as only three other states had a one-year statute of limitations.[23] Proponents of the change argued that the short, one-year statute of limitation resulted in the unnecessary filing of many potential lawsuits that would have settled without filing. Opponents argued that increasing the statute of limitations would increase claims settlement costs, drive up insurance premiums, and would result in more stale claims being litigated. In adopting the change, the legislature stated a specific finding that "[m]any such matters would be resolved without the need to resort to litigation if California's statute of limitations permitted such actions to be filed within two years, as the vast majority of other states provide for a longer time to resolve claims short of litigation."[24]

After the extension of the statute of limitations, there was a significant reduction in the total number of filings of higher value Unlimited Civil Injury/damage cases. The extension went into effect in the middle of fiscal year 2002–03 (gray column in Figure 7.6). Unlimited Civil Auto Injury/damage filings had been rising in the previous five fiscal years (orange line in Figure 7.6). In the fiscal year the change took effect, Auto Injury/damage filings dropped almost 6 percent. Filings dropped another 33 percent in the first full fiscal year after the change took effect, the largest percentage single year drop in 41 years. Total Auto Injury/damage filings dropped another 13.5 percent in the second full fiscal year after the change. Filings rose almost 10 percent in the third fiscal year, but changed very little over the next four fiscal years. Auto Injury/damage total filings were 37 percent lower in the five years after the change stabilized compared

---

22. 2002 Cal. Stat. ch. 448, § 2, adding Cal. Code of Civ. Proc. § 335.1.
23. *Senate Floor Analysis*, Cal. Legislature, SB 688, Sept. 12, 2002, at 5.
24. 2002 Cal. Stat. ch. 448, § 1(b).

to the five years before the change. This amounted to an average of more than 17,000 fewer filings per year statewide.

There was also a reduction of total filings of Unlimited Civil Non-auto Injury/damage cases (blue line in Figure 7.6) when the new statute of limitations became effective. However, the drop was less pronounced. Filings had been relatively steady before the change. Filings dropped less than 2 percent in the fiscal year during which the change took effect. In the first full year after the change, filings dropped more than 14 percent, the largest single year percentage drop in 41 years. Filings dropped another 13 percent in the second full fiscal year. Filings were essentially flat for the next several years after the change. The Non-auto Injury/damage filing level was almost 20 percent lower in the five years after the change compared to the five years before the change. This amounted to an average of more than 5,000 fewer filings per year statewide.

FIGURE 7.6 CALIFORNIA UNLIMITED CIVIL INJURY/DAMAGE TOTAL FILINGS, CHANGE IN STATUTE OF LIMITATIONS

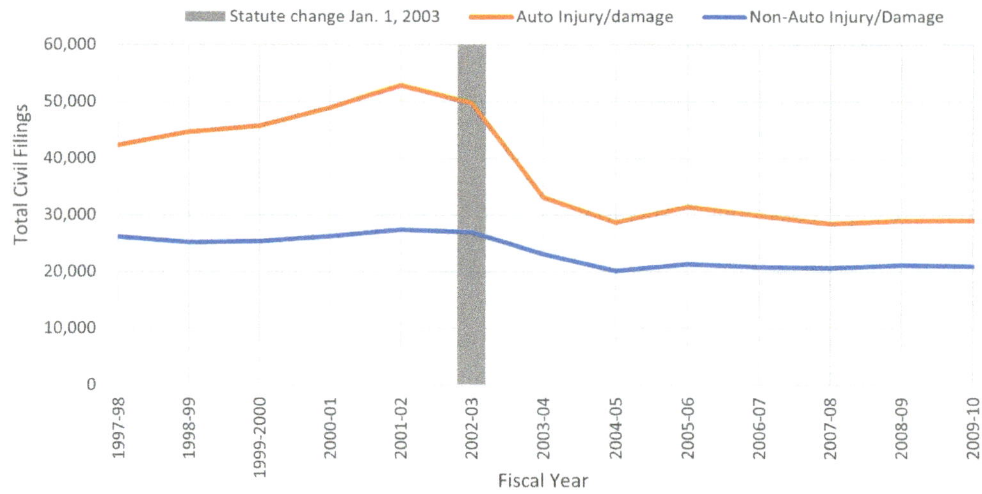

The change in the statute of limitations only applied to Injury/damage cases involving personal injury or wrongful death. It did not apply to property damage cases for which the statute of limitations was three years.[25] The statewide proportion of property-damage-only Injury/damage cases was not known. Filing data supplied by the Orange County (CA) Superior Court for calendar years 2007 and 2017 suggested property-damage-only Injury/damage cases were 17–21 percent of all Unlimited Civil Injury/damage cases. Statewide information about Injury/damage cases filed as Limited Civil cases was also not available. Filing data supplied by the Orange County (CA) Superior Court for calendar years 2007 and 2017 suggested Injury/damage cases constituted only 5 to 6 percent of all Limited Civil cases, and that property-damage-only Injury/damage cases were 6 to 9 percent of all Limited Civil Injury/damage cases. This suggests that the volume of cases for which there was no change was not so large as to obscure the nature of the change for Injury/damage cases for which the change did apply.

25. Cal. Code of Civ. Proc. § 338.

7.2.4 Minnesota Limitation on Hip Pocket Filing

Prior to 2013, Minnesota was one of a very few states where a civil action could be commenced by service of the complaint on the defendants without first filing the case with a court—referred to as "hip pocket filing." There was no time limit within which a case had to be filed in court after service. The lack of a limitation for filing was assumed to result in fewer court filings to the extent that cases settled after service, but without a filing in court. In 2001, a legislative auditor's evaluation of district courts found that one-third of judges and 42 percent of attorneys surveyed considered hip pocket filing practice to be effective in avoiding case filings.[26]

In a 2011 report, the Civil Justice Reform Task Force contained a discussion of hip pocket filing, including the likely impact on total filings of establishing a one-year limitation.[27] A footnote summarized the experience of other states with similar filing practices.[28] Comments from debt collection firms suggested that imposing a limit might triple consumer debt case filings. Others suggested that the increase in filings would be somewhere between 20 percent and 100 percent each year. Based on the recommendation of the Task Force, the Supreme Court amended a rule of court[29] to require all non-family civil cases to be filed within one year of the service on defendants. The requirement became effective on July 1, 2013.

When a one-year limitation was adopted, two effects were anticipated. First, there would be a one-time spike in filings of those cases that were more than a year old since service and had not yet settled. Second, on an ongoing basis, there would be a higher level of total filings from those cases that previously might have settled more than one year after service without having been filed in court. The actual changes in total filings was not what was expected, and the changes varied significantly by case category.

The most noticeable change was in total filings of Minor Civil[30] cases (orange line in Figure 7.7). Contrary to the expectation that filings would rise, total Minor Civil filings dropped noticeably in the year the change became effective. Minor Civil filings had been slowly dropping since 2008. In 2013, filings dropped almost 20 percent (a total of 11,145 cases), the largest single year drop in 25 years. Filings dropped another 5 to 6 percent in each of the next two years. There were more than 16,000 fewer filings in the third year. In the fourth year, filings began a very slow rise. The impact of the

26. Minn. Office of the Legislative Auditor, PROGRAM EVALUATION REPORT, DISTRICT COURTS, Report # 01-02, Jan. 2001, at 103. The Auditor's report also noted: "Minnesota tends to have fewer civil filings per judge than comparable states: Minnesota had 854 civil filings per judge in 1998, compared with 962 median civil filings per judge in seven comparable states. One possible explanation for the lower civil filings was Minnesota's practice of 'hip pocket filing,' which allows a person to serve another with a civil lawsuit without first filing it in court; such cases that settle were not included in the count of civil filings per judge." (p. 23).

27. Recommendations of the MINNESOTA SUPREME COURT CIVIL JUSTICE REFORM TASK FORCE, FINAL REPORT, Dec. 23, 2011.

28. *Id.* at 21, n.8.

29. Minn. Supreme Court Administrative Order ADM10-8052, ADM09-8009, and ADM04-8001, *Order Relating to the Civil Justice Reform Task Force, Authorizing Expedited Civil Litigation Track Pilot Project, and Adopting Amendments to the Rules of Civil Procedure and the General Rules of Practice*, filed May 8, 2013, amending MINN. R. CIV. PROC. r. 3.01 and 5.04(a).

30. For Minor Civil cases the figures exclude filings of Implied Consent (associated with DWI cases), several case types associated with enforcement of existing judgments, and Conciliation (small claims) cases.

change was a reduction of filings, not the one-time spike in filings or step-up in total filings that had been predicted.

FIGURE 7.7 MINNESOTA TOTAL COMPARABLE CIVIL FILINGS, HIP POCKET FILING LIMITED TO ONE YEAR ON JULY 1, 2013

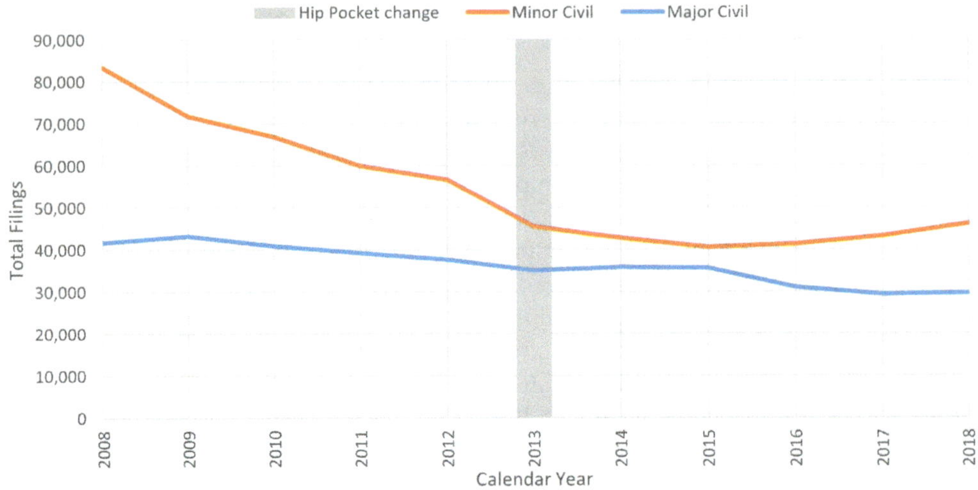

Looking at subcategories of Minor Civil cases, the drop in 2013 was primarily a drop in Default and Confession of Judgment filings (blue line Figure 7.8). Default and Confession filings had dropped steeply since 2008. They dropped more than 32 percent in 2013 (more than 10,000 cases), and dropped a further 5 to 6 percent in each of the next two years. The other case subcategories also dropped, but not as much in magnitude or percentage. Unlawful detainer/eviction filings (green line in Figure 7.8) dropped almost 5 percent in 2013 (about 1,000 cases), then another 8 percent in 2014 and over 6 percent more in 2015. Enforcement of judgment filings (burnt orange line in Figure 7.8) had been dropping for several years, dropping less than 1 percent in 2013, but dropping almost 5 percent in 2014. The Other Minor Civil category filings[31] (yellow line in Figure 7.8) dropped about 1 percent in 2013, but rose about 5 percent in each of the next two years. Again, there was no one-time spike and no step-up in total filings for these case subcategories.

Note that the drop prior to the change was the tail end of the Great Recession surge, which may have obscured the impact of the change. Filings were dropping in all five states during this period. It may be that there was no "backlog" of served, but unfiled, cases at this stage of the recession recovery. It may also be that cases were already being filed less than a year after service, particularly in Default and Confession cases.

31. This subcategory included Change of Name and Appointment of Trustee cases.

FIGURE 7.8 MINNESOTA MINOR CIVIL FILINGS WITHOUT CONCILIATION, HIP POCKET FILING LIMITED TO ONE YEAR ON JULY 1, 2013

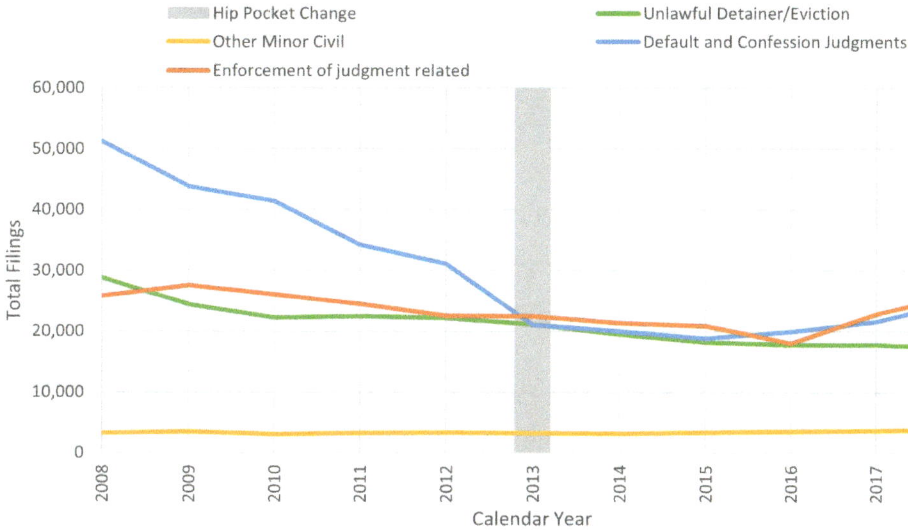

Total filings of Major Civil[32] cases rose very slightly after the change in 2013 (blue line in Figure 7.7). Total filings had been falling for several years before the change in 2013. Total filings dropped more than 6 percent in 2013, the year in which the change took effect. The drop was not particularly large; drops in that range had occurred before 2013. Total filings rose almost 2 percent in 2014, the first full year after the change, then dropped very slightly in 2015. Thereafter, total Major Civil filings continued to drop, including a drop of 12 percent in 2016. While the slight increase in 2014 might have constituted a spike, it was very small. The drop in filings thereafter suggested no step-up in filings. The change in total filings of Major Civil cases after 2013 varied significantly by case subcategory.

Total filings of all Major Civil Contract cases peaked in 2010, having risen more than 58 percent since 2005. The rise was associated with the Great Recession, discussed in Chapter 9. Filings then dropped each year through 2013 (blue line in Figure 7.9). In 2014, as predicted, Contract filings spiked. Although the total filing level was slightly higher than the peak in 2010, the spike was much smaller than predicted, less than 19 percent. While a step-up in filings was also predicted, total filings actually dropped from 2015 to 2017. Total filings in 2017 and 2018 were comparable to total filings during the 2003 to 2005 period prior to the Great Recession.

32. For Major Civil cases, the filing figures exclude Forfeiture and Habeas Corpus case types, which are associated with criminal cases.

FIGURE 7.9 MINNESOTA MAJOR CIVIL CONTRACT SUBCATEGORY FILINGS, HIP POCKET FILING LIMITED TO ONE YEAR ON JULY 1, 2013

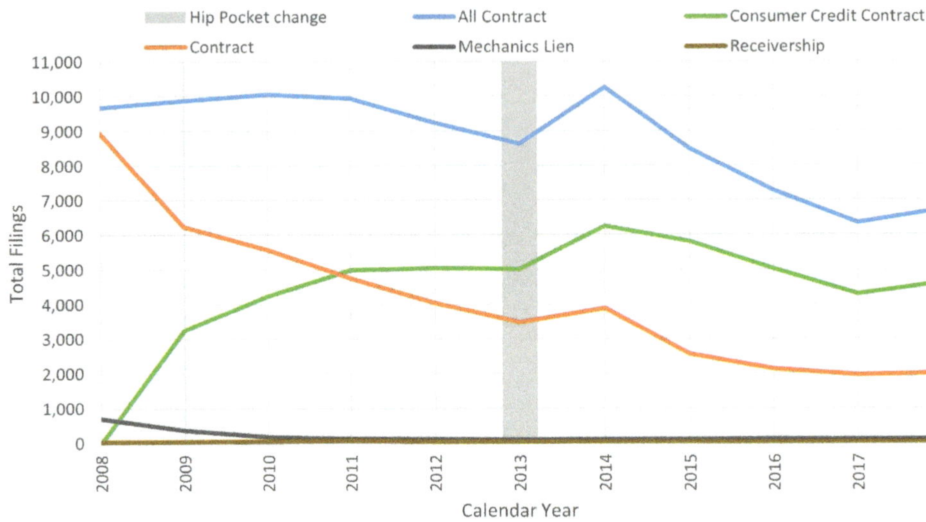

Figure 7.9 displays the total filings for four subcategories of Contract cases. The subcategories of Consumer Credit Contracts (green line) and Contracts other than Consumer Credit (burnt orange line) both spiked after the change. Consumer Credit Contract case filings increased more than 24 percent in 2014. This was consistent with the predictions of consumer collection attorneys noted by the Civil Reform Task Force in its 2011 report. However, filings dropped more than 7 percent in 2015, and dropped again in 2016 and 2017. The total filings in 2017 and 2018 were below the total filings in 2011, 2012, and 2013, indicating no step-up increase in filings. This was contrary to the predictions noted in the 2011 Task Force report.

There was another possible contributing factor to the jump in Consumer Credit Contract filings in 2014. In addition to the limitation on hip pocket filing in 2013, there was a change in the law regarding burden of proof in assigned debt collection filings requesting a default judgment.[33]

Non-consumer credit Contract cases (burnt orange line in Figure 7.9) had been dropping for the last four years and dropped 14 percent in 2013. Filings then spiked 12 percent in 2014, and then dropped 34 percent in 2015. Again, the spike in filings was not as great as had been predicted and there was no step-up increase in total filings.

Total filings of the other subcategories of contract cases, Mechanics Liens and Receiverships, were also affected by the limitation of hip pocket filing, but the number of cases was very small. Mechanics Lien total filings (black line in Figure 7.9) dropped 24 percent in 2013, rose almost 13 percent in 2014, then fluctuated through 2017. Receivership cases (brown line in Figure 7.9) rose 10 percent in 2013, dropped more than 36 percent in 2014, and dropped almost 50 percent through 2018. There was a spike in total filings in the year after the change, but no step-up in total filings.

---

33. 2020 MINN. STAT. § 548.101, added by 2013 Minn. Laws ch. 104, § 3.

Major Civil Injury/damage cases of all types also showed a spike in 2014, the year after the 2013 change (blue line in Figure 7.10). The surge occurred mostly in a few injury/damage subcategories. Again, there was no step-up in filings, rather, they continued to decline.

FIGURE 7.10 MINNESOTA MAJOR CIVIL INJURY/DAMAGE FILINGS, HIP POCKET FILING LIMITED TO ONE YEAR ON JULY 1, 2013

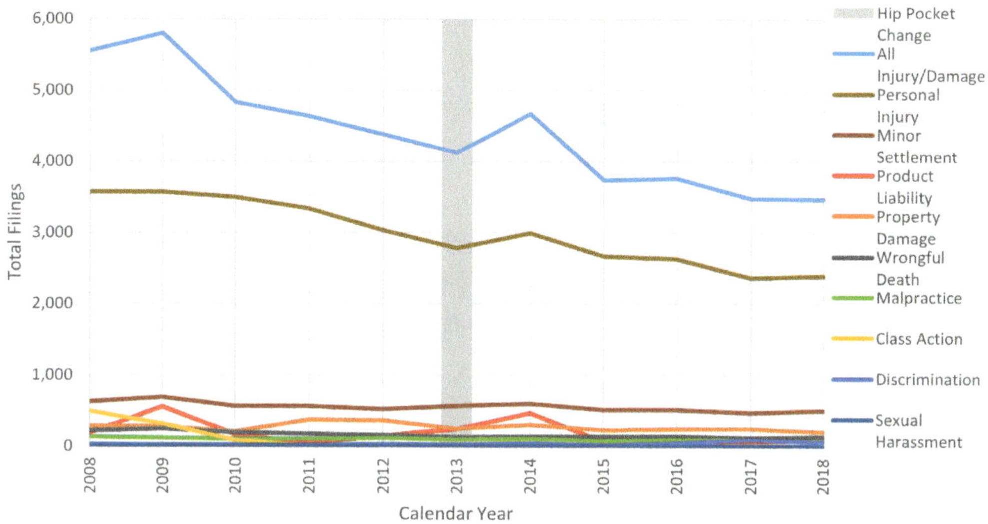

In terms of percentage change in 2014, the largest change was in Product Liability cases (red line in Figure 7.10). However, the number of filings had fluctuated considerably since 2008. Filings in 2009 were more than twice those in 2008. Filings fell in each of the next two years by more than 70 percent. Then the number doubled again in 2012. In 2013, filings increased 69 percent, and another 90 percent in 2014. In 2015, filings dropped 86 percent. Although filings increased in 2013 and 2014, when the limitation in hip pocket took effect, other factors also appeared to have had an impact.

The case subcategory next in terms of total filings was Personal Injury cases (brown line in Figure 7.10). Personal injury filings had been dropping steadily since 2008, including in 2013. They jumped more than 7 percent in 2014, then began dropping again in 2015. The filings trended down during the entire period, except for the spike in 2014. The other case subcategories (sexual harassment, discrimination, property damage, malpractice, minor settlements, and wrongful death) also exhibited one-time spikes in 2014, but the increase in number of filings was very small, ranging from two to 55 cases per year.

8

State Court Characteristics

In addition to looking at civil case filings over time, across states, and across counties within states, we looked at three factors that might be expected to affect civil filing levels. First is the organization of trial courts in each state. The second is the level of the initial civil filing fee in each state. The third is the number of active lawyers in a state. In all three instances we did not find any discernable relationship between the factor examined and the filing levels in the state.

8.1 Trial Court Structure and Civil Case Filings

8.1.1 Overview

Historically, states established multiple types of trial courts in every county. Typically there was a trial court with general jurisdiction and one or more courts that were limited to hearing specific categories of civil cases, for example, cases with a low dollar amount in controversy or landlord/tenant disputes. Since the 1960s, there has been a national trend, urged by the American Bar Association's Standards for Court Organization Standards,[1] to consolidate all trial level courts in each county into a single, unified trial court. The goals of a unified trial court structure were to improve the performance of trial courts, in particular, regarding timeliness, efficiency, consistent implementation of the law (with all judges being required to be lawyers), and the management of resources provided to the courts.[2] In addition, having only one trial court in a county for all case types was less confusing to potential litigants and the public.

1. Standards Relating to Court Organization: Standards of Judicial Administration, Vol. I (1990 ed. ABA), NCJ Number 128491.

2. *See, e.g.*, Steven W. Hays & Cole Blease Graham, Jr., eds, Handbook of Court Administration and Management (1993).

Studies of the impact of court unification looked for benefits such as more current calendars, faster case processing, higher case clearance rates, greater flexibility in the use of judicial officers, and greater administrative efficiency.[3] Neither the explanations and justification for a single type of trial court nor studies of the impact of court unification explicitly addressed the impact on case filings. Implicitly, a more prompt, effective, and efficient trial court could encourage filings. Conversely, a slow, ineffective, or inefficient trial court could discourage filings. Did the merger of trial courts in a county affect the numbers of civil case filings?

Of the five states examined here, California, Illinois, and Minnesota have a unified trial court structure—one type of trial court in each county. Ohio has two types, and Texas has four types of trial courts. Figure 8.1 displays the total civil filings in all five states from 1994 to 2019. Examining total filings across these five states does not suggest that unified trial courts have different patterns of filings over time. In the three unified states, California's pattern fluctuated more than all the other states, and Minnesota and Illinois fluctuated the least. All five states had surges associated with the Great Recession, but the patterns were different. Ohio's surge began earlier and lasted longer than in the other states. California's surge started later and rose more steeply. Illinois and Texas had similar patterns around the Great Recession. In the last five years, Texas filings rose appreciably, both Ohio and California total filings rose slightly, and Illinois and Minnesota were flat. While the data only includes five states, no pattern of total filings distinguished unified trial court states from multiple trial court states.

FIGURE 8.1 TOTAL CIVIL FILINGS, COMPARABLE CASE CATEGORIES

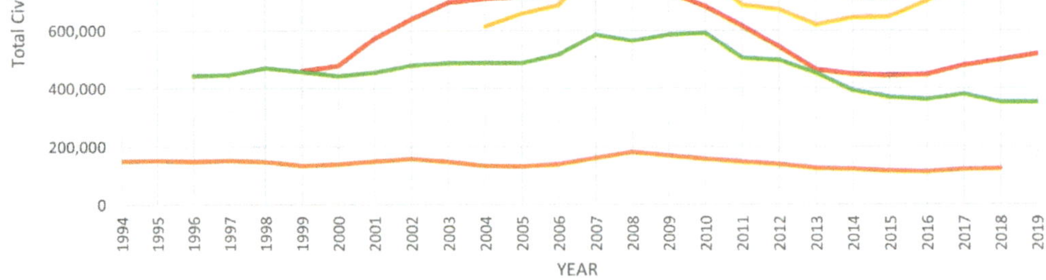

There was also no apparent relationship when per capita filing levels were examined (Figure 8.2). Ohio had the highest per capita filing levels. Texas, California, and Minnesota had the lowest, and very similar, per capita filing levels. Illinois per capita filing levels were in the middle. Per capita filing levels in all five courts peaked in

3. *See, e.g.*, William Raftery, *Judicial Unification and Its Impact on Efficiency*, INST. FOR COURT MGMT., ICM Fellows Program, 2015–2016 Court Project Phase, May 2016, and Carl Baar, *Trial Court Unification in Practice*, 76(4) JUDICATURE 179–84, (Dec.–Jan. 1993), NCJ Number 141563.

2007 or 2008, associated with the Great Recession discussed in Chapter 9. There was a second peak in 2010 in Texas and Illinois. Ohio and Texas per capita filing levels rose beginning in 2015, but so did those of California and Minnesota, although not quite as steeply. Again, there do not appear to be differences in per capita filing levels based on the number of trial courts.

FIGURE 8.2 COMPARABLE CIVIL FILINGS PER 100K POPULATION

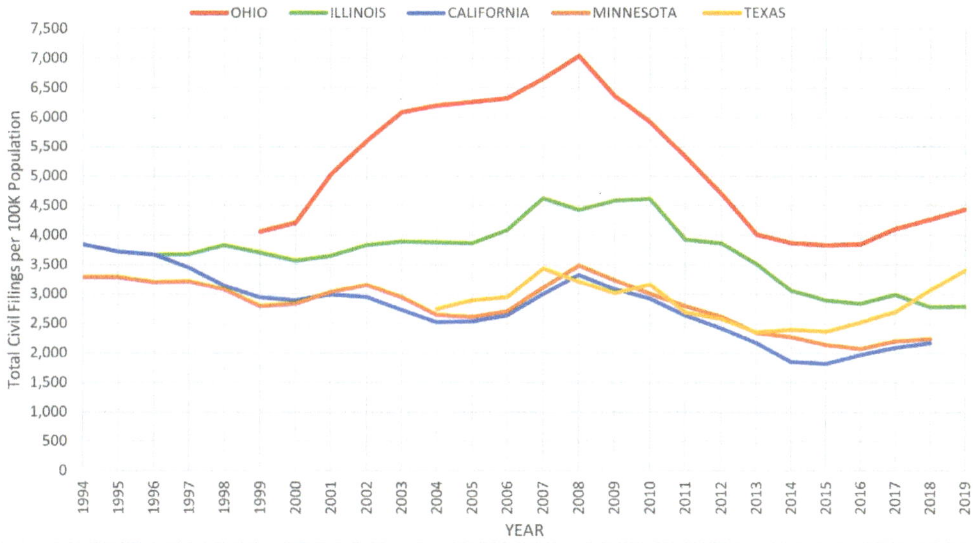

What happened to filing levels when multiple trial courts were consolidated into one trial court? Although three of the five states studied here, California, Illinois, and Minnesota, transitioned to a unified trial court structure, filing data across the unification period was only available in California. Consolidation of trial courts in Illinois occurred in 1964. It occurred in Minnesota between 1983 and 1987. Both those events preceded the filing data provided for this study, precluding a before/after data comparison. Data was available for a before/after analysis of the impact of trial court consolidation in California, where unification took place between 1998 and 2001.

8.1.2 California

The merger of trial courts in California evolved slowly.[4] Since 1879, there had been one general jurisdiction superior court in each of the 58 counties and one or more limited jurisdiction courts in each county. Prior to 1950, there were six types of limited jurisdiction courts.[5] A constitutional amendment in 1950 reduced the number of limited jurisdiction courts to two types: justice courts and municipal courts. By 1970, there were 75 municipal courts and 244 justice courts.[6] Serious study of consolidation began in 1970.

4. For a full discussion of the history of trial courts, see Larry Sipes, COMMITTED TO JUSTICE, THE RISE OF JUDICIAL ADMINISTRATION IN CALIFORNIA, Cal. Administrative Office of the Courts, 2002, hereinafter COMMITTED TO JUSTICE.

5. Harry N, Scheiber, *Innovation, Resistance, and Change: A History of Judicial Reform and the California Courts, 1960–1990*, 66 SO. CAL. L. REV. 2049, 2077 (1992).

6. COMMITTED TO JUSTICE, *supra* note 4, at 106.

A ballot measure to allow consolidation of all trial courts in each county was proposed in 1992,[7] but not approved by the legislature.[8] However, in 1994, the voters approved a constitutional amendment to convert justice courts to municipal courts.[9]

Another proposed constitutional amendment to merge the municipal and superior courts into one superior court in each county was introduced in 1995. A report had been prepared looking at the possible impacts of consolidation of the courts pursuant to the proposed constitutional amendment.[10] The report addressed the issue of filings only by noting the recent decline in municipal court criminal filings, potentially freeing up judicial officers in those courts to hear other matters.[11] The report did not otherwise address the possible impact of consolidation on case filings generally. That amendment was rejected by the voters.

In 1998, a constitutional amendment authorizing the merger to one trial court in each county was finally adopted by the voters.[12] It became effective June 3, 1998. The amendment required a majority of the judges in the existing municipal and superior courts to approve a merger in their county. Many courts immediately voted to unify. Judges in 50 of the 58 counties had voted to unify by the end of 1998. The largest court, Los Angeles, voted to merge on January 22, 2000, and the last court to merge voted on February 8, 2001.

Legislation implementing consolidation required the Judicial Council of California to "assess the effectiveness and efficiency of those trial court systems that have unified."[13] A report assessing consolidation was completed in September 2000.[14] The analysis provided an overview of the short-term impact of unification in four areas: (1) the utilization of judicial resources, (2) the organization and efficiency of court staff, (3) the efficiency of court operations, and (4) the quality of services provided by the courts (e.g., case backlogs, pace of litigation, service to the public). The analysis found positive impacts on availability and flexibility of judicial resources and court staff, and improvements in court operations and case processing. The analysis did not examine the impact of consolidation on the volume of case filings.

The effect of consolidation on filings was mixed across civil case types. Table 8.1 and Figure 8.3 display changes in filing levels before, during, and after consolidation. The higher-value Unlimited Civil filings reversed a slow decline and increased during and after consolidation. Filings of lower-value Limited Civil cases declined during and following consolidation. The ongoing decline in Small Claims case filings was accelerated.

Total civil filings had risen slightly before consolidation, due to a significant increase in Limited Civil filings. During the period when the trial courts were voting to merge, total filings went down, then up. The Dot.com Recession was occurring during

7. Cal. Senate Const. amend. 3 (SCA 3) 1992.

8. Committed to Justice, *supra* note 4, at 112–14.

9. Cal. Senate Const. amend. 7 (SCA 7) 1994; *see* Committed to Justice, *supra* note 4, at 114.

10. Robert Tobin, Alexander B. Aikman, Gwendolyn H. Lyford, Frederick G. Miller, & Dale A. Sipes, California Unification Study, NCSC, Feb. 1994.

11. *Id.* at 14.

12. Proposition 220 amending Cal. Const. art. VI.

13. Cal. Gov't Code § 68113(d).

14. Mary Anne Lahey, Bruce A. Christenson & Robert J. Rossi, Analysis of Trial Court Unification in California, Final Report, American Institutes for Research, Sept. 28, 2000, https://www.courts.ca.gov/documents/928rept.pdf.

this same time frame, which is discussed in Chapter 9. After consolidation, through FY 2018–19, total filings were down 14 percent, attributable largely to the significant drop in Small Claims filings. Unlimited Civil filings were down before consolidation, then rose both during and for a short period after consolidation. Limited Civil filings had been rising steadily before consolidation, dropped 14 percent during consolidation, then rose only slightly after consolidation. Small Claims filings were dropping before consolidation. The drop continued, but slowed, during consolidation, then accelerated after consolidation. By FY 2018–19 Unlimited Civil filings were at levels below those prior to consolidation. Limited Civil filings fluctuated, but at a lower level than before consolidation. Small Claims were also lower after consolidation.

FIGURE 8.3 CALIFORNIA CIVIL FILINGS LEVELS DURING TRIAL COURT UNIFICATION FROM FY 1997–98 TO 2000-01

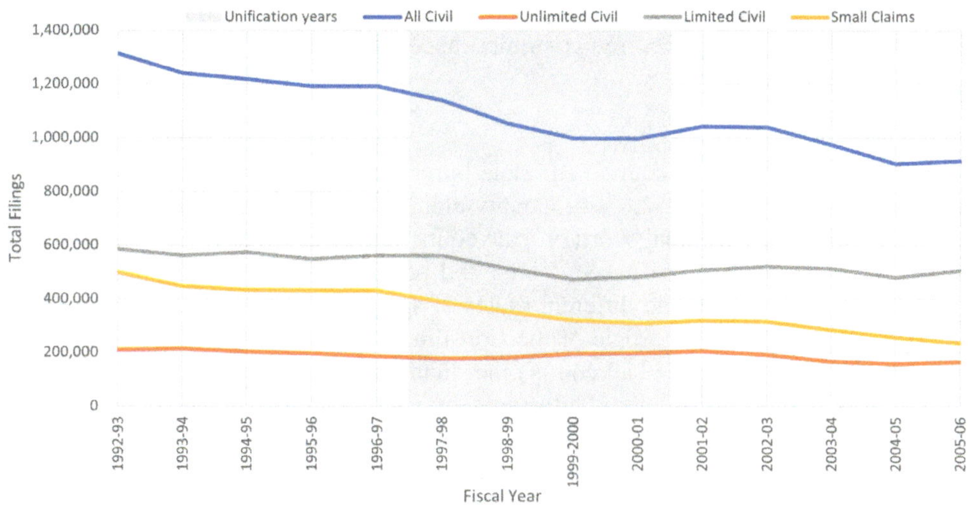

TABLE 8.1 CALIFORNIA—CHANGE IN TOTAL FILINGS AT THE TIME OF UNIFICATION

Time frame	All Civil	Unlimited Civil	Limited Civil	Small Claims
Before unification FY 1978–79 to FY 1997–98	+5 %	-8%	+46%	-22%
During unification FY 1997–98 to FY 2000–01	-12%	+11%	-14%	-20%
After full unification FY 2000–01 to FY 2018–19	-14%	+10%	+1%	-51%
From beginning of unification, FY 1997–98, to FY 2018–19	-25%	+22%	-13%	-61%
Overall FY 1978–79 to FY 2018–19	-21%	+12%	+27%	-70%

8.1.3 Minnesota

The Minnesota Constitution established district courts[15] with original jurisdiction in all civil and criminal cases[16] and authorized the legislature to create trial courts in addition to the district courts. Over time, several types of limited jurisdiction courts were established, including county courts, municipal courts, probate courts, and justice of the peace courts. Probate courts in most counties were merged with county courts in 1971.[17] The municipal[18] and justice of the peace courts[19] were consolidated into the county courts as of July 1, 1977. The probate courts in Hennepin and Ramsey Counties became part of the district courts in these counties in 1982.[20] Authority for the county courts to merge with the district courts was established in 1982,[21] but it required a majority of the judges in each court to agree to the merger. The courts in only one district had approved a merger by 1984. The courts in several more districts voted to merge by 1986, and the balance of the districts voted to merge in 1987.[22] All of this merger activity took place before the filings data made available for this study, so it was not possible to see whether any filing changes occurred contemporaneously with unification.

8.1.4 Illinois

The number of different trial courts in Illinois burgeoned from the adoption of the 1870 Constitution until 1964. In 1962, Cook County alone had 208 courts: circuit court; superior court; family court; criminal court; probate court; county court; city, village, town, and municipal courts; justice of the peace courts; and police magistrate courts. Many courts had overlapping jurisdiction and different routes of appeal.[23] In 1962, the voters approved a new Article VI, the judicial article of the Constitution, that went into effect January 1, 1964. The amendment abolished all courts other than the circuit courts, which became the trial court of unlimited jurisdiction. Unfortunately, filing data made available for Illinois does not cover the period during which consolidation occurred, so it was not possible to observe any filing changes that occurred contemporaneously with consolidation.

8.1.5 Future Consolidations

Since efforts to consolidate trial courts may continue, in particular for fiscal and efficiency reasons, states should consider the possible impact on filing levels when considering consolidation. This will require more analysis of past consolidations in an effort

---

15. MINN. CONST. art. VI, § 1

16. MINN. CONST. art. VI, § 3.

17. 1971 MINN. LAWS, ch. 951, § 1.

18. Former Chaps. 488, and 488A, repealed by 1977 MINN. LAWS, ch. 432, § 49.

19. Justice of the Peace was merged into County Courts by 1977 MINN. LAWS, ch. 951, § 35. The Justice of the Peace position, former § 487.35, was abolished by 1977 MINN. LAWS, CHAP. 432, §§ 27 and 49.

20. 1982 MINN. LAWS, ch. 398, § 3.

21. 1982 MINN. LAWS, ch. 398, § 8. Former ch. 487 establishing County Courts was repealed by 2006 MINN. LAWS, ch. 260, art. 5, § 54.

22. Robert J. Sheran & Douglas K. Amdahl, *Minnesota Judicial System: Twenty-Five Years of Radical Change*, 26(2) HAMLINE L. REV. 219–376, 235–36 (Winter 2002).

23. David F. Rolewick, A SHORT HISTORY OF THE JUDICIAL SYSTEM OF ILLINOIS, Administrative Office of the Illinois Courts, 1971 ed., at 19.

to identify which case categories appear to have been affected. Going forward, states should then collect more detailed filing data for those case categories that are likely to be affected by consolidation.

8.2 Initial Civil Filing Fee and Civil Filing Levels

8.2.1 Overview

One barrier to access to justice are filing fees that must be paid to initiate a case. Simply stated, if an aggrieved party cannot afford the initial filing fee, and therefore chooses not to file a case, access to justice is denied. Traditionally, filing fees have been thought to be so small in comparison to the other costs of civil litigation (e.g., attorney's fees and expert witness costs) that they have been considered a "rounding error." At what amount does the initial filing fee become such a barrier, particularly for self-represented litigants?[24] Based on a survey of households in 2017, the Federal Reserve found that, if faced with an unexpected expense of $400, 40 percent of adults would not be able to cover it from cash, savings, or credit card. This was down from 50 percent in 2013. Could this be another instance of what we know "that just ain't so"? Are these fees sufficiently large that they constitute a "cost of justice" that influences the use of court services?

We gathered data on the history of filing fees for various types of civil filings over the time of our study in each of the five states. We derive three findings from this data:

- The variation in filing fees within a state—even where there has been a serious effort to create statewide uniformity—is bewildering.
- There is no relationship between the overall level of civil filing fees in a state and the per capita civil filings in that state for high-value, low-value, or small claims civil filings.
- In the two states in which we have relatively consistent filing fee data over the time period of our study, we do not observe any consistent pattern of filing changes associated with filing fee increases (or, in one state, a decrease).

The impact, if any, of the amount of the initial filing fee on filing levels in a state may be obscured to the extent the filing fee varies across courts within the state. The most common source of inconsistency in these five states had to do with how courts were funded. If the majority of trial court expenses are paid by the county, as opposed to the state, initial filing fees usually varied by county. While authority to impose a fee is generally based on state statute, the statutes generally give counties discretion to set the amount of the filing fees within a range or up to a maximum amount.

---

24. While it is clear that self-representation has increased markedly in recent decades, the most widely quoted statistic—"at least one party is unrepresented in 76% of civil cases"—does not necessarily translate to 76 percent of filings. The data shows that defendant/respondents—not plaintiff/petitioners who initiate cases—are the party most often unrepresented or that failed to appear at all. Paula Hannaford-Agor, The Landscape of Civil Litigation in State Courts, NCSC, Civil Justice Initiative, 2015, https://ncsc.contentdm.oclc.org/digital/collection/civil/id/168/rec/20. The combination of Boddie v. Connecticut, U.S. 371 (1971), United States v. Kras, U.S. 434 (1973) and Ortwein v. Schwab, 410 U.S. 656 (1973), established that a court system could condition access on a would-be litigant's paying a mandatory (non-waivable) filing fee, but that the due process clause required an exception for cases involving constitutional rights that could be effectuated only by resort to the courts.

Most states also had "add-ons" to the base civil filing fee. The add-ons generally related to the funding of specific court expenses, for example, automation of court operations, fees to fund new courthouses, and court security fees. Other add-on fees were collected for specific activities within a case, for example, electronic filing of documents, jury fees, and court reporter fees. Occasionally, add-on fees were collected to fund services not directly related to the funding of court operations nor operated by the courts, for example, alternate dispute resolution programs, legal assistance programs that serve only a subset of litigants, and equal access funds. There were even add-on fees collected in civil cases to support programs related to other types of cases, for example, to support a child custody exchange program or a domestic relations legal fund. The variance in initial filing fee and variety of add-on fees made it more difficult to assess the impact of filing fees on filing levels in a state.

We observed a wide range of initial civil filing fees in the five states studied. For higher-value or major civil cases, the initial filing fee was $285 in Minnesota, $350 in Texas, and $435 in California. In Illinois, the fee was $366 in Cook County and $316 in the other counties. In Ohio, the range was from $200 to $350. We would expect to find that filing fee increases would have less of an impact on the level of filings of higher-value civil cases than on those with lower value because they would be more likely to involve lawyers and parties with more assets. Indeed, we found that the amount of the initial fee was unrelated to filing levels. For example, the per capita filing levels were almost identical in California and Minnesota, and twice as high in Texas.

For lower-value or minor civil cases, the filing fee amount was lower, but the range of initial filing fees was much greater. It was $54 in Texas justice courts, $90 to $123 in Ohio municipal courts, $266 to $357 in Illinois courts, $285 for Minor Civil cases in Minnesota, and $370 for Limited Civil cases in California. The per capita filing levels for these cases ranged from 817 in Minnesota to 3,092 in Ohio. Again, states with higher initial filing fees did not appear to have lower per capita filing levels.

The spread of initial filing fees for small claims cases was smaller. It was $37 to $78 in Ohio, $54 in Texas, $50 to $75 in California, $65 in Minnesota, and $89 or $265 (Cook County) in Illinois. For this case type, the data contradicted the hypothesis that higher filing fees lead to lower filings. The per capita small claims filing levels were the lowest in the state with the lowest initial filing fee, but proportionately much greater in the states with higher fees. The per capita filing levels were 246 in Texas, 380 in Ohio, 382 in California, 897 in Minnesota, and 1,086 in Illinois.

During the years covered by our study, in response to the variety and range of filing fees in the state, four of the five states, California, Illinois, Ohio, and Texas, established a task force or working group to study filing fees and make recommendations about the amount, uses, and uniformity of filing fees in the state. The resulting reports about civil filing fees often used terms such as "complex," "dizzying," and "byzantine" to describe the patchwork of civil filing fees in counties in a state, in particular, in states where trial courts were primarily locally funded, as opposed to state funded. None of the studies directly addressed the issue of the effect of initial filing fees on filings.

In two states, California and Minnesota, data was available about the change of initial civil filing fees over time that could be compared with civil filing levels. There was no discernable pattern when comparing filing fees and filing levels in either state. Sometimes filing levels were rising when fees were increased, and sometimes filing levels were falling. Two states is a very small sample size, so the fact that we do not see any relationship over time in the relationship between civil filing fees and civil filing levels is insufficient to conclude that no such relationship exists.

8.2.2 California

Prior to unification of the trial courts and state assumption of all trial court funding, filings fees varied across California counties. State funding of trial courts became effective in 1998. The trial courts in each county were merged by early 2001. In December 2003, the Chief Justice appointed a Court Fees Working Group to review civil fees and make recommendations regarding the fee structure. In December 2004, based on the Working Groups' efforts, the Judicial Council sponsored legislation to establish a uniform civil fee structure for the state.[25] The legislation was adopted and took effect January 1, 2006.[26] It streamlined and simplified the civil fee structure by combining surcharges and add-on fees that varied by county into one uniform statewide filing fee structure. As a result, the same fees are assessed in all 58 counties. There are additional fees added to the base fee for multiple filings by one plaintiff, for specific case categories, for example, complex cases, and, in only a few counties, for courthouse construction debt payments.

The following discussion and figures compare per capita filing levels and basic civil filing fees for each broad civil case category for each year since 2000. The fees in the figures only include the base fee.

When the initial filing fee increase became effective in 2006, Unlimited Civil filings increased dramatically (Figure 8.4). However, this was also the start of the hump associated with the Great Recession. Filings were flat when the fee was increased in 2009 and 2010. The increase in 2012 occurred after filings had already started declining post-2008. If there was any impact from an increase in the filing fee during these two decades, it appeared to be overwhelmed by other factors occurring at the same time.

FIGURE 8.4 CALIFORNIA UNLIMITED CIVIL FILINGS PER 100K POPULATION AND UNLIMITED CIVIL FILING FEES

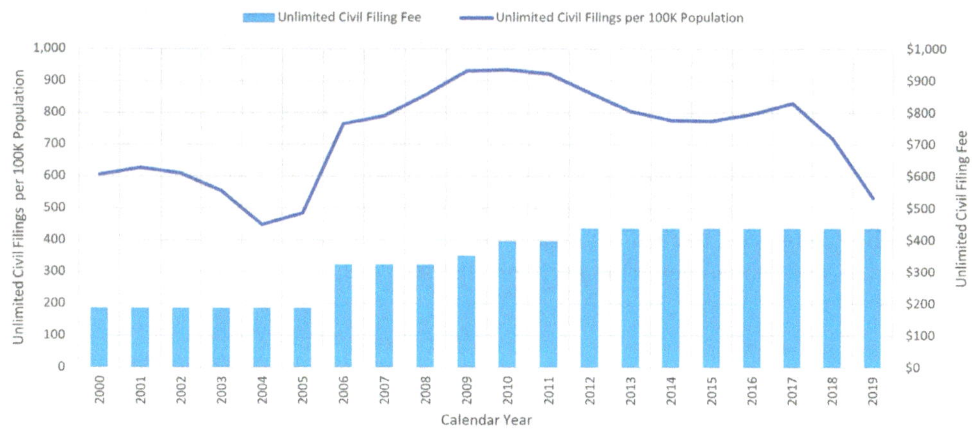

25. Cal. Admin. Office of the Courts, FACT SHEET UNIFORM CIVIL FEE STRUCTURE, April 2008, https://www.courts.ca.gov/documents/uniformcivilfee.pdf.

26. Uniform Civil Fees and Standard Fee Schedule Act of 2005, 2005 CAL. STAT. ch. 75 (AB 145) codified at CAL. GOV'T CODE §§ 70600 *et seq.*

A similar pattern appears regarding the increases in the Limited Civil initial filing fee (Figure 8.5). The filing fee increase in 2006 occurred at the same time as the dramatic pre-2008 rise in filings. The fee was increased twice, in 2009 and 2010, during the downslope of the Great Recession hump. The filings decline began before the increases occurred, so it is unclear what contribution they made to that decline. The filing levels changed significantly between 2010 and 2019 when there was no change in the fee.

FIGURE 8.5 CALIFORNIA LIMITED CIVIL FILINGS PER 100K POPULATION AND LIMITED CIVIL FILING FEES

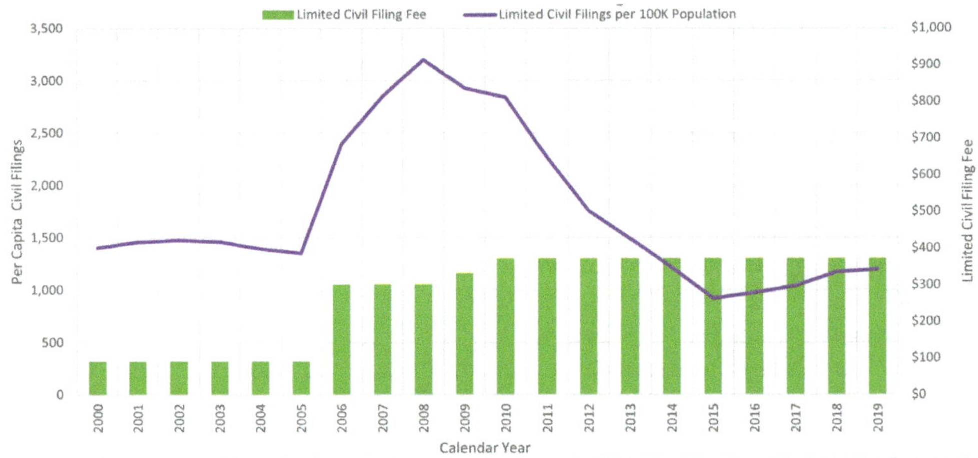

Prior to 2006, there was only one filing fee for a small claims case, regardless of the amount of damages claimed. It was $8 as of January 1, 1992,[27] raised to $15 as of September 1992,[28] then raised to $20 as of January 1, 1998.[29] As part of the Uniform Civil Fees and Standard Fee Schedule Act that became effective January 1, 2006, the fee was split. The fee was $30 if the claim was $1,500 or less, and $50 if it was more than $1,500.[30] The fee was split again as of January 1, 2008, adding a fee of $75 if the claim was more than $5,000.[31]

The pattern associated with per capita small claims filings and filing fee increases was mixed (Figure 8.6). Per capita small claims filings were level for several years at the start of the Great Recession when the fees were increased. Filings had been declining before this, and started declining again in 2010. Filings continued to decline through 2015, while filing fees were unchanged. No data is available to assess any possible impact of the split fees in deterring higher-value small claims filings.

27. 1991 Cal. Stat. ch. 915, § 4, codified at Cal. Code of Civ. Proc. 116.230.

28. 1992 Cal. Stat. ch. 696, § 4, Trial Court Realignment and Efficiency Act.

29. 1997 Cal. Stat. ch. 850, § 4, Lockyer-Isenberg Trial Court Funding Act of 1997.

30. 2005 Cal. Stat. ch. 75, § 18, Uniform Civil Fees and Standard Fee Schedule Act, codified at Cal. Gov't Code §§ 70600 et seq.

31. 2007 Cal. Stat. ch. 738, § 3.

FIGURE 8.6 CALIFORNIA SMALL CLAIMS FILINGS PER 100K POPULATION AND SMALL CLAIMS FILING FEES

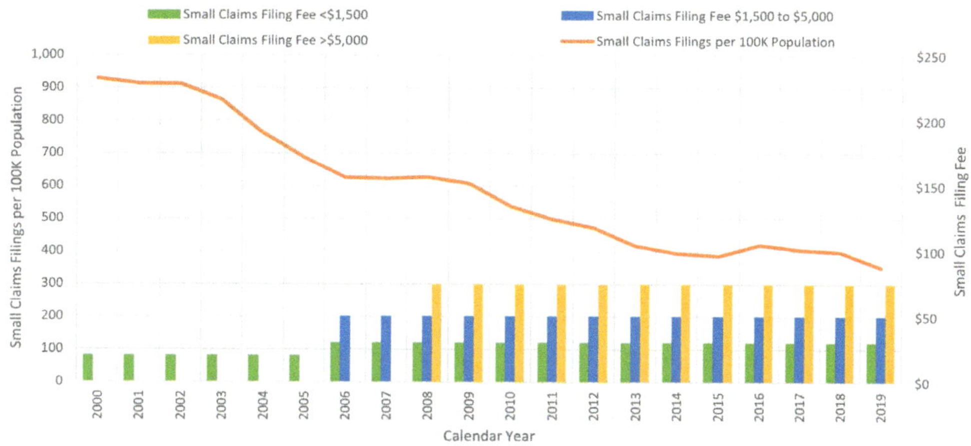

8.2.3 Illinois

The circuit courts in Illinois are organized and operated on a county basis. Financing of the courts is shared by the state and the counties. Revenue to pay for court services is provided from a variety of sources: case filing fees, court-imposed fines and assessments, other fees collected by the courts, state revenue, and county property taxes. Prior to 2019, numerous state statutes authorized counties to impose fees that often included discretion as to the amount of the fee. Consequently, civil filing fees were not uniform across the state.

In 2013, the Illinois legislature created the Statutory Court Fee Task Force to "conduct a thorough review of the various statutory fees imposed or assessed on . . . civil litigants."[32] The Task Force included judges, legislators, circuit clerks, and members of the private bar from across the state. The Task Force issued a report in 2016 that stated, with respect to civil fees:

> Illinois imposes a dizzying array of filing fees on civil litigants. . . . Skyrocketing fees in civil cases in recent years have effectively priced many of our state's most economically vulnerable citizens out of the opportunity to participate in the court system. . . . In virtually all civil . . . proceedings, wide county-to-county variations in the fees and costs for the same type of proceedings injects additional arbitrariness and unfairness into the system.[33]

The Task Force proposed simplifying and streamlining the existing fee provisions in various statutes. In 2018, the legislature approved a bill that, among other changes, consolidated and amended the civil fee statutes.[34] The statutes were amended to establish

32. Access to Justice Act, Pub. Act 098-0351, §25, effective Aug. 15, 2013.

33. Statutory Court Fee Task Force, Illinois Court Assessments. Findings and Recommendations for Addressing Barriers to Access to Justice and Additional Issues Associated with Fees and Other Court Costs in Civil, Criminal, and Traffic Proceedings, Executive Summary, at 1.

34. Criminal and Traffic Assessment Act, Pub. Act 100-987, effective July 1, 2019.

four schedules for filing fees for civil cases.[35] There were two fee amounts for each schedule. One amount was for counties with a population of more than three million, which only included Cook County, and the second amount was for all other counties.

The act delegated to the Supreme Court the assignment of civil case categories to each schedule. The Supreme Court's order[36] assigned most civil case categories, where the amount in controversy was $15,000 or more, to Schedule 1. Arbitration and Law-Magistrate cases where the amount in controversy was less than $15,000, small claims cases where the amount in controversy was more than $2,500, and eviction cases, except those seeking possession, were assigned to Schedule 2. Small claims cases where the amount in controversy was $2,500 or less and eviction cases seeking only possession were assigned to Schedule 3. The fee for Schedule 1 cases was not to exceed $366 in Cook County, and $316 in the other counties. The fee for Schedule 2 cases was not to exceed $357 in Cook and $266 in other counties. The fee for Schedule 3 cases was not to exceed $265 in Cook and $89 in other counties.

In 2021, the Illinois Supreme Court established a new Task Force to propose further measures regarding the basis on which fees and assessments were imposed. The Task Force issued a report in 2023 that identified several existing fees collected in addition to the base civil fee, which resulted in variations in fees assessed across counties.[37] Examples of these fees included the Court Automation Fund,[38] the Court Security Fee,[39] the Dispute Resolution Fee,[40] and the Law Library Fee.[41] The changes proposed by the new task force are being reviewed by the Supreme Court.

Data was not readily available of the basic civil filing fees in each of the 102 counties over the time period for which filing totals were provided, so a comparison of filing fees and filing levels was not possible.

8.2.4 Minnesota

The trial courts in each county in Minnesota were consolidated to one district court by 1987. State funding of all trial courts became effective in July 2005. Filing fees in Minnesota were basically uniform across all counties by 1994. Some add-ons are allowed, for example, a technology fee, and for some add-ons the amount varies by county, for example, a law library fee. Minnesota was unique in that it was the only one of the five states where the filing fee for major civil cases was recently reduced.

As in California, there was no obvious relationship between the per capita filing levels and the amount of filing fees in Minnesota (Figure 8.7). Major civil filings were rising and falling from 1994 to 2002, when the filing fee was unchanged. Filings were

---

35. Pub. Act. 100-1161, effective July 1, 2019, amending 705 ILL. COMP. STAT. 105/27.1b(a)(1).

36. In the Supreme Court of Illinois, In re: Civil Assessment Schedules, M.R. 28741, February 1, 2023.

37. Illinois Supreme Court Statutory Court Fee Task Force, REPORT ON IMPLEMENTATION OF 2016 TASK FORCE RECOMMENDATIONS AND ADDITIONAL PROPOSED MEASURES FOR ADDRESSING BARRIERS TO ACCESS TO JUSTICE AND EXCESSIVE FINANCIAL BURDENS ASSOCIATED WITH FEES AND COSTS IN ILLINOIS COURT PROCEEDINGS, Jan. 1, 2023, https://ilcourtsaudio.blob.core.windows.net/antilles-resources/resources/6228d82a-c843-4211-adfa-02a6171655a9/2023_Statutory_Court_Fee_Task_Force_Report.pdf.

38. 705 ILL. COMP. STAT. 105/27.3a(1), range $1 to $25.

39. 55 ILL. COMP. STAT. 5/5-1103, up to $25.

40. 710 ILL. COMP. STAT. 20/3, $1.

41. 55 ILL. COMP. STAT. 5/5-39001, range $2 to $21 through Dec. 31, 2021.

falling in 2003 and 2004, when the fee was raised. Filings rose in association with the Great Recession when the fee was unchanged. The fee was raised in 2009, during a period when filings had been dropping steadily. However, when the fee was lowered in 2017, filings rose in that year and the next, although it is unknown what other factors may have contributed to the rise in filings. Other states had a similar increase in those years without a change in their filing fees.

FIGURE 8.7 MINNESOTA MAJOR CIVIL FILINGS PER 100K POPULATION AND FILING FEES

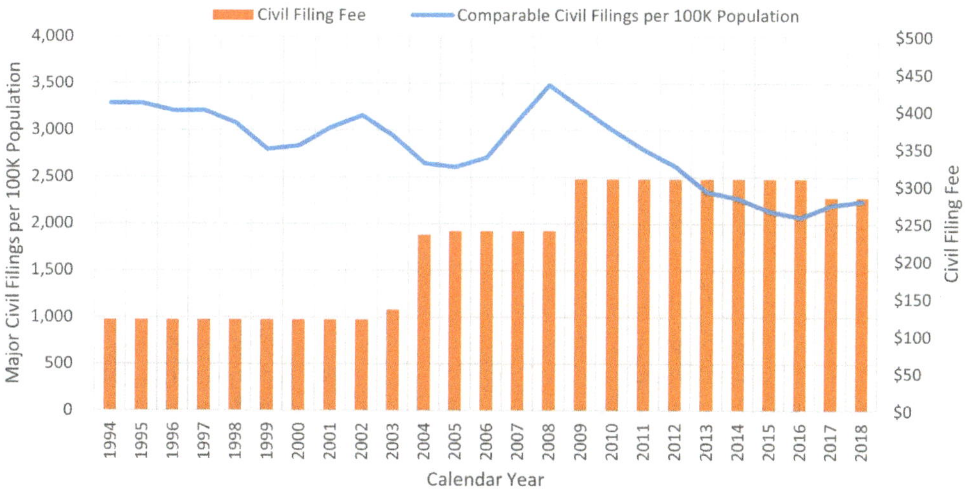

Effective August 1, 1993, there were two filing fees for "conciliation cases"—Minnesota's term for small claims cases—based on the amount of damages claimed. For claims of less than $2,000, the fee was $15, and for claims of $2,000 or more, the fee was $25.[42] The fees were raised to $25 and $35, respectively, as of August 1, 2002.[43] As of July 1, 2003, the split fees was abolished, and the fee raised to $50.[44] In 2009, the fee was raised to $65.[45]

Again, there does not appear to be any association between per capita conciliation filings and fee increases (Figure 8.8). Filings were dropping prior to 1999 when the fees were unchanged. The fee was unchanged when the filings rose during the Great Recession. Filings were already falling when the filing fee was last raised in 2009. Filings continued to decline through 2016, then rose slightly, although the filing fee was unchanged.

42. 1993 Minn. Laws ch. 192, § 93.
43. 2002 Minn. Laws ch. 220, art. 11, § 7.
44. 2003 Minn. Laws 1st Spec. Sess. ch. 2, art. 2, § 3.
45. 2009 Minn. Laws ch. 83, art. 2, § 24.

FIGURE 8.8 MINNESOTA CONCILIATION FILINGS PER 100K POPULATION AND FILING FEES

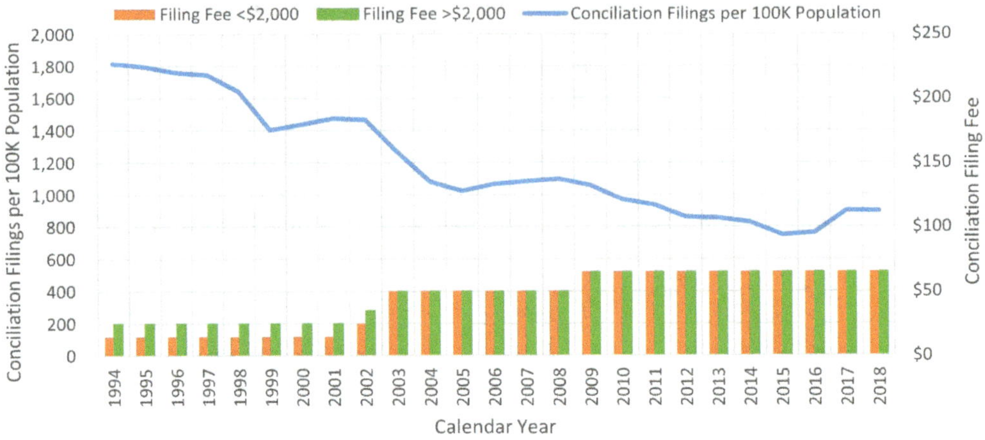

8.2.5 Ohio

The costs of the Ohio judiciary are shared between the state and the counties. Judicial salaries are a shared cost of the state and counties. All other expenses are county funded. The funds supporting the trial courts come from three sources: (1) state and local governments, (2) court fees and costs paid by litigants, and (3) grant monies from public and private sources.

Civil filing fees in Ohio are set by the legislature. Basic filing fees are different for each level of trial court. In addition, the legislature has authorized various "additional" fees to fund either the operation of specific programs,[46] automation of the clerk's office,[47] or to operate specific courts.

A Joint Committee to Study Court Costs and Filing Fees was created in 2006 by the Ohio General Assembly to examine and make recommendations regarding filing fees and court costs in civil and criminal actions and proceedings.[48] The Joint Committee included judges, legislators, clerks of court, court administrators, and attorneys. The Joint Committee released a report in 2008.[49] The report included a table of all fees and costs that could be assessed in all types of cases in the courts of common pleas, municipal courts, and the court of claims. The table runs for 17 pages. The report made a number of recommendations, although none called for the consolidation or standardization of civil fees in the trial courts.

We examined available fee schedules from several courts in the state to determine the typical first filing fee in civil cases. In the courts of common pleas, the initial filing fee for a civil case ranged from $200 to $350. In municipal courts, the initial filing fee

46. For example, OHIO REV. CODE §§ 2303.201(E)(1) and 1901.26(B)(1).

47. OHIO REV. CODE §§ 1901.261(B)(1), 1907.261(B)(1), 2101.162(B)(1), 2151.541(B)(1), 2153.081(B)(1), 2301.031(B)(1), and 2303.201(B)(1).

48. Ohio Laws, 126th General Assembly, Substitute H.B. 336, eff. Jan. 18, 2007.

49. REPORT AND RECOMMENDATIONS OF THE JOINT COMMITTEE TO STUDY COURT COSTS AND FILING FEES, July 2008, www.supremecourt.ohio.gov/Publications/JtCommCourtCostsReport.pdf.

for cases other than small claims ranged from $90 to $123. For small claims cases, the range was from $37 to $78.

8.2.6 Texas

The costs of operating the Texas judiciary are shared between the state and the counties. The State funds a base salary for district judges and salary reimbursements for certain constitutional and statutory county court judges. The State also pays for, or supplements, some other expenses of the judicial branch, for example, juror pay, basic civil legal services, and technology, including electronic filing. Most counties supplement the base salary of judges of district courts. Counties pay the salary of constitutional, statutory, and justice court judges and the operating costs, including staff salaries, for district courts, constitutional and statutory county courts, and justice courts.

Civil filing fees in Texas have many components established by state statute. Some components are a fixed amount, but are only required to be collected in some courts, for example, a judicial support fee or a court reporter fee. Other components are collected only in some counties and vary in amount, for example, a civil court facility fee, a courthouse security fee, an ADR fee, or an appellate judicial system fee. Thus, the total filing fee for a category of civil cases in a court in a particular county depends on decisions by the county commissioners or court clerks. As a result, fees are not uniform across the state.

Legislation was adopted in 2021 to consolidate and standardize collection of fees in civil cases.[50] Although there are still some added fees in some courts and counties, as of January 1, 2022, the basic total consolidated state and local fee for civil cases in district and county courts was set at $350, and the basic total consolidated state and local fee for justice courts was set at $54.

Data on the filing fees and filing levels in each of the 254 counties over time was not readily available, so a comparison of filing fees and filing levels was not possible.

8.3 The Number of Active Lawyers in a State and Civil Filings

As we looked for ways to explain the phenomena of civil filing levels that we have observed in the five states, one hypothesis that was testable was that there has been a reduction in the number of lawyers over time, or in the number of lawyers per capita, leading to fewer civil filings. This hypothesis would not account for the increasing role of self-represented persons in the civil justice process. On the other hand, self-represented persons are disproportionately defendants or respondents rather than the initiators of civil lawsuits.

We asked the entities responsible for maintaining the roster of attorneys in each of the five states to provide us with the number of lawyers in active status in each of the years for which we have civil filings data for that state. Four of the states responded positively to our request. Minnesota declined to provide the information but referred us

50. 2021 Tex. Acts 87th Reg. Sess., ch. 472 (S.B. 41), § 1.03, eff. Jan. 1, 2022.

to the judicial branch annual reports where we were able to find the number of active attorneys for the last five years of the study period. Note that the number of lawyers included all lawyers in active status, some of whom may be practicing law in criminal, family, probate, or other non-civil case types, and some may not be actively practicing law at all. Nonetheless, this provided a first pass look at the relationship between the total number of lawyers in active practice and civil filing levels.

Figure 8.9 shows the number of lawyers in active status in the five states over the periods for which we have civil filings data. The active bar grew fastest in California—the state with the most significant decrease in total civil filings during the period of time we studied.[51] Texas and Illinois also showed growth over the time of the study. The other two states were relatively flat.

FIGURE 8.9 NUMBER OF ACTIVE ATTORNEYS

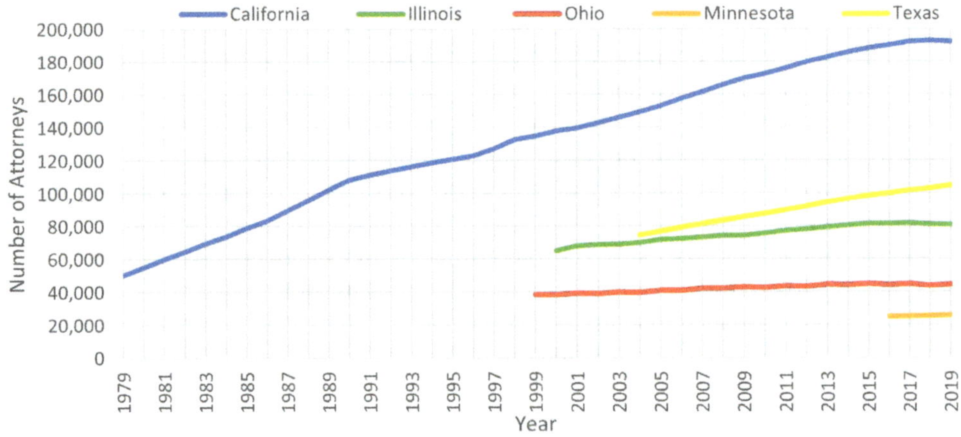

Figure 8.10 shows the number of active bar members per 100,000 population in each of these states. By this measure, Illinois is the most "lawyered" of the five states and also shows the highest rate of growth relative to population in the number of active bar members over the period of the study. Although the differences in per capita lawyers are not as striking as the differences in per capita civil filings discussed in Chapter 2, they did surprise us, with Illinois having almost 50 percent more active lawyers per capita than Ohio and Texas. None of these trends match the per capita civil filing trends for these states. In particular, the California data for per capita lawyers is the inverse of its data for per capita civil filings—the former growing steadily while the later falls just as steadily.

51. The California State Bar official from whom we obtained this data was perplexed by the decline in the number of lawyers in active practice after 2017, which was inconsistent with the growth during those years of the membership of the California bar. Perhaps there was a growth in the number of lawyers employed in jobs not requiring bar membership.

FIGURE 8.10 NUMBER OF ACTIVE ATTORNEYS PER 100K POPULATION

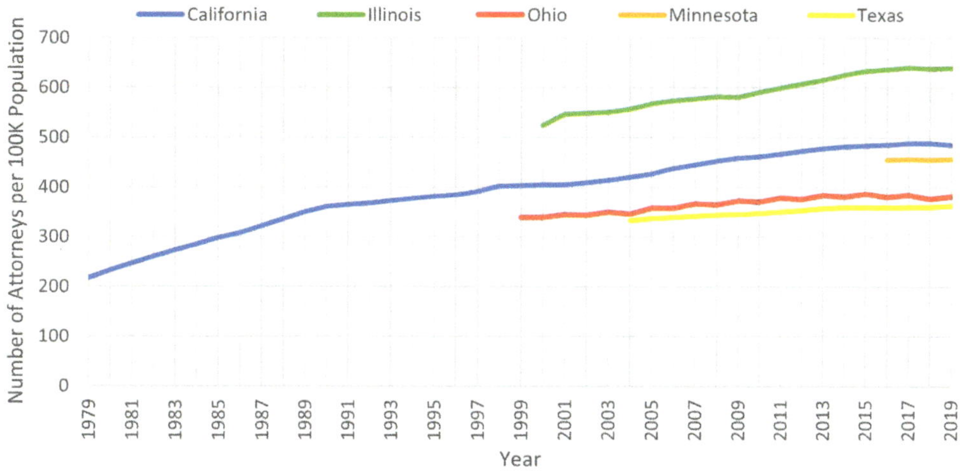

Figure 8.11 shows the civil filings per active lawyer over the period of time for which we have data. The chart is remarkably similar to the chart for overall civil filings. It shows the gradual, persistent drop for California and the huge impact on Ohio filings associated with the Great Recession. There are the same smaller "humps" for the other three states for which we have significant data. As in the charts for overall civil filings, Texas is the only state showing an overall increase in civil filings per active bar member over the course of the study.

FIGURE 8.11 TOTAL CIVIL FILINGS PER ACTIVE ATTORNEY

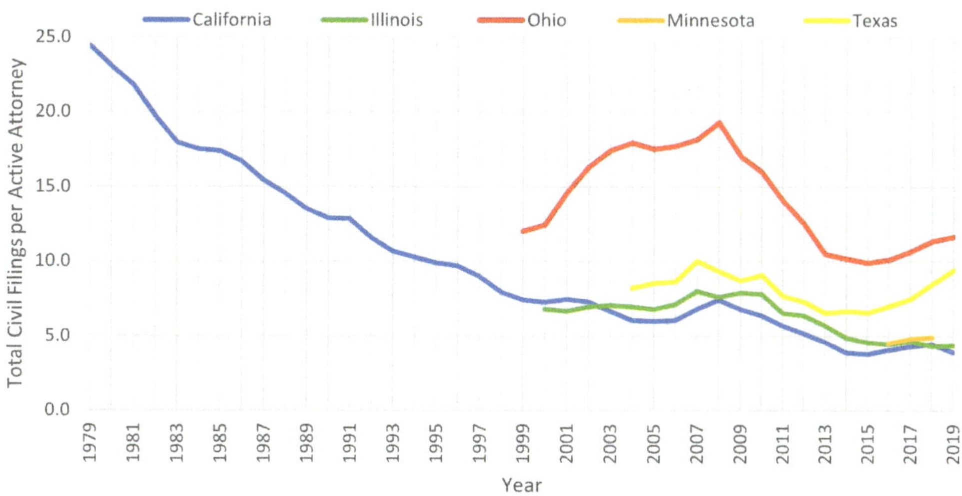

Figure 8.12 shows the high-value Injury/damage filings per active lawyer over the period of time for which we have data. High-value Injury/damage cases are more likely to have lawyers representing the parties. Again, the long-term drop in California is repeated. Interestingly, there is no hump associated with the Great Recession in any of the four states with data covering that period. Instead, the filing levels are relatively

flat. Not knowing how many of the lawyers practice civil law makes interpretation of this problematic.

FIGURE 8.12 TOTAL HIGH VALUE INJURY/DAMAGE FILINGS PER ACTIVE ATTORNEY

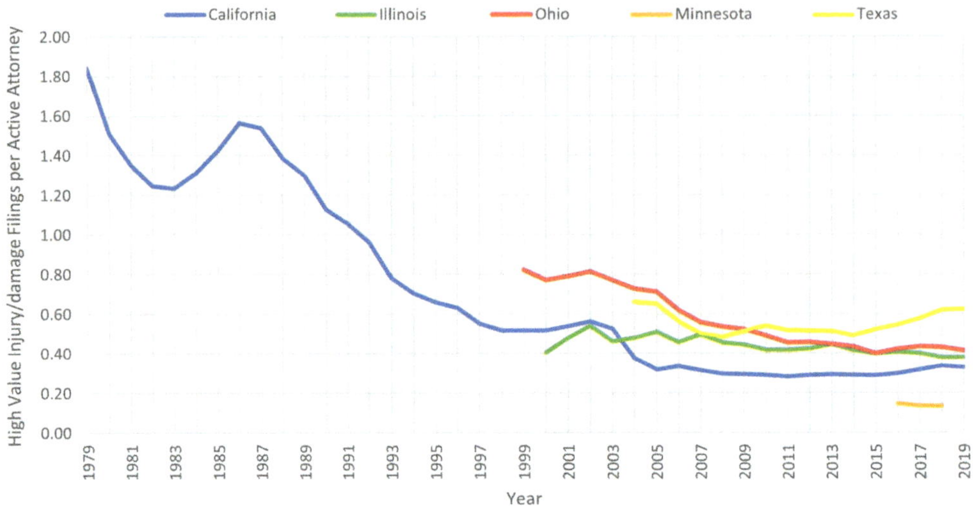

Our conclusion from this analysis is that the size of the active bar has no impact on the civil filing levels. Whatever factors are at play are simply causing individual lawyers to file more or fewer civil cases at different points in time. Over the time period we studied, it has tended to be fewer.

9

Impact of Economic Recessions on Civil Filings

9.1 Overview

Changes in the economic conditions in a state would be expected to cause fluctuations in court filings. However, the impact of economic conditions on filings may be a complicated mix of confounding actions. In a healthy economy, there might be more filings to the extent potential plaintiffs think they are more likely to recover from defendants. Conversely, there might be fewer filings because potential plaintiffs chose not to pursue a case because times are good. When economic times are bad, potential plaintiffs may choose not to pursue a case thinking they would be unlikely to recover damages. Conversely, potential plaintiffs might pursue a case they would not pursue in good times because they need the money from a recovery. Predicting an impact would involve a lot of uncertainty.

Depending on the sectors of the economy affected, the impact of a recession on different case categories of civil filings may vary widely. To the extent filings reflect business activity, filings associated with business transactions might drop during and after a recession. At the same time, economic woes might increase filings from failed or unconsummated business transactions. The number of people unemployed, and the extent of their legal woes, would depend upon the economic sector suffering a recession. For example, higher unemployment among lower-income populations might increase eviction filings, whereas higher unemployment among homeowners might increase foreclosure filings.

A change in filings might begin to occur before a recession is "officially" declared if the economy started to slow sooner or unemployment increased earlier. A change in filings might also continue for a time after the recession was officially over if unemployment continued or the recovery was slow.

Since FY 1978–79, the earliest year for which filing data was available for our study, there have been five nationwide economic recessions, using the National Bureau of Economic Research (NBER) definition. The dates of the five recessions are:[1]

- During the first six months of 1980;
- From July 1981 to November 1982;
- From July 1990 to March 1991—referred to here as the Savings and Loan Recession;
- From March to November of 2001—referred to here as the Dot.com Recession; and
- From December 2007 to June 2009—referred to here as the Great Recession.

To the extent that data is available for each of these time frames, we have analyzed the change in total civil filings in the five states during each of these recessions. The recessions are addressed in chronological order. Where more detailed filing data is available, we have looked at specific subcategories of civil cases exhibiting filing fluctuations associated with a recession. States may have experienced local recessions or economic downturns in addition to the national recessions just noted. Southern California experienced a recession associated with the collapse of the aerospace industry that began before, and extended past, the Great Recession. Since filing data for this period was available, we explored whether civil filings changed during this period as well.

Several states responded to increases in filings associated with a recession by establishing task forces, committees, or work groups to address sudden increases in certain categories of filings. Their task was to identify changes in substantive law, legal procedures, case management practices, or technology to better resolve these cases. Examples include programs addressing foreclosures, evictions, and debt collection. We have noted a few programs in these five states, although it is difficult to attribute a change in filing levels to the implementation of a program. The programs focused on the resolution of cases once filed, not on the filing of cases, although there may have been an indirect impact on decisions to file.

9.2 Filing Changes during Early Recessions in California

Only filing level data from California was available for the recessions in 1980 and 1981–82, and the Savings and Loan Recession in 1990–91. Total filings by major case category across these three recessionary periods are displayed in Figure 9.1. For all three recessions, the pattern of per capita filings was the same as that of total filings, with more of an overall downward tilt because the state's population was growing quickly. There is no consistent pattern across the major case categories. The changes of each major category during these three recessions are discussed next. Much more detail about the case subcategories within each major category would be needed to describe the variance observed.

1. Nat'l Bureau of Econ. Res., *Business Cycle Dating*, https://www.nber.org/research/business-cycle-dating. *See also* Kimberly Amadeo, reviewed by Brian Barnier, History of Recessions in the United States, Causes, Length, GDP, and Unemployment Rates, updated May 29, 2020.

Looking at total Small Claims filings, the pattern appears to be that total filings increased slightly during recessions (dark blue line in Figure 9.1). Total Small Claims filings rose in the first year of all three of these recessions, ranging from 2 to 9 percent. They rose in the second year during two of the three recessions, but not after the 1981–82 recession. The increases during both the FY 1981–1982 and the Savings and Loan recessions coincided with increases in the small claims jurisdiction (discussed in Chapter 5). After the 1981–82 and the Savings and Loan recessions, total filings dropped to levels below the pre-recession levels, and continued a long slow drop through FY 2018–19.

FIGURE 9.1 CALIFORNIA CIVIL FILINGS BY MAJOR CASE CATEGORIES ACROSS RECESSIONS

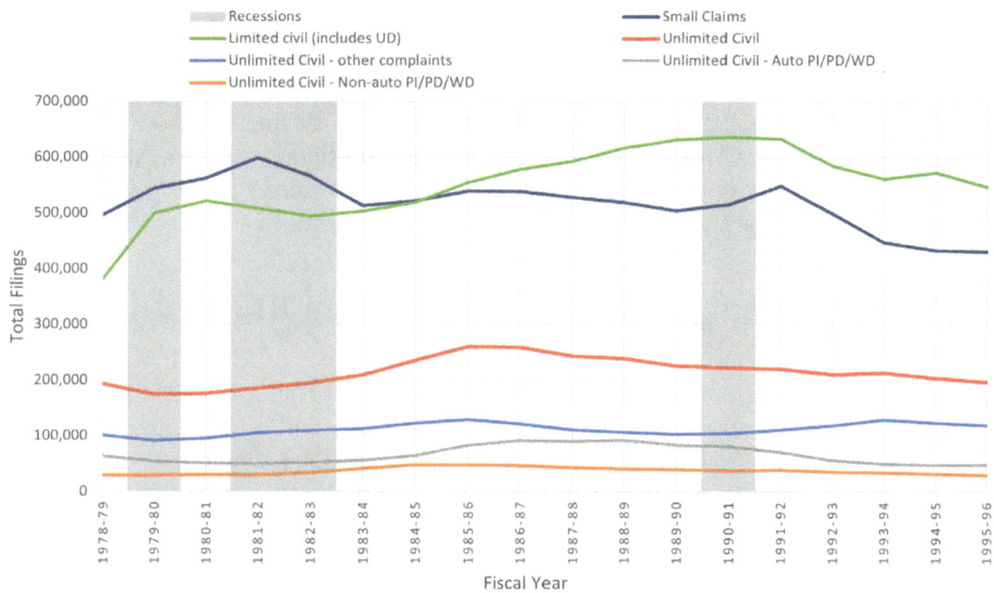

In the long view, total Limited Civil filings were rising through all three of these recessions, although not continuously (green line in Figure 9.1). Filings rose sharply during the 1980 recession, almost 31 percent. However, this was the same period in which the jurisdictional limit was increased (discussed in Chapter 7). Filings rose again the next year, but not as much. During the first year of the 1981–82 recession, Limited Civil filings dropped 5 percent, then rose steadily for the next eight years, including through the Savings and Loan Recession, peaking in FY 1991–92. Thereafter filings dropped until the Great Recession began.

Looking at all Unlimited Civil filings, there did not appear to be a consistent filing pattern through these early recessions (red line in Figure 9.1). There was a dip in filings during the 1980 recession, but filings were rising during the 1981–82 recession, peaking in FY 1985–86. There was then a gradual drop in filings that continued through the Savings and Loan Recession and until FY 1997–98.

The Unlimited Civil–Other case category includes a number of case subcategories that might explain some of the fluctuations during recessions. The category includes cases related to mortgage foreclosures as well as contract, unlawful detainer, and collection cases involving more than $25,000. These case categories likely fluctuate with the economy, particularly during a recession. Total Unlimited Civil–Other filings dropped 9 percent during the 1980 recession (blue line in Figure 9.1). Filings then rose for the next seven years, including through the 1981–82 recession. They peaked in FY 1985–86, having risen almost 29 percent from the pre-1980 recession level. After the peak, filings gradually dropped a total of 20 percent going into the Savings and Loan Recession, after which filings rose for three years, then started a decline.

Total filings for Unlimited Civil Auto Injury/damage cases displayed no consistent pattern during these three recessions (gray line in Figure 9.1). Filings were already dropping before the 1980 recession. Filings dipped slightly through both the 1980 and 1981–82 recessions. Filings then rose for the next three years. Going into the Savings and Loan Recession, filings were again dropping, and they continued a downward trend for the next five years, to a level below that 17 years earlier.

Unlimited Civil Non-auto Injury/damage filings were essentially flat through the 1980 recession and into the 1981–81 recession (burnt orange line in Figure 9.1). In the second year of that recession, filings began a rise that continued for the next four years. Filings dipped slightly during the Savings and Loan Recession. After this recession, filings dropped slowly to a level below the level 17 years earlier.

9.3 Filing Changes during the Dot.com Recession

The Dot.com Recession occurred from March to November of 2001. It was triggered by the closure of many new dot.com businesses. The 9/11 attack that fall stalled the recovery. While the national GDP became positive by the end of 2001, unemployment continued to be high, peaking at 6.3 percent in June of 2003. Figure 9.2 displays the total comparable civil filing levels from 1999 to 2016 in the five states. The peach column represents the official period of the Dot.com Recession. Only four states can be compared for this recession, as the Texas data set starts in 2004.

In general, filings were either flat or dropped very slightly before the official start of the Dot.com Recession, increased slightly during the recession, peaking in 2002 or 2003, after the end of the official period. Filings then dipped in California and Minnesota before rising into the Great Recession period. The increases tend to be lesser-value cases, particularly contract cases.

In California, total civil filings increased across the dot.com recession period (blue line in Figure 9.2). Filings then dropped in the next two years. However, year-to-year percentage changes in filing levels during the period of the recession were not greater than changes in other years when there was no recession. The increased filings during this period were primarily Limited Civil and Small Claims cases. Unlimited Civil–Other filings also increased, starting sooner, in FY 1999–2000, and declining sooner, in FY 2002–03. Unlimited Auto Injury/damage filings rose slightly, but this may have been attributed to a change in the statute of limitations (discussed in Chapter 7).

In Illinois, both total filings and per capita filings dropped from 1999 to 2000 (green line in Figure 9.2). Filings then increased slightly during the two years of the Dot.com Recession. Thereafter, filings continued a slow rise for the next several years. Lesser-value Law ≤ $50,000 filings were at a low point in 2000, but then began a rise that continued to a peak during the Great Recession. Chancery filings, including foreclosures, were rising across this period, and continued to rise to a peak in 2010. Higher-value

FIGURE 9.2 TOTAL COMPARABLE CIVIL FILINGS DURING RECESSIONS

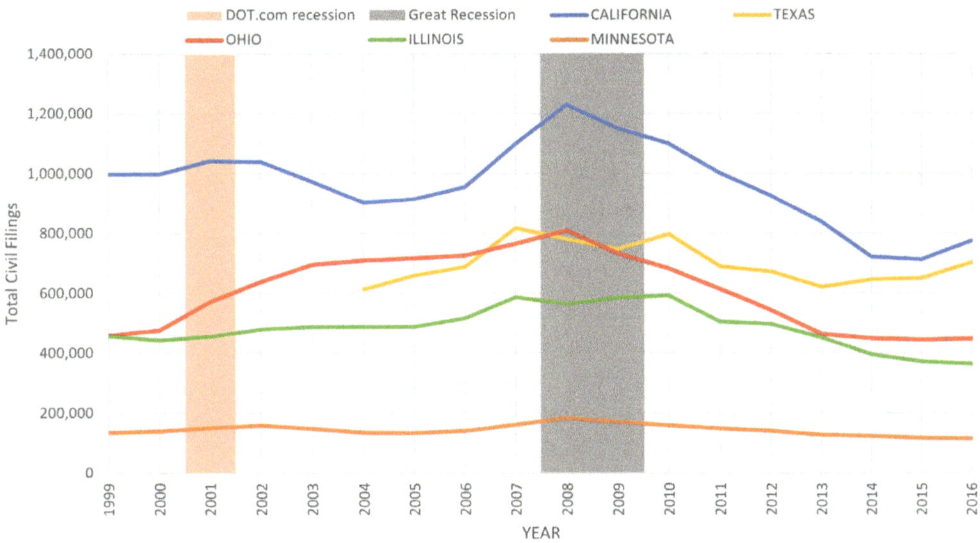

Law > $50,000 filings increased slightly in 2000, but the percentage increase was no greater than in several other years when there was no recession.

In Minnesota, both total and per capita filing levels slowly increased through the dot.com period (orange line in Figure 9.2). Filings peaked in 2002, and then dropped for the next three years. The Major Civil subcategories of Contract and Civil Other–Miscellaneous were rising before the Dot.com Recession. Civil Other–Miscellaneous filings peaked in 2002. Contract filings peaked in 2003. The Minor Civil subcategory of Default and Confession of Judgment jumped in 2001 and peaked in 2003. Unlawful Detainer/Eviction cases began a slow rise in 2001 that continued through the Great Recession. Conciliation filings (small claims cases) also rose in 2001, 2002, and 2003, then dropped.

Total filings in Ohio rose slightly in 2000, then rose sharply in the two years of the Dot.com Recession (red line in Figure 9.2). Unlike in the other three states, there was no flattening or dip in total filings between the Dot.com Recession and the Great Recession. Instead, the rise in filings continued steadily for seven years, peaking in 2008 during the Great Recession. The steepest increase during the Dot.com Recession were Contract and Other Civil cases in municipal and county courts, and Foreclosure cases in the courts of common pleas. Injury/damage filings in the courts of common pleas were flat or declining during this period, but rose slightly in the municipal and county courts.

9.4 Filing Changes during the Great Recession

The filing pattern of each of the five states includes a roller coaster associated with the Great Recession. The official dates of the recession were from December 2007 to June 2009. However, the filing pattern changes associated with this recession spanned a much longer period. Figure 9.2 shows the total filing levels in the five states from 1999 to 2016. The gray column represents the official period of the Great Recession.

The start of the total filings roller coaster associated with the Great Recession did not begin in the same year across the five states. It began earlier, in 2001, in Ohio and Illinois. In California and Minnesota, filings did not begin to rise until 2005 or 2006. Since the earliest available filing data is in 2004, we do not know when the rise began in Texas. Total filings in all five states peaked in either 2007 or 2008. Illinois and Texas had a second peak in 2010. By 2013, total filing levels in all five states were at or below the levels when the rise began. California and Illinois filings continued to drop until 2015. Four states, not including Texas, all had per capita filing levels in 2016 lower than in 2000.

The steepest one-year rise and fall in each state were near the peak of the recession in four of the five states. In Illinois and Texas, the steepest rise was in the year filings peaked. In California and Minnesota, the steepest rise was the year before the peak. In Ohio, the steepest one-year increase was when the roller coaster began, seven years before the peak. The steepest one-year drop was not always as close to the peak. In Illinois, the steepest drop was the year after the second peak and, in Texas, two years after the second peak. The steepest drop was four years after the peak in Minnesota, five years in Ohio, and six years in California.

The percentage increase in total filings from the start of the roller coaster to the peak was significant. The increase in California, Illinois, and Minnesota was similar, in the 30 to 35 percent range. It was much higher in Ohio, at 70 percent. The drop from the peak to the lowest subsequent filing level was similar for four states, between 36 percent and 45 percent. It was much smaller in Texas—only 22 percent.

The differences in case categories across the five states and the broad categories in several states made it difficult to generalize what categories of cases contributed to the rise in filings during the Great Recession. Generally, it was the lower-value civil cases that surged during the recession. Where known, the case categories that included contract cases, consumer credit, and debt collection cases clearly surged. Where separately counted, eviction and foreclosure cases surged in some states, but not others. Injury/damage cases, particularly higher-value cases, did not rise significantly, if at all, during the recession. Small Claims cases rose only in Illinois. Specific categories can be identified in some states and are discussed in more detail in the sections that follow.

Another impact of the Great Recession was that some courts closed courthouses or concentrated cases in fewer courthouses in response to budget cuts. Some California courts that closed or concentrated cases experienced a decline in lower-value Limited Civil filings when the closures occurred.

9.4.1 California

The roller coaster pattern associated with the Great Recession began in FY 2005–06 and peaked in FY 2008–09. Total filings then dropped continuously until FY 2015–16. The decline after the peak was more gradual than the rise to the peak. The greatest one-year increase was almost 15 percent, from FY 2006–07 to FY 2007–08. The largest one-year drop was almost 14 percent, from FY 2013–14 to FY 2014–15. These were the largest one-year changes for the entire 41-year period for which data was available.

The large increase was primarily due to lesser value Limited Civil cases (green line in Figure 9.3). Unlimited Civil–Other Complaints cases (brown line) also contributed, peaking in FY 2009–10, but at a much lower level. Small Claims cases (purple line) also rose slightly in 2008–09. Unlimited Civil–Injury/damage cases (blue and dark gray lines) were essentially flat during this period.

FIGURE 9.3 CALIFORNIA TOTAL CIVIL FILINGS BY MAJOR CASE CATEGORY BEFORE, DURING AND AFTER THE GREAT RECESSION (DECEMBER 2007 TO JUNE 2009)

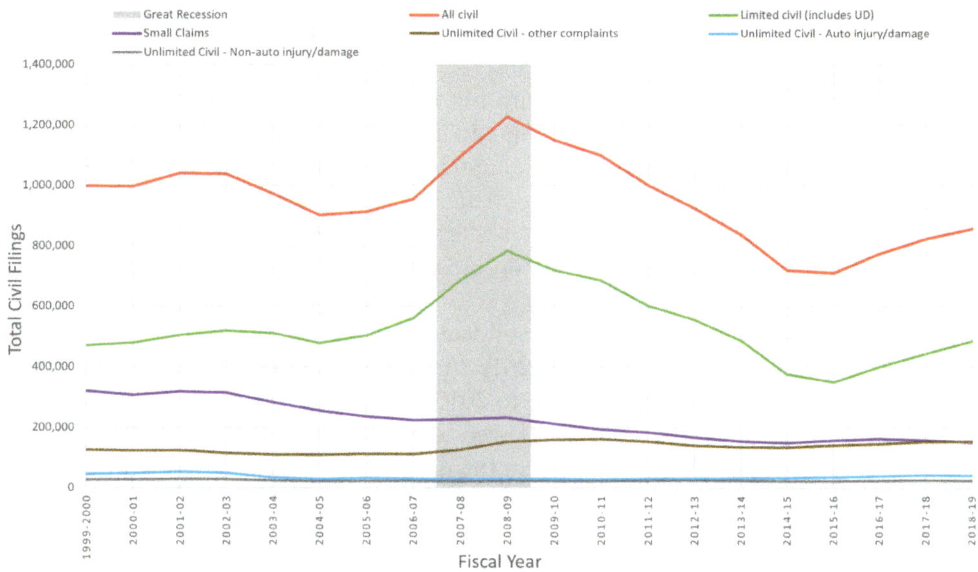

Limited Civil cases were the largest contributor to the roller coaster pattern (green line in Figure 9.3). These are the lesser-value civil cases of all categories: debt collection, other contract, unlawful detainer, and Injury/damage cases. More detailed subcategory filing data for all of these years was not available on a statewide basis. However, a study of Limited Civil filings during the years leading up to the recession, FY 2003–04 to FY 2007–08, provided some insight.[2] Filings of contract cases and unlawful detainer cases grew steadily over the period. In the last year of that study, FY 2007–08, contract cases filings grew by 33 percent and filings of unlawful detainer cases grew 17 percent. Injury/damage filings were flat or declining over the period. The Orange County Superior Court reported that residential unlawful detainer cases peaked in 2008 and then fell 30 percent by 2015. Debt collection cases in Orange peaked in 2010 and then declined 72 percent by 2015.

The Unlimited Civil–Other Complaints category included cases related to mortgage foreclosures, unlawful detainer, contract, and collection cases involving more than $25,000 (brown line in Figure 9.3). Filings in these categories might be expected to increase during a recession. More specific filing totals for subcategories of this category were not available. However, filing data from the Orange County Superior Court

2. Dag Macleod, Data Points: Civil Filings Fuel Continued Growth in Trial Court Caseload, Cal. Admin. Office of the Courts, Office of Court Research, Aug. 2009, https://www.courts.ca.gov/documents/datapoints09.pdf.

indicated that Breach of Contract/Warranty and Other Collections cases, but not foreclosure cases, rose sharply from FY 2006–07 to FY 2009–10, then dropped sharply the following fiscal year.

The contribution of Small Claims filings to the roller coaster associated with the Great Recession was minor (purple line in Figure 9.3). Small claims cases rose slightly in FY 2007–08 and FY 2008–09. However, the increases were quite small, and not the largest one-year increase during the 41-year period for which data was available. Filings of these cases had been declining before FY 2008–09, and continued to decline for the next six fiscal years.

There were several counties in California that closed branch courthouses hearing Limited Civil cases or concentrated Limited Civil case hearings in fewer courthouses after the Great Recession began. Large counties that shifted hearings of Limited Civil cases to fewer courthouses included Los Angeles, San Diego, Orange, Riverside, and Fresno. Some smaller counties also shifted where Limited Civil cases were heard. Looking at total Limited Civil filing levels, court closures did not appear to noticeably reduce total filings.

Orange County Superior Court consolidated hearings of Limited Civil cases from five branch courts to three, as of July 1, 2013.[3] Figure 9.4 shows total filings for Limited Civil cases in Orange County from 2000 to 2019. It was not apparent that the shifting of cases had an impact on filings, as filings were dropping steadily from 2010 until 2015. The drop from 2013 to 2014 was less than the drop from 2012 to 2013, and the same as the drop from 2014 to 2015.

FIGURE 9.4 CALIFORNIA TOTAL LIMITED CIVIL FILINGS IN ORANGE COUNTY SUPERIOR COURT

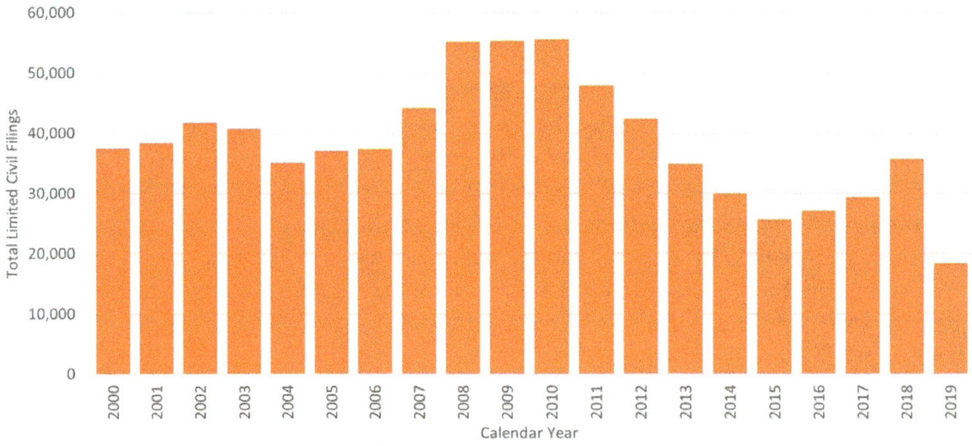

3. Orange County Superior Court closed its Laguna Hills Justice Center, moving Limited Civil cases to the Harbor Justice Center per Cal. Gov't Code § 68106, notice filed Apr. 29, 2013, https://www.courts.ca.gov/documents/68106-orange-20130430-Laguna-Hills.pdf. Limited Civil cases were moved from the North Justice Center to the Central Justice Center, notice filed Apr. 29, 2013, https://www.courts.ca.gov/documents/68106-orange-20130430-NJC.pdf.

Fresno Superior Court was another large court that consolidated Limited Civil filings from seven courthouses to one courthouse in July and August of 2012.[4] Figure 9.5 shows total filings for Fresno County from 2000 to 2019. As with Orange County, the closures occurred during a steady drop in filings that began in 2009 and continued until 2015. However, the greatest year-to-year drops during that period were from 2011 to 2012 and 2013 to 2014, not in 2012, the year the closures took effect.

FIGURE 9.5 CALIFORNIA TOTAL LIMITED CIVIL FILINGS IN FRESNO COUNTY SUPERIOR COURT

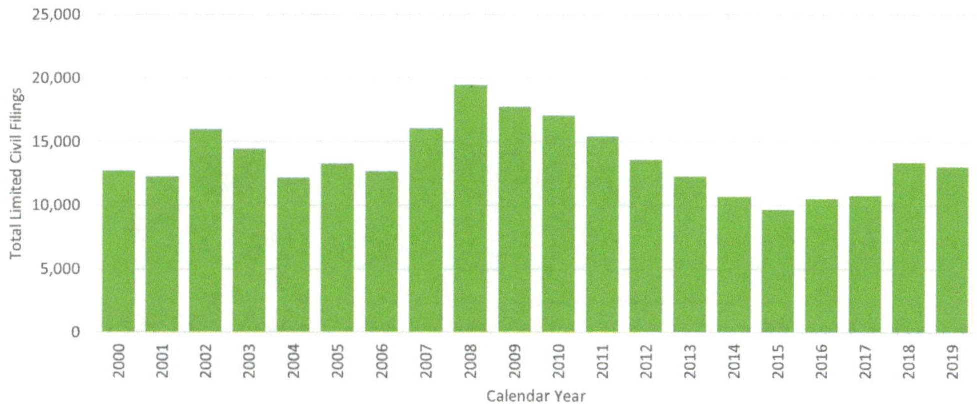

9.4.2 Illinois

In Illinois, the roller coaster associated with the Great Recession began much earlier than in the other states, had two peaks, then declined steeply. Total filings began rising in 2001. In 2006, the rise accelerated, peaking in 2007 (blue line in Figure 9.6). Filings dropped in 2008, rose to a second peak in 2010, then dropped sharply. By 2013, total filings were at the same level as in 1996. The largest single-year increase was from 2006 to 2007, almost 14 percent. The largest single-year drop was almost 15 percent, from 2010 to 2011.

4. Fresno closed the branch courts in Coalinga, Firebaugh, Reedley, Sanger, and Selma on July 30, 2012. Clovis and Kingsburg branch courts were closed effective Aug. 6, 2012, closure notice dated May 25, 2012, https://www.courts.ca.gov/documents/Fresno-20120525-closure-notification.pdf.

FIGURE 9.6 ILLINOIS TOTAL COMPARABLE CIVIL FILINGS BY MAJOR CASE CATEGORY BEFORE, DURING, AND AFTER THE GREAT RECESSION (DECEMBER 2007 TO JUNE 2009)

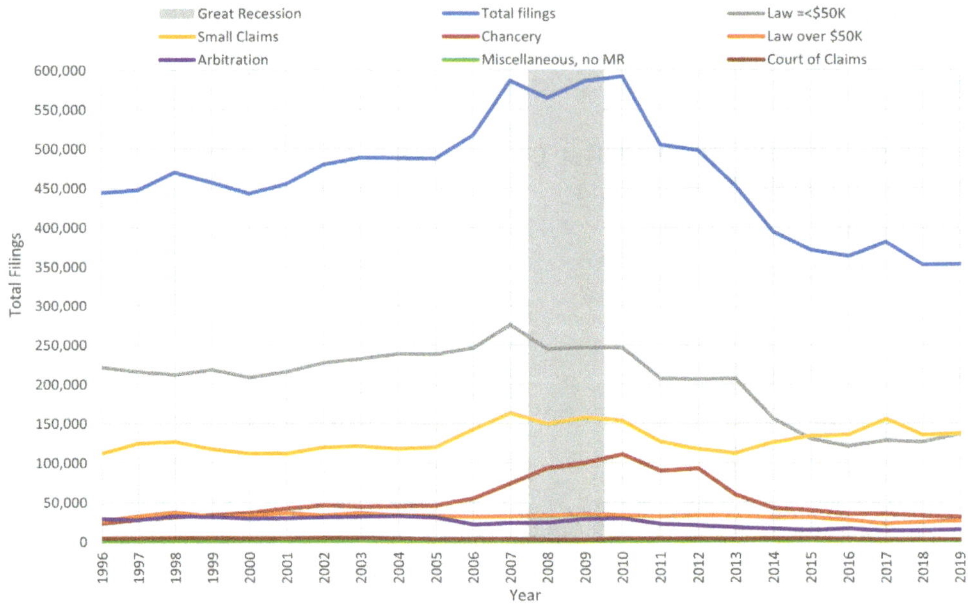

The first peak in 2007 was largely the result of an increase in cases valued at or below $50,000 (gray line) and Small Claims filings (yellow line). This was the only state of the five where Small Claims cases rose during the Great Recession. The second peak in 2010 was associated with a surge in Chancery cases (red line), which began to rise in 2007 and peaked in 2010. The cases valued above $50,000 (orange line), Arbitration (purple line), Miscellaneous Civil, no MR (green line), and Court of Claims (brown line) cases were flat or declining during the Great Recession.

The category of Law ≤ $50,000 includes a variety of case categories where the claim for damages is less than or equal to $50,000. This includes injury and damage suits, contracts, confession of judgment, eviction and tenant-related suits, but not foreclosures or property-related suits. Because of the range of cases included, it is not possible to identify which of these subcategories had increased filings during this period. Interestingly, the surge of total filings of Law cases with a value above $50,000 during the Great Recession was clearly only in Cook County (Chicago) (red line in Figure 9.7). The total filings of the cases with a value above $50,000 in the rest of the state were essentially flat during the Great Recession (purple line).

The second case category that rose significantly during the Great Recession were Chancery cases. This case category includes foreclosures (mortgages, security interests in personal property, and mechanics liens), title to real property, trusts, and other complaints for equitable relief.[5] Chancery filings statewide had been rising steadily since at least 1996, rose sharply beginning in 2006, and peaked in 2010 (blue line in Figure 9.8). Filings dropped in 2011, then peaked again in 2012. Filings dropped very steeply in

5. Administrative Office of the Illinois Courts, Manual on Record Keeping, 3d ed., effective Apr. 1, 2017, pt. 1, § C, at 1.

2013 and 2014, when the total filings were below the level in 2002. In contrast to Law ≤ \$50,000 cases, the surge patterns in Cook County (red line) and the rest of the state (green line) were the same for Chancery cases.

FIGURE 9.7 ILLINOIS CIVIL FILINGS LAW ≤ \$50,000 BEFORE, DURING, AND AFTER THE GREAT RECESSION (DECEMBER 2007 TO JUNE 2009)

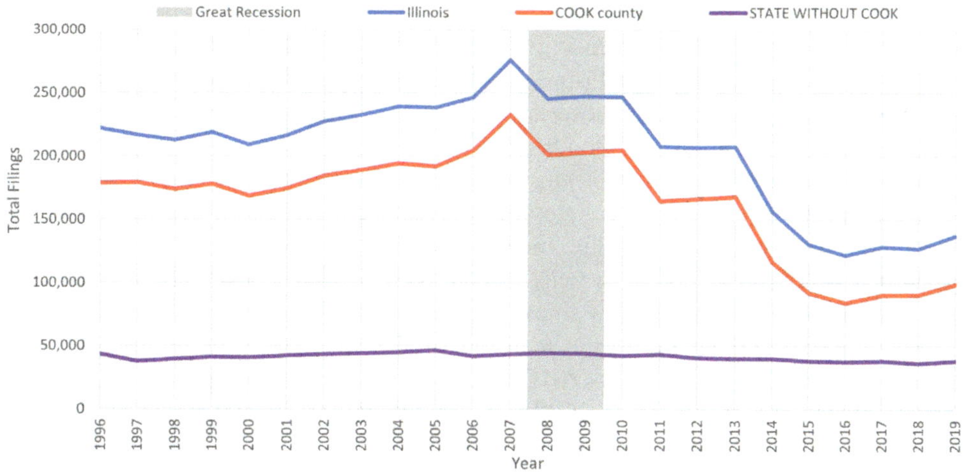

FIGURE 9.8 ILLINOIS CHANCERY FILINGS BEFORE, DURING, AND AFTER THE GREAT RECESSION (DECEMBER 2007 TO JUNE 2009)

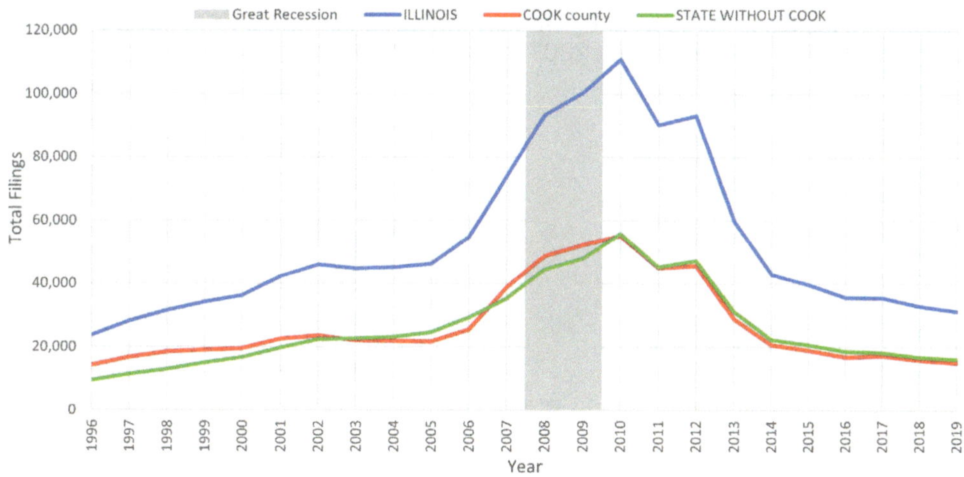

Because there was no separate subcategory of mortgage foreclosure cases, it is not possible to identify the extent to which the increased Chancery filings were mortgage foreclosure cases. However, the increase was noted in the judiciary's annual reports. In 2011, the Supreme Court formed a Special Supreme Court Committee on Mortgage Foreclosures[6] to study the foreclosure procedures in response to "the drastic increase in mortgage foreclosure cases and the resultant burden on judicial circuits throughout the

6. Supreme Court of Illinois, 2011 Annual Report of the Illinois Courts Administrative Summary, A Message from the Chief Justice, § 1, at 4.

state."[7] The Committee, consisting of judges, attorneys, and bankers, was charged with developing a uniform procedural structure that would ensure fairness and the appropriate use of foreclosure proceedings across the state. The Court also expanded its approved residential mortgage foreclosure mediation programs to more counties.

In 2013, based on the work of the Special Committee, the Supreme Court adopted new rules governing the foreclosure process.[8] The new rules were intended to improve homeowners' knowledge of the process and avoid deceptive practices by lenders.[9] The rules established requirements for mortgage foreclosure mediation programs and obligations lenders must follow in foreclosure proceedings, in particular, regarding documentation and notices. By the time these new rules were adopted, total Chancery filings were dropping rapidly, and continued to drop through 2019.

The third case category contributing to the Great Recession roller coaster in Illinois was Small Claims cases. The rise statewide began in 2005, peaked in 2007, dipped in 2008, and peaked again in 2009 (blue line in Figure 9.9). By 2013, total filing levels had dropped below levels in 2005. The peak in 2007 was driven primarily by increased filings in the smaller counties (yellow line), not in Cook County (red line) or the adjacent five large counties (green line). Filings in the smaller counties subsequently declined. The surge in filings from 2006 to 2010 in the four large counties surrounding Cook County contributed to the peak in 2009 that continued into 2010. Cook County Small Claims filings did not contribute to this surge, although the surge in Law ≤ $50,000 cases was primarily from Cook County, as already discussed. The increase in small claims filings after 2013 was attributable largely to their rapid growth in Cook County—for which we have not been able to provide an explanation.

FIGURE 9.9 ILLINOIS SMALL CLAIMS FILINGS BEFORE, DURING, AND AFTER THE GREAT RECESSION (DECEMBER 2007 TO JUNE 2009)

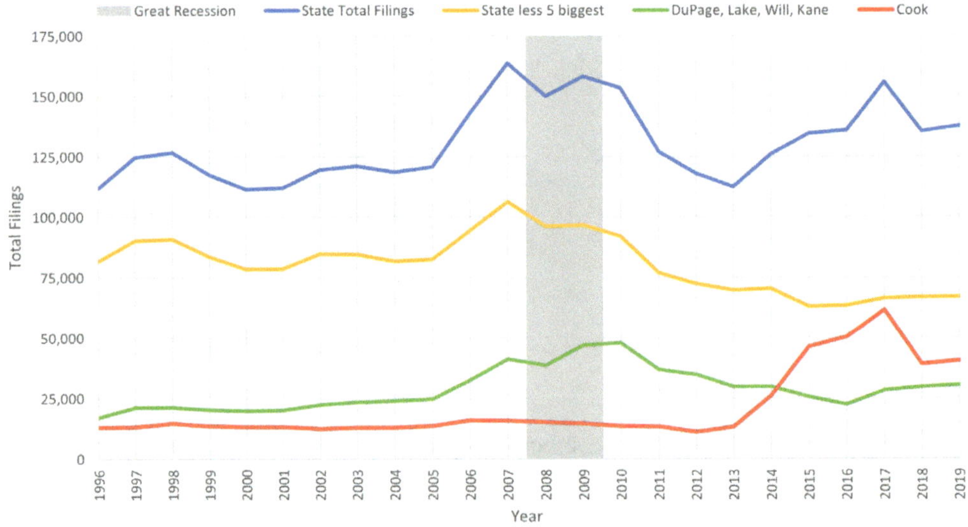

7. Illinois Supreme Court Rules, r. 99.1, Committee Comments, Mar. 1, 2013.

8. Illinois Supreme Court Rules, r. 99.1, r. 113, and r. 114, effective May 1, 2023.

9. Supreme Court of Illinois, 2013 Annual Report of the Illinois Courts Administrative Summary, A Message from the Chief Justice, § 1, at 4.

9.4.3 Minnesota

In Minnesota, the roller coaster associated with the Great Recession began in 2006, rose sharply to a peak in 2008, then receded more gradually through 2016 (red line in Figure 9.10). By 2013, total filings were less than the total filings in 2005. The largest single-year increase was from 2006 to 2007, almost 16 percent. The largest single-year drop was almost 10 percent, from 2012 to 2013, later in the cycle than in the other states.

The roller coaster associated with the Great Recession was preceded by a smaller, shorter roller coaster pattern that began in 2000, peaked in 2002, and flattened out in 2004. The case categories contributing to this rise were Minor Civil cases (burnt orange line), Conciliation (small claims) cases (green line), and, to a much lesser extent, Major Civil cases (blue line). The source of this bump is unclear. It began after the Dot.com Recession was officially over.

The case categories contributing to the roller coaster associated with the Great Recession were primarily Minor Civil cases (burnt orange line) and, on a much smaller scale, Major Civil cases (blue line). Conciliation cases (green line) rose slightly, but were declining steadily.

FIGURE 9.10 MINNESOTA TOTAL COMPARABLE CIVIL FILINGS BEFORE, DURING, AND AFTER THE GREAT RECESSION (DECEMBER 2007 TO JUNE 2009)

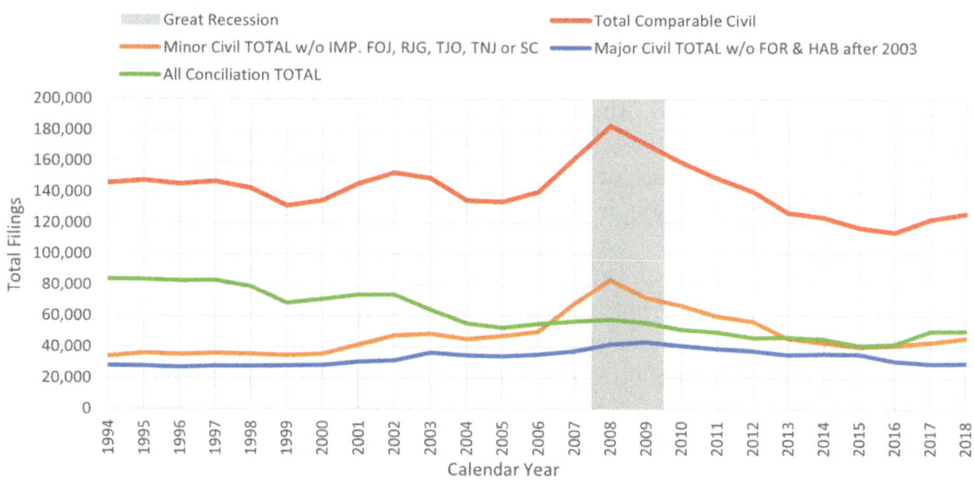

The rise in Minor Civil cases associated with the Great Recession was mostly in Default and Confession of Judgment cases (blue line in Figure 9.11). These filings rose sharply from 2006, more than doubling to a peak in 2008. From 2008 to 2013, these filings declined more slowly than they had risen. It is not clear what case subcategories this included. In other states, a default judgment is a type of disposition, not a case category. Default judgments could occur in any category of case where the defendant does not file an answer within a specified time period. In other states, defaults occur disproportionately in debt collection and eviction cases.

Unlawful detainer/eviction cases (green line) also contributed to the surge. They rose steadily from 2000 to a peak in 2008, rising 168 percent. Thereafter they declined sharply for two years, then more slowly. By 2010, eviction filings were at about the same level as in 2000. From 2000 to 2018, filings were down almost 20 percent.

FIGURE 9.11 MINNESOTA SELECT MINOR CIVIL FILINGS BEFORE, DURING, AND AFTER THE GREAT RECESSION (DECEMBER 2007 TO JUNE 2009)

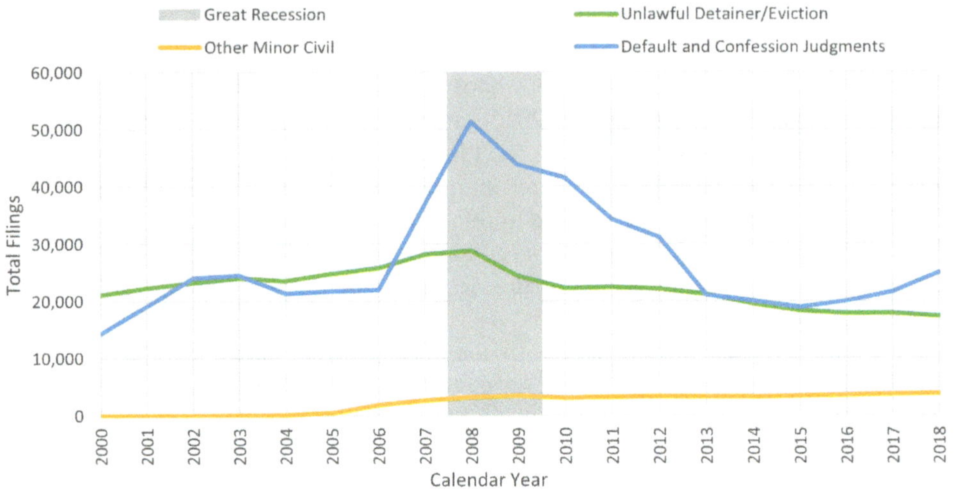

Unlawful detainer/eviction cases are more frequent in areas with a greater proportion of rental units—cities and urban areas. Sorting unlawful detainer/eviction filings by county, the bulk of the statewide Unlawful detainer/eviction filings occurred in the two large population counties, Hennepin and Ramsey, and the seven surrounding urban counties.[10] From 1994 to 2018, the percentage of all Unlawful detainer/eviction cases filed in these urban counties began at 91 percent and dropped to 72 percent in 2018. Hennepin District Court's share of all Unlawful detainer/eviction filings dropped from 51 percent to 32 percent, although Hennepin County included only 22.5 percent of the state's population in 2019.

The labels of the case subcategories of Unlawful Detainer/Eviction cases were changed beginning in 2003. Prior to 2003, the term Unlawful Detainer was used. Beginning in 2003, the term Eviction was used. This coincides with a change in the terms used in statutes related to landlords and tenants.[11] In the statistical reports, there was an overlap in use of the two descriptions from 2003 to 2008, as MNCIS, the trial court case management system, was implemented. It was unclear whether the change was exclusively a matter of terminology or something more substantive in terms of subcategories included in this case category.

The contribution of Major Civil cases to the roller coaster during the Great Recession was less pronounced, and peaked in 2009 (Figure 9.12). The primary case categories contributing to a rise were All Property related (blue line) and All Contract cases (red line). Miscellaneous Major Civil filings (black line) surged a little in 2008. The other categories were declining or comparatively flat during the Great Recession.

---

10. Anoka, Carver, Dakota, Scott, Sherburne, Washington, and Wright counties.

11. For example, Minn. Laws of 2003, ch. 2, art. 2, § 15, changed the term "unlawful detainer" to "eviction" in the conciliation court jurisdictional statute, MINN. 2020 STATS, § 491A.01, subdiv. 4(10).

FIGURE 9.12 MINNESOTA MAJOR CIVIL TOTAL FILINGS BY CATEGORY BEFORE, DURING, AND AFTER THE GREAT RECESSION (DECEMBER 2007 TO JUNE 2009)

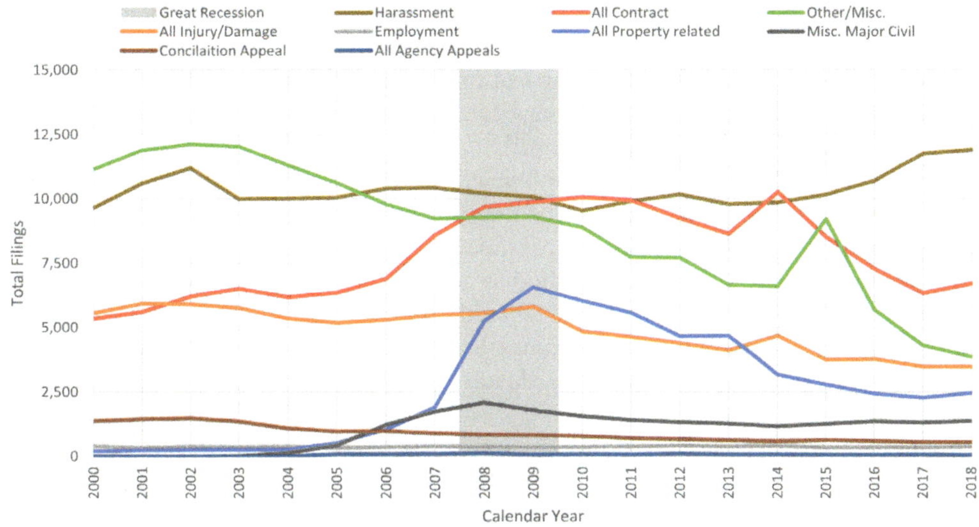

One Major Civil case category contributing to the surge associated with the Great Recession was Contract and Consumer Credit cases (Figure 9.13). The category of Contract was separated into several subcategories beginning in 2003. All Contract case subcategories fluctuated, but were rising from 1994 through 2006. Beginning in 2006, filings rose very quickly until 2008. The rise beginning in 2006 was Mechanic's Lien filings (green line), which surged for the next two years. From 2009 forward, the driving categories were Contract (burnt orange line) and Consumer Credit filings (red line). All Contract cases (blue line) rose more slowly to a peak in 2010, then started dropping to a low in 2013.

FIGURE 9.13 MINNESOTA MAJOR CIVIL CONTRACT FILINGS BY CATEGORY BEFORE, DURING, AND AFTER THE GREAT RECESSION (DECEMBER 2007 TO JUNE 2009)

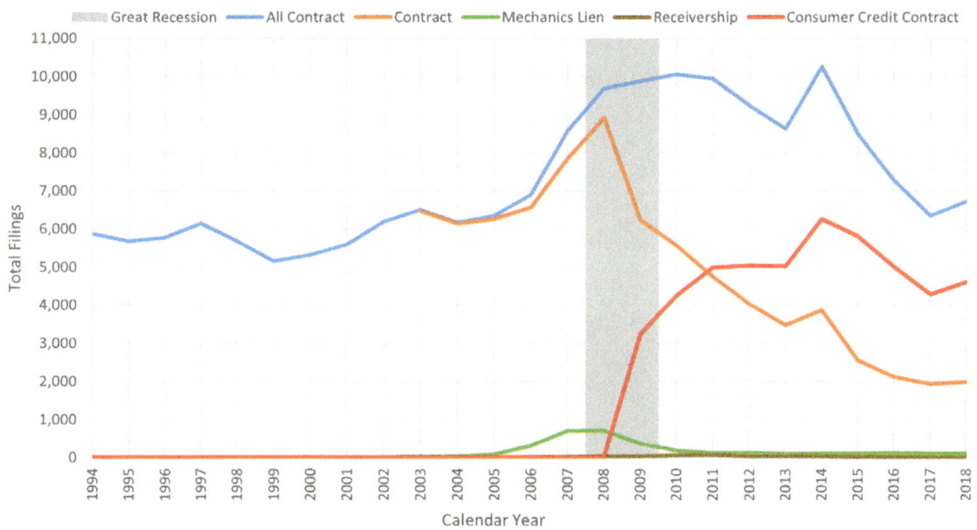

There was a sharp rise in total Contract filings in 2014, post-recession (blue line). There are two possible contributors to this jump. In 2013, a requirement was added that cases served, but not filed, had to be filed within one year, or were deemed dismissed. This is discussed in more detail in Chapter 7. The jump in 2014 was most likely cases that had previously been served but now had to be filed to avoid dismissal.[12] In addition, there was a change in the law in 2013 regarding burden of proof in assigned debt collection filings requesting a default judgment.[13]

In May 2019, Ramsey County implemented a program for consumer credit cases with the goal of reducing the number of required appearances for parties, and achieving resolution within 180 days. The streamlined calendar was developed with input and consensus from attorneys representing both creditors and debtors. Since implementation of the calendar, most cases have been resolved after only one appearance, reducing the inconvenience of appearing multiple times for creditors and debtors.[14] As this was a post-filing program, the impact on filing levels is unclear. To the extent litigants anticipated the program, it may have reduced filings. Conversely, the effectiveness of the program may have encouraged filings to take advantage of the benefits.

The other Major Civil category contributing to the Great Recession hump were Torrens cases. The Torrens system is an alternative land registration system.[15] After a title registration proceeding, the court issues a Certificate of Title. After a Certificate of Title has been issued, there are times when the court must correct the certificate. The most common correction is when title has been transferred by a mortgage foreclosure sale. After a foreclosure sale regarding Torrens property, the new owner must complete a procedure known as a "proceeding subsequent to registration." Torrens filings rose steeply in 2008 and 2009, then declined more gradually through 2018. It is unknown whether the filings are original Torrens actions or proceedings subsequent to registration.

9.4.4 Ohio

Total civil filings in Ohio showed a longer, slower roller coaster pattern during the Great Recession than did the other states (Figure 9.14). The increase began in 2001, several years earlier than in the other states. The largest year-to-year increase, almost 20 percent, was at the beginning, from 2000 to 2001. The peak was in 2008. The largest single-year drop was almost 9 percent, from 2008 to 2009. The roller coaster pattern flattened in 2013 when the total filing level was below the level in 2000.

---

12. See discussion Chapter 7 about changes in hip pocket filing laws.
13. MINN. STAT. § 548.101 (2020), added by Minn. Laws of 2013, ch. 104, § 3.
14. REPORT TO THE COMMUNITY, THE 2019 ANNUAL REPORT OF THE MINNESOTA JUDICIAL BRANCH 17.
15. MINN. STAT. ch. 508.

FIGURE 9.14 OHIO TOTAL CIVIL FILINGS IN COMMON PLEAS, COURT OF CLAIMS, AND MUNICIPAL AND COUNTY COURTS BEFORE, DURING, AND AFTER THE GREAT RECESSION (DECEMBER 2007 TO JUNE 2009)

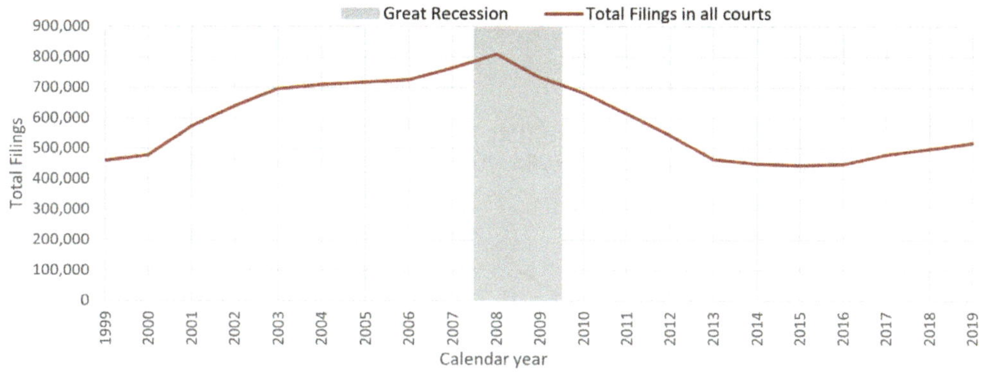

The bulk of the surge in total filings, particularly early, was in the municipal and county courts (MCC), not including Small Claims cases (blue line in Figure 9.15). The court of common pleas (CCP) (green line) experienced a shallower roller coaster in total filings. It started more slowly, peaked in 2009, and declined more slowly. Small Claims filings (burnt orange line) did not contribute to the roller coaster. They experienced a long-term decline, with a slight increase from 2001 to 2005 and in 2006 and 2007.

FIGURE 9.15 OHIO TOTAL CIVIL FILINGS BY COURT BEFORE, DURING, AND AFTER THE GREAT RECESSION (DECEMBER 2007 TO JUNE 2009)

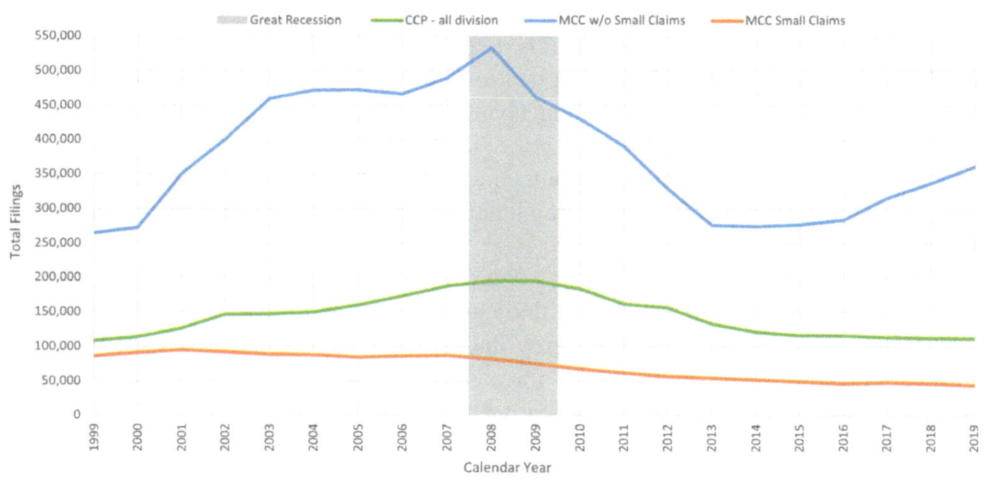

The significant increase in municipal and county court filings was from two case subcategories—Contracts and Other Civil (Figure 9.16). The early rise was attributable primarily to Other Civil cases (green line). This subcategory included minor civil matters that were usually quickly resolved, for example Applications for Appointment of Trustee and Transfers of Judgment.[16] The Contract category (red line) included cases

16. Instructions for Preparation of Statistical Report Forms, Municipal and County Courts — Individual Judge Report 4.

that involved liability on promissory notes, including confession of judgment or collection of accounts due.[17] Total Contract case filings showed a steady increase from 1999 to a peak in 2008. Filings then dropped faster than they had risen until 2013. Filings in 2013 were slightly higher than filings in 1999. Filings slowly increased for the next three years, then rose sharply beginning in 2017.

FIGURE 9.16 OHIO TOTAL FILINGS MUNICIPAL AND COUNTY COURTS BEFORE, DURING, AND AFTER THE GREAT RECESSION (DECEMBER 2007 TO JUNE 2009)

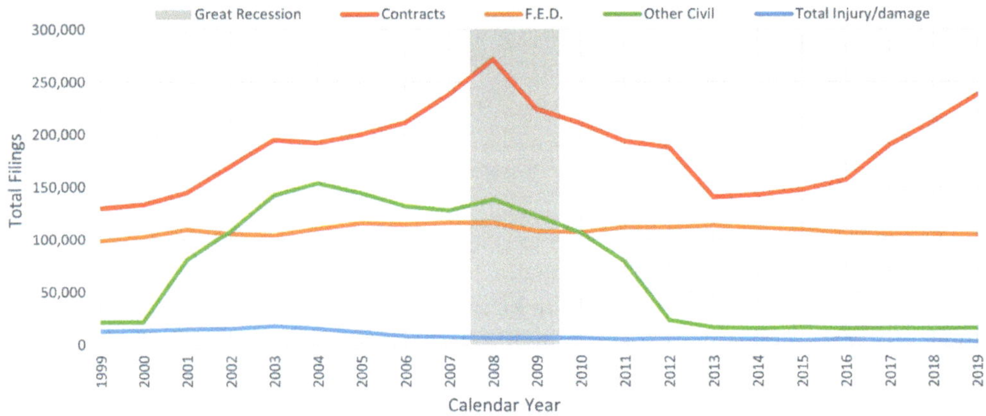

Forcible Entry and Detainer (F.E.D.) cases (burnt orange line) did not surge during the Great Recession. F.E.D. cases are summary proceedings for restoring possession of real property to one who was wrongfully kept out or wrongfully deprived of possession.[18] The category also included applications for the release of deposited rent payments (rent escrow).[19] The F.E.D. filing level in 2019 was about the same as the level in 1999.

Similarly, Injury/damage cases (blue line) did not contribute to the surge. There was a peak in 2003, but by 2005 filing levels were below the 1999 level, and were 74 percent lower in 2019.

The court of common pleas case categories experiencing a surge during the Great Recession were Foreclosures (yellow line) and Other Civil cases (blue line) (Figure 9.17). Injury and damage cases (dark gray line) experienced minor increases from 2001 to 2005, but were declining steadily through 2019. Admin./Workers Compensation appeals (light blue line) were also relatively flat for the period.

---

17. Instructions for Preparation of Statistical Report Forms, Municipal and County Courts — Individual Judge Report 3.

18. F.E.D. cases were initiated under Ohio Rev. Code, § 1923(A) or § 5321.03. Municipal court subject matter jurisdiction over F.E.D. cases is specified in Ohio Rev. Code § 1901.18(8). County Court subject matter jurisdiction over F.E.D. cases is specified in Ohio Rev. Code § 1907.031(6).

19. Instructions for Preparation of Statistical Report Forms, Municipal and County Courts — Administrative Judge Report 4.

FIGURE 9.17 OHIO COURT OF COMMON PLEAS TOTAL FILINGS BY CASE CATEGORY BEFORE, DURING, AND AFTER THE GREAT RECESSION (DECEMBER 2007 TO JUNE 2009)

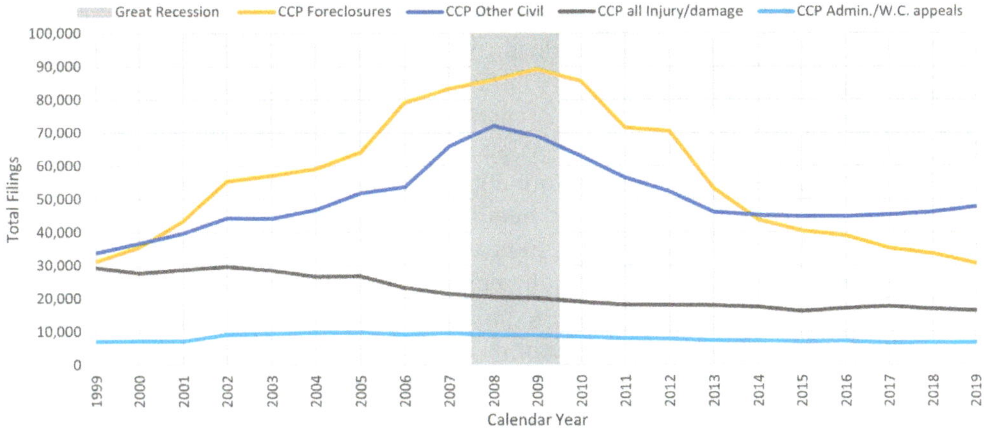

In Ohio, Foreclosure cases involve the enforcement of a lien, mortgage, trust deed, or "other similar instrument in any method provided by law."[20] The filings include all types of foreclosures, and do not distinguish between residential, commercial, tax, or other types of foreclosures. From 1999, Foreclosure filings experienced a sharp rise until 2002, a slower rise for three years, and then a sudden jump in 2006. In 2007, the number of foreclosure cases exceeded the total number of felony criminal cases in the state.[21] Foreclosure filings peaked in 2009, then fell, with sharp drops in 2011, 2013, and 2014. The drop in 2013, almost 25 percent, was the largest single-year drop in the 20-year period. Foreclosure filings dropped only 2 percent over 20 years; however, they dropped almost 66 percent since the peak in 2009.

The surge in foreclosure filings was discussed in two "Spotlights" in annual statistical report summaries.[22] The Spotlight in 2008 identified the ten counties with the highest growth in foreclosure filings from 1999 to 2008. The growth in filings in these counties ranged from 308 percent to 536 percent. However, all were relatively small counties in terms of total filings; the range was from 201 to 1,306 filings in 2008. The Spotlight also identified nine counties with at least 2,000 filings. The growth in these counties was not as high, ranging from 148 percent to 209 percent, with the higher figures in the smaller of the counties on the list. The three largest counites, Cuyahoga, Franklin, and Hamilton, had lower foreclosure growth rates, 157 percent, 168 percent, and 173 percent, respectively. The 2008 Spotlight noted that the surge in filings did not appear to result in a sustained backlog, as the clearance rate[23] only dropped below 90 percent in 2006. The Spotlight also noted that the number of defaults in foreclosure

20. Instructions for Preparation of Statistical Report Forms, Court of Common Pleas—General Division, Form A, at 2.

21. This was noted in the Message from the Chief Justice in OHIO COURTS SUMMARY 2008.

22. 2008 Ohio Courts Statistical Summary 53–56 and 2009 Ohio Courts Statistical Summary 53–54.

23. The clearance rate is the ratio of terminations to new filings, reactivations, and transfers in a year. A clearance rate of 100 percent indicates in a given year the court was terminating the same number of cases as were filed in a year (not the percentage of cases filed in a year that were terminated that year).

cases rose during this period, with a significant rise in 2006, while dismissals fell. The Spotlight offered that this pattern suggested "borrowers were increasingly unable to effect a negotiated outcome of their case."[24]

The Spotlight in 2009 looked farther back in time as well as providing an update on the then current status of the caseload. A separate category for Foreclosures cases had been introduced in 1990. From 1990 to 2009, the number of new foreclosure filings statewide had increased 311 percent. A chart was provided that showed the filings had decreased slowly from 1990 to 1995. A steady increase in filings began in 1996 and continued to 2002. The rise slowed from 2002 to 2005, then rose sharply in 2006. The Spotlight noted with concern that the number of pending foreclosure cases had been growing at a faster rate than filings in 2008 and 2009.

In response to the surge in filings, the Foreclosure Mediation Model was introduced in February 2008.[25] The objective of the program, which was referred to as "Save-the-Dream," was as much to keep people in their homes as to reduce the burden of these cases on the courts. The model was developed by a Foreclosure Working Group that included judges, magistrates, mediators, attorneys, legal aid representatives, educators, mortgage bankers, and representatives of homeowners.[26] The mediation model was designed to assist courts in determining which cases were appropriate for mediation based on information from the homeowner and the lender. Within a year, all counties were offering mediation as an option in foreclosure cases, and reported very high settlement rates from implementation of the model.

The mediation program was introduced when the filings were peaking. It is difficult to assess the impact of the program on filings. The nature of the program, triaging options for the parties after a case was filed, suggests it might increase filings, rather than decrease them. Alternatively, the options available in the program may have resulted in resolution of potential foreclosure cases before filing. The program began when filings were beginning to decrease. It did appear to help the courts address the backlog of cases.

In early 2020, the Ohio Office of Court Services convened a group "to analyze projected caseloads, create strategies for backlogs, and modernize court operations through technology" in response to anticipated increase in foreclosure filings as a result of the pandemic.[27] The report from the group noted that foreclosure cases had steadily declined from the peak in 2009 until the end of 2019.[28] In anticipation of an influx of filings and the possibility of a developing backlog, the group suggested that courts implement mediation programs or other settlement programs to address the plight of delinquent borrowers facing likely foreclosure.[29]

The second category of cases in the CCP that experienced a rise associated with the Great Recession were Other Civil cases. These included contract disputes, debt collection, employment-related matters, requests for equitable relief, civil rights actions, and

24. 2008 Ohio Courts Statistical Summary 56.

25. The Supreme Court of Ohio Annual Report, 2008, at 17–18.

26. The Supreme Court of Ohio Annual Report, 2007, at 60.

27. Ohio, Foreclosures & Civil Justice Report & Recommendation, June 2020, at 1.

28. Ohio, Foreclosures & Civil Justice Report & Recommendation, June 2020, at 2–3. Interestingly, the data showed that foreclosure cases tended to peak in the first quarter of each year.

29. Ohio, Foreclosures & Civil Justice Report & Recommendation, June 2020, at 6.

some property-related cases, for example, landlord/tenant issues but not foreclosures. From 1999, Other Civil filings experienced a steady rise until 2005, then a sudden rise in 2007, peaking in 2008, followed by a drop until 2013. Other Civil total filings were up almost 41 percent over the 20-year period, but dropped almost 34 percent from the peak in 2008. Greater detail of the subcategories of Other Civil filings was not available. However, data from other states suggests contract and debt related filings are much greater in volume than employment, civil rights, or property cases. Thus, the surge in filings during the Great Recession were more likely contract and debt cases.

9.4.5 Texas

Total civil filings in Texas showed a modest roller coaster pattern during the Great Recession. Since the data set begins in 2004, it is unclear when the increase associated with the Great Recession began. During the period for which data was made available, the largest one-year change in total filing levels was associated with the Great Recession. The largest year-to-year increase was from 2006 to 2007. The roller coaster pattern ended in 2013.

Figure 9.18 displays the total filings by level of court. The largest contribution to the roller coaster was from the justice court cases, not including Small Claims cases (blue line). The roller coaster pattern of Justice court filings ended in 2013, after which filings rose from 2004 to 2016. Both district courts (green line) and county courts (burnt orange line) exhibited a shallower roller coaster pattern. By 2012, total filing levels in these two courts dropped below the filing levels in 2004. Small Claims cases (yellow line) were declining from 2004 until 2013 when the jurisdiction was augmented.

Texas was one of two courts that had two peaks of total filings during the Great Recession. The peak in 2007 was a combination of justice court and county court cases. The peak in 2010 was a combination of justice court and district court cases.

FIGURE 9.18 TEXAS TOTAL CIVIL FILINGS BY COURT BEFORE, DURING, AND AFTER THE GREAT RECESSION (DECEMBER 2007 TO JUNE 2009)

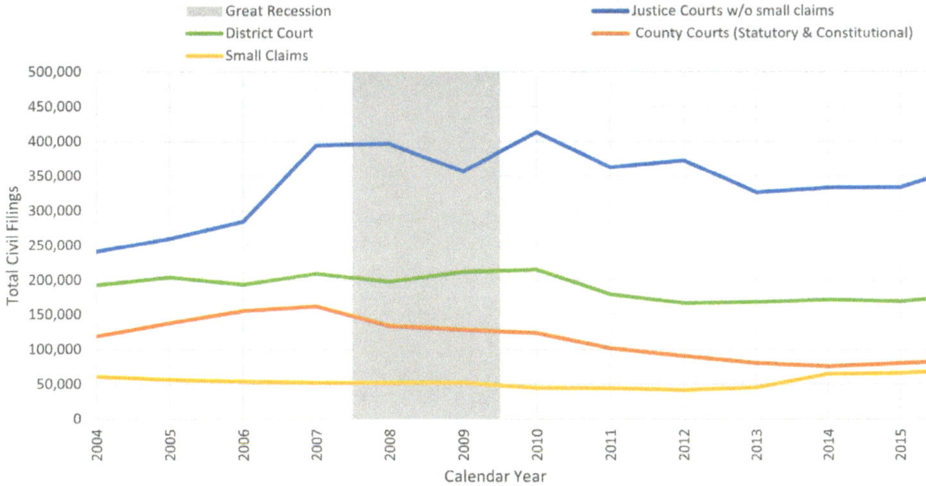

Drilling down into more granular case categories in these courts reveals that the two peaks during the Great Recession were surges in Debt and Contract case filings. Figure 9.19 displays the total filing for these case categories in all three courts. The biggest increase was in Other Civil and Debt cases in justice courts (burnt orange line). Filings increased 119 percent from 2006 to 2007. Debt cases in county courts (blue line) peaked in 2007. Other Civil and Debt cases in justice courts and Contract cases in district courts (green line) peaked in 2010, the second peak in total filings. By 2013, total filing levels for these case categories were almost down to pre-rise levels.

FIGURE 9.19 TEXAS TOTAL CONTRACT AND DEBT FILINGS BEFORE, DURING, AND AFTER THE GREAT RECESSION (DECEMBER 2007 TO JUNE 2009)

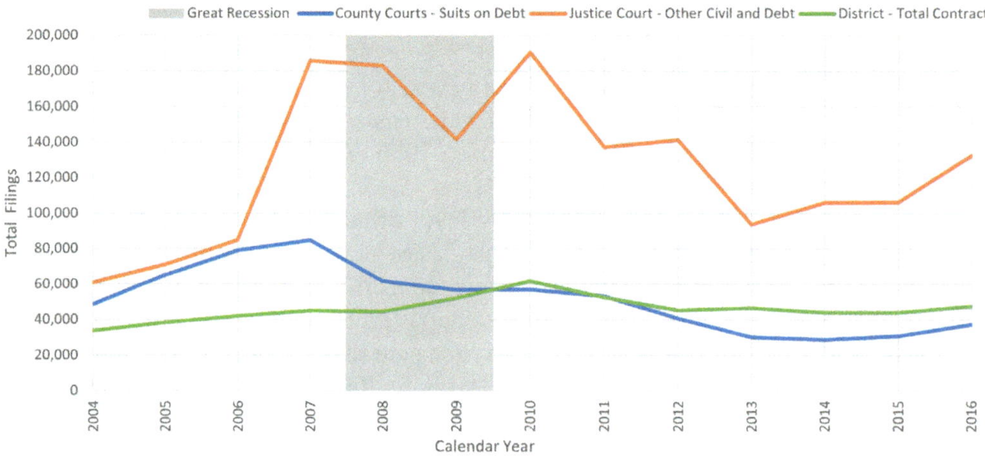

Injury/damage cases did not exhibit the same roller coaster pattern during the Great Recession. Figure 9.20 displays total Injury/damage filings combined for district and county courts. Both courts used the same definitions for the two subcategories of Injury/

FIGURE 9.20 TEXAS TOTAL INJURY/DAMAGE FILINGS IN DISTRICT AND COUNTY COURTS BEFORE, DURING, AND AFTER THE GREAT RECESSION (DECEMBER 2007 TO JUNE 2009)

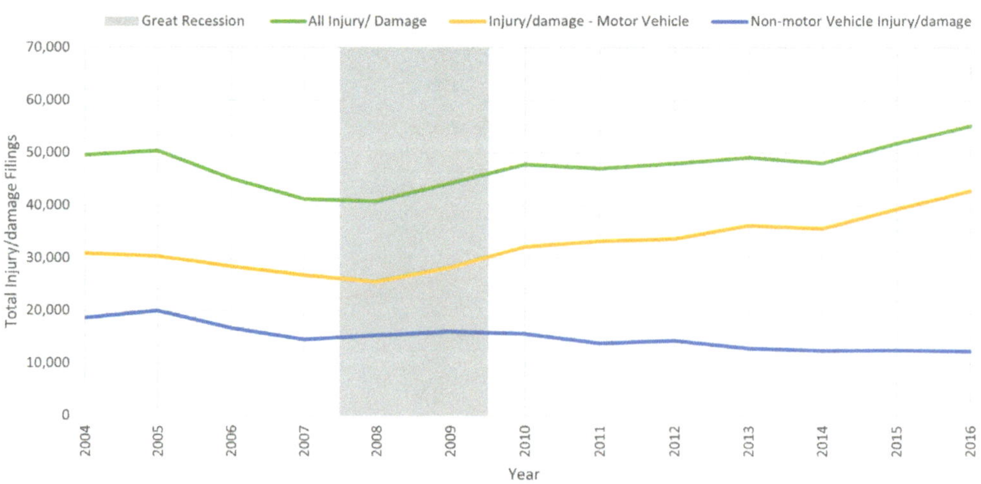

damage cases: Motor Vehicle and Non-motor Vehicle. There was also substantial overlap in subject matter and monetary jurisdiction of the two courts. Non-motor vehicle Injury/damage cases peaked in 2005, then steadily dropped over the next ten years by a total of 38 percent. Motor vehicle Injury/damage filings dropped 17 percent from 2004 to 2008, then rose steadily through 2016 when the filings were 68 percent higher.

9.5 Impacts of a Regional Recession—The Collapse of the Aerospace Industry in Southern California

The demise of the aerospace industry in Southern California after the turn of the century provides a view of changes in filing levels during a local recession. Since World War II the aerospace industry (private, military, and space) had been a major employer in Los Angeles, Orange, and San Diego Counties. Many of the employees lived in neighboring counties of Riverside and San Bernardino where there was less-expensive housing. At the end of the Cold War, the aerospace industry nearly collapsed. Between 2004 and 2014 "there was a 16.4 percent decline in employment in the aerospace industry throughout Southern California."[30] UCLA economists later reported that the near collapse "made the region the center of a severe statewide recession. More than a million people, many of them aerospace workers and their families, decamped for other states."[31] Since this collapse started before but continued into the Great Recession period, it is more difficult to sort out the effects of the Great Recession on other parts of California, or to compare the effect of the Great Recession in California with the other four states.

The impact of this exodus of industry and people on filing levels was most apparent as to Limited Civil filings and, in Riverside, also as to Unlimited Civil filings. Moreover, the impact was not in the manner expected. To the extent filing levels were a function of population, a significant loss in population might be expected to result in a drop in total filings. However, during this recession, when there was a significant dislocation of people and businesses, there was an increase in filing levels for several years.

The change in lower-value Limited Civil filings was the most dramatic during the 2004–14 period (Figure 9.21). Filings began to rise in 2006 in all of the courts. All of the courts, except Ventura, showed a significant increase in filings from 2006 to 2015. Los Angeles (light blue line) had a very sharp rise, peaking in 2008, followed by a sharp fall of filing levels in 2011. By 2013, filing levels were below the levels from 2000 to 2005. Increases in San Diego (brown line) and Riverside (black line) followed a similar pattern. Riverside's was steeper in the beginning and ended sooner, in 2012. San Diego's also began sharply, but lasted longer, and dropped more slowly, ending in 2015. Although the total filings were approximately the same, San Diego had a much larger population (3.3 million in 2019) than Riverside (2.4 million). San Bernardino's rise (dark blue line) also began in 2005, peaked in 2008, dropped significantly in 2009, then continued to slowly drop, and ended in 2015 at a level below the 2005 filing level.

---

30. Alexander Nguyen, *Southland's Aerospace Industry Continues to Decline: Report*, PATCH (updated Mar. 1, 2016, 6:30 p.m. PT), https://patch.com/california/redondobeach/southlands-aerospace-industry-continues-decline-report.

31. Dan Walters, Commentary: A Tale of Two Regions: In California's economy, North trumps South — for now, August 13, 2017, https://calmatters.org/housing/2017/08/tale-two-regions-californias-economy-north-trumps-south-now/.

Unfortunately, filing levels for case subcategories within Limited Civil are not available. This information would have provided some insight as to the categories of cases that increased during this period. For example, Limited Civil cases include the subcategories of collection cases and eviction cases. The volume of both categories of cases would be sensitive to the economy, credit availability, and unemployment, all of which would vary significantly before, during, and after a recession.

FIGURE 9.21 CALIFORNIA TOTAL LIMITED CIVIL FILINGS IN SOUTHERN CALIFORNIA COUNTIES BEFORE, DURING, AND AFTER THE GREAT RECESSION (DECEMBER 2007 TO JUNE 2009)

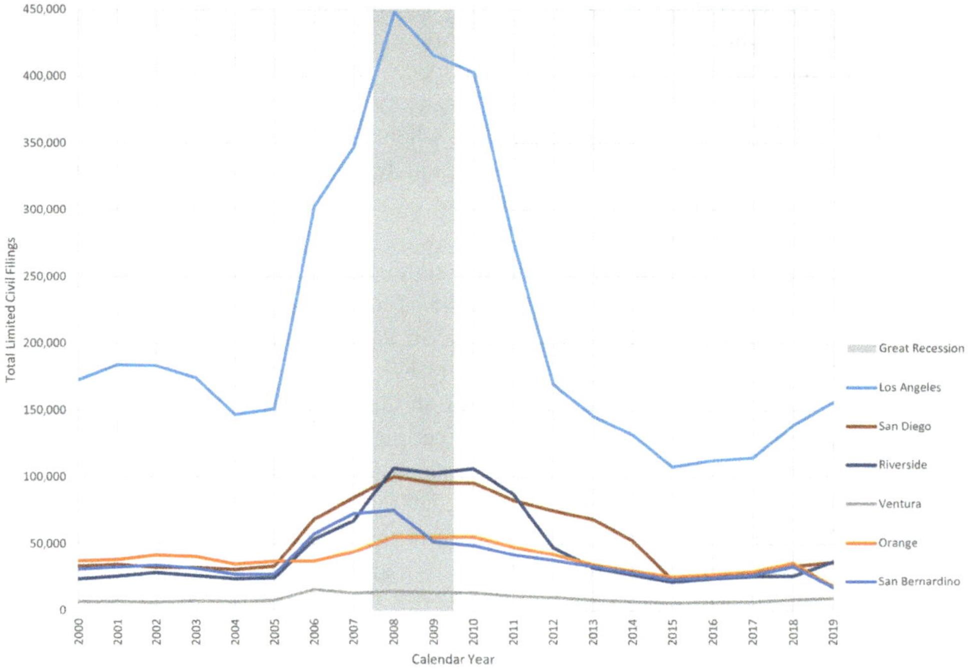

During the period from 2004 to 2014, higher-value Unlimited Civil filings showed three patterns in the six counties (Figure 9.22). The most striking pattern (and one that did not appear elsewhere in California or in the other four states) was in Los Angeles County (blue line) where the higher-value Unlimited Civil filings rose sharply and stayed higher longer than in the other counties. Los Angeles filings rose steeply in 2006, peaked in 2011, dipped, then peaked again in 2017. The second pattern was in Riverside (red line) and San Bernardino (green line) Counties where the roller coaster was not as long as in the other courts. Filings began to rise in 2006, peaking in 2007 in San Bernardino and in 2009 in Riverside. San Bernardino was dropping by 2008 and Riverside by 2011. Both then leveled off not much above 2004 levels by 2013. The third pattern was in Orange County (burnt orange line) and San Diego County (dark brown line) where the roller coaster was at a lower level, but lasted longer. Filings began rising in 2006, but not as steeply. Orange peaked in 2009 and stayed at that level through 2018. San Diego peaked in 2011 and stayed at a higher level through 2017. Ventura County filings (black line) rose slightly in 2005 and 2006, then stayed relatively flat through 2019, at a level higher than the early 2000s.

FIGURE 9.22 CALIFORNIA TOTAL UNLIMITED CIVIL FILINGS IN SOUTHERN CALIFORNIA COUNTIES BEFORE, DURING, AND AFTER THE GREAT RECESSION (DECEMBER 2007 TO JUNE 2009)

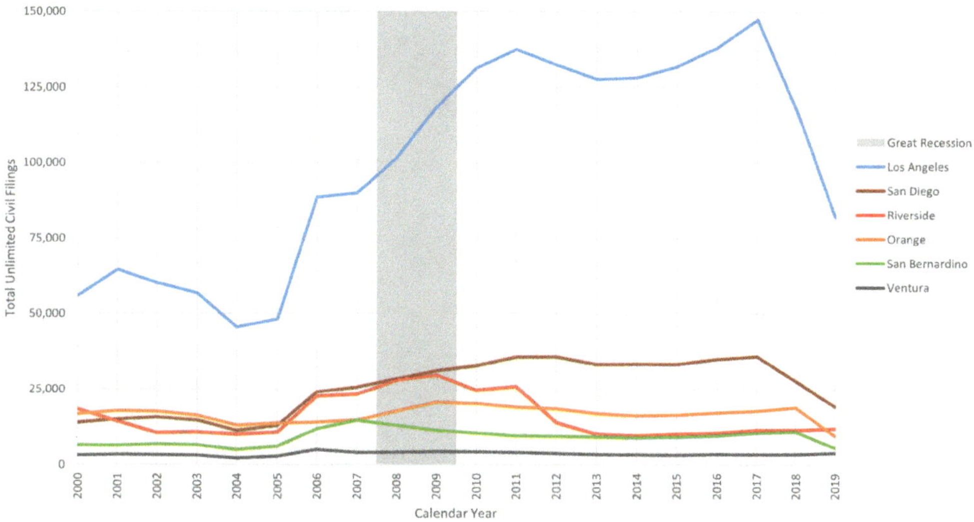

Total Small Claims filings for these six courts in this period did not show any changes associated with the aerospace collapse (Figure 9.23). All of the courts showed a flat or slightly rising filing level through 2003, then a long decline throughout the rest of the period. Los Angeles's decline was the steepest, and begins in 2004. None of the courts showed a small claims roller coaster in the 2004 to 2015 period as seen for Unlimited Civil and Limited Civil filings.

FIGURE 9.23 CALIFORNIA TOTAL SMALL CLAIMS FILINGS IN SOUTHERN CALIFORNIA COURTS BEFORE, DURING, AND AFTER THE GREAT RECESSION (DECEMBER 2007 TO JUNE 2009)

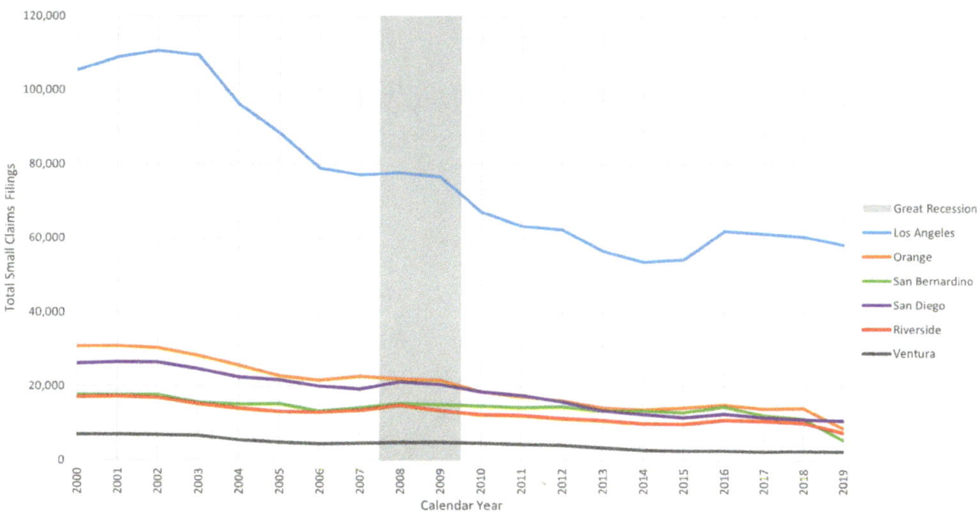

10

Observations and Recommendations

10.1 So What? What Did We Learn from This Study?

We began this study by taking a long view of what is happening regarding new civil case filings in state trial courts. We looked at filing levels over time, across states, and within states. We examined the impact of legislation, procedural changes, case management programs, and characteristics of the judiciary on filing levels. We have exposed "known knowns" that "just ain't so," provided some insight about "known unknowns," and revealed a few "unknown unknowns" regarding civil filing levels. The patterns we have uncovered are sometimes unexpected and often baffling.

Overall, our study found that total civil filings declined in four of the five states, and some have been declining for a very long time. These findings are consistent with National Center for State Courts (NCSC) data indicating many states have experienced a decline in all types of filings, not just civil filings. Our study also revealed that filing levels vary significantly over time, across states, and within states. The levels appear to be unrelated to population, geography, or demographics. Changes in the law assumed to affect filing levels often did not. New strong case management programs may have shortened disposition times and reduced litigation costs, but they did not affect filing levels.

Nor is the impact of national or local business cycles on filing levels obvious. Some recessions appeared to have little or no impact on filing levels, others a large impact, perhaps depending on what part of the economy is involved. The Great Recession appears to have had a large impact, but not in the manner expected. Some types of filings would have been expected to rise as a result of the shrinking economy, for example, small claims, evictions, and debt collection, because people had lost jobs and business slowed. Instead, we found these types of filings rose before the economy was officially declared to be in recession, then declined during the declared recession period. Perhaps these categories of cases are a leading indicator of a recession that affects wide swaths of the economy, not a simultaneous or lagging indicator.

Our experience suggests that most judges, court managers, and lawyers have little or no notion of the phenomena we observed. They are unaware of significant decline in filing levels over time. Their worldviews are too insular—focused on their own areas of practice or their own caseloads. Given the changes in filing levels uncovered here, the legal profession, judges, courts, and legislatures need to understand the larger trends and their implications.

But what are the implications? Our study did not lead us to conclusions about why civil filings have been declining. Nor did it provide evidence to show whether declining filings represent normal, historical fluctuations, a positive development, or a reason for alarm. If the filings decline were due to a general improvement in the fairness of business practices and less contentious interpersonal relationships, that would be a cause for celebration. We are not aware of any studies that would support that hypothesis. Rather, several recent, large-scale public surveys indicate that there is a serious problem with people either not realizing they have a legal problem, not being able to find their way into the legal system, or not able to successfully navigate the process. Given these problems, the judiciary and the bar should reconsider how to engage the public in order to better fulfill its role of providing equal access, as well as equal justice, to all. Otherwise, there is the risk of the judiciary becoming less relevant in society.

The recommendations to address these problems are organized in three stages in this chapter. The first stage is how the judiciary can improve the collection of data about civil case filings to provide better answers to questions. The second stage posits filing levels as a measure of court performance and addresses their analysis. The third stage addresses how the judiciary and the bar should engage the public to address the problems they encounter.

In the first stage, the judiciary needs to better understand the trends revealed here about what is happening to filing levels. First, case categories should be identified that are more relevant to understanding and managing the work of trial courts. In addition, data should begin to be collected about the types of litigants involved in lawsuits. Filing data should be collected and made available based on shorter time periods, for example, by month as well as by year, and by individual courts.

At the next stage, the more detailed filing level information should be analyzed by judges, court managers, legislators, and others to assess the effectiveness of laws, court rules, and case management programs and to design more effective approaches to assisting litigants in navigating the legal system.

The third stage involves reimaging how to engage the public and formulate new strategies to help people with legal problems find a way to reach a just resolution of their problems.

10.2 Identify More Useful Case Categories

We begin the recommendations at a very basic level. The most obvious recommendation from this study is for courts to start collecting new case filing data based on more particularized case categories that allow useful analysis of filing trends.

Most case type categories currently used for counting filings do not measure much that is useful for understanding or explaining changes in filing levels. Nor are they useful for predicting future filing levels. Existing categories often combine several case types, each with different filing patterns and levels, into broad categories that muddle any explanatory or analytical value. Existing categories also tend to be organized by areas of law as taught in law school—torts, contracts, landlord-tenant, property, and so on—that have little to do with managing cases. Many existing categories are also based on a mix of legal theory and amount of damages alleged.

Instead, states should identify and begin to count new case filings using categories that will assist in:

1. Understanding the incoming and pending workload of the court;
2. Assessing the trial courts' need for resources—judicial, staff, and fiscal—to appropriately resolve the cases that are filed;
3. Evaluating the impact and effectiveness of case management practices;
4. Evaluating the impact and effectiveness of proposed or new legislation or rules of court, and
5. Evaluating the impact of events such as natural disasters.

Developing new categories will undoubtedly be an iterative process. It would begin with too many categories, and, as information is developed, selection of those categories that are most relevant to the types of analysis suggested earlier.

10.2.1 Proposed New Case Categories

There are several possible criteria for identifying useful case categories for counting and analytical purposes. The criteria may overlap, resulting in categories that incorporate several factors that may affect filing levels. For example, consumer debt cases are a high-volume case type that fluctuates significantly with economic conditions and are governed by some unique procedural laws.

High-volume cases. The most common type of filings should be identified, regardless of the amount of time required to resolve individual cases. Based on current assumptions about what cases are most common, initial categories should include consumer debt collection, injury/damage cases involving vehicles, eviction cases, and foreclosure cases. Although each individual case in these categories may not require a lot of judge time, these cases represent the greatest public contact with the civil justice system as litigants.

Cases for which filings fluctuate significantly year-to-year or based on the health of the local economy. Case categories that tend to fluctuate year-to-year create challenges for the allocation of judges and court resources and for this reason need to be separately counted. Again, consumer debt, eviction, and foreclosure case filings may fluctuate more based on economic conditions, as opposed to Injury/damage cases or eminent domain cases.

Cases subject to unique substantive and procedural laws and rules that are not applicable to civil cases generally. Examples include non-family protective order, class action, equity, and eminent domain cases. Another category in this group would be cases subject to new laws, court rules, or case management programs, for example, as a result of tort reform legislation, or new pleading and proof requirements. Only by separately tracking these cases can an analysis be made of the efficacy of the changes in laws or case management programs.

Cases that take a disproportionate amount of judicial resources. Although these cases may be few in number, relative to other categories, each case my require much more judicial resources to resolve than simpler, higher-volume cases. Examples include toxic torts, malpractice cases, and complex business cases. Counting these separately will provide more useful information for assigning cases and assessing the need for resources. Cases such as malpractice are easily ascertained at the time of filing. Complex cases may not be identified at filing, but become apparent early in the litigation process.

Courts should continue to report filing levels for the broader case categories that have been used historically. This can be accomplished by aggregating the filing counts for the new categories that were included in the old categories, but now separately counted. This would maintain a level of continuity of filing data when looking back in time, yet permit more useful analysis going forward. The filing levels of the new, more detailed categories should be available for analysis even if not all are included in annual reports.

Finally, case type terminology and categories should be **purged of old common law and Latin terms**. Examples of case categories and terms that neither litigants nor the general public can understand include: cognovit, detinue, distress for rent, ejectment, escheat, forcible entry and detainer, habeas corpus, lis pendens, mandamus, mechanics lien, mittimus, ne exeat, quo warranto, remittitur, replevin, torrens, tort, and trover. Ideally, a new set of terms replacing the common law and Latin terms should be developed to provide consistency across states.

10.3 Start Counting Litigant Categories

Recent studies have reported the mix of litigants has changed, and the level of self-represented litigants has risen significantly. For example, the proportion of cases in civil and family law where at least one party is self-represented is roughly 75 percent.[1] Self-represented defendants are more common than self-represented plaintiffs. Knowing the status of litigants may guide the development of new strategies for assisting them in knowing about and navigating the legal system.

Other examples are changes in the proportions of individual versus organizational litigants, and changes in the type of organization involved. One example of this is the shift from banks and credit card companies to debt collection organizations as plaintiffs in consumer debt cases.[2] Does this vary by case category? How has this changed over time? Is the mix affected by recessions? Do recessions have different impacts based on which part of the economy is affected, for example, the Dot.com Recession versus the Great Recession. Perhaps different procedural rules should apply to different types of litigants to facilitate the prompt and just handling of their cases. For this reason, it would be useful to know who is using the courts.

---

1. Nat'l Ctr. for State Courts, THE LANDSCAPE OF CIVIL LITIGATION IN STATE COURTS, 31–33, 2015, https://www.ncsc.org/~/media/Files/PDF/Research/CivilJusticeReport-2015.ashx, and Nat'l Ctr. for State Courts, FAMILY JUSTICE INITIATIVE: THE LANDSCAPE OF DOMESTIC RELATIONS CASES IN STATE COURTS, 2018, https://ncsc.contentdm.oclc.org/digital/collection/famct/id/1544/rec/1.

2. The Pew Charitable Trusts, HOW DEBT COLLECTORS ARE TRANSFORMING THE BUSINESS OF STATE COURTS, 2020, https://www.pewtrusts.org/-/media/assets/2020/06/debt-collectors-to-consumers.pdf.

Knowing who the litigants are is as important as knowing what the filing levels are in understanding the way in which the use of the courts changes over time. In order to achieve this, courts should **count the number of each type of litigant in new filings**. The count should include both the number of plaintiffs and defendants, whether they are a person, business, or other type of organization, and whether they are represented by an attorney. Most case management systems already require entry of the name of every party, as well their attorney, if they are represented. Tools are available that can distinguish people and various forms of businesses. Knowing the pattern of litigants is important when assessing the need for, and when developing, new procedures and strategies to assist litigants, especially self-represented litigants.

Counting self-represented litigants is complicated by the fact that the representation status often changes during the life of a case. The National Center for State Courts statistical reporting guidelines call for a case to be designated as "self-represented" if one or more parties in the case were not represented by a lawyer at any time during the life of the case.[3] New filing counts would reflect the representation status when the case is initiated. Updating of the status would be necessary when analyzing the resolution of cases, as opposed to the filing of cases.

10.4 How to Count More Detailed Categories of Civil Cases

Accurately counting more detailed case categories will require a re-engineering of the case category determination process. Currently, most courts identify the case category of new cases either through a clerk's review of the initial complaint or petition or the litigant's designation of the case category. The litigant's designation occurs either through use of a civil cover sheet required to be filed with the initial complaint or petition or during the data entry for e-filing of the initial complaint or petition. Clerks may review the litigant's choice of category, particularly if the choice is "Other." Modifying this manual, mostly paper-based case category selection process would be challenging, requiring new rules, forms, and modifications to case management and data warehouse systems, and training of court staff, lawyers, and litigants. This is probably why changes occur so infrequently. However, there are now options for revising the process.

New technology tools are available that should be used to identify more detailed case categories. Software tools are now available that can help in the categorization of new filings. The software tools can easily, quickly, and reliably extract case category information from the text in electronic documents. These tools should be trained, and maintained, by teams of court staff, lawyers, and data analysts to properly categorize cases. Such software tools are already in use. They have been used for years to identify and redact information in court documents that are subject to privacy and access rules.[4]

---

3. Nat'l Ctr. for State Courts, Court Statistics Project, State Court Guide to Statistical Reporting, ver. 2.2.2, updated Jan. 5, 2023, at 34, https://www.courtstatistics.org/__data/assets/pdf_file/0031/88735/State-Court-Guide-to-Statistical-Reporting.pdf.

4. For examples of redaction software, see Stephen Cooper, *The Best Redaction Software and Tools. Privacy Regulations Require Companies to Protect Information from Disclosure While Also Expecting*

They are also being used to provide analytics to lawyers about cases.[5] While collecting information from documents raises several issues about privacy and access, acceptable solutions are available.[6] To the extent electronic documents are available in cases filed in past years, information should be collected to build data sets covering a longer time frame. A few courts or states should work with vendors to develop these tools and make them available for use by all courts.

The accuracy of case filing counts is also important.[7] Problems of missing or mis-identified cases should be addressed through **periodic random audits of filing reports**. If a new case is not counted or is mis-categorized, for whatever reason, it does not affect the subsequent processing of that case. Since the initial reporting category is not significant, there is a risk of it being less accurate than data that is relied on for ongoing case management. Hence it is recommended that periodic random audits of case filing data reports be conducted, at least until comprehensive electronic data collection is established. The audit should address the total filings reported, as well as the case category counts. The audits will reveal inconsistencies, as well as errors, in reporting. More accurate data engenders greater trust in the data by other courts, the public, researchers, and the other branches of government.

In order to best assess the critical question of whether changes in legislation, court rules, court decisions, or case management programs have an impact on filing levels, filing data must be available based on the implementation date of changes. For this reason, if **case filing data should be collected and made available by shorter time frames than one year**. Filing data available by month, as opposed to by year, would allow analysis of the changes that may have been implemented at any point during a year. Changes can become effective at the start of a calendar year, fiscal year, or legislative cycle. For example, most new laws in California take effect on January 1 of the year after adoption. In Texas, most new laws take effect on September 1 of the year of adoption. Judicial decisions can occur at any point in a year, suggesting data availability at least by month.

Often new case management programs are begun as pilot programs in one or a few courts. In order to assess the impact of the program on filing levels, it would be necessary to have filings for each of the pilot courts from before and after the implementation date. In order to effectuate this, **case filing data should be collected and reported by individual court jurisdictions within a state**. If cases are assigned to a judge for all purposes at the time of filing, collection and reporting should be available at the judge level. Availability of filings by court would also allow analysis of the impact of natural

---

Businesses to Protect Data. Redaction Software Helps with Solving This Problem, COMPARITECH, Feb. 28, 2023, https://www.comparitech.com/data-privacy-management/best-redaction-software-and-tools/.

5. K. Firth-Butterfield & K. Silverman, *Artificial Intelligence—Foundational Issues and Glossary*, ARTIFICIAL INTELLIGENCE AND THE COURTS: MATERIALS FOR JUDGES ARTIFICIAL INTELLIGENCE, LEGAL RESEARCH, AND JUDICIAL ANALYTICS, AMERICAN ASSOCIATION FOR THE ADVANCEMENT OF SCIENCE (AAAS) (2022) https://doi.org/10.1126/aaas.adf0782.

6. Amer. Acad. of Arts & Sciences, MEASURING CIVIL JUSTICE FOR ALL. WHAT DO WE KNOW? WHAT DO WE NEED TO KNOW? HOW CAN WE KNOW IT?, 2021, https://www.amacad.org/sites/default/files/publication/downloads/2021-Measuring-Civil-Justice-for-All.pdf.

7. Nat'l Ctr. for State Courts, Court Statistics Project, DATA GOVERNANCE GUIDE, ver. 1.0, 2019, at 21–25, https://www.courtstatistics.org/__data/assets/pdf_file/0031/23899/data-governance-final.pdf.

or human-caused events affecting only one or a few courts, such as hurricanes, floods, wildfires, earthquakes, local recessions, 9/11-type terrorist attacks, and pandemics.

Filing counts should separately report new case filings from reopened, transferred, or returned cases. Case filing reports often report a filing number that includes cases that have been transferred, remanded, reopened, or recategorized, as well as new cases. The reason for the inclusion of these cases in addition to new cases is that they do represent additional work for the courts to which the cases are now assigned. They also need to be counted in order to balance pending caseload totals, as the cases were counted as "disposed" based on prior activity in the case or in another court where the case originated. It is therefore appropriate to include them in the filing number in an annual report.

Unfortunately, little information is available about what portion of filings reported are actually new cases. Of the five states studied here, only Ohio reported new filings separately in their annual reports. Data from Ohio indicates that cases other than new filings represented between 6 and 12 percent of reported total filings over a 19-year period, a significant proportion relative to annual fluctuations in total filings.

For the purposes of analysis contemplated in these recommendations, **there should be a separate count of just new filings**. The count of new cases should exclude the following cases, as they had already been counted once when the case was originally filed:

1. Cases transferred between courts or judges, including change of venue;
2. Cases re-designated, for example, when a case was coordinated with other cases, designated as a complex case, or the case category changed;
3. Cases "remanded" from an appellate court following appeal;
4. Cases reinstated, reactivated, reopened, or restored after being closed or placed on an inactive status, for example, because of a bankruptcy filing by a party, or
5. Subsequent proceedings to enforce the judgment obtained in an original proceeding.

In some states, a case seeking the right to recovery is counted as a new filing, and then subsequent proceedings to enforce any judgment awarded are also counted as new filings. Counting subsequent proceedings that require judicial resources is appropriate for judicial workload purposes, but they should not be counted as a new filing since the case has already been counted once as a new filing.

When a set of relevant case categories are developed, **the new categories should be used by all trial courts in a state**. The same categories should be used regardless of monetary or other jurisdictional boundaries defining trial courts. Uniform categories should also be used even if rolled up to broader case categories that have historically been reported, such as Unlimited Civil and Limited Civil in California, Law ≤$50,000 and Law >$50,000 in Illinois, or Major Civil and Minor Civil in Minnesota. Consistent categories across all courts will allow analysis within a case category, as well as across states, of the impact of changes in decisions, laws, rules, case management practices, and economic conditions.

10.5 Filings as a Court Performance Measure

Courts should engage in more sophisticated analysis of case filing levels to assess the effectiveness of court performance. The analysis of filing data reported in this book demonstrates what can be learned about the impact, or lack thereof, of legislation, court rules, and case management programs. Existing examples of judiciary efforts to develop this capability include the interactive dashboards available through the NCSC Court Statistics Project[8] and through other interactive dashboards, such as the Ohio judiciary website.[9] One recent example of an effort to analyze the impact of a program on filing levels is the Ohio Court Services group looking at foreclosure filings.[10]

If the judiciary does not engage in these types of analysis, others will do it, and, perhaps, for purposes contrary to the rule of law and equal access to justice. The private sector already offers analytics to examine the performance of the courts, including assessments of individual judges and courts.[11] One academic study examined how an extraneous factor—when the judicial officer last ate—affected judicial decisions.[12] It will be difficult to constrain this type of analysis, although France has outlawed analytics about decisions of judicial officers.[13]

Additional recommendations regarding the analysis of filings to identify and remove barriers to access follow. However, we also want to make courts and researchers aware of the limitations of some of the ways filings have traditionally been used when examining courts.

Extreme caution should be used when predicting statewide filing levels based on data from the large courts in a state, a sample of courts in a state, or just those courts that can readily generate data from electronic court records. The wide variance of filing levels across courts within a state and over time make it problematic to predict statewide filing levels from a sample of the courts in the state.

Population is not a good predictor of filing levels. The analysis here finds very little correlation between total population and filing levels. It may be that an examination of population demographics, for example, proportion of renters versus homeowners or income levels, will reveal some relationship.

Caution should be used when reporting changes in filing levels over time. The length of the time period comparing filing levels can result in very different conclusions. For example, total civil filings in FY 2018–19 in California were up 2 percent over the last five years, down 30 percent over the last ten years, down 19 percent over the last 20 years, and down 21 percent over the last 40 years.

Predicting or estimating judgeship, staff, or budget needs from filings can be problematic. As discussed more extensively in Chapter 2, methodologies that use raw

---

8. https://www.courtstatistics.org/court-statistics/interactive-caseload-data-displays/csp-stat.

9. https://www.supremecourt.ohio.gov/courts/services-to-courts/court-services/dashboards/.

10. Ohio, Foreclosures & Civil Justice Report & Recommendation, June 2020.

11. Rick Merrill, *Top 5 Most Important Judicial Analytics Metrics*, A.B.A. J., Oct. 11, 2021, https://www.abajournal.com/columns/article/top-5-most-important-judicial-analytics-metrics, and John Focciola & Nicholas Miganelli, *Artificial Intelligence, Legal Research, and Judicial Analytics*, Artificial Intelligence and the Courts: Materials for Judges: Artificial Intelligence, Legal Research and Judicial Analytics, American Association for the Advancement of Science (AAAS) (2022), https://doi.org/10.1126/aaas.adf0787.

12. Shai Danziger, Jonathan Levav, & Liora Avnaim-Pesso, *Extraneous Factors in Judicial Decisions*, 108(17) PNAS 6889–92 (Apr. 26, 2011), http://www.pnas.org/content/pnas/108/17/6889.full.pdf.

13. Section 3: Concilier la publicité des décisions de justice et le droit au respect de la vie privée, Art. 33, as amended 2019 [Conciliating the Publication of Judicial Decisions and the Right to Respect for Private Life], https://www.legifrance.gouv.fr/jorf/article_jo/JORFARTI000038261761.

filings to estimate the number of judges or staff, or amount of funding needed by a court, are, at best, trailing indicators of need, and inherently flawed. There are at least five problems. First is the time lag—at least a year—between when filings increase and when additional resources might become available. Second is the reluctance and near impossibility for a court to reduce the number of judges or staff when filings suddenly decline, especially if it may only be temporary. The third problem is that significant year-to-year fluctuations in filing levels can result in significant fluctuations in estimated need for judges, staff, or funding. Fourth is a possible shift in the mix of filings in a case category that affects the amount of resources needed when the methodology parameters are not adjusted in a timely manner. The fifth problem is when changes in substantive or procedural laws, or implementation of new case management programs, render the methodologies' parameters obsolete.

10.6 Engaging the Public Regarding the Use of Courts

The long-term decline in civil filings documented here and elsewhere requires serious attention. As suggested at the beginning of this chapter, it is unlikely the decline in civil filings can be attributed to a general improvement in the fairness of business practices, or less-contentious interpersonal relationships. Rather, there is evidence of a staggering gap in unmet legal needs that could account for the decline in filings. Recent surveys by several organizations have documented the unmet civil legal needs of the public and provide some indications of why they are not being met. A review of the survey findings points to possible alternatives for addressing the unmet legal need.

10.6.1 Extent of Unmet Legal Need

How great is the unmet legal need? A 1992 American Bar Association survey suggested as many as half of American households experienced at least one significant civil justice situation at any given time.[14] The Legal Services Corporation (LSC) has an ongoing initiative measuring the unmet civil legal needs of low-income Americans.[15] Surveys were conducted in 2005,[16] 2009,[17] 2017,[18] and 2022.[19] The 2017 survey contacted approximately 2,000 adults in households at or below 125 percent of the federal poverty

14. Rebecca L. Sandefur, *What We Know and Need to Know About the Legal Needs of the Public*, 67 S.C. L. Rev. 443, 445 (2016), citing Amer. Bar Assoc., Consortium on Legal Servs. & the Public, Legal Needs and Civil Justice: A Survey of Americans; Major Findings from the Comprehensive Legal Needs Study (1994).

15. Legal Services Corporation, Justice Gap Research, https://www.lsc.gov/initiatives/justice-gap-research.

16. Legal Services Corporation, Documenting the Justice Gap in America, 1st ed., Sept. 2005, 2d ed., June 2007, https://lsc-live.app.box.com/s/zb2hn2xm0ewmsubckbtpo9jjegxruwfp.

17. Legal Services Corporation, Documenting the Justice Gap in America: The Current Unmet Civil Legal Needs of Low-Income Americans, 2009, https://www.lsc.gov/sites/default/files/LSC/pdfs/documenting_the_justice_gap_in_america_2009.pdf.

18. Legal Services Corporation, The Justice Gap: Measuring the Unmet Civil Legal Needs of Low-income Americans, 2017, https://www.lsc.gov/sites/default/files/images/TheJusticeGap-FullReport.pdf.

19. Legal Services Corporation, The Justice Gap: The Unmet Legal Needs of Low Income Americans, 2022, https://justicegap.lsc.gov/the-report/.

level. The survey found that 71 percent of low-income households had experienced at least one civil legal problem in the last year. Moreover, 86 percent reported that they received inadequate or no legal help for the problems encountered in the last year. The 2019 survey contacted 5,000 American households and found higher levels of unmet needs of low-income households; 74 percent of the households experienced at least one civil legal problem in the previous year, and 92 percent did not receive enough, or any, legal help.

In the late spring of 2019, the State Bar of California conducted a comparable survey of 3,885 Californian households at all income levels, not just low-income.[20] The survey found that 55 percent of all California households and 60 percent of low-income households experienced at least one civil legal problem in the previous year. Overall, 85 percent of households received no or inadequate legal help to resolve their civil legal problems. Rates were similar among low-income households, 86 percent, and higher income households, 84 percent.

In the fall of 2019, HiiL and IAALS partnered to conduct a study of access to justice in the United States.[21] They asked 10,058 people about legal problems they experienced in the last four years, what they did to solve those problems, and whether they felt they had reached a fair resolution. The survey found that 66 percent of the population experienced at least one legal issue in the past four years. Only 49 percent of the problems were reported to be completely resolved. Another 22 percent were expected to be resolved, leaving 22 percent unresolved.

Significantly, the proportion of people with unmet legal needs appears to have increased during the period of declining civil filings.

10.6.2 Most Common Civil Legal Problems

These surveys also identified the most common types of civil legal problems people reported experiencing. Focusing on types of civil legal problems examined in this book, the most common problems reported, not in order of volume, were personal injury and property damage, work and employment (unsafe working conditions, unfair or discriminatory treatment in the workplace, and difficulty getting paid for work), financial (debt collection), housing (foreclosure, eviction, rent and lease issues, and landlord failure to maintain property in good repair), consumer disputes, and neighbor disputes. Family law issues were also prominently mentioned in these surveys; we have not included those cases in our analysis of civil filings.

---

20. California State Bar, The California Justice Gap: Measuring the Unmet Civil Legal Needs of Californians, Nov. 2019, https://www.calbar.ca.gov/Portals/0/documents/accessJustice/California-Justice-Gap-Report.pdf.

21. The Hague Institute for Innovation of Law (HiiL) and The Institute for the Advancement of the American Legal System (IAALS), Justice Needs and Satisfaction in the United States of America 2021 Legal Problems in Daily Life, 2021, https://www.hiil.org/wp-content/uploads/2019/09/Justice-Needs-and-Satisfaction-in-the-US-web.pdf.

10.6.3 Why Are Needs Not Being Addressed?

Survey respondents described numerous reasons for not seeking or receiving help for their legal problems. The reasons given were not always mutually exclusive, but, collectively, they are daunting. However, they do provide a roadmap of sorts as to where to direct activities to reduce the unmet legal need identified by the surveys. The reasons noted by survey respondents included the following:

- Many people **do not know that the problem they experienced was legal in nature and could be resolved through the legal system**.
- A significant portion of people **decided to deal with the problem without getting** help.
- Some people were **afraid to pursue legal action**.
- Related to this was a concern expressed about their **ability to find a lawyer** they could afford if they needed one. Professor Bill Henderson of the Indiana University Maurer School of Law has documented the decline of the sector of the bar serving individuals, as opposed to businesses and government.[22] Between 2012 and 2017, law firm revenues reported to the Census Department rose from $225 to $246 billion, but revenues from individuals dropped by $7 billion. Only a quarter of lawyer revenue is derived from individuals (of all income levels). In a 2017 report,[23] CLIO, the law firm billing software company, summarized the billing data for 60,000 solo practitioners and showed their precarious financial situations, billing on average only 2.3 hours per day and collecting only 70 percent of that. The bar is not currently organized to serve the needs of ordinary people.
- Even if they located a lawyer, concerns about the **cost of legal help** is a significant barrier to seeking legal help. Anecdotally, the cost of litigation, relative to the benefits, is the most common barrier to litigation cited by lawyers.
- If a case was filed without the assistance of a lawyer, many found that **navigating the legal process** was daunting. The legal process was designed by lawyers for use by people represented by lawyers. Many studies have shown that self-represented litigants in particular encounter barriers at every step of the process to obtain legal remedies for which they are eligible.
- Another problem is that people **just don't have time** for litigation. They are overwhelmed with life. This is less true for higher-income people, who can afford lawyers and afford to wait for a remedy. Anecdotally, self-represented litigants report spending enormous amounts of time initiating and pursuing a case, in part because it requires a mini legal education, self-taught.
- A more serious problem arises from potential litigants **perceptions about the fairness and efficacy of the civil legal system**. Higher income individuals have more confidence in the civil legal system and are more likely to believe that they can use the civil legal system to protect and enforce their rights. Lower income people are less likely to feel that they can use the courts to protect themselves and that they are treated fairly by the courts. This is corroborated

---

22. Bill Henderson, *The Decline of the PeopleLaw Sector* (037), LEGAL EVOLUTION, NOV. 19, 2017, https://www.legalevolution.org/?s=Decline+of+the+PeopleLaw+Sector.

23. https://www.clio.com/resources/legal-trends/2017-report/.

by annual polls conducted by the National Center for State Courts.[24] The 2022 poll revealed that state courts have reached an all-time low in positive public perception. Only 60 percent of respondents have confidence in the state courts, and only 43 percent believe that courts are providing equal justice to all.

- Finally, the **public awareness of the role of courts and what they can do has diminished.** When the country was young, court proceedings were a form of public entertainment where people saw the problems that could be resolved in court and what the outcomes might be. As the population increased and became more urbanized, public attention dropped. As a result, the role of the court in providing information and direction to people on the rule of law and how to behave weakened. What the media chose to publicize were the aberrant, exceptional cases, like the McDonald's hot coffee case. Movie and television series portrayals of court processes and trials have also had a negative effect. The nature and outcome of the vast majority of cases are not publicized. Having lost the connection to the courts, the public's sense of the role of courts diminished.[25]

10.6.4 Where Do People Go for Help?

When people did seek help for legal problems, they turned to a variety of sources for information and assistance. Some did seek help from lawyers or the courts, although some responded that they were unable to get help there, or they felt the help they received did not or would not help with the issue. Many sought assistance from non-legal sources. The most common sources were family members, friends, medical and mental health professionals, religious or spiritual leaders, police officers, and insurance companies. In addition, people sought help from the internet, with mixed success. When considering options for addressing the unmet legal needs, understanding where people turn for help can identify better strategies for reaching people in need of legal help.

10.7 A Vision for a Different Relationship between the Courts and Their Customers

If an automobile dealer experiences a decline in the number of customers visiting the sales lot and buying a car, that is a matter the dealer must address to stay in business. What are the causes of the reduced demand? Is the model of car the dealer is selling going out of fashion, or is it losing market share because of the introduction of cheaper products by a competitor? Or is it a falling reputation of the car model's quality. Perhaps the dealership's post-sales service has developed a negative reputation. Or is it the

---

24. Nat'l Ctr. for State Courts, State of the State Courts, https://www.ncsc.org/consulting-and-research/areas-of-expertise/court-leadership/state-of-the-state-courts.

25. Daniel Small, *Reversal of Roles on Access to Courts*, A.B.A. J., Feb. 9, 2022, https://www.americanbar.org/groups/litigation/publications/litigation_journal/2021-22/winter/reversal-roles-access-courts/ and Brandy R. Manning, *Storytelling for Advocates and Judges: How and Why We Should Incorporate Storytelling Techniques and Themes into Our Work*, A.B.A. J., Feb. 4, 2022, https://www.americanbar.org/groups/judicial/publications/appellate_issues/2022/winter/storytelling-for-advocates-and-judges/.

manufacturer's or the dealer's lack of advertising, or effective advertising, or of advertising using the best medium for reaching potential customers?

The courts are facing a similar predicament; they are losing their civil justice customers. What can be done differently to bring them back? Several states have begun efforts to address the "justice gap" in a systemic fashion. We will not attempt to summarize these strategies and initiatives here. They are evolving rapidly. Recognizing that the courts and the legal profession cannot, and perhaps should not, close the justice gap by their efforts alone, we nonetheless focus on ways that they can do their part.

Our suggestion that courts use civil filings as a performance measure would focus the courts and the legal profession on the experience of their customers. The first step should be an attempt to identify, and maximize, those things that attract civil justice customers and, conversely, to identify, and minimize, those things that deter those customers.

Here are a few examples of ways in which courts can focus on improving their services to maintain their customer base.

- **Recognize that courts are a service and not a place.** Richard Susskind has long advocated that courts stop identifying their services with their physical courthouse.[26] The Covid-19 pandemic triggered profound changes in live court proceedings, enabling persons to appear remotely rather than in person. It turns out these appearance options enable a much larger percentage of self-represented parties to participate in hearings. It also appears that judges, lawyers, and litigants are now comfortable in interacting remotely on all sorts of matters—with each other as well as with the court. Maintaining and increasing remote services should be a cornerstone of a customer-focused mindset that will increase the base of satisfied customers.
- **Schedule court proceedings for the convenience of the parties.** One way to expand access to services is to extend court hours of operation. Offering expanded hours of service demonstrates the court's willingness to adapt to litigants' schedules, which should build trust and confidence in the judicial system. The National Center for State Courts recently published a toolkit supporting this approach.[27]
- **Analyze court data to identify the bottlenecks in the legal processes that thwart rather than facilitate court users.** Where do self-represented litigants get stuck in the process? What processes are unnecessarily complicated? What assistance would best help litigants get past this barrier? A good example is dismissals for failure to prosecute. Courts monitor civil case progress. If a case is not preceding as it should—which generally means there has been a failure to complete a step required for the court to timely hear the matter on the merits—the courts will often enter a dismissal for failure to prosecute. Failure to complete service of process is a common basis for such dismissals. Courts view these dismissals as the consequence of litigant failures. In most instances,

26. Richard Susskind, Online Courts and the Future of Justice, New York, 2019, online ed., Oxford Academic, https://doi.org/10.1093/oso/9780198838364.001.0001.

27. Nat'l Ctr. for State Courts, Alternative Court Hours Toolkit, Mar. 2023, https://www.ncsc.org/__data/assets/pdf_file/0029/88616/Alternative-Court-Hours-Toolkit-.pdf.

it is not a failure of the litigant, but a failure of the court process—the litigant can't figure out what to do. Since courts should be more interested in resolving cases on their merits, they should change the process or find ways to provide sufficient assistance to unrepresented litigants to avoid these dismissals. Tom Tyler's research on procedural fairness[28] demonstrates that litigants care more about the fairness of the process than on whether or not they are the prevailing party.

- **Maximize the use of technology to enhance the experience of their customers.** In 2018, the Institute for the Advancement of the American Legal System published *Eighteen Ways to Use Technology to Better Serve Their Customers.*[29] The publication notes that courts actually benefit more from technologies designed for their customers than from those designed to improve their internal processes. One example is deploying an application allowing lawyers and parties to schedule their own hearings without having to talk to court staff. Not only does this produce court dates that are more convenient for the parties, but it also relieves court staff of the labor of calling and clearing hearing dates with the parties. Another promising tool is the use of text messaging to alert litigants (and lawyers) of the required next step in the litigation process, including reminders until the step has been completed or an appointment with the self-help center, or a court hearing, has been set, to keep the case on track toward resolution.
- **Identify ineffective or outmoded legal procedures and new, alternative procedures that are easier to use and more effective.** One example has to do with methods of service of process. Historically, service had to be personal. If the party could not be personally served, service by publication was permitted. Service by publication has become meaningless with the demise of newspapers. The proliferation of electronic communications tools suggests that electronic service should now be permitted, preferably through multiple channels. If the point is to give someone notice of a lawsuit, every means available should be used to ensure actual notice.
- **Maximize court self-help services.** Most large courts today have well-staffed offices established explicitly to provide services to unrepresented litigants. They provide procedural guidance, identification of appropriate forms, help filling them out, and review of completed forms. Their effectiveness depends on the court empowering them to provide the broadest scope of service possible—effectively countering the instinctive reaction of court personnel to refuse to give "legal advice."[30] A number of states have created statewide self-help centers providing remote services to supplement those provided in local courts

---

28. *See* John Hagan & Valerie P. Hans, *Procedural Justice Theory and Public Policy: An Exchange*, 13 Ann. Rev. Law & Soc. Sci. 1–3 (Oct. 2017), https://www.annualreviews.org/doi/full/10.1146/annurev-lawsocsci-121416-011426.

29. John M. Greacen, *Eighteen Ways to Use Technology to Better Serve Their Customers*, IAALS (Oct. 30, 2018), https://iaals.du.edu/publications/eighteen-ways-courts-should-use-technology-better-serve-their-customers.

30. For a recent review of the guidance provided to court staff for this work, see https://judicature.duke.edu/articles/legal-information-vs-legal-advice-a-25-year-retrospective/.

and to ensure that such services are available to rural customers. While they are helping litigants, self-help centers should examine court policies and practices to identify the bottlenecks that prevent litigants from navigating the process, and propose alternatives to better serve the litigants.

- **Work with the organized bar to enhance the availability of legal services for individuals.** It is clear from the CLIO data cited earlier that solo and small firm lawyers are struggling. New approaches are needed to link them to potential customers needing their help. Limited scope representation, which entails lawyers assisting persons to represent themselves, is a service option that needs to be made widely available. Lawyer referral services, for the most part, use archaic technology and wholly lack an advertising component. Mobilizing the bar to provide more effective representation to individuals cannot be left to the initiative of individual practitioners.

In addition to improving services, the judiciary and the bar should engage in greater outreach to the public. If people do not know that courts can help them with their legal problem, they will not turn to courts for help. Courts have not actively engaged in this, in part because of a sense that it violates their neutrality. However, failure to do so isolates the judiciary and diminishes its relevance. Here are ways that courts can reach out without impinging on their neutrality.

- **Build public trust and confidence through timely, accurate, and understandable communication.** The Conference of State Court Administrators recently released a policy paper[31] that recommends courts should:
  - Publish summaries of court decisions directed to a general audience;
  - Expand transparency especially in high profile cases;
  - Respond promptly to bad information;
  - Use a restrained response to undue criticism of courts or a specific judicial officer;
  - Increase social media presence; and
  - Continue to expand civics education activities.
- **Provide information to the public about what the courts can do and how to use them.** The position of Public Information Officer (PIO) is now well established, at least in large courts. Its role is usually limited to handling media and social media relations and, occasionally, educational sessions regarding the role of the court. However, it should also include educating the public about the remedies a court can provide and how to access them. Personal injury lawyers have demonstrated the value of billboard, television, and online advertising. While this may seem extreme, courts seeking to increase their use should consider the same or similar processes to provide the public with a very different view of what courts and lawyers are about. An area of the court's work that could be a first place to experiment with this approach would be small claims

31. Conference of State Court Administrators (COSCA), Courting Public Trust and Confidence: Effective Communication in the Digital Age, 2023, https://cosca.ncsc.org/__data/assets/pdf_file/0020/86015/COSCA-Policy-Paper-Courting-Public-Trust.pdf.

court. Our data shows that this process—designed to help ordinary people resolve their ordinary legal problems—is disappearing through nonuse.[32]

- **Educate the public about changes in the law that may be relevant to solving their legal problems.** For example, the analysis here shows little impact from changes in the monetary jurisdictional limits of courts, particularly small claims court. Could this be due to the lack of broad scale notice to the public about the change? A person may have not used small claims court because they thought their damages were above the limit, based on old information about the limit.
- **Educate the helpers to whom people turn about using the courts.** The national surveys found that people often seek help from non-legal people in their community, not from lawyers or the courts. An example of a major national effort along this line is Frontline Justice,[33] a bipartisan national project focusing on creating a cadre of "justice workers" in our communities to help people identify and address their legal problems.

The pandemic showed that courts are capable of rapid and effective change—when they accept that it must take place. If courts can be motivated by the reality that the decline in civil filings is a sign of their declining significance in American life, they should be able to identify and implement many additional steps to improve the experience of their customers. The need to do so is made clear by insights provided by two of our profession's thought leaders. Gillian Hadfield wrote "People who feel as though the rules don't care about them don't care about the rules."[34] And Bill Henderson says "We have entered a period where we are either going to redesign our legal institutions or they will fail. . . . Step one is acknowledging the magnitude of the problem."[35]

32. See Matthew G. Smith, *Promoting Public Awareness of Court Resources by Advertising*, NCSC Trends 2022, at 41.

33. https://www.frontlinejustice.org/.

34. Gillian Hadfield, Rules for a Flat World 79 (2017).

35. Bill Henderson, *The Decline of the PeopleLaw Sector* (037), Legal Evolution, Nov. 17, 2009, https://www.legalevolution.org/?s=Decline+of+the+PeopleLaw+Sector.

APPENDIX

Methodology

A description of the sources and contents of the case filing data is provided here. It begins with a general discussion applicable to all five states. This is followed by a description specific to each of the five states.

Sources of Data

The project requested each participating state to provide a data set of aggregate statewide civil filing totals for as many years as the state deemed to be consistent regarding case category definitions. The goal was to collect data beginning in at least 2000, through 2019, which four of the five states were able to provide. The data sets represented the population of all civil filings, not a sample. The statewide filing data sets contain no data about individual cases or individuals, only the number of each category of cases in each type of trial court. The data in the data sets did not allow reverse engineering to discover personally identifiable information about any individual involved in any case.

The data set was requested from the state court administrator's office. In all five of the participating states, there were state statutes or rules of court requiring all courts or judges to report caseload statistics monthly or quarterly to the state court administrator's office. In all five states here, the state court administrator's office promulgated regulations specifying what data to report and what categories to use. Many courts in these five states submitted the reports manually on paper forms, but in many counties, particularly the larger counties, data was submitted electronically.

The state court administrator's offices in all five states reported that they reviewed the data submitted by courts for obvious types of errors—missing data or data that was significantly "out of range" compared to previous submissions. Any concerns noted were brought to the attention of the reporting court or judge, who may, or may not, submit corrections. In none of the five participating states was there a formal audit by the state court administrator's office of data submitted by a court, although there may have been audits at the local level. Another source of possible consistency errors occurred when a court moved to a new case management system or shifted from a manual to an electronic reporting process.

Initially states were asked to provide civil filing data based on the same year time frame as was reported in their annual reports. For added states, data was requested based on calendar years. In retrospect, it would have been better to request one-year time frames consistent with when changes in state statutes and rules of court took effect to allow more specific analysis of the impact of changes in the law.

We asked participating states for the total number of cases filed in each type of trial court for each year disaggregated by the case type categories required to be collected and reported. We did not ask for finer breakdowns of case type if it was not reported to the state court administrator's office. In a few instances, the lack of detail made it difficult to explain fluctuations in filing levels observed in the aggregate data.

Only New Filings Included

The focus of the study was on new cases filed in the trial courts. The data request to the state court administrator's office was for new filings only. The following cases were not considered new cases, as they had already been counted once when the case was originally filed:

1. Transferred between courts or judges, including change of venue;
2. Re-designated, for example, when a case was coordinated with other cases, designated as a complex case, or the case category changed;
3. "Remanded" from an appellate court following appeal; or
4. Cases "reinstated," "reactivated," "reopened," or "restored" after being placed on an inactive status, for example, because of a bankruptcy filing by one of the parties.

Only two states, Ohio and Texas, were able to provide numbers of just new cases. The total filings data in California, Illinois, and Minnesota included some of the categories just listed. The volume of cases not counted as new filings, as just defined, varied from a small ratio to a more substantial ratio of "new" filings depending on the state, as discussed later. Annual reports often reported total filing figures that include many of the types of filings just described, along with new filings, because these cases represented additional work for the courts and judges. For Ohio and Texas, the focus on only new cases in this analysis accounted for differences in the filing numbers analyzed here and the total filing numbers reported in their annual reports.

Civil Case Categories

In order to analyze filing data that was more comparable across the five states, some categories of filings that were regarded as civil in one or more of the states, but not in the others, were excluded.

In all five states, the following broad case types were excluded: probate, trusts, conservatorship, guardianships, mental health, civil commitment, mental competency, family law (including stay away or protective orders), child support, adoptions, domestic violence, juvenile dependency, juvenile delinquency, criminal (felony, misdemeanor, and infractions), traffic, enforcement of local ordinances, and parking cases.

Cases seeking equitable relief were included. Appeals from one trial court to another trial court that were reported were included. The volume of these case types was generally small compared to the more common civil case types.

Where possible, filings in the following case categories were excluded, as noted later in the descriptions about each state. In some of the states, the category of "other civil cases" or "other civil petitions" included cases that were not considered civil in the other participating states. For example, petitions for stay away orders involving members of a family or certain relationships were counted as a civil case in some states and as family law cases in other states. Cases related to criminal proceedings were excluded. Examples include habeas corpus writs, bond forfeiture, search warrants, matters relating to various types of surveillance, forfeitures or seizure of property, extradition, contempt in criminal cases, expunction, loss of occupational license, interstate probation transfers, foreign subpoenas, petitions for relief from a firearms disability related to criminal cases, and victim protective orders.

Unit of Count for a Civil Case

Generally a civil case was counted and reported when an original complaint, petition, or other originating pleading was filed, regardless of the number of (1) plaintiffs, petitioners, defendants, respondents, or other parties; (2) causes of action involved; or (3) parcels of land involved. In some states, there was no clear definition about how to count cases with multiple causes of action or parties.

Who Decides the Case Type Category

The question of who decided the appropriate case category for a new case filing varied with how the filing occurred. When filings were submitted on paper, the clerk entering new case information into a case management system reviewed the filing and chose a case type. To aid the clerk, two states (California and Minnesota) had adopted "civil cover sheets" that were required to be filed with the originating document. The cover sheet required the filing party to choose a case category from the list on the cover sheet (California) or a list on the court's website (Minnesota). This shifted the case category selection from the court to the party filing the case. With the introduction of e-filing, the party entering data to e-file the complaint generally chose a case category from a list provided as part of the data entry steps to transmit the originating document.

Either the filing party or the court's data entry clerk could make mistakes in selecting the appropriate case type category. One source of error could result when a case had more than one cause of action and could fit in more than one category. This was generally addressed in the reporting instructions to the court or the instructions to the party. Typically the instructions indicated that the choice should be a more specific rather than a more general category, and reflect the primary cause of action if there were several.

A second type of error occurred when the person selecting the category just choose "other" instead of a more specific appropriate category. If a filing party chose "other," the clerk's office might review the filing and change the category. In addition, a party filing a responsive pleading could designate a different, or more specific, case category.

No effort was made here to attempt to identify the probable level of either type of error. Nor was an analysis made to look at whether filing category proportions changed when the identification of the case category shifted from the court clerk to the filing party.

Changes in Case Type Categories over Time

Over the long time frames involved in this study, participating states occasionally changed case reporting categories. Generally, the number of categories was increased, with new categories being separated from existing, more general categories. In some instances, the newly separated categories might be shifted from one broader case category to another, for example, from "Other Civil" to "Contract." These changes are discussed when they are relevant to the analysis of filing data.

Population Estimates

In order to convert filings to a measure more comparable across the participating states, the total filing numbers were recalculated as filings per 100,000 population, referred to as per capita filings. The population estimates were obtained from the U.S. Census Bureau's Population Estimates Program (PEP).[1] The PEP program provides population estimates for the whole state and counties within the state. The population estimates for each year were obtained from the Intercensal Estimates[2] for each decade.

Sources and Descriptions of Case Filing Data by State

California

Sources of data. Two data sets were provided by the Judicial Council of California (JCC). One included total statewide filings by fiscal year (FY) from FY 1980–81 through FY 2018–19, a period of 39 years. This data set included total statewide filings of all case types in all trial courts. Civil filing data for the 1978–79 and 1979–80 fiscal years was obtained from the annual reports produced by the JCC, resulting in a 41-year time frame. Total statewide small claims filing data for FY 1976–77 and FY 1977–78 were also obtained from annual reports, resulting in a 43-year data set for small claims filings. A second data set was provided of civil filing data by county for each calendar year for the period 2000 to 2019—a period of 20 years.

Case filing data was collected by each superior court and reported to the JCC on a monthly basis. The data from each court was compiled in a data warehouse with a consistent structure and definitions referred to as the Judicial Branch Statistical Information System (JBSIS). There was a detailed manual for data collection and reporting into JBSIS.[3]

1. U.S. Census Bureau Population Estimate Program, https://www.census.gov/programs-surveys/popest/about.html.

2. See discussion at https://www.census.gov/programs-surveys/popest/guidance.html.

3. Judicial Branch Statistical Information System Manual, ver. 3.0, effective July 2018 [hereinafter JBSIS Manual].

New cases included. In addition to original filings, the data set included change of venue, reclassified cases, cases restored to the court's control after being counted as removed from the court's control, and cases reopened after being counted as terminated.[4] Cases reopened for post-termination actions (for example, for enforcement of judgment) and cases transferred between judges within a court were not counted in filing totals provided by the JCC.

Case categories included and excluded. There were three broad categories of civil cases included: Unlimited Civil, Limited Civil, and Small Claims. The categories were based on both the case type and the amount of damages alleged. Unlimited cases alleged more than $25,000 in damages and Small Claims had a damage cap of $10,000. Appeals in Small Claims matters and appeals from Limited Civil judgments were heard in the superior court and counted as new filings and were included in the analysis. Both Unlimited Civil and Limited Civil case types included Enforcement of Judgment actions for which filings were not separately reported. Asset forfeitures were included in the Other Civil Complaints subcategory of Unlimited Civil filings. The Orange County Superior Court provided more granular data on filings for 2007 and 2017. In both years, asset forfeitures were 0.1 percent of civil filings and enforcement of judgment filings were about 1 percent of all civil filings.

Definition and unit of count for a civil case. A civil case was broadly defined as "lawsuits brought to redress private wrongs, such as breach of contract or negligence, or to enforce civil remedies, such as compensation, damages, and injunctions."[5] The unit of count for a civil case was defined as the filing of a complaint or petition regardless of the number of plaintiffs, defendants, or respondents or causes of action. Civil cases that contain multiple plaintiffs, defendants, or respondents were counted as a single filing.[6] If a civil property case contains multiple parcels in the complaint, it was to be counted as a single filing.[7]

Who decides the case type categorization? Since 1996, a party filing a lawsuit was required to file a Civil Case Cover Sheet[8] with the original complaint.[9] The cover sheet required the filing party to choose one category that best described the case. The categories provided on the cover sheet corresponded to the categories the courts used when reporting filings to the JCC. If a case was filed electronically, the e-filing system required the filing party to select a case type from the same list that was on the civil cover sheet.

Changes in case type categories over time. All of the data provided by the JCC staff and used in this report followed the post-2002–03 subcategories of civil cases.

Prior to FY 2002–03, there were two civil case subcategories for non-PI/PD/WD (personal injury/property damage/wrongful death) cases, one called "Other Civil Complaints" and a second called "Other Civil Petitions." Beginning in FY 2002–03, cases in these subcategories were reallocated. Department of Child Support Services filings

---

4. JBSIS Manual at 99–101 (Unlimited Civil cases) and 51–56 (Limited Civil cases).
5. JBSIS Manual at 49 (Limited Civil cases) and 89 (Unlimited Civil cases).
6. JBSIS Manual at 41 (Limited Civil cases) and 89 (Unlimited Civil cases).
7. JBSIS Manual at 52 (Limited Civil cases).
8. Civil Case Cover Sheet, Judicial Council Mandatory Form CM-010, rev'd July 1, 2007.
9. Cal. R. of Ct., tit. 3 Civil Rules, Div. 3 Filing and Service, Chap. 3 Papers to be Served, Rule 3.220. Case cover sheet.

previously counted in the Other Civil Petitions subcategory were now reported in a new subcategory, "Family Law Petitions," along with other miscellaneous family law petitions previously reported in Family Law. The remaining nonfamily petition filings were now combined with the Other Civil Complaints subcategory in a new subcategory renamed "Other Civil Complaints and Petitions." This subcategory includes Civil Harassment petitions and Workplace Violence petitions.[10] Domestic violence and Elder/Dependent Adult Abuse petitions were counted under Family law.[11]

Appeals to superior court in Limited Civil cases (civil or criminal) were reported as Civil Appeals, not civil cases. Civil filings also did not include habeas corpus (criminal or other) filings. Small claims appeals were reported under Civil Appeals prior to FY 2003–04, and as a subcategory of civil cases beginning in FY 2003–04.

Prior to FY 1998–99, there was a separate subcategory of General Civil cases for Eminent Domain cases. These were subsequently counted in the Civil–Other Complaints subcategory.

Illinois

Sources of data. The Administrative Office of the Illinois Courts (AOIC) provided civil filing data for the calendar years 1996 to 2019. The data file included quarterly case filings for all civil case categories by county and year. Case filing data for the court of claims for the same time period was obtained from the Illinois Office of the Secretary of State which oversees the court of claims.

The Illinois Constitution authorizes the Supreme Court to require collection of caseload data about the work of the courts.[12] The Supreme Court promulgated an administrative order,[13] requiring monthly reporting of caseload data by the court clerks. A statute requires the clerks to provide the data required by the Supreme Court.[14] The AOIC issued a manual on recordkeeping,[15] instructing the clerks on what data to report.

New cases included. In addition to each initial complaint or petition filed, the new filing count included cases where there was a change of venue, change of place of trial, initial filing of a foreign judgment, and a case remanded by a reviewing court if the case is assigned a new case number.[16]

Case categories included and excluded. The data set provided included two categories of "law" cases, distinguished by the amount of damages alleged, and a set of specific case categories. The categories included a category of Arbitration cases that applied only in circuit courts that had adopted the program, and could include a variety of cases from other categories. Cases categorized as Order of Protection (code OP) were not included, as these cases could relate to family or criminal cases, not just civil

10. JBSIS Manual, *supra* note 3, at 96.

11. JBSIS Manual, at 141.

12. Ill. Const. art. VI, § 2.

13. Supreme Court of Illinois, General Administrative Order on Recordkeeping in the Circuit Courts, M.R. 1218, adopted May 20, 1968. A copy of the order is included in the Manual on Recordkeeping, Administrative Office of the Illinois Courts, Third Edition, effective April 1, 2017, at i.

14. 705 Ill. Comp. Stat. 125/1 (1963).

15. Manual on Recordkeeping, Administrative Office of the Illinois Courts, 3d ed., effective Apr. 1, 2017.

16. *Id.* at pt. 3, Introduction, at 1–2.

cases.[17] This case category included petition for order of protection, civil no contact order, firearms restraining order, and stalking no contact order when filed separately from an existing case.

The category of Miscellaneous Remedy (code MR) was also excluded from the analysis. The category constituted almost 5 percent of total statewide civil filings for the study period. The category included a number of case categories included in the other states, for example, change of name, review of administrative decisions and writs of certiorari, mandamus, quo warranto, and prohibition. However, it was estimated that these cases were probably about a quarter of the cases included in the category. The bulk of cases included in the MR category related to criminal cases, which were excluded in the other four states, for example, search warrants (estimated to be more than half the cases), probation interstate transfers, foreign subpoenas, forfeitures of seized property, matters relating to various types of surveillance, and so on.[18] Note that beginning in 2022, the category was split into two categories, one related to civil cases (code MR), and categories related to criminal cases (code MX).[19]

Definition and unit of count for a civil case. There was no formal definition of a civil action. A case number is assigned at the time the first document in a case is filed in the clerk's office,[20] except for the annual tax sale, for which only one case number was assigned each year.[21]

Who decides the case type categorization? In Illinois, the clerk determines the case type category at the time the case is filed if the case contains two or more counts that appear to fall under more than one case category.[22] If a case is filed electronically, the filer chooses a category from a list of case subcategories.[23]

Changes in case type categories over time. The case categories used here were those revised effective January 1, 1996.[24] Several new case categories were added. In addition, the amount of the claim distinguishing the two categories of Law cases, L and LM, was raised to $50,000.[25] The Manual on Recordkeeping was significantly revised, effective January 1, 2022.[26] There were revisions to the case category codes,[27] but these took effect in 2022, and did not apply to the data provided for this study.

---

17. *Id.* at pt. 1, § B, at 4.

18. A list of the cases included in this category is found at MANUAL ON RECORDKEEPING, *supra* note 15, pt. 1, § C, at 4.

19. A list of the cases included in each of these categories is found at MANUAL ON RECORDKEEPING, ADMINISTRATIVE OFFICE OF THE ILLINOIS COURTS, 4th ed., ver. 4.4, effective Ja. 1, 2022, updated Mar. 15, 2022, pt. 1, § C, at 17 (MR) and 18–19 (MX).

20. MANUAL ON RECORDKEEPING, *supra* note 15, pt. 1, § B, at 1.

21. *Id.*, subsec. 5 at 6.

22. Administrative Office of the Illinois Courts, MANUAL ON RECORDKEEPING, 3D ED., effective Apr. 1, 2017, pt. 1, § B, at 1.

23. The comprehensive listing of subcategories, referred to as the eFileIL Trial Court Public Facing Codes, http://efile.illinoiscourts.gov/Trial-Court-Configuration-Standards.htm.

24. MANUAL ON RECORDKEEPING, *supra* note 22, at iii.

25. *Id.*

26. Administrative Office of the Illinois Courts, MANUAL ON RECORDKEEPING, 4TH ED., ver. 4.4, effective Jan. 1, 2022, update effective Mar. 15, 2022.

27. *Id.* pt. 1, § C, at 15–17.

Minnesota

Sources of data. The Minnesota Judicial Branch provided a data set that consisted of calendar year filings for the years 1994 to 2018—a period of 25 years. The data was disaggregated by county as well as by case type. Total court filings for Major Civil and Minor Civil cases for 2019 were obtained from the 2019 Annual Report, extending the study period to 26 years for total filings in these two categories.

A state statute required the state court administrator to collect and report statistics on the business transacted by the courts.[28] District court administrators are required to "comply with the requests of the state court administrator for statistical or other information relating to the courts of the judicial district."[29] Court administrators are required to comply with any request from a district administrator for statistical information.[30]

New cases included. In addition to new filings, the data set included cases reactivated from an inactive status and reopened for additional proceedings.

Case categories included and excluded. In Minnesota there were two broad categories of civil cases, Major Civil and Minor Civil. The categories were based on case type and not on the amount of damages alleged. Within each broad category, certain case types were excluded from some analyses because they were not counted as civil cases or were not counted as new filings in the other states studied. The subcategories of Major Civil excluded were "Habeas Corpus" and "Forfeiture" for which separate filing totals began to be reported in 2003. In the other states, these were considered criminal filings. The Minor Civil subcategories excluded from analyses were "Implied Consent" and "Enforcement of Judgment." An Implied Consent case was defined as a "Petition for judicial review of a driver's license revocation as the result of a Driving While Impaired citation or complaint."[31] The Enforcement of Judgment case type subcategory included enforcement of an order or judgment already obtained in another case which were not counted as new filings in the other states. The subcategories of Enforcement of Judgment were Transcript of Judgments (judgments from a conciliation court filed in district court for satisfaction of indebtedness, whether from within the county, or from another county), Restitution Judgments, and Foreign Judgments.

Definition and unit of count for a civil case. A civil action is a lawsuit that involves money, injury, or damages, property, civil rights, or other noncriminal matters. There is only one form of civil action.[32] There is no explicit definition of the unit of count. However, the practice appeared to be that each case filed was counted as one case, regardless of the number of causes of action, number of parties, or number of parcels of land involved in the case.

Who decides the case type categorization? Minnesota required a Civil Cover Sheet[33] to be filed by the initial filing lawyer.[34] Question 13 of the Cover Sheet required the lawyer to indicate the case type based on a list in the Handout Case-Type-Index.[35]

---

28. 2020 MINN. STATS. § 480.15, subdiv. 5.
29. 2020 MINN. STATS. § 484.68, subdiv. 3(4).
30. 2020 MINN. STATS. § 484.17, subdiv. 3.
31. Minn. HANDOUT CIVIL CASE TYPE INDEX–MINN. R. CIV. P., Rev. 1-29-2021, at 5.
32. MINN. R. CIV. P. r. 2, One Form of Action.
33. Form CIV-117, PDF, rev. 1/2020.
34. MINN. GEN. R. PRAC. 104.
35. HANDOUT CIVIL CASE TYPE INDEX—MINN. R. CIV. P., Rev. 1-29-2021.

Once the initial civil cover sheet was filed, opposing lawyers or unrepresented parties could submit their own cover sheets with a different case type destination.

Changes in case type categories over time. There were some changes in case type categories during the study period. A number of new categories were added beginning in 2003. Filing totals for the new categories grew over the next few years, stabilizing by 2008. Consumer Credit Contract (CCC) appeared as a separate case category in 2008. Reduced Mortgage Redemption (RMR) appeared as a separate case category in 2017.

Ohio

Sources of data. The Ohio judiciary initially provided a data set consisting of statewide civil filing data for calendar years 1999 to 2018—a period of 20 years. The data was disaggregated by court, case type, and county. Statewide total filing data for 2019 disaggregated by court and case type was provided later. The filing totals for the court of common pleas were for the General Division only. Court filing data for the case types Change of Name, Wrongful Death, and Minor's Settlement heard in the probate division of the court of common pleas was obtained from the annual Court Statistical Summaries or the annual Ohio Courts Statistical Reports for 1999,[36] 2009,[37] and 2019.[38] The court filing data for court of claims cases was also obtained from annual Court Statistical Summaries or the annual Ohio Courts Statistical Reports.

Cases filed in the trial courts were generally randomly assigned to a judge almost immediately,[39] and remained on that judge's calendar until terminated or transferred.[40] Each trial court judge was obligated to report caseload statistics to the Supreme Court's Case Management Section every month for the cases assigned to him or her.[41] In municipal and county courts, the administrative judge was required to file a monthly report for any cases not individually assigned to a judge.[42] Prior to 2014, judges submitted reports on paper forms. Starting July 1, 2013, judges could submit reports through the eStats electronic portal.[43]

New cases included. The data set included only new filings, not transferred, reactivated, or re-designated cases. Beginning in 2014, the Annual Court Statistical Summary reports provided filings for "incoming cases," which included cases transferred, reactivated, or re-designated, in addition to new filings.[44] A comparison of transferred, reactivated, and re-designated cases to new filings reported in annual reports suggested that these three types of cases represented as little as 6 percent and as much as 12 percent of all filings between 1999 and 2018.

Case categories included and excluded. In Ohio, all case types heard in the general division of the court of common pleas were included in the analysis here. Three

36. The Ohio Courts Summary 1999, at 136.
37. Ohio Courts Statistical Summary 2009, Appendix 59.
38. Ohio Courts Statistical Summary 2009, Appendix 56.
39. Rules of Superintendence for the Courts of Ohio, r. 36.011(B).
40. Rules of Superintendence for the Courts of Ohio, r. 36.01(B).
41. Rules of Superintendence for the Courts of Ohio, r. 37.
42. Rules of Superintendence for the Courts of Ohio, r. 37.03(A).
43. Described in the Ohio Courts Statistical Summary 2012, at 26–27. The eStats home page is at https://www.sc.ohio.gov/JCS/casemng/statisticalReporting/.
44. Ohio Courts Statistical Summary 2019, at 3.

categories of cases filed and heard in the probate division of the court of common pleas were also included, because they were counted as civil cases in the other four states. These were Wrongful Death, Minors' Settlements, and Change of Name. In addition, civil cases filed in the court of claims against the state of Ohio, were also included.

Appeals from municipal[45] and county courts[46] were heard in the court of appeals and therefore not included in the trial court filings. Ancillary proceedings were not counted as cases.[47]

Definition and unit of count for a civil case. A civil case was defined as a complaint, petition, or administrative appeal filed in the court of common pleas, municipal court, or county court.[48]

There was no explicit description of what to count as a separate case. However, the definition of a case as a "complaint, petition, or administrative appeal" implies that each filing was counted as one case, regardless of the number of causes of action, parties, land parcels, and so on, that were involved.

Who decides the case type categorization? In Ohio, the clerk determined the case type category at the time the case was filed. The monthly statistical form instructions stated that when a civil case may be reported in more than one category, it is to be reported only in the category that represents the principal issue in controversy. If, based on subsequent pleadings or case activity, staff determines that the case was classified incorrectly, on the next monthly report the case should be terminated in the original case category, and a "reclassified" filing should be added with the correct classification.[49]

Changes in case type categories over time. No changes in case categories occurred during the time frame the data set was provided.

Texas

Sources of data. The Texas Office of Court Administration (OCA) provided a data set containing the civil case filing data for each type of trial court for each case type reported for each of the calendar years 2004 through 2019—a period of 16 years. There was a separate data set for each of the four types of trial courts, disaggregated by county and case type.

State statutes authorize the Texas Judicial Council to require courts to report statistics on caseloads.[50] The Judicial Council has adopted Rules regarding reporting requirements for case filing data.[51] The Rules require each district court clerk, county clerk, justice of the peace, and municipal judge to submit reports monthly to the OCA.[52] The

45. Ohio Rev. Code § 1901.30.

46. Ohio Rev. Code § 1907.30.

47. Ohio Courts Statistical Summary 2018, at 52.

48. Rules of Superintendence for the Courts of Ohio, r. 2(A)(1).

49. Instructions for Preparation of Statistical Report Forms, Court of Common Pleas—General Division—Form A, Rev'd Dec. 6, 2019, at 2, and Instructions for Preparation of Statistical Report Forms, Municipal and County Courts—Individual Judge Report, at 2.

50. Tex. Gov't Code, §§ 71.019, 71.035.

51. Tex. Admin. Code, tit. 1 Administration, pt. 8 Texas Judicial Council, ch. 171 Reporting Requirements Sources of Case Filing Data.

52. Tex. Admin. Code § 171.2.

rules also list the civil case categories to be counted,[53] but do not include the definitions of the categories. Detailed instructions for reporting by each court have been prepared by the OCA.[54]

New cases included. The data set included only new filings, not reopened or reactivated cases. New filings were described as "cases that were filed with the court for the first time during the reporting period." [55] Total filings of reopened and reactivated cases were also reported to the OCA. The annual report for FY 2019 indicated "reactivated" and all "other cases added" represented 14.8 percent of "new cases filed" in district court, 3.5 percent of "new cases filed" in statutory county courts, and 1 percent of "new cases filed'" in justice courts.

Case categories included and excluded. In Texas, two categories of cases in the district and county courts that were counted as civil cases were excluded from the data sets and the analysis here. One category was "civil cases related to criminal proceedings." This category included bond forfeiture, seizure, habeas corpus, expunction, nondisclosure, occupational license, seizure and forfeiture, extradition, contempt in criminal cases, writ of habeas corpus in criminal cases, and petitions for relief from a firearms disability related to criminal cases. The second category excluded was "all other civil cases." This category included petitions for relief from a firearms restriction and certain involuntary mental health commitment cases.

Definition and unit of count for a civil case. There was no specific definition in statute or court rules of a civil case. The appendix to the annual reports defined a Civil Docket: "A civil case, unlike a criminal case, does not depend on the number of persons involved. Instead, each separate suit, normally commenced by the filing of the plaintiff's original petition, defines an individual civil case."[56] A civil case was considered commenced by the filing of the plaintiff's original petition.[57] A civil case was counted and reported when an original petition, complaint, or other pleading was filed, regardless of the number of persons, other parties, or causes of action involved.[58]

Who decides the case type categorization? In civil cases, the OCA strongly recommended that clerks require the attorneys or the litigants filing a case to complete a case cover sheet so that the attorney or litigant was responsible for identifying the nature of the case.[59] In the fall of 2008, the Texas Judicial Council adopted a model case

---

53. Tex. Admin. Code, § 171.4(b)(2)(A) for District Court, § 171.5(b)(2)(A) for Statutory County Courts, § 171.6(b)(2)(A) for Constitutional County Courts, and § 171.1(b)(2) for Justice Courts.

54. For district courts: Office of Court Administration, Texas Judicial Council, Official District Court Monthly Report Instructions, Sept. 20, 2019; for statutory county courts: Office of Court Administration, Texas Judicial Council, Official Statutory County Court Monthly Report Instructions; for Constitutional County Courts: Office of Court Administration, Texas Judicial Council, Official Constitutional County Court Monthly Report Instructions; and for justice courts: Office of Court Administration, Texas Judicial Council, Official Justice of the Peace Monthly Report Instructions.

55. Annual Statistical Report for the Texas Judiciary for FY 2020, Appendix, at 1.

56. Annual Statistical Report for the Texas Judiciary for Fiscal Year 2019, Appendix, at iii.

57. Tex. R. Civ. P. 22.

58. Tex. Admin. Code § 171.3(b).

59. *See* Frequently Asked Questions District and County-Level Court Reports, Effective Sept. 1, 2010.

cover sheet for use by the district courts and county level courts.[60] A cover sheet for justice court cases was adopted effective May 1, 2013.[61] If no cover sheet was filed, the clerk determined the type of case.

Changes in case type categories over time. The case categories reported were substantially revised in 2003, which explains why the data set begins in 2004. There were a number of changes in case type categories during the study period. A number of new case type categories were added beginning in 2010 and in 2013. The changes in 2010 occurred as a result of a Judicial Data Project mandated by the legislature[62] and the Texas Judicial Council. The project made its recommendations in the spring of 2008,[63] and, after approval by the Texas Judicial Council, the changes went into effect on September 1, 2010.[64]

---

60. Annual Report for the Texas Judiciary, Fiscal Year 2009, at 66.
61. Tex. R. Civ. P. 502.2(b).
62. In the General Appropriations Act, art. IV, OCA, TX JC Rider 7.
63. Annual Report for the Texas Judiciary, Fiscal Year 2009, at 65.
64. Annual Report for the Texas Judiciary, Fiscal Year 2011, at 39.

About the Authors

Alan Carlson

Alan Carlson has worked as a court executive and management consultant in state trial courts for 47 years. He served as Court Executive Officer (court administrator, clerk of court, and jury commissioner) in both the Orange County and San Francisco Superior Courts, as Executive Officer of the Monterey County Superior Court, and Assistant Executive Officer of the Alameda County Superior Court. He has also served as President of Justice Management Institute (court management consultants), Director of Court Services at the Judicial Council of California, and as a Staff Attorney at the National Center for State Courts. He has a JD from the University of California, College of Law, San Francisco, and a BS in industrial engineering and operations research from the University of California at Berkeley.

Alan has worked in four California Superior Courts for a total of 26 years. For 23 years he was the court administrator reporting directly to the judges of the court, and for 15 of these years he also served as the clerk of the court. He has served under 30 Presiding Judges and Chief Justices during his career. Among his accomplishments in these courts are the merger of two levels of trial courts into a unified trial court, implementation of e-filing, the shift to an all-electronic record, business process re-engineering of all trial court operations, and development of portals to assist self-represented litigants in small claims and divorce cases.

As a court management consultant, Alan has worked on projects in 43 state trial courts at the county or city level and 19 state Supreme Courts in 33 states and one foreign country. Areas of particular expertise include criminal case flow management, trial court funding, trial court governance, the development and implementation of policies for public access to court records, and drafting privacy and civil liberties policies for criminal justice systems.

Recently, Alan has written and spoken about what has happened to civil case filings over the last 16 to 41 plus years in five states and the benefits and risks of artificial intelligence applications in the justice system.

Alan has received numerous professional awards for his work in the field of judicial administration, including the following:

- Ernest C. Friesen Award, The Justice Management Institute, August 20, 2019
- Distinguished Service Award, California Judicial Council, August 25, 2016
- Warren E. Burger Society, National Center for State Courts, November 2012
- Award of Merit, National Association for Court Management, 2012

- Robert B. Yegge Award for Outstanding Contribution in the Field of Judicial Administration, American Bar Association, 2010

Significant publications:

- What Is Happening to State Trial Court Civil Filings? The Unsolved Riddles, with John Greacen (ABA, forthcoming 2023).
- *Imagining an AI Supported Self-help Portal for Divorce*, 59(1) The Judges' Journal 26–28, 30 (Winter 2020), http://maestro.abanet.org/trk/click?ref=z1 1aidwdq5_0-3f447x3f5995x04806&.
- *Using Artificial Intelligence and Big Data to Develop Tools Used in Courts*, November 2019, unpublished.
- *A Taxonomy of Risks Using AI/ML Models*, October 23, 2019, https://medium .com/@AlanCarlson/a-taxonomy-of-risks-using-ai-ml-models-81026dfe1f5e.
- *Financial Management of Courts*, in The Improvement of the Administration of Justice, ch. 18 (8th ed., ABA, 2016).
- *Adequate, Stable, Equitable, and Responsible Trial Court Funding: Reframing the State vs. Local Debate*, with Prof. John K. Hudzik & Kate Harrison, Nat'l Inst. of Just., NCJ Number 223973 (Fall 2008), https://www.ojp .gov/library/publications/adequate-stable-equitable-and-responsible-trial-court -funding-reframing-state.
- *Public Access to Court Records: Guidelines for Policy Development by State Courts*, Nat'l Ctr. for State Courts (August 2002), https://cdm16501.con tentdm.oclc.org/digital/collection/accessfair/id/221.
- *Managing to Reduce Delay*, with Larry Sipes, Teresa Tan & Alex Aikman, Nat'l Ctr. for State Courts (1980), https://ncsc.contentdm.oclc.org/digital /collection/ctadmin/id/35/rec/1.
- *Justice Delayed, The Pace of Litigation in Urban Trial Courts*, with Thomas W. Church, Jo-Lynne Q. Lee & Teresa Tan, Nat'l Ctr. for State Courts (1978), https://ncsc.contentdm.oclc.org/digital/collection/ctadmin/id/0/rec/2.

John Greacen

John Greacen has worked in multiple roles in the justice system for 55 years, including the following:

- Clerking for a federal appellate judge
- Teaching at two law schools (University of Arizona and American University)
- Practicing with a major law firm (Kirkland & Ellis) in Washington, DC, and as a solo practitioner in rural New Mexico (admitted to practice in Arizona, Colorado, District of Columbia, and New Mexico)
- Serving as a court executive for the U.S. Court of Appeals for the Fourth Circuit, the U.S. Bankruptcy Court for the District of New Mexico, and as Director of the Administrative Office of the Courts for New Mexico
- Serving in leadership positions in six justice improvement organizations (Project Director, University of Arizona College of Law, revising the rules of criminal procedure for Arizona; Deputy Director of the National Institute for Law

Enforcement and Criminal Justice; Director of the National Institute for Juvenile Justice and Delinquency Prevention; Director of Programs, Police Foundation; Acting Director, Institute for Advanced Studies in Justice at American University; and Deputy Director for the National Center for State Courts)
- Consulting for 21 years with courts and access to justice entities in 36 states and four foreign countries as Principal of Greacen Associates, LLC, Regina, New Mexico

John has served in volunteer leadership roles in the American Bar Association (chair of the Criminal Justice Section and of the Lawyers Conference of the Judicial Division), Conference of State Court Administrators, the Federal Court Clerks Association, Global Justice Information Network Advisory Committee Infrastructure Standards Working Group, Institute for the Advancement of the American Legal System, Legal Internet Working Group, National Association of Appellate Court Clerks, National Association for Court Management, National Commission on Correctional Health Care, National Conference of Bankruptcy Clerks, National Institute of Corrections, National Judicial College, New Mexico State Bar, New Mexico Access to Justice Commission, Organization for the Advancement of Structured Information Standards, the President's Commission on Mental Health, Self-Represented Litigation Network, and the Lindrith/Llaves Volunteer Fire Department.

John has received numerous professional awards over the course of his career:

- Meyer Elkin Essay Award for the best article published in the Family Court Review 2020
- Ernest J. Friesen Award from the Justice Management Institute for "vision, leadership, and sustained commitment to the achievement of excellence in the administration of justice" 2017
- Organization for the Advancement of Structured Information Standards Distinguished Contributor Award 2013
- New Mexico State Bar "Pioneer" Award 2000
- Membership in the National Center for State Courts' Warren E. Burger Society
- National Association for Court Management Award of Merit 1999
- Director's Award for Outstanding Leadership Administrative Office of U.S. Courts 1992
- Attorney General's Special Achievement Award U.S. Department of Justice 1975
- Editor in Chief, Arizona Law Review 1967–68
- Ralph W. Aigler Award for greatest contribution to the College of Law 1968

His publications include the following:

- WHAT IS HAPPENING TO STATE COURT TRIAL COURT CIVIL FILINGS? THE UNSOLVED RIDDLES, with Alan Carlson (ABA, forthcoming 2023).
- *Legal Information vs. Legal Adviçe: A Twenty-five Year Retrospective*, 106(2) JUDICATURE 48 (2022).
- *Supporting Self-Represented Litigants and Access to Justice: How does ODR Fit In?*, 6(2) INTERNATIONAL JOURNAL OF ONLINE DISPUTE RESOLUTION 170 (2019).

- *Ensuring the Right to Be Heard: Guidance for Trial Judges in Cases Involving Self-Represented Litigants*, with Michael Houlberg, INST. FOR THE ADVANCEMENT OF THE AMERICAN LEGAL SYSTEM (November 2019).
- *Eighteen Ways Courts Should Use Technology to Better Serve Their Customers*, INST. FOR THE ADVANCEMENT OF THE AMERICAN LEGAL SYSTEM (October 2018); also published in 57(4) FAMILY COURT REVIEW 515 (October 2019).
- *Access from Anywhere: Report Finds Courts Effectively Deliver Remote Self-Help Services*, with Katherine Alteneder & Stacey Marz, 32(3) COURT MANAGER 14 (Summer 2017).
- *Remote Appearances of Parties, Attorneys and Witnesses—A Review of Current Court Rules and Practices*, prepared for the Self-Represented Litigation Network (March 17, 2017).
- *From Market Failure to 100% Access: Toward a Civil Justice Continuum*, with Amy Dunn Johnson & Vincent Morris, 37 UNIVERSITY OF ARKANSAS LAW REVIEW 1 (2016).
- *Serving Self-Represented Litigants Remotely—A Resource Guide*, prepared for the Self-Represented Litigation Network (July 1, 2016).
- *Self-Represented Litigants, the Courts, and the Legal Profession—Myths and Realities*, 52 FAMILY COURT REVIEW 662 (July 2014).
- *Using Technology to Enhance Access to Justice*, with James E. Cabral, Abhijeet Chavan, Thomas E. Clarke, Bonnie Rose Hough, Linda Rexer, Jane Ribadeneyra & Richard Zorza, 26(1) HARVARD JOURNAL ON LAW & TECHNOLOGY (Fall 2012).
- *Confidentiality, Due Process, and Judicial Disqualification in Unified Family Courts: Report to the Honorable Stephanie Domitrovich*, 46(2) FAMILY COURT REVIEW 340 (April 2008). Judge Domitrovich was chair of the Children and Family Law Committee of the ABA's National Conference of State Trial Judges.
- *Draft Standards for Electronic Filing Processes*, 2(6) E-FILING REPORT 1 (Glasser LegalWorks, May 2002).
- *"A Handbook for Courts" Book Review of Steelman, et al., Caseflow Management, The Heart of Court Management in the New Millennium*, with Julia H. Barnes, JUDICATURE 85(5) Judicature 249 (March–April 2002).
- *State Court Administration, in* THE IMPROVEMENT OF THE ADMINISTRATION OF JUSTICE (7th ed., ABA, 2002).
- Column in American Bar Association's *Judges Journal:* "An Administrator's Perspective"
    - *Judicial Leadership*, Summer 2001, at 41.
    - *Relationships between Judges and Court Administrators*, Fall 2001, at 38.
    - *Trial Court Governance*, Winter 2001, at 40.
    - Developing *Performance Measures for Trial and Appellate Courts*, Spring 2002, at 40.
    - *The Impact of Self-represented Litigants on Trial Courts—Testing Our Stereotypes against Real Data*, Summer 2002, at 32.
    - *Let Us Dispense with the Myth That America Needs or Wants Generalists*, Fall 2002, at 45.

  - *The Status of Unbundled Legal Services*, Spring 2004, at 39.
  - *Working with the Legislature during the Court Appropriations Process*, Summer 2004, at 30.
  - *Measuring a Trial Court's Criminal Caseflow Management—Clearance Rates and Failures to Appear* (2006).
  - *Judicial Fitness—A Broad View* (2006).
  - *A Fresh Look at Our System for Providing Civil Legal Assistance* (2006).
  - *Court Administration: Backlog Performance Measurement—A Success Story in New Jersey*, Vol. 46, No. 1, at 42 (2007).
- *Judicial Techniques for Cases Involving Self-Represented Litigants*, with Rebecca A. Albrecht, Bonnie Rose Hough & Richard Zorza, 42(1) JUDGES' JOURNAL 16 (ABA, Winter 2003).
- *Unified Family Courts: Recent Developments in Twelve States,* with Julia Hosford Barnes, 42(2) JUDGES' JOURNAL 10 (ABA, Spring 2003).
- *Statewide Planning for Court Security*, with Robert Klein, 576 ANNALS OF THE AMERICAN ACADEMY OF POLITICAL AND SOCIAL SCIENCE 109 (July 2001).
- *Legal Information Versus Legal Advice: Developments during the Last 5 Years*, 84(4) JUDICATURE 198 (Jan–Feb 2001).
- *How Fast, Fair, and Cheap Should Courts Be? Instead of Letting Lawyers and Judges Decide, New Mexico Asked Its Customers* 82(6) JUDICATURE (May–June 1999).
- *Social Security Numbers in State Court Information Systems*, COURT TECHNOLOGY BULLETIN (Nov./Dec. 1998).
- *No Legal Advice from Court Personnel: What Does That Mean?*, 34 THE JUDGES JOURNAL 10 (Winter 1995) (also published in *The Court Manager* 35 (Winter 1995).
- *The Increasing Number of Litigants Proceeding without Lawyers, How Should the Courts and the Bar Respond?*, with Joyce Stowers, STATE BAR OF NEW MEXICO, BAR JOURNAL (Sept./Oct. 1995).
- *Court Rules Related to Technology*, THE COURT MANAGER (Spring 1995).
- *Has Your Court Administrator Retired? Without Telling You?,* THE COURT MANAGER (Winter 1991). Manuscript co-winner of first prize in the open competition for papers at the Second National Conference on Court Management, September 1990.
- *What Standards Should We Use to Judge Our Courts?*, 72(1) JUDICATURE (1988).
- *Use of Electronic Mail in Appellate Courts*, with Blend, McCulloch & Schrinel, 10(3) STATE COURT JOURNAL (1986).
- *The Role of the Police: Should It Be Limited to Fighting Crime?*, PROGRESS IN POLICING: ESSAYS ON CHANGE (1980).
- *Arbitration: A Tool for Criminal Cases?*, 2(1) BARRISTER (Winter 1975).

Index

H

I

N

T

U

V

W